THE LAWYER'S GUIDE TO
Fact Finding
ON THE
Internet

Carole A. Levitt

Mark E. Rosch

(First Edition entitled **The Internet Fact Finder for Lawyers:
How to Find Anything on the Net**
by Joshua D. Blackman and David Jank)

Law Practice Management Section
MARKETING • MANAGEMENT • TECHNOLOGY • FINANCE

Commitment to Quality: The Law Practice Management Section is committed to quality in our publications. Our authors are experienced practitioners in their fields. Prior to publication, the contents of all our books are rigorously reviewed by experts to ensure the highest quality product and presentation. Because we are committed to serving our readers' needs, we welcome your feedback on how we can improve future editions of this book. We invite you to fill out and return the comment card at the back of this book.

Screen shots reprinted with permission from their respective owners. All rights reserved.

Cover design by Jim Colao.

Nothing contained in this book is to be considered as the rendering of legal advice for specific cases, and readers are responsible for obtaining such advice from their own legal counsel. This book and any forms and agreements herein are intended for educational and informational purposes only.

The products and services mentioned in this publication are under or may be under trademark or service mark protection. Product and service names and terms are used throughout only in an editorial fashion, to the benefit of the product manufacturer or service provider, with no intention of infringement. Use of a product or service name or term in this publication should not be regarded as affecting the validity of any trademark or service mark.

The Law Practice Management Section, American Bar Association, offers an educational program for lawyers in practice. Books and other materials are published in furtherance of that program. Authors and editors of publications may express their own legal interpretations and opinions, which are not necessarily those of either the American Bar Association or the Law Practice Management Section unless adopted pursuant to the bylaws of the Association. The opinions expressed do not reflect in any way a position of the Section or the American Bar Association.

Printed in the United States of America.

Library of Congress Cataloging-in-Publication Data

Levitt, Carole A.
   The lawyer's guide to fact finding on the Internet / Carole A.
   Levitt, Mark E.   Rosch.-- 2nd ed.
      p. cm.
      Includes index.
      ISBN 1-59031-274-0
      1. Legal research--United States--Computer network resources.
      2. Legal research--Computer network resources.
      3. Internet   research. I. Rosch, Mark E. II. Title.
   KF242.A1L48 2004
   025.06'34--dc22
                          2003028017
07 06 05 04 03   5 4 3 2 1

Discounts are available for books ordered in bulk. Special consideration is given to state bars, CLE programs, and other bar-related organizations. Inquire at Book Publishing, American Bar Association, 750 N. Lake Shore Drive, Chicago, Illinois 60611.

Contents at a Glance

Contents

Chapter 4: Search Tools   83

Chapter 5: General Factual Research   123

About the Authors

Carole Levitt

Carole Levitt is a nationally recognized author and speaker on Internet legal research. She has over twenty years of extensive experience in the legal field as a law librarian, legal research and writing professor (Pepperdine University School of Law), California lawyer, and Internet trainer. She is a skilled online searcher, focusing on legal, public record, investigative, and business research.

As president and founder of Internet For Lawyers (**www.netfor lawyers.com**), she provides customized Internet legal research training to legal professionals (with continuing legal education credit). Ms. Levitt has made Internet legal research presentations at the LegalWorks and the LegalTech Technology conferences; the annual meetings of the American Bar Association, the National Association of Bar Executives, the Association of Continuing Legal Education, and the California State Bar Association; the worldwide Gibson, Dunn & Crutcher corporate lawyer retreat; and at law firms, bar associations, and library associations throughout the United States.

She is a regular contributor to the *Los Angeles Lawyer* magazine's "Computer Counselor" column (reaching twenty-five thousand lawyers throughout California) and has also written for the following magazines and newsletters: the *Internet Lawyer, Computer and Internet Lawyer, Research Advisor, Nashville Lawyer*, the *Bottom Line* (publication of the State Bar of California Law Practice Management and Technology Section), as well as the Web sites Internet For Lawyers, FindLaw, CEB Case N Point, and LLRX.

Ms. Levitt is a member of the state bar associations of Illinois and California and of the Los Angeles County Bar Association. She is the chair of the State Bar of California Law Practice Management and Technology Section and also serves on the executive board of the Los Angeles County Bar Association Law Practice Management Section. Additionally, Ms. Levitt is a member of the Association for Continuing Legal Education (ACLEA). She served as the vice-president of the four-hundred-member Southern California Association of Law Libraries.

Ms. Levitt received her Juris Doctor from the John Marshall Law School, where she graduated with distinction and was a member of the school's law review. She earned her bachelor's degree in political science and her master's degree in library science at the University of Illinois. Ms. Levitt can be contacted at **clevitt@netforlawyers.com**.

Mark Rosch

As vice president of marketing for Internet For Lawyers (IFL), Mr. Rosch is the developer and manager of the Internet For Lawyers Web site. He is the editor of IFL's newsletter, and he writes and speaks about legal technology for firms, and about how to use the Internet for research and marketing.

Mr. Rosch provides electronic-marketing consulting services to solo practitioners and law firms of all sizes who seek to create online marketing efforts or increase the effectiveness of their current efforts. He has also helped law firms and legal consultants optimize their Web sites to improve their search-engine rankings. During his sixteen years of marketing experience, Mr. Rosch has developed, implemented, and supervised the publicity, promotions, and marketing campaigns for numerous and varied clients, from the prestigious legal Web site LLRX.com to new media developers. Currently he provides Web-management consulting to the State Bar of California Law Practice Management and Technology Section Web site.

Mr. Rosch has written on the subject of building and managing effective Web sites for the Legal Marketing Association and *Los Angeles Lawyer* magazine. Mr. Rosch has also written about the application of computer technology to the law office for *Law Office Computing, Los Angeles Lawyer*, and the *Los Angeles Daily Journal*, among other publications. He has presented at the annual meetings of the ABA, the National Association of Bar Executives, the Association of Continuing Legal Education (ACLEA), the State Bar of California, and in-house at various firms.

Previously, as vice president for public relations for E! Entertainment Television networks, Mr. Rosch was responsible for developing and supervising all publicity strategy and its implementation for the E! Entertainment Television cable network, as well as for Style, the company's newest network.

Prior to E!, Mr. Rosch was vice president of the Weissman/Angellotti public relations firm, working on numerous projects, including all television specials, events, and activities of the Academy of Television Arts and Sciences (including the prime-time Emmy Awards), and new media projects including the launch of the Academy's first Web site in 1995, as well as numerous feature films, including *Like Water For Chocolate.*

Mr. Rosch is a member of the ACLEA and the ABA, in addition to serving as a member of the board of directors of the Entertainment Publicists Professional Society. He has also served as a member of the Academy of Television Arts and Sciences public relations steering committee, the Television Publicity Executives Committee, and the American Film Institute.

He graduated from Tulane University in New Orleans with a bachelor's degree in sociology. Mr. Rosch can be reached at **mrosch@netforlawyers.com.**

Introduction

In 1999, we combined Carole's dual background as a lawyer and law librarian with Mark's background in marketing and his penchant for technology to create Internet For Lawyers and teach lawyers how to use the Web effectively and efficiently. To create our first seminars and training materials, we reviewed a lot of Internet research books to find the most useful sites for lawyers that were available for free on the Internet. In all of the books we used, we never found an Internet research book that was everything we thought such a book should be.

When the ABA asked us to write a new edition of Joshua Blackman's *The Internet Fact Finder for Lawyers*, our goal was to write a book that would save researchers time and money and help them avoid frustration. We looked at it as our chance to write the book we had been searching for, but never found—and our chance to correct all the pet peeves we found in other books. We wanted to share what we learned about the best of the hundreds of Web sites we've used while conducting real-world research or while testing for evaluation purposes.

The following is a rundown of the pet peeves we've had with other Internet research books, and an explanation of how we hope this book overcomes those shortcomings in order to empower you to become a more efficient and effective researcher.

But, Is It Free?

The authors of the other Internet research books rarely warned us if the Web site they were describing was a pay site. There's nothing more bothersome than going to a site expecting to find these other information for free, and instead being greeted by a registration and payment screen asking for your credit card. On the other hand, these other authors usually also failed to bother to clue us in when a site was free.

We know, as it is with most anything, that price is a major consideration when deciding between alternative research resources—and we all agree that free is better (all other things being equal!). Our first goal, then, was to label the Web sites we included in the book to show whether they are free (or free but requiring registration) or pay. Some sites have different levels of access. For example, a Web site might offer some limited information for free and then charge for more extensive information (such as those sites that are free to search but require a paid subscription to view the full text of search results). Some sites are completely free, while others, though costing no money, require registration to access all or part of the sites.

However a Web site is arranged, it's good to know before you get there. We label the sites with the icons shown below to indicate what kind of access is offered. If we use more than one icon, it means the site offers varying levels of access.

$ Pay   Free   Registration Required

We also tell you when free is not better—that is, when you're not going to find it for free or when free won't be the most efficient route. In such instances, we recommend a pay site. We want to save you time and money by clueing you in—in advance.

So, What's the Purpose of this Site?

Some of the authors of other books we reviewed simply pointed to a laundry list of Web sites but failed to describe their contents or indicate the purposes of the sites. Our second goal was to provide an overview of each site's content and to suggest in what situations the Web site should be used. When applicable, we also suggest alternative sites. We want to save you the frustration of visiting Web sites that don't have the content you need or don't allow you to search in the manner you want. For example, if you need to know the owner of a certain piece of real estate in Los Angeles, we recommend a pay site to find that information, and explain that while the Los Angeles County assessor's office offers a free, searchable Web site, it doesn't allow you to search by owner's name, only by the property address. Even then, the free site does not provide the owner's name—only the assessed value.

What's with This Alphabetical List of Titles?

Some Internet research books we looked at listed Web sites in alphabetical order by the name of the site. A research book is not useful if it's simply an alphabetical list. Even one of the authors of this book, who is a librarian by training and who lives and dies by alphabetical order, doesn't find it useful when organizing a research book— in fact, she abhors it! And this is from someone who organizes her spice rack (and even the credit cards in her wallet) alphabetically.

We want to save you time and money by thinking the way you do. So, our third goal was to organize by subject. Researchers don't think in alphabetical title order—they think in subject order. To make this book more useful, we have chosen to organize it in subject order.

But, Which Sites Are We Recommending, and Where Should You Start?

Even those few authors who did organize their books by subject couldn't stay completely away from alphabetical order. They always seemed to revert to an alphabetical list of Web sites within each subject when it would have been more meaningful to organize in a way that showed the reader in which order they should use the sites, starting with the most useful. The reader seeks and depends on the judgment of the author, who is the expert searcher. The author is there to guide searchers down the superhighway—to draw the road map, showing the searcher which sites to stop and visit in order to gather the most useful information.

Our fourth goal was to list the Web sites in a meaningful order within each topic. Thus, our list of sites begins with what we judge to be

the best starting-point sites. We want to save you time and money by listing sites in a way that quickly displays our judgment of each site—by
showing you which ones to begin with, and then which sites to visit next.
We only show you the best sites.

Are There any Tips or Tricks to Using This Site?

Most other Internet research books failed to provide practical tips and
tricks about the Web sites listed in the book. Our book is designed to save
searchers from the wrong turns, dead-ends, and even wrong destinations
that we encountered along the way while evaluating the sites. To do this,
we include tips about the best aspect of each site (content and functionality) and a how-to for those sites that have great content but are not
intuitive to use. For example, some Web sites bury the search function, or
its most useful information. Some sites use cryptic labels for parts of the
site.

Our goal is to uncover that information and those features for you—
to translate those sites for you. We want to save you time and money by
detailing the information we learned by visiting and testing out the hundreds of sites included in this book.

Show Me the Site

Finally, most authors failed to display the Web sites that they
described! The Internet is a graphic-intensive medium, chock-full of icons
and links—not just text. When getting driving directions, most people
find it useful to look at a map while the instructions are being given. It's
the same with the Internet. So, rather than just describe Web sites, we
also provide screen shots of the more important sites, or the ones that
have some hidden trick.

This book is written in a style that mixes narrative with a standard-
ized template presentation. First, we give you an introduction to the topic
in a narrative fashion, and then we highlight the best sites in a template
format so you can quickly learn about each individual Web site. The template, as shown below, displays the site name, whether it's free or not, its
URL, its purpose, its content, our view of the site, and our tip or tips for
using the site.

Internet For Lawyers

Articles, tips, and links: Online CLE: **$**

http://www.netforlawyers.com

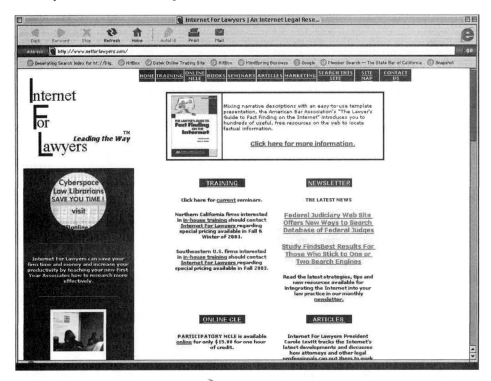

Figure I-1. **netforlawyers.com** is the Web site of the authors. It provides articles and tips about conducting Internet legal research and also promotes their live seminars, many of which are based on the content of this book.

Purpose: To provide information to the legal professional about how to use the Internet for legal, business, and investigative research.

Content: The site offers articles about Internet research and also has online CLE courses to help you hone your Internet research skills by having you test out the sites discussed in the CLE articles in order to answer the quiz questions. Some of the articles explain how to find free case law on the Internet, how to find information about companies, and how to find free public records.

Our View: It's our site, so we're probably a bit biased, but here goes! You'll like the clickable links included in the articles—it makes it easy for you to visit the sites for your own research. The online CLE quizzes are probably the least expensive you'll find on the Internet at $15 per credit hour.

Tip: Use the blue tabs at the top to navigate the site, or click on SEARCH THIS SITE to search with keywords. The TRAINING tab informs you about in-house courses and the SEMINARS tab tells you in which city (from Alaska to Atlanta) you can attend an Internet For Lawyers bar-association-sponsored seminar (and in March 2004, look for us on the East Coast).

How to Use the CD

To make it easier to locate and access the sites you want to use in the book, we have included a CD-ROM that includes links to all of the sites discussed in the book. The sites are all indexed, by name and by topic so you can easily navigate to them without typing URLs into your browser! The index is included as a PDF file and requires the free Adobe Acrobat Reader to view. See Chapter 2 for more information on using Acrobat effectively to get the most out of this index.

Also provided are some of the helpful checklists featured in the book, including a Source Credibility Checklist, a handy Methodology Checklist, and more. These are included as Microsoft Word files so that you can copy them to your hard drive, print them out and make notations for your own Web searches.

Keeping Up to Date

We have been teaching legal professionals where to find the information they need on the Internet at seminars for more than four years, so nobody knows more than we do that useful new sites appear on the Internet daily. That's why we are working with the ABA to keep you up-to-date on these developments.

We have developed a monthly, companion update service for this book to inform you of the newest sites and useful new developments at old favorites. This update will be delivered to your e-mail inbox every month, so you can print out the pages and keep them with your copy of the book, or near your computer for easy access. More information about subscribing to this service is available online at **http://www.lawpractice.org/ factfinder.**

*CHAPTER*ONE

Using the Internet for Factual Research

War Stories from Internet Fact Finders

In legal practice, research involves *much* more than the case law, statutes, and regulations explained in law school. For example, medical malpractice lawyers need to know about anatomy, and how to find medical experts. Product liability lawyers need to know how to find corporate family trees to deduce parent-subsidiary relationships, and to trace the path of a product—from manufacturing to distributorship to sales—in order to ascertain liability. The Internet is extremely well-suited to such fact-finding. This book is aimed at factual research only. While we may discuss some legal research and government sites, it is because those sites can be used for digging up *factual* information.

For example, in Chapter 9, "Finding and Backgrounding Expert Witnesses," we talk about court opinions, but only in the context of using court-opinion databases to find experts who are referenced in cases that have similar facts to your case and for which you are seeking an expert. When we talk about bills and legislative histories in that chapter, once again it is not in the legal context, but in the context of finding experts who have testified about a certain matter in a pending bill, or been referred to in a legislative report about a similar issue you are involved with. In the discussion of dockets in Chapter 8, "Accessing Public Records," we talk about how to use dockets for client development, recruiting, and learning about the opposition lawyer or even the judge you're going before. Once again, we are not discussing dockets from a legal-research perspective.

If you're not yet convinced that you should bother with the Internet, or if you're uncertain whether anything of practical value is available on the Internet, below are a few examples from practicing lawyers describing how they've used the Internet to find factual information to solve problems. In most of the war stories, we note the lawyer's name. But if a matter is still ongoing, to protect the confidentiality of the parties (and in one case an innocent dog) we need to shield the lawyer's name.

War Story: Drunk Driving

Wes Pittman of Pittman & Perry, P.A., in Panama City, Florida (wes@pittmanfirm.com), describes how he finished a trial for which he used the Internet to generate some ideas for opening statements and summations. He said that it worked "marvelously well."

"I represented a plaintiff in a personal injury case. The defendant was a drunk driver who crossed the center line of a highway one dark rainy night and struck her car head-on. I had a claim not only for compensatory but also for punitive damages. Under Florida law, we are permitted to argue that punitives are to deter flagrant conduct by the defendant and by others, and we are able to argue that the conduct is pervasive, etc., much like in other jurisdictions. I needed to use only one search phrase, 'drunk driving,' to generate forty-nine-thousand-plus hits and to find, within the first twenty-five, two great ideas to use. Both ideas related to the widespread practice of drinking while driving and how it has become a joking matter. I took it one step further, of course, to say in closing that the only way to keep people like the defendant from continuing to make drunk driving a joke is to send a message by a punitive award.

"The two hits which were so useful were about a card game called 'Drunk Driver, Drunk Driver' in which successive cards are dealt, each accompanied by the consumption of an entire drink, until the driver 'safely makes it off the road' (all the cards are dealt). [The second useful site included] an article that at first sounded serious enough in its title to divert me to it. [I thought I might] want to print it for use in future product liability cases. Its title was something like 'The Steering Propensities of Pickup Trucks at Highway Speeds.' As I read the article, I quickly learned that the author had written the three-page paper as a (poor) joke to describe how a pickup has become 'the only beer-guided vehicle in the country,' how pickups stall in front of bars, how to balance a beer to keep it from spilling in the crotch, etc."

Pittman's use of the Internet to easily find examples of how our culture perceives drunk driving, and then his using that information to demonstrate to the court the strength of his arguments, perfectly demonstrates the Internet's great strength. Because the Internet enables virtually anyone to publish material for the world to see, it makes a remarkably rich repository.

While professional researchers can take the time to search the database sites Dialog or LexisNexis to find pertinent articles, most people have neither the expertise to search those databases (especially Dialog), nor wish to pay for access. Online databases generally are collections of commercial publications, professional journals that are peer reviewed, and newsletters. While there is undeniable value in such collections, they also necessarily omit vast bodies of data and knowledge that, before the Internet, had little to no distribution. In addition, such databases do *not* include articles written "as a joke," the very articles that proved most useful to Pittman to make his point that drunk driving is considered a joke when, in fact, it's a deadly serious problem.

Before the Internet, Pittman may have been able to search Dialog or LexisNexis for published articles on the subject, or he may have sought to collect anecdotal information on the subject, but it's unlikely he could have done either from the comfort of his office on the weekend, within a short period of time, for virtually no cost. The informal information he personally collected from the Internet, which proved useful for defending his client, was only available from the unique "library" we know as the Internet. And, to share with the jury that he received forty-nine-thousand-plus hits by searching for the phrase "drunk driving" is more impressive than saying, "I spoke to a few people about 'drunk driving' and they said . . ."

The fact is that the Internet is rich with free, valuable information that legal professionals and anyone else can conveniently access day or night. It's simply become an easy way to get smart fast about topics we may otherwise know nothing about. It's one thing to know the law on a given subject; it's another to be armed with the factual information required to make a winning argument. Besides getting ideas for an opening or closing as Pittman did, the Internet is just the place to find a useful statistic or the perfect quote to use in that opening or closing.

War Story: Case Research and Lawyer Referral

Several lawyers volunteered anecdotes describing how the Internet is being used in law offices across the country to solve research problems.

Bruce L. Dorner (callmylawyer@choiceonemail.com), who practices law in Londonderry, New Hampshire, relates these recent incidents:

"I had a client who was seriously injured in a propane explosion. I searched the Internet for references to propane. Once I filtered down to the better items, I found a link to the home page for the American Gas Association (**http://www.aga.com**). They had all the standards of the industry posted, including comments about the particular appliance implicated in my case. Best of all, there was a phone number and an Internet mail address for further information. I got some good materials for the case."

Disappearing Sites

An attempt to recreate Dorner's search several years later found that the Aga.com site was no longer the site of the American Gas Association, but now belonged to a private international gas company, Linde Gas. That site, obviously, would be of no help to Dorner if he needed the same information today. What happened to the American Gas Association site? On February 15, 1999, the American Gas Association changed its URL to **http://www.aga.org** (they changed ".com" to ".org"). Their old URL was purchased by Linde Gas, but used only as a "redirect" to Linde's corporate site at **http://www.lindegas.com**. This type of information can be discovered by tracking the original URL through Archive.org (**http://www.archive.org**), an amazing site that you can read more about in the "Finding Extinct Pages" section of Chapter 4, "Search Tools."

Dorner has another story. "Another client wanted to adopt a child. A third party told him about a prospective birth mother in Tennessee, and my client thought this might be worth pursuing. My client needed the name of a lawyer in Tennessee who handled interstate adoptions. A quick trip to the West Legal Directory (**http://www.wld.com**) and a search using the phrase 'interstate adoption' produced the information in just a few minutes."

Lawyer Searches

Recreating this adoption search also revealed that the original URL used was no longer valid. The old URL redirected to another site—FindLaw's lawyer directory (**http://lawyers.findlaw.com**) that contained the same information as the old West Legal Directory site. (Since its purchase of FindLaw in 2001, West now posts its directory there).

Now, searching for the phrase "interstate adoption" was no longer possible. Instead, only a preselected set of practice areas was available for use as search terms (and interstate adoption was not one of them). Also, the site now requires you to select not only the practice area from the list, but also to indicate the state and city.

Lawyer searches can also be conducted at an online version of the printed Martindale-Hubbell directory (**http://www.martindale.com**). Searching at the Martindale site is more flexible, because you are not limited to preselected practice areas. (Click the ***Location/Area of Practice*** tab on the site's home page). You can also search nationally, internationally, or statewide. Searching for the two words "interstate adoption" for Tennessee returned no results. It was necessary to insert the Boolean connector AND between the words "interstate" and "adoption" to find lawyers who listed interstate adoption as their area of practice. While none were currently listed as practicing in Tennessee, the search returned numerous names of lawyers in other states.

War Story: Immigration Cases

Greg L. Siskind, of Siskind, Susser, Haas & Chang in Tennessee, explains how his firm uses the Internet for various nonlegal questions relating to their immigration cases:

"[We have used the Internet for] finding documentation to support human rights violation claims in connection with an asylum case (we actually found specific references in an obscure UN document to the torture of our client by the government of Equatorial Guinea).

"We have located expert witnesses for our cases; we have gotten procedures sent to us by e-mail from officials at various U.S. consulates around the world; [and] we frequently submit National Interest Waiver green-card applications that require a demonstration that the applicant's work will provide a substantial, prospective benefit to the U.S. The key to winning these cases is documentation, and we often find articles and other support material on the Internet."

War Story: Weather Evidence

Michael C. Zusman (mikez@evanszusman.com), who practices commercial litigation with emphasis on securities, real property, and creditor's rights, describes how one of his partners "was preparing to try a case involving an allegedly defective concrete floor laid by our client. One of the issues was whether the concrete was poured on a day where our client knew or should have known that the weather was too warm for the concrete to set properly. I hopped on my PC and, after linking around for a while, located a Web site for the Oregon Climate Service (**http://www .ocs.orst.edu**) and obtained the name and e-mail address for our state climatologist, George Taylor. He responded, and I was able to obtain hour-by-hour temperatures for the relevant locality on the day in question which, as I recall, my partner was able to introduce into evidence."

War Story: A Law Librarian's Unusual Search

When a lawyer needed to discover the manufacturer of an item responsible for burning down a client's farm, he turned to the ultimate Internet fact finder—his law librarian. The item that was responsible for burning down the farm was a white heated pet bowl, which, unfortunately, had met the same demise as the house, making the research a tad tricky. Despite that, the law librarian took up the challenge. (Because this matter is an ongoing case, and to protect the innocent dog, we have changed the color of the bowl and are not using any of the names of the cities, manufacturers, hardware stores, the lawyer, the law librarian—or the dog).

The librarian first began his search by using a general search at Yahoo! with the phrase "heated dog bowls." He began looking at some of the search results. The first one he found that sold heated dog bowls was **http://www.petco.com**. It had a picture of a blue heated dog bowl, but not a white one. The librarian then turned to his law-librarian mailing list for some suggestions. Here is his story:

"Four days ago I asked for help [from a law-librarian list] to find a specific model of a white heated dog bowl (which burned down the farm). I received over twenty-five replies from the list . . . providing . . . sites with heated dog bowls—undoubtedly, pet lovers were attracted to the search by the pictures of cute dogs and cats. Indirectly, they were all helpful. Thanks!!! Yesterday, I purchased two of the correct models (one for testing by an expert, the other for demonstrative evidence).

"The key to the find was to distinguish the marketing chain: (1) *manufacturing* from (2) *wholesale distribution* from (3) *retailing*.

"Most of the leads [from the list] were to retailers on the Internet. By themselves, the Internet retailers did not solve the problem. Most pictures on the Internet were of bright blue bowls (a visual expert ruled out color blindness by our client). EBay had started a cut-and-paste service of all products by type, but it looked like that Internet service had just started building its database [so it wasn't useful]. Then we analyzed all the retailers and narrowed the search down to three manufacturers (X, Y, and Z). Then we obtained written lists of all products made by each manufacturer and compared them with their Web sites and some of the more comprehensive sites of the retailers.

"We discovered one product on manufacturer Z's product list that was *not* shown on Z's Web site or any retailer Web site. We called the manufacturer (posing as a pet groomer) and asked for the product—of course, they had none in stock, but did provide us with a list of wholesale distributors in our area. None of the distributors, however, were in the [current] phone directories. One, however, was listed in an old city directory. The distributor had a small downtown office just two blocks from our office. With the specific model number, the distributor confirmed that he had fifty-two of the bowls in a nearby warehouse. The warehouse supplied the part number and local hardware stores to whom it distributed [the bowls]. We called several of the retail hardware stores. Of course, none stocked heated pet bowls in the heat of August. So we ordered two bowls from one hardware store. Eureka!!! They are the model that burned down the farm."

Jumpstarting a Search on the Internet

This is a great example of how the power of the Internet and a searcher's good use of various search strategies coalesced to successfully use the Internet to hunt down what seemed like an impossibility. Fact finders should take note of these search strategies: (1) because he had no idea of where to begin, and knew he would need to cast a wide net, he chose a general search engine; (2) he entered very specific keywords into the general search engine so he could zero in on the specific item; and (3) he took advantage of an Internet mailing list he had joined earlier (for law librarians from around the world). From the search-engine search he was able to start identifying manufacturers and retailers of the item. From the mailing list, he received numerous suggestions of more names of retailers who sold this type of product. He was then able to immediately turn to the retailers' product catalogs by finding their Web sites. From their sites, he was able to search for pictures of a white heated pet bowl and compile a list of retailers' phone numbers to start making phone calls to learn about the distribution chain. This is a also a great example of using information found via the Internet to jump-start what otherwise would have been a tedious manual search through product directories at a library, in the hopes that they would even have pictures of the product—and in color.

Yet, it's important also to realize the role that old-fashioned research played here—from obtaining print copies of the product lists in case the lists on the Internet weren't complete (which, as it turned out, they weren't), to thinking about who else to ask for assistance (in this case, fellow librarians) to making dozens of phone calls to manufacturers, retailers, and distributors—mostly from phone numbers found on the Internet, but also from printed directories.

War Story: The Internet Advantage

What is the advantage of using the Internet? Why not go the route before there was the Internet—the library? Why use the Internet at all? Lawyer Ted Claypoole (**http://www.wcsr.com/FSL5CS/lawyers/ lawyers430.asp**), who is the senior member of the Technology and Commerce practice group at Womble Carlyle (a firm with 450 members and offices throughout the Southeast and mid-Atlantic), answers these questions this way:

"[I use the Internet for] convenience and a broad general search to find what is out there. If I want to get a feel for what is going on in the area, I can sit down in the comfort of my own home and take an hour or two in the evening with the radio or TV on and do a general search and get some very good ideas of where I might want to go. I usually do not consider that a serious search. I still think it has advantages though. I think it will continue to have advantages to that and as you move forward, if you look at it as not a serious search you will find the sites that have what you want. In other words, if I am on it even once a week, and looking at legal topics, I will eventually know that Emory University (an example used before) has Sixth Circuit opinions—I bookmark that, and the next time I want Sixth Circuit opinions and I am home and I want to word-search them, I can go to that site. It just takes far more time than it is worth to actually say that 'I am going to do all this research on the Web.' You would spend way more time than you would need to. If you know where you are going already, then it is a very good tool. If you do not know at all what is out there and you want to get an idea, it is a very good tool."

All of these Internet research war stories have common threads: in each one, the researcher really had no idea of where to begin his search and simply threw some key words out to a general search engine. In each case, one Internet link led to another, until each person found their answer, whether directly from the Internet or indirectly. For those who got their answers indirectly from the Internet, the Internet quickly pointed them to the persons who held the answers.

We hope that this book can help you figure out where to begin your search. As you read through Chapter 3, "Search Strategies," and Chapter 4, "Search Tools," you'll get a sense for how to use general search engines effectively. Then, as you read through the subject-oriented chapters, you'll learn about specific sites that may hold the answer to your question. We'll also attempt to tell you how to use those sites, and not simply point you to them to find your own way.

Distinguishing Legal Research from Factual Research

This is a book about Internet fact finding for the legal researcher. Among the first steps in learning how to conduct factual research on the Internet is distinguishing between factual and legal research, and learning where to find the factual sources. Legal research on the Internet seems to be more organized than factual research on the Internet. So, the online-legal-researcher-turned-Internet-factual-researcher may find that conducting factual research on the Internet is more of a challenge.

Utilizing the Internet effectively is a challenge for any type of researcher. Unlike a traditional library, with catalog access to every book and every book shelved in order, the Internet is more like a vast highway where someone tossed billions of books out the car window in no particular order, and where catalog records are kept of some, but not of others. From this smorgasbord of sources strewn about the information superhighway, we are continually challenged to bob, weave, and select carefully, knowing that some of the information cannot even be accessed because it's not cataloged (indexed) by a search engine.

Differences in Research Terms

Legal researchers and factual researchers use similar terms in describing their sources. While both speak in terms of *primary, secondary*, and *tertiary* sources, these terms have very different meanings to each group.

Primary, Secondary, and Tertiary Research Sources Compared

	Factual Reasearch	**Legal Research**
Primary	• Obtained by either conducting in-person interviews with experts, litening to taped recordings of seeches or commentaries, or requestng permission to view some piece of original documentation not available from another source. • Consulting with primary sources can sometimes be referred to as "going to the source" or "getting it from the horse's mouth."	• Sources of law—compilations of legislation, regulations, and court opinions. • Includes state and federal statutory codes, municipal ordinances, constitutions, the Code of Federal Regulations, case law (court opinions), etc., whether found in books or databases.
Secondary	• Data that is compiled, organized, and distributed publicly for mass consumption. • Includes books, newspapers, magazines, journals, published papers, public speeches, directories, reference guides, and almanacs (to name just a few); electronic formats of these materials are also secondary sources.	• Materials that discuss, illuminate or otherwise provide reference to primary materials. • Includes law journals and legislative committee hearing transcripts, which provide commentary, explanation and guidance to the law, but not necessarily access to the full-text of statutes or case law and treatises (that may provide narrative overviews of an area of law, or references to case law and statutes).
Tertiary	• Materials or sources referred to by other primary or secondary sources. • Includes sources referred to by footnotes, bibliographies, quotations, or other mentions in primary or secondary sources.	• Materials that direct the researcher to other primary or secondary sources; also known as "finding tools." • Includes case digests and statutory indexes (to direct researchers to primary source materials) and legal periodical indexes (to direct researchers to secondary source materials such as law reviews or legal newspapers.

How a Factual Researcher Uses Sources

When you don't know much about a topic, secondary factual sources are generally good places to *start* conducting research because they lead to primary sources that, in addition, lead to other sources, which the factual researcher refers to as tertiary sources. Secondary legal sources can also be a good place to start legal research for the same reasons—because they lead the legal researcher to primary sources (cases, statutes, and regulations) for citing to a judge, and also lead to other secondary legal sources.

Let's say a factual researcher is researching e-mail spam. He starts by conducting a quick search of the Electronic Privacy Information Center (EPIC) Web site, (**http://www.epic.org**) and finds an article, "SPAM: Unsolicited Commercial E-Mail," that's full of good information. This article is a *secondary* source.

The article refers to Timothy Muris, chairman of the Federal Trade Commission (FTC), who released a new privacy agenda for the agency. The article also refers to a book by David Sorkin, *Technical and Legal Approaches to Unsolicited Electronic Mail.* The references to the agency's new privacy agenda and to Sorkin's book are both *tertiary* sources, because they were referenced in a secondary source. (A legal researcher would label these sources secondary.)

If the factual researcher phones Muris and Sorkin and interviews them, they become *primary* sources. If the legal researcher phones them, they remain secondary sources. If either of these people refers the legal researcher to a statute, regulation, or case about the topic, these become primary sources when the legal researcher locates them.

Judging Sources for Worth and Credibility

To determine which sources are worthy of use for a research project, the expert researcher needs not only to judge their worth by assessing their relevance and quality, but to judge also their credibility. Distinguishing the relevant and credible sources from the irrelevant and suspect sources is a critical research skill, especially so when using the Internet—where anyone can (and anyone does) publish. See the section "Internet Source Credibility" later in this chapter to learn how to apply the credibility test to material found on the Internet.

> The most valuable skill an Internet researcher can have is to know when *not* to use the Internet.

When to Use the Internet

Prior to jumping onto the Internet, knowing how accessible a resource is in a nonelectronic format can save lots of time. If you are about to invest time in accessing, searching, and sifting through Internet sources, it ought to be worth the trip. There is no better testament to the need to choose the right resource than watching a colleague pull a copy of the *World Almanac* right off the shelf sitting next to you while you are hyperlinking through home pages, and seeing him flip to the page with the data you are looking for in less than half the time it takes you to find it online.

However, if an Internet surfer can verify the toxicity of an accidental overdose of an over-the-counter drug by accessing a pharmaceutical encyclopedia online that is not located on the shelf right next to you, then the Internet has more than proved its worth as a research tool.

> On the other hand, it can also be said: always use the Internet— everyone else is.

In fact, lawyers may run the risk of competency claims if they do not have access to and make use of the Internet. At least one federal court has held that in order to avoid negligence, and to satisfy due diligence considerations, lawyers should be plugged into the Internet. Seventh Circuit Judge Kanne wrote that in the context of a Securities Exchange Act Rule 10b-5 securities fraud action, "nondisclosure of enacted or pending legislation and industry-wide trends is not a basis for a securities fraud claim" because the information was in the public domain and accessible to the plaintiff. "In today's society, with the advent of the information superhighway, federal and state legislation and regulations, as well as information regarding industry trends, are easily accessed. A reasonable investor is presumed to have information available in the public domain, and there-

fore Whirlpool is imputed with constructive knowledge of this information." (*Whirlpool Financial Corporation v. GN Holdings, Inc.* [7th Cir. 1995]
at **http://www.law.emory.edu/7circuit/sept95/95-1292.html**.).Reading
this decision might make you think that this chapter might be more aptly
titled "Always Use the Internet—Everyone Else Is."

Lawyers have an obligation to clients (and to themselves, in order to
remain competitive) to have access to the most comprehensive, cost-
effective research resources. The Internet provides an unparalleled opportunity to find the facts relevant to legal issues.

Maintaining an Edge over Research

The researcher's judgment must remain sharp when determining
whether to use the Internet for fact finding (or for legal research). Maintaining an edge over research is a process of continually asking yourself
what types of sources you need and where you might find them.

Internet Methodology Checklist

1. What type of information do I need?
2. What sources do I need in order to locate the information?
3. What is the likelihood of finding these sources on the Internet?
4. How immediately can these sources be accessed elsewhere, if at all?
5. What will the research cost, in time and money?

This thought process may appear to be painstaking at the outset, but
it is crucial to the researcher, especially if there are limitations on time
and expense. When well integrated into the research mix, this Internet
Methodology Checklist becomes second nature to the researcher, and
often can be processed in no time. It is, in fact, not very different from the
step-by-step approach employed for many years by researchers using
printed materials. It is at the heart of truly effective Internet use, and is
mastered not simply by learning how to surf the Internet like a pro, but by
remembering to think like a researcher. The checklist can be applied to
both legal research and fact-finding research.

We'll use the following fact pattern to illustrate how to use the Internet Methodology Checklist for legal research and fact-finding research:
Let's say you are working on a case that involves a school-bus accident. A
child was injured in the accident. It appears that her injuries were caused

from the seat belt that she was wearing on the school bus. The child and her parent want to know who's liable.

❑ *Checklist Item 1: What Type of Information Do I Need?*

To put this question into law school exam lingo, "What is the call of the question?" To start assessing liability, the legal researcher in you decides that the first bit of information you need is to figure out *why* there were seat belts on this school bus to begin with. When you rode a school bus, there were no seat belts. You're going to need legal data and information to answer the following question:

- Did the school bus company install seat belts because a new law was passed mandating their installation in school buses, or did they install them on their own, without any mandate?

The factual researcher in you has other questions. You're going to need factual data and information to answer the following questions:

- What type of seat belt was it (lap or shoulder)?
- Who manufactured it? Who installed it?
- Was it manufactured or installed defectively?
- Were other children injured on the bus?
- Were they wearing seat belts?
- Have there been similar accidents?
- Were children in those other accidents injured by the seat belts?

❑ *Checklist Item 2: What Sources Do I Need in Order to Locate the Information?*

The following legal sources are needed to locate information about whether a law was passed recently that mandated seat belts on school buses:

- Codes (probably state, but possibly local or federal)
- Bills (if it's a new statute, it might not be in the code yet, so you'll need to search current bills)
- Legislative history (to find the intent behind the law and to learn if there was any conflicting data as to whether it is safe to place seat belts on school buses)
- Newspaper articles (there were probably articles written about this new law)

The following factual sources are needed to locate the answers to all the other questions relating to the manufacture and installation of the seat belts, and statistics about other similar accidents:

- Product directory (to help identify the seat belt manufacturer and other manufacturers of similar products)
- Company Web site (to see if the manufacturing specs are on any of the manufacturers' sites, and to learn about this specific company structure so you know who to name)
- Government statistics (about school bus and seat belt accidents)
- Articles from newspapers or journals about safety issues concerning placing seat belts on school buses and about similar accidents (and cases) elsewhere
- Newsgroups or Internet mailing lists (to find unofficial or informal reports about school bus and seat belt accidents)

❏ *Checklist Item 3: What Is the Likelihood of Finding these Sources on the Internet?*

The likelihood is high that you'll find many of these legal and factual research sources on the Internet, but you'll need to verify that they are current and credible sources. It won't do any good to rely on an old code, for instance, especially if you suspect that this is a new law.

The following federal legal sources are on the Internet, and they are free:

- U.S. Code
- Bills
- Legislative history

The following state legal sources are likely to be on the Internet, and free (this varies from jurisdiction to jurisdiction):

- Codes
- Bills
- Legislative history
- Local codes and ordinances

The likelihood is high that the following factual resources will be on the Internet for free:

- Bus accident and injury statistics—probably in some government agency Web site related to transportation (see Chapter 6, "Government Resources Online," Chapter 17, "Statistical Research," and Chapter 18, "Transportation Research")
- Articles about school bus and seat belt safety issues and other accidents and cases (see Chapter 9, "Finding and Backgrounding Expert Witnesses," to learn how to find experts' articles)
- Company Web sites (see Chapter 10, "Company Research")

- Product directories (see Chapter 10, "Company Research")
- Newsgroups (such as Google Groups) and Internet e-mail lists. The Internet is the only likely place where you might get information directly from the source by searching newsgroups and e-mail lists (see Chapter 3, "Search Strategies," and Chapter 10, "Company Research")

❏ *Checklist Item 4: How Immediately Can these Sources Be Accessed Elsewhere, if at All?*

Codes: If you have ready access to any of the codes in print, start there. Otherwise, start searching the Internet. Most (if not all) free sites with codes lack case annotations. Even though you can immediately access both the code and the case annotations at a pay site, we wouldn't advise starting with a pay site. Instead, use the free Web sites to find the statute's citation. In case it takes a while to find the citation, you can do it without worrying about the cost of being on a pay site. However, once you find the citation, then turn to a pay database and enter the citation to find annotations.

Local codes: Most people don't have ready access to local (county or city) codes and it's hardly worth a commercial publisher's effort to try to place every municipality's code online—the money is just not there. It's more likely that the local codes, if online at all, can be found on a free site on the Internet.

Statistics and company Web sites: It's unlikely that you have immediate access to injury statistics or information about seat belt manufacturers at your fingertips, and there's no saying that you can find these resources more quickly on a pay site than on the free Internet. Obviously, a company's Web site won't be immediately accessible anywhere but on the free Internet.

Articles: Magazine articles are unlikely to be immediately accessible in print. You might try a free site on the Internet first (such as FindArticles.com), but you may want to turn to a pay database of articles, where more articles and more years' worth of articles are indexed. For newspaper articles, try a few free sites first, but you'll need to search each newspaper's site one by one (unless you know how to access a free newspaper index that searches many simultaneously—see the section "Free Internet Access to Library Databases and Catalogs" in Chapter 5, "General Factual Research"). For newspaper articles, we also recommend using a pay site where you can search hundreds of newspapers in one simultaneous search.

❏ *Checklist Item 5: What Will the Research Cost, in Time and Money?*
It will cost you less money to use the free Internet to find the statute's citation, and because it's usually less expensive to do a citation search than a keyword search in a pay database, you will spend less money if you first find the statute's citation, then use a pay database to find case annotations.

It should cost you little time and no money to search for the company Web site on the Internet. However, if you need very detailed information about the corporate structure, in order to know who to name in the suit, a pay database may be the quicker way to go. We recommend the Directory of Corporate Affiliations database for an instant answer (found on Lexis or Westlaw). Granted, you could piece the information together through various sources on the free Internet (see Chapter 10, "Company Research," and Chapter 11, "Competitive Intelligence Research"), but it may take too long and end up costing you in billable hours.

Finding statistics will probably be less costly on free sites than in a pay database, but in both cases it might be time-consuming, so this might be the perfect research project for a "virtual law librarian" (see the section "Getting Help: Expert Research Support" in Chapter 3, "Search Strategies").

Finding Something Responsive to Your Research

As you can see from the sample search above, you may be able to retrieve most of the information for free from the Internet. This is because the Internet's breadth has continued to widen, and it is becoming a first stop for research of all sorts (including traditional legal research) and particularly for factual research. The openness of the Internet, which enables virtually anyone to publish, has resulted in a continually expanding collection that covers the scope of human knowledge. This is not to say that you can find *everything* on the Internet, but that it's likely you'll find something responsive to your research—something that will point you in a productive direction, even if it does not actually answer your precise question.

Lack of Documentation on the Free Internet

With the openness of the Internet, however, comes the caveat that not everything on the Internet is current or credible (see the section on "Internet Source Credibility" in this chapter). This is where the pay databases sometimes have an advantage over the free Internet sites—you can pretty much assume the pay sites' data is credible and current without doing the extra checking you might need to do when using a free source. Documentation is still somewhat lacking at the free sites on the Web. If you need documentation regarding the credibility or currency of the data found in pay databases, there's 24-7 customer service to provide the answers. (Fee-based Internet customer service is just evolving for the legal professional—see the section on "Getting Help: Expert Research Support" in Chapter 3, "Search Strategies.")

Internet Source Credibility

A good researcher needs to be a sleuth, someone who specializes in finding facts, in understanding why some facts can't be found, and in figuring out whether any of the found facts are credible. Surrounded by today's ocean of information on the Internet, a lawyer now needs to be a "cybersleuth." Lawyers need to be able to look through endless buckets of data to find the relevant drops. We are faced with so many data sources that simply keeping track of them, let alone vouching for their credibility, can be overwhelming. Just because a search engine brings you back Web site results doesn't mean the information at the sites comes from credible sources or is necessarily quality information. Anyone can put up a Web site (or a Web log), post to a newsgroup or an advice site, or join an Internet mailing list, and say anything he wants.

One of the tenets of sound research technique is that a healthy ounce of skepticism is worth a pound of information. There is an adage in accounting that states, "Figures don't lie, but liars figure." The computer-expert version is "Garbage in, garbage out." For most researchers, the adage can be stated even more simply: "Just because it's published doesn't mean it's true." Regular users of the Internet recognize that sentiment. The Internet puts a means of instantaneous worldwide publication at everyone's fingertips, from established commercial publishers to school-children.

Case in point: In a two-week period, "Lawguy1975" dispensed 939 legal answers to 943 questions posed on Askme.com (which was an advice site at the time). By mid-July, Lawguy1975 was the number-three-rated expert in criminal law on AskMe.com. Beneath him in the rankings were 125 licensed lawyers and a wild assortment of ex-cops and ex-cons. When asked why he hadn't answered the other four questions out of the 943 posed, "Traffic law," he said. "I'm sorry, I don't know traffic law." Lawguy1975 finally came clean and admitted on Askme.com that he wasn't a lawyer, just Markus Arnold, a 15-year-old kid with an obvious penchant for Court TV. He didn't know about traffic law because, at age 15, he hadn't learned how to drive . . . yet. (Arnold's exploits were included in the book *Next: The Future Just Happened*, by Michael Lewis.)

So, your job is to evaluate a site's credibility before relying upon the information. How do you do this? The easiest way is to use this book for suggested Web sites. The authors of this book have tested the sites and evaluated them—not only for content, but also for credibility—before recommending them.

There are also a number of Web sites that offer advice on determining the credibility of other sites you find on your own. Consumer Union's Consumer WebWatch site offers a set of recommended guidelines for Web sites to follow (**http://www.consumerwebwatch.org/bestpractices/ index.html**). The site also offers a report on its 2002 research survey, "A Matter of Trust: What Users Want From Web Sites" (**http://www.con sumerwebwatch.org/news/1_abstract.htm**). Other sources for guidelines for testing Web site credibility include **http://www.webcredibility.org/ guidelines**, and LLRX's article "Getting It Right: Verifying Sources on the Net" (**http://www.llrx.com/features/verifying.htm**).

For other Web sites that you encounter, try running them through the following checklist to see how they stand up.

Internet Source Credibility Checklist

1. Can you tell the site's owner, editor, or authors when you visit the site?
2. Run the domain name through a registry database to discover the owner.
3. Verify credentials by doing an independent search, not just by relying upon what is given on the site.
4. Discover who else relies on a particular site by conducting a link search.
5. How fresh is the content?
6. What is the quality of the content?
7. Is the site missing any content? Is it as complete as its print version (if there is one)?
8. Verify all information by trying to find the same data at another site.
9. Ascertain the top-level domain (TLD) to help decide credibility.
10. Document your search.

❑ *Checklist Item 1: Can You Tell Who the Site Owner Is When You Visit the Site?*

Look for a publication statement on the site to ascertain the owner, editor, and authors. Be suspicious if you don't find it easily. A credible site owner should post his name and contact information in a readily visible place on the site in case you want to verify the owner's identity or contact him via e-mail or phone. We've contacted site owners countless times to ask about their credentials or the currency of their data, or even to let them know that links weren't working.

When we went to the Jurist.law site (**http://jurist.law.pitt.edu/ about.htm#Masthead**), for example, it was easy to find out that it was hosted by the University of Pittsburgh and that the site editors and founder were a group of law professors (although when we noticed one of their names was "Lawless" we were momentarily concerned about creditability!).

❑ *Checklist Item 2: Run the Domain Name through a Registry Database to Discover the Owner*

To *try* to discover who is behind a Web site, type the URL into a registry such as Better-Whois (**http://www.betterwhois.com**) or Allwhois (**http://www.allwhois.com**). Allwhois also provides links to other countries' registries. If you only know a partial domain name and are also unsure of the TLD, use DomainSurfer.com (**http://www.domainsurfer.com**). The reason why we emphasized "try" in the first sentence of this paragraph is because no registry, for a variety of reasons, seems to be "completely complete." A registry may claim to be the "most complete 'whois' service on the Internet," but this doesn't mean complete as in "comprehensive"—just the most complete that it can be, given all the obstacles. It's difficult to create a comprehensive registry because registries may receive less-than-complete records when a domain is registered, and most registries only cover the most popular TLD types such as .com, .net, or .org, thus leaving out many records from the less popular TLD's such as .biz or .museum.

Even if you do find the registration statement, it's hard to say whether you have found the site owner because anyone can list themselves as the contact person on the registration statement—the site owner, the IT manager, or the Web site's outside designer.

❑ *Checklist Item 3: Verify the Owner or Author's Credentials by Doing an Independent Search*

Don't just rely on the information that is given on the site. If the site owner says he's a lawyer in California, run his name through the California bar association's member records to verify his license and review his discipline record. If the site owner claims to be an author, run his name through the Library of Congress online catalog (**http://catalog.loc.gov**) and its copyright database (**http://www.loc.gov/copyright/search**).

❏ *Checklist Item 4: Discover Who Else Relies on the Site*

Sometimes the best way to verify credibility is to see who thinks highly enough of the site to link to it from another site. For example, to

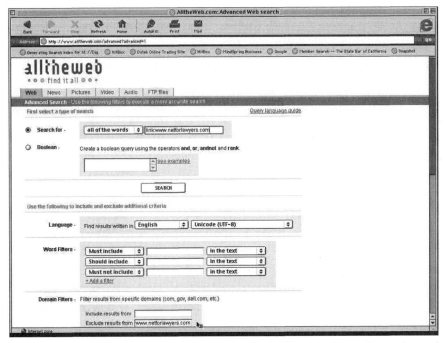

Figure 1-1. The Alltheweb search engine allows you to determine what other sites link to a site you are interested in.

see if others rely upon a site called www.sitename.com, conduct a link search using the Alltheweb search engine. Using Alltheweb's Advanced Search page, enter "link:www.sitename.com" in the **all of the words** query box and also enter the same URL (**www.sitename.com**) in the **Domain Filter-Exclude Results From** query box.

❏ *Checklist Item 5: How Fresh Is the Content?*

Look for a statement saying when the site as a whole was last updated. Also look for publication dates for the articles or other material posted on the site. For example, on April 22, 2003, we visited the

Jurist.law site (**http://jurist.law.pitt.edu/index.htm**) and found a 2003 copyright statement at the bottom of the home page. We then looked for a publication date for any of the material posted on the site and found exact dates that indicated when each piece of information had been added (such as "added 4/18/03"). There were also news stories with the current date (4/22/03). All this indicated that the site was being kept fresh.

❑ *Checklist Item 6: What Is the Quality of the Content?*

Is the content one-sided or objective? One-sided information might be acceptable if it's being used to persuade. For example, the Electronic Privacy Information Center (EPIC) states that it is "a public interest research center . . . established . . . to focus public attention on emerging civil liberties issues and to protect privacy, the First Amendment, and constitutional values." Is this site biased? You bet. But, as noted above, it clearly states its bias on its home page by way of its purpose message. Is the information of high quality? Yes—it's just presented from a privacy advcate's viewpoint.

❑ *Checklist Item 7: Is the Site Missing Any Content? Is It as Complete as Its Print Version (if There Is One)?*

Ever since the *Tasini* decision, many publications have had to remove individual author's articles from their Web sites (*New York Times Co. v. Tasini*, 533 U.S. 483 [2001]). Thus, many Web sites are no longer as complete as their corresponding print versions. Sometimes the opposite occurs—a Web site may contain more content than the print publication. This is the case with sites that continually update throughout the day.

❑ *Checklist Item 8: Verify All Information by Trying to Find the Same Information at Another Site*

Just by reviewing your results, you can often tell that the information is being published at many sites. Does this make it any more credible? Not necessarily, but you can click on a few of the sites and apply the credibility test. We typically don't verify information if we've already run the site through a credibility test, or if someone else whose judgment we trust has done so. Whom do we trust? People who test out sites before writing about them. These are some of the sites where we know the authors test sites before recommending them: Virtual Chase, SearchEngineWatch, Search Engine Showdown, LLRX, and Netforlawyers (just add a .com to each to visit the sites) and the ABA's Site-tation (**http://www.lawtechnology.org/site-tation**).

❏ *Checklist Item 9: Ascertain the TLD to Help Decide Credibility*

Does the TLD indicate it's a government (.gov), educational (.edu), or commercial (.com) site?

Can you trust a site with a .gov TLD? The U.S. General Services Administration Federal Technology Service (GSA FTS) validates each .gov top-level domain name before registering it. It's likely then that a site with the .gov TLD is actually sponsored by the government. We say "likely" because on Jan. 24, 2003, the GSA was faced with the first "hijacking" of a .gov TLD, and pulled the domain of AONN.gov after CNET site (**http://news.com**) questioned the site's governmental status.

Even when you're sure a .gov site is authentic, there are other aspects of credibility that must be considered, such as whether the information on the site is current. For example, the U.S. Code is published by two governmental entities—the House of Representatives and the Government Printing Office (GPO)—but the House site is the more current (**http://uscode.house.gov/usc.htm**). On April 22, 2003, the GPO site (**http://www.access.gpo.gov/congress/cong013.html**) was current only up to laws that took effect on January 2, 2001, while the House site showed dates of 2002.

Another credibility issue is whether the information on a government site is the "official" record? For example, many court sites warn that their site is for informational purposes only and that the information is *not* the official record. This is especially true for courts that publish their slip opinions because the court can later modify the opinion.

Can you trust the .edu TLD? Just because an academic institution sponsors a site doesn't mean an academician is writing the content. Case in point: we did a search using the words "lemon" and "law" and came up with a .edu site with a page written by an elementary school child, who liked lemonade and root beer and wanted to be a law professor when he grew up! Needless to say, this site didn't help us with our lemon-law questions. Not all such instances will be as obvious, unfortunately.

Therefore, as with all information sources, data retrieved from the Internet must be viewed with skepticism until its credibility has been verified. Any cybersleuth can access data sources. But if you are after genuine knowledge, only a *good* cybersleuth knows to judge credibility before relying on the data.

Can you trust well-known pay resources? Even pay resources can contain errors. While you don't have to go through the same credibility checklist to identify owners and sponsors of pay resources (such as Lexis-

Nexis or Westlaw), you still need to verify the veracity and currency of the information you find there.

❏ *Checklist Item 10: Document Your Search*
Keep a copy of the pages you will be relying upon so you can prove credibility to others.

Free Versus Pay Resources

Although Lexis, Westlaw, and other legal research, fee-based databases originally provided access only to the law, they have added reams of factual information to their databases. Though you can now turn to them for factual research, the best researchers know that there are often many ways to access the same information for free on the Internet. Sometimes the information you seek will only be found in a free Internet source (such as a small-town newspaper that a pay database wouldn't bother to index). On the flip side, the best researchers also know that sometimes it's worth the money to use pay databases (even if you think the information can be found for free on the Internet).

The Myth of the "All-Comprehensive" Database

Although a savvy searcher knows how to evaluate which method (free or pay) is the best route to take, the *really* savvy searcher knows that there is no such thing, even in a pay environment, as a definitive and comprehensive database (in scope and content) for any area of knowledge. For example, there is no pay database that will search every type of public record that was ever filed, in every government agency, and in every jurisdiction.

The savvy searcher also knows that whether using free or pay databases, the type and amount of information available varies greatly from jurisdiction to jurisdiction. Some states, such as Florida, have a wide variety of public records available for free on the Internet (such as Uniform Commercial Code filings (UCC), trademark owner names, corporate records, and annual reports), and they also provide a large amount of information in each record by placing the image of the original public record online (**http://ccfcorp.dos.state.fl.us**). Other states may not provide access to the same data Florida does, or may provide some of it free and require payment for some.

And finally, the savvy searcher knows that to conduct what comes closest to a comprehensive search sometimes involves all, or a combination of, the following:

- Pay database searching
- Free Internet searching
- Print resource searching
- Hiring expert researchers
- Contacting the source, such as a government agency or an individual, via:

    - In-person visit
    - Phone call
    - E-mail message
    - Letter

When to Use Pay Databases

We recommend using pay databases in the following instances:

- **If it's going to be quicker than surfing the Internet.** You might know exactly where to find the information in a pay database because you've been there before, or perhaps you need to document that the data is credible and current, and you don't have time to evaluate a free Internet source (documentation is usually better on the pay sources).

- **If you need older data.** Pay databases often offer earlier date coverage. The free Internet is fairly new compared to pay databases, many of which have been around for at least twenty-five years. Thus, the pay databases are more comprehensive in scope because they have been building their archives longer than the free sites have.

- **If you need to perform a somewhat complex search.** Pay sites often have better search functions—allowing for easier access to data (and sometimes the only, or the only reasonable, access), such as:

    - Performing national or multistate searches
    - Searching a broad swath of unrelated material (for example, searching through thousands of articles in hundreds of individually owned newspapers or magazines)
    - Field searching (by name, date, and so on)

- **If the information is only available at a pay source**.
  - A pay database may have purchased a certain category of public records from a government entity and created an on-line product where one did not exist before
  - A pay database may have purchased publicly available information to fill in any information gaps in public records
  - A pay database is commonly known as the only source—such as a D & B company or a credit report for a private company

Examples of Pay Database Searches

Below are some examples of the types of searches best suited to pay sites.

National and Multistate Searching

If a searcher wants to search a corporation in every state in which it is registered (and therefore needs to find the registered agent in each state), a multijurisdictional secretary of state search using the corporation's name is in order. If the searcher needs to discover in which state a company is incorporated or licensed to do business, again, a multijurisdictional secretary of state search by the corporation's name is in order. Neither of these types of simultaneous multistate searches can be done for free on the Internet. Conceivably, you could search the free Internet, state by state, but in a time and cost analysis, it would not be worth your while. Thus, a pay site is the best (and only reasonable) option. Also, not every state has posted its corporate records for free on the Internet, but the records are likely to be available in a pay database.

Field Searching

Field searching allows you to search with almost any nugget of information, or with a combination of nuggets. For example:

- If you *only* know someone's Social Security number and need to find his or her name, address, and phone number, you can perform a reverse search on a fee-based database that provides a Social Security number search field.
- When searching using a name is getting you nowhere and you suspect the spelling provided to you was wrong, if you have any other nugget of information (such as a Social Security number, a phone number, or an address), entering that information into the appropriate field to conduct a reverse search can get you the correct spelling.

- If you need to know if a specific person is a registered agent in a state, this typically requires a pay search, because most free sites don't provide multiple-field searching options where you can search by either a corporation's name or a registered agent's name. Most free sites only allow you to perform a one-field search, and that is typically a corporation name search. Most pay sites also allow you to also conduct a registered agent name field search. (However, in Florida, you *can* search by a registered agent's name for free at Florida's Secretary of State site. Thus, it never hurts to first visit a state's free site to review the search functions.)

Advanced Searches

Pay sites allow sophisticated and flexible types of searches, such as the following searches of public records:

- In a single search, being able to search one public-record category for one or more states (for example, searching using an individual's name through all online real estate records nationwide to marshal his or her assets)
- In a single search, being able to search through multiple public-record categories in unrelated agencies in one or more states (for example, searching on an individual's name to find all of his or her property records, bankruptcies, liens, and judgments)

Publicly Available Information at Pay Sites

The content found in a fee-based database is usually more comprehensive than that of a free public-record database, because pay sites add data from publicly available information that was voluntarily provided to nongovernmental entities. This information is extracted from sources such as a product warranty cards, where purchasers divulge income, gender, and age; phone directories; utility customer lists; and so on.

Examples of Major Pay Databases

Throughout the book, we refer to pay databases, such as Lexis, LexisONE, Westlaw, Choicepoint, Accurint, Merlin, eInfoData, and KnowX. We discuss specific aspects of the data available on these pay sites when it relates to the chapter's subject, and we indicate when it's best (or necessary) to use the pay sources. For example, in the section on real estate records in Chapter 8, "Accessing Public Records," we discuss free real estate assessor sources first. But if a jurisdiction doesn't have this data online for free, or if the pay database has a better search feature, we discuss the pay database too. In some of the chapters, we introduce pay databases in addition to the major ones noted above.

When to Use Free Internet Sources

Below are just some of the myriad situations when it's best to use the free Internet. Throughout this book, we give examples of each type of situation listed below, and suggest specific free Web sites to use to find the factual answers. Use a free site in these circumstances:

- If you don't need a comprehensive search, only a targeted one
- If the free site provides more information than the pay site
- If you have a lot of clues about a person or if he has a unique name
- If you want both official and unofficial information—such as rumors or opinions about a company, a product, an event, or a person, or to see what nuggets of information "pop up"—use the following free Internet sources:

  - Search engine
  - Newsgroup
  - Your subject's Web site
  - Your subject's Web log (also known as a "blog")
  - Internet mailing list
  - Archive of magazine or newspaper articles
  - Conference papers

- If you're looking for very local or regional information
- If you're looking for up-to-the-minute (literally) news—some search engines and some sites add news continually throughout the day (see the section on news in Chapter 5, "General Factual Research")
- If you're looking for other types of up-to-the-minute information such as:

  - Stock quotes
  - Time
  - Weather
  - Sports scores

- If you're looking for anything that might have been created in the following file formats:

- Microsoft Word
- Microsoft Excel (spreadsheets)
- Microsoft PowerPoint (presentations)
- Adobe Portable Document Format (PDF)

- If you're looking for government information, such as:

  - Public records
  - Statistics
  - Reports

- If you're looking for forms

- If you're looking for something created privately and later posted to the Internet, such as:

  - Brochures
  - Newsletters
  - Family trees
  - Conference papers

Examples of Searches on Free Sites

Targeted Search

If a searcher needs to locate a company's corporate record, and only needs to search one specific state, the free route usually is satisfactory if that state's secretary of state database is free on the Web. In this case, it doesn't pay to search virtually the same database at a pay site. To easily link to all states that do provide free corporate record databases over the Web, use the National Association of Secretaries of States metasite (**http://www.nass.org/sos/sos.html**) or Residentagentinfo.com (**http://www.residentagentinfo.com**). For more details on these two databases, see Chapter 10, "Company Research."

Free Site with More Information

In state trial-court docket databases, some of the pay sites may only contain the party name and the docket number, while the free government sites may also contain the lawyers' names and the case disposition (and sometimes even more).

However, even though the free site may have more information, you still might first need to use a pay site to get to the free information because the pay site offers better searching! For example, if you only have the party's name, and the free docket site doesn't allow for party name field searching (it only allows docket number field searching), a pay site comes in handy because it typically allows for party name field searching. By doing a party name field search at the pay site, you can discover the docket number. Then to find more information, such as the attorneys of record or the disposition, you can visit the free site and search by the newly found docket number. It's a roundabout method, but one we've had to use.

If the first key to successful, efficient research is to first know where to start—in a pay database or free on the Internet—the next step to success is deciding which specific sources to use. For instance, if using the free Internet, in which Web site or search engine should you start your research? See Chapter 3, "Search Strategies," and Chapter 4, "Search Tools," for tips on how to begin to identify specific sources.

Citing Internet Resources

For insight into how to cite to a Web site, *The Bluebook: A Uniform System of Citation, Seventeenth Edition* finally provides some solutions beyond the *Bluebook's* sixteenth edition's examples of journal articles only (see Rule 18 in the *Bluebook*). The *Bluebook* discourages citing to Web sites unless the materials are unavailable in printed form because sites are so transient and can disappear from the Internet. If no one is able to find and verify your citation to a Web site, you will not be able to rely upon it any longer for your argument.

Although the *Bluebook* is not online, a basic guide to the *Bluebook* entitled *Introduction to Basic Legal Citation*, by Peter Martin, with examples on how to cite Internet sources, can be found at Cornell University's Web site, **http://www.law.cornell.edu/citation**. To find examples, click on **How to Cite** (in the left column) and then click on **Electronic Sources**.

Martin also refers to an alternative citation manual for examples on citing electronic sources, the *ALWD Citation Manual: A Professional System of Citation* (2000), written by the Association of Legal Writing Directors.

An electronic citation should consist of all the elements required by the *Bluebook* for any of the basic document types found in print, followed by the appropriate signal ("available at" or "at") with a direct address to the online source. "Available at" is the appropriate signal to use before the Web site citation if you are citing to both the printed and the Web site versions. For example, you would cite to a print version of U.S. Supreme Court case that is also found on the Cornell site in this manner:

Hill v. Colorado, 200 U.S. 404 (2000), *available at* **http://supct.law.cornell.edu/supct/html/98-1856.ZS.html**.

If the electronic source is the only known source, use the signal "at":

Smith v. Jones *at* **http://supct.law.cornell.edu/supct/html/98-1856.ZS.html**.

If citing only to the electronic source, even when the material is also available in a printed source, no explanatory signal is used:

Hill v. Colorado, **http://supct.law.cornell.edu/supct/html/98-1856.ZS.html**

To cite to articles on the Web, provide the following: (1) the name of the author, (2) the title of the article, (3) the URL in angle brackets (< >), and (4) the publication date if available (or the most recent modification date of the site or the date you visited the site). For example:

Levitt, Carole, How to Use the Internet for Legal Research (last modified September 20, 1999) <**http://www.netforlawyers.com**>

If a journal appears only on the Internet, include (1) the volume number, (2) the title of the journal, (3) the sequential article number, and (4) the paragraph number (if doing pinpoint citing). For example:

Levitt, Carole, How to Use the Internet for Legal Research, 3 *Net for Lawyers* L.J. 1, par.8 (July 20, 1999) <**http://www.netforlawyers.com/levitt.html**>

A word about using angle brackets to set off URLs: opinion on this is divided into two camps. The first camp believes in following *The Chicago Style of Manual,* which does not favor using angle brackets because they can cause confusion (Web site designers also use angle brackets as part of Web page mark-up languages, such as HTML or XML). The other camp thinks angle brackets are useful to show where a URL begins and ends. To avoid the mark-up language confusion and to indicate where the URL begins and ends, in this book we often place URLs in parentheses.

In 1996, the American Bar Association (ABA) approved a resolution recommending that courts adopt a uniform public domain citation system "equally effective for printed case reports and for case reports electronically published on computer disks or network services." About twelve states and the Sixth Circuit Court have adopted the ABA's resolution for uniform citation. For a full copy of this report, go to **http://www.abanet.org/tech/ltrc/research/citation/report.html**. (The American Association of Law Libraries published the *Universal Citation Guide* to implement the ABA's resolution. To order this book, see **http://www.aallnet.org/products/pub_universal.asp**.)

The following example is offered by the ABA for citation to a federal court of appeals decision found on a Web site:

   Smith v. Jones, 1996 5Cir 15, ¶ 18, 22 F.3d 955

The ABA instructs that if a case is only available on the Internet, print it out for opposing counsel and the court.

Finally, if you don't find a specific rule or example in any of these sources, provide as much information as you can and print out a copy of the material (as the ABA instructs you to do for cases on the Internet) or use citation examples from either of the two nationally recognized general citation style manuals, *The Chicago Manual of Style* or the *American Psychological Association* (APA) *Publication Manual*. The APA manual has a Web page about electronic references at **http://www.apastyle.org/elecref.html.** The Chicago Manual is not online, but its frequently-asked questions (FAQs) page (**www.press.uchicago.edu/Misc/Chicago/cmosfaq/cmosfaq.html**) offers helpful Internet citation tips, and the editors welcome your questions. Their replies may come as individual responses or may appear on the FAQ page. Here is an example of a *Chicago Manual* citation for a private e-mail message:

   Ford, Cory <cford@soil.com>, "Soil Ecology Discussion," private e-mail
   message to author. 7 March 1998.

Internet Copyright Issues

All we can definitively say about copyright and the Internet is that as courts try to superimpose traditional copyright rules (Title 17 of the U.S. Code) onto the digital world, the two concepts will continue to clash, and the rules will be constantly shifting. When copyright laws were written, no one dreamed that books, articles, and other text, and even music, images, and videos would be posted in cyberspace on this thing we call the Internet.

Ask a typical Internet user about copyright and the Internet and you'll probably get the reply that if it's on the Internet for free, then it's free to copy! This, of course, is patently wrong if the material is copyrighted (unless it fits within fair use), but it's the common belief (or hope) of most Internet users.

When digital data appears on a computer screen, is it considered to be

- A copy?
- Distribution?
- Publication?

- Public display?
- Fair use?

Or, do these questions only arise when the digital material is actually printed out as a hard copy?

Ownership of Digital Rights to Freelance Work: The Tasini Decision

Digital rights are now typically a standard part of a freelancer's contract, but when contracts were signed over a decade ago, they were not. In *New York Times Company v. Tasini*, 533 U.S. 483 (2001), the U.S. Supreme Court ruled that print publishers must seek copyright permission from freelancers before placing their work into an electronic database. This decision has affected many Web site archives that contained freelancers' articles from over a decade ago because many works have now been taken off line. While this decision was a victory for freelancers, it was a loss for researchers who can no longer rely on digital archives necessarily being complete.

Ownership of Digital Rights to an Author's Works

The case of Rosetta Books also dealt with the question of digital rights. Rosetta Books paid various authors for the electronic publishing rights to their books. Random House then filed suit, claiming those rights were already theirs by virtue of agreements from twenty to forty years before, when each author granted to Random House the exclusive right to "print, publish and sell in book form." Random House asserted that those agreements should be interpreted as including the right to publish those books in an e-book format. Random House's appeal, from the denial of a preliminary injunction that sought to enjoin Rosetta Books from selling the e-books that it claimed it had exclusive rights over, was affirmed by the Second Circuit in *Random House v. Rosetta Books*, 283 F.3d 490 (2002). Eventually, the pending litigation was settled, with no financial payment made by either party. Instead, they agreed to partner in developing the e-book market. The question of who owns digital rights to an author's work if digital technology was not even imagined when the contracts were signed remains unanswered.

In-line Linking and Framing

Is it fair use for sites to use in-line linking or frames to display content that actually resides on a third party's server? Not according to the Ninth Circuit and its decision in *Kelly v. Arriba Soft Corporation*, 280 F.3d 934, (9th Cir. 2002). In *Kelly*, the Arriba (now Ditto.com) search engine located and reproduced Kelly's images as thumbnails on the Arriba Web site, and also displayed Kelly's full-sized images on the site using in-line linking and framing. This means, basically, that Arriba linked to the image on Kelly's server, but placed an Arriba frame around the image so it looked as though it was posted on Arriba's site. Although Arriba did not *copy* Kelly's Internet images onto its site (and thus did not violate Kelly's right of reproduction under fair use), the Court held that Arriba did infringe on Kelly's copyright because it unlawfully *distributed* and publicly *displayed* Kelly's images. The Copyright Act protects against unlawful distribution and public display of copyrighted material.

Screen Shots

Does using a screen shot of a Web site for illustrative purposes (as we do in this book) invoke copyright issues? The Ninth Circuit faced a somewhat similar issue in a "comparison advertisement" case. In *Sony Computer Entertainment America v. Bleem*, 214 F.3d 1022 (9th Cir. 2000), the court had to decide "whether the unauthorized use of a 'screen shot'—a frozen image from a personal video game [in this case]—falls within the fair use exception to the law of copyright." The court stated, basically, that there was no market in screen shots and held that use of the screen shot was fair use, explaining that:

1. Although Bleem is . . . copying Sony's copyrighted material for the commercial purposes of increasing its own sales . . . there is very

little corresponding loss to the integrity of Sony's copyrighted material.

2. A screen shot is merely an inanimate sliver of the game.

3. A screen shot is such an insignificant portion of the complex copyrighted work as a whole.

4. Bleem's use of a handful of screen shots in its advertising will have no noticeable effect on Sony's ability to do with its screen shots what it chooses.

What if those screen shots are of government Web sites? Does the concept that the government cannot copyright its data because it is in the public domain change in cyberspace? When we wrote for copyright permission to show a screen shot of the government's FedStats Web site (**http://www.fedstats.gov**), the reply was, "Fedstats is in the Public Domain, therefore no special permission is needed to link to our site or place a screen shot on your site or in your publication." Just as we thought. But there are some other intellectual property issues to consider when taking screen shots of government Web sites, such as trademark issues, as pointed out by the reply from the U.S. Security and Exchange Commission (SEC) **EDGAR** site (**http://www.sec.gov/edgar.shtml**) when we sought copyright permission to publish a screen shot of **EDGAR**. "While the Commission has no copyright interest in the web page, it does own a trademark in the **EDGAR** name and logo . . ." However, the commission went on to say that "a display of the name or logo incidental to publication of an image of the web page in a book about Web sites is unlikely to cause public confusion . . ."

The Internet and the Entertainment Industry

When the ruling in *Napster* was made in favor of the entertainment industry, it was hoped by the industry that the issue of downloading copyrighted music had finally been put to rest (*A&M Records, Inc. v. Napster* 284 F.3d 109 9th Cir. 2002). But, as of April 2003, a new case now poses another threat to the entertainment industry's music and movie copyrights. In *MGM v. Grokster*, No. 01-08541 (C.D. CA 2003), Judge Wilson ruled that Grokster is not liable for copyright infringement merely because buyers of its software can copy copyrighted music and movies (thus infringing on copyrights) because the Grokster networks do not monitor or control what people do with the software (unlike Napster, which did). The judge stated that Grokster is no more liable for copyright infringement than Sony was for distributing the Betamax VCR (**http://www.grokster.com/files/030425_order_on_motions.pdf**). Suing each individual infringer is an option, but probably not the most cost-effective and time-effective way of eradicating copyright infringement.

Copyright Clearance Center

Using the Copyright Clearance Center (CCC), you can request permission to reproduce copyrighted material (**https://www.copyright.com**). From articles and book chapters, to Web sites, e-mails, and more, CCC manages the rights to over 1.75 million works of more than 9,600 publishers and hundreds of thousands of authors. Over 10,000 corporations and thousands of government agencies, law firms, document suppliers, libraries, educational institutions, photocopy shops, and bookstores use CCC to clear rights. You can search CCC's online catalog to discover if a work is registered: if it is, you can find out what it would cost to reproduce the work and then instantly have CCC clear the rights you need. The cost depends on how many copies are to be reproduced and for what purpose (to use in a newsletter, for a brochure, and so on).

Other Copyright Issues

These are only a few of the issues confronting lawyers involved in copyright and the Internet. For a look at myriad issues in this area, see the Electronic Frontier Foundation site (**http://www.eff.org**).

*CHAPTER***TWO**

Internet Tools and Protocol

Browsers and Favorites

Web Browsers: A Quick View

- A browser is a program that allows you to view pages on the Internet.
- Browsers (such as Microsoft Internet Explorer or Netscape Communicator) often come pre-installed when you purchase a new computer.
- The different browsers have many similar characteristics . . . and some subtle differences.
- You can cut and paste material from visited sites.
- You can use the Find function to locate text in a long Web page.
- You can bookmark sites you find especially useful to make them easy to return to.

Pick the Browser That Best Suits Your Needs

Besides the software that dials into your Internet Service Provide (ISP), the single most important piece of software required for surfing the Internet is the Web browser, also referred to as simply the browser.

The browser is the computer program that allows users to reach out onto the Internet, locate innumerable Web pages on any number of topics, and translate these computer documents from their HTML programming language into the graphical Web sites we are now all used to seeing.

While all Web browsers perform basically the same functions, they each have their own characteristics. Netscape was first-to-market with a commercial version of a graphical Internet browser with the introduction of its Navigator browser in 1994. Realizing the importance of the Internet as an information platform, Microsoft introduced its Internet Explorer browser the following year. Exhibiting some of the marketing savvy (and muscle) that has made it the largest software publisher in the world, Microsoft went on to capture the lion's share of the browser market. In December 2002, OneStat, a provider of Internet usage statistics, reported that "Microsoft's Internet Explorer has a total global usage share of 95%," while "the global usage share of Netscape is 3.0%" (**http://www.onestat.com/html/aboutuspressbox15. html**). This ongoing competition between Netscape and Microsoft for browser market share has resulted in an incredibly rapid evolutionary pace. For a while, new versions of Navigator and Explorer were being released every six months or so. It is pointless to discuss these features here in any depth, since any information may soon be irrelevant.

It is worth noting, however, the essential browser features that a researcher ought to be familiar with:

- Browsers provide the ability to bookmark favorite Internet sites and easily access those bookmarks.
- Arrows in the upper left-hand corner of the browser window allow you to move back and forward between Web pages you have viewed.
- Like many other programs, browsers offer you the ability to cut text from sites you visit and paste it into your own word processing documents (such as Microsoft Word or Corel WordPerfect). This can be a very handy feature.
- Another excellent browser feature is the ability to conduct a text search on any Web page viewable in your browser, using the Find Function.

Practical Point

Let's say you're conducting research designed to challenge your opponent's expert witness. If the expert is a physician, you might click over to the American Medical Association site (**http://www.ama-assn.org**) to get the expert's basic background. Once you find her address, school attended, and other basics, you might highlight the data with your mouse, copy it using the Ctrl+C sequence (hold down the Ctrl key, and hit C), open your word processor (either a new or existing document), and paste the information (using Ctrl+V) onto the dossier page you're building.

Practical Point

Suppose you're interested in adding to your law firm's corporate clients. As part of the preparation for your marketing effort, you'd like to look into a particular target company's recent legal matters. Assuming your target is a public company, you might start by looking at the relevant portion of the SEC 10-K filing, (Part 1., Item C. Legal Proceedings). So, you could click over to the SEC's EDGAR site (**http://www.sec.gov/cgi-bin/srch-edgar**), and pull up the 10-K. Then, if you're using Navigator or Explorer, you could hit Ctrl+F (hold down the Ctrl key, and hit F) to invoke the Find tool. Note that this tool searches only the document that appears in the browser window. It does not search the entire Internet the way search engines like AltaVista and Google do. When the Find search window pops up, type "legal proceedings" (upper or lower case—it doesn't matter), hit the Enter key, and you should be taken to the Legal Proceedings section of the 10-K.

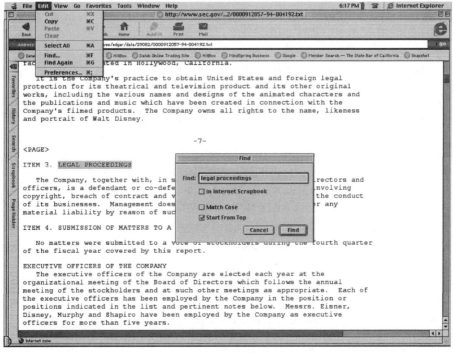

Figure 2-1. Here is a demonstration that uses the Find search tool to locate the Legal Proceedings section of a Walt Disney Company 10-K from the SEC's EDGAR site.

Figure 2-2. To do a similar search when viewing a PDF document on the Internet, click the Binocular icon on the special Adobe® Acrobat Reader® toolbar that opens near the top of your Web browser window whenever you're reading a PDF document. Adobe product screen shot reprinted with permission from Adobe System Incorporated.

Practical Point

Many government documents are posted on the Internet in the Adobe Portable Document Format (PDF). While these documents can be viewed in your browser (if you have installed the Acrobat Viewer plug-in), they are searched differently than described above. An additional toolbar is seen (see Figure 2-2) when the browser displays a PDF document. On this toolbar is a Binocular icon that is used to search the PDF. Clicking that icon brings up the search box into which you type your search term. Clicking Ctrl+F will bring up the browser's Find box, but it will not actually find your search term even if it is in the PDF document. (To make matters even more confusing, not all PDF documents are searchable—even when clicking the Binocular icon and entering search terms. This is dependent on how a document was originally created.)

Choosing a Web browser boils down to personal preferences. Especially given the Microsoft versus Netscape battle for desktop supremacy, the leading browsers are functionally nearly identical. You may have a preference, however, for the way Netscape handles bookmarks, or for the screen layout employed by Internet Explorer. To each his own.

Those without the luxury of an in-house computer support staff must decide for themselves whether to follow the software developers and regularly update their chosen browser by downloading each new version as soon as it becomes available. Often, the newest version of any program can be plagued by small problems known as bugs. As these bugs are discovered and repaired, the browser's creators periodically issue "patches" that must be downloaded and installed on your computer to fix the known bugs. Putting off the updating for a while and waiting for the bugs to be fixed in subsequent versions can cut down on headaches for experienced and novice computer users alike.

Internet Explorer

http://www.microsoft.com/windows/ie

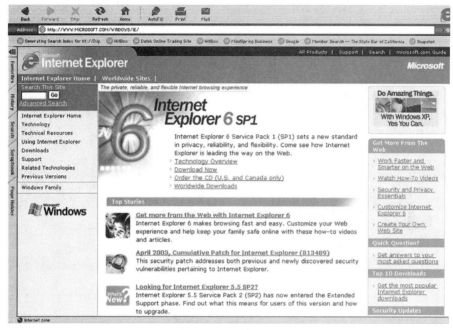

Figure 2-3. Microsoft's Internet Explorer is the most-used Web browser in the world.

Purpose: Software necessary to access Web sites.

Content: Most computers sold commercially come pre-installed with a Microsoft operating system (such as Windows XP), and the latest version of the Internet Explorer (IE) browser. Recent additions to Internet Explorer include Auto Address Completion (which presents a list of possible matches for a URL you are typing from previous URLs you have visited) and improved handling of Internet programming standards to insure that pages are displayed as their designers intended.

Our View: According to some statistics, there's a better than 90 percent chance that this is the browser you're currently using. By virtue of Microsoft's dominance in the software publishing industry, Internet Explorer is the de facto Web browser standard.

Tip: The browser is available as a free download for Windows
               and select handheld operating systems. In June 2003,
               Microsoft announced that it would no longer be developing
               new versions of its Internet browser for Apple operating systems.

Netscape Communicator

http://wp.netscape.com/computing/download

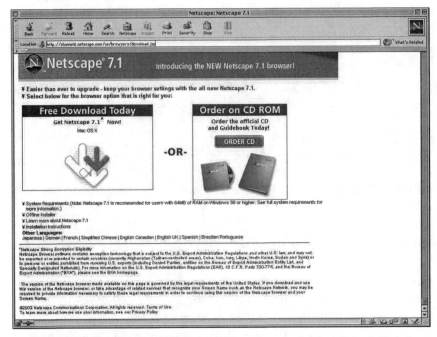

Figure 2-4. Netscape introduced the first commercial (graphical) Web browser
in 1984. This is version 7.1.

Purpose: Software necessary to access Web sites.

Content: With each new version released, the perceptible differences
               between Internet Explorer and Netscape Communicator
               become fewer and fewer. In 1998, Netscape was purchased
               by America Online (AOL).

Our View: Versions of the browser since 1998 have shown more
               and more integration with AOL services like e-mail and

Instant Messenger. Other recent additions include Web page saving, group bookmarks, full-screen mode (which devotes more screen space to Web page content) and pop-up blocking. Some people prefer to use it, and its accompanying e-mail application (Netscape Messenger), because it is not as often the victim of malicious viruses as is Internet Explorer.

Tip: The browser is available as a free download for Windows, Apple, and Linux operating systems.

Mozilla

http://www.mozilla.org

Purpose: Software necessary to access Web sites.

Content: Mozilla was the original code name for the browser that became Netscape Navigator and Communicator. In January 1998, Netscape Corporation announced that it would make the source code for the Netscape browser freely available. Since then, volunteer software developers around the world have revised and refined that original code to create a new browser also known as Mozilla. (This is what is known as an "open source" project.)

Our View: Mozilla includes many of the most up-to-date features of the more well-known browsers, as well as variations on those features. Users familiar with either Internet Explorer or Netscape Communicator will be very comfortable with Mozilla.

Tip: The browser is available as a free download for Windows, Apple, and Linux operating systems. For more informtion on how Mozilla differs from other Internet Browsers, see the article "101 Things that the Mozilla Browser Can Do that IE Cannot" at **http://www.xulplanet.com/ndeakin/ arts/reasons.html**.

Opera

http://www.opera.com/download

Purpose: Software necessary to access Web sites.

Content: The Opera browser has long been popular with "power" Internet users. They praise the program's small size and the speed with which it opens Web pages. Opera is available for most major operating systems, including Windows, Apple, Linux, OS/2, and select handheld computers.

Our View: The paid version ($39) adds e-mail technical support and OperaMail (an e-mail application) in addition to removing the ads.

Tip: A free version (which includes banner advertising) is available for download from Opera. For a more in-depth discussion of the benefits of the Opera browser, see the e-Week article "Opera Stands at the Head of Browser Class" at **http://www.eweek.com/article2/0,3959,857333,00.asp**.

Safari

http://www.apple.com/safari

Purpose: Software necessary to access Web sites from a Macintosh computer.

Content: This is Apple's new Mac OS-X-only Web browser.

Our View   The Apple engineers have added a number of refinements to the basic browser functions. These include a "naming sheet" that allows bookmarks to be easily and immediately named and put into folders for easy access and a "snapback" feature. If you've linked from one site to another, to another, and so on, snapback takes you back to the last page where you typed a URL into the address bar at the top of the browser.

Tip: The browser is available as a free download from Apple.

iCab

http://www.icab.de/dl.php

Purpose: Software necessary to access Web sites.

Content: ICab is another Apple-only browser from Germany. It is available for operating systems from 7.1 through the current OS X.

Our View: Devotees appreciate iCab's small size, fast page loading, and its search tool that users can configure to use their search engine of choice.

Tip: A free version is available for download. A Pro version with added features is available for $29.

Bookmark Your Favorite Sites

All Web browsers allow you to create your own list of Web sites that you find particularly useful. Internet Explorer calls these Favorites. Netscape Communicator calls them Bookmarks. Selecting Bookmarks or Favorites on subsequent Internet sessions takes you directly back to the bookmarked site. Because Internet Explorer is the most widely used browser, we will outline the process of adding Favorites when using that browser. The process is similar in other browsers.

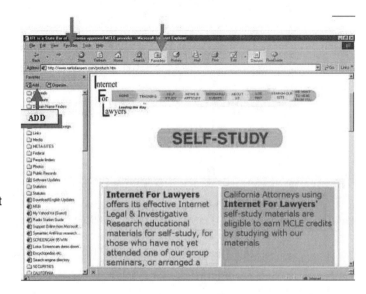

Figure 2-5. To create a Favorite in Internet Explorer, select Favorites at the top of the screen, and then **Add to Favorites**.

To create a Favorite in Internet Explorer, select Favorites at the top of the screen, and then Add to Favorites. Internet Explorer then displays the name of the site in a name dialog box. You can change the name (if you would rather call it something else) by clicking into the Name box and typing in your new name. Click OK, and the site will be added to your Favorites list.

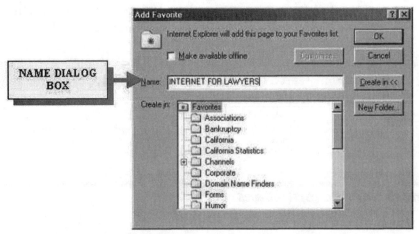

Figure 2-6. Internet Explorer's Favorites **Name** dialog box.

As you add Favorites, your list can grow quite long. Just as you do with other documents on your computer, you can arrange your Favorites into folders (and subfolders) to help you easily locate the one you're looking for.

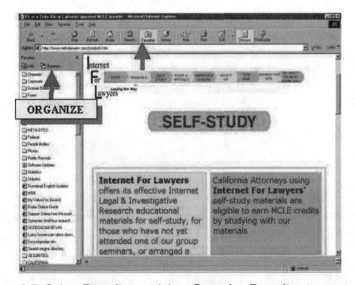

Figure 2-7. Select **Favorites** and then **Organize Favorites** to create folders to classify your Favorites to find them more easily.

Using the **Organized Favorites** dialog box, you can move a Favorite into an existing folder or move it into a newly created folder, rename a Favorite, rename a folder, delete a folder, or delete a Favorite. You can organize your folders by jurisdiction (International and Foreign), by subject (Corporate), by types of materials (Public Records or Forms), or by a combination (by jurisdiction and subject, such as California Statistics), or by any other system that is useful to you.

Netiquette and Internet Ethics

Netiquette

Most lawyers are familiar with the term "netiquette," which is the code of proper behavior online. Generally, the rules of netiquette date back to the earliest days of the Internet. Those rules, which came together in the days when Usenet newsgroups were the "killer app" that drew people online, have evolved and expanded to cover all electronic communication, including e-mail sent directly to others and to Web sites, in addition to behavior on Internet mailing lists and discussion groups.

Generally, these rules include the following:

- The use of capital letters is the online equivalent of SHOUTING. DON'T DO IT!
- Don't send messages with a vague subject line (or no subject at all).
- Keep messages concise. (For discussion groups, you should also append "Long Response" to the subject for those who might not want to read a long response.)
- A brief "signature" (four or five lines) identifying yourself and including your contact information is acceptable (and not viewed as advertising) and has come to be expected.
- Don't regularly forward jokes (particularly long or risqué jokes) to people who have not asked you to send them.
- If you don't have anything nice to say, don't say anything at all. (Negative messages, particularly in newsgroups or discussion groups, are referred to as "flames." They're considered a no-no and can elicit more flames in return, touching off a "flame war.")
- Be aware whether you're clicking the **Reply** or the **Reply All** button!

While this list is not comprehensive, it's a good place for any "netizen" to start.

The Invention of Spam

No discussion of netiquette would be complete without mention of "spam"—that bane of nearly everybody with an e-mail address. For those who may not be familiar with the term, spam refers, essentially, to electronic junk mail—unsolicited e-mail messages that are trying to sell you something you probably don't want.

There is no agreed upon origin of the spam label. According to the Internet dictionary Webopedia (**http://www.webopedia.com**):

> . . . the generally accepted version is that it comes from the Monty Python song, 'Spam spam spam spam, spam spam spam spam, lovely spam, wonderful spam . . . ' Like the song, spam is an endless repetition of worthless text. Another school of thought maintains that it comes from the computer group lab at the University of Southern California who gave it the name because it has many of the same characteristics as the lunchmeat Spam:
>
> - Nobody wants it or ever asks for it.
> - No one ever eats it; it is the first item to be pushed to the side when eating the entree.
> - Sometimes it is actually tasty, like 1% of junk mail that is really useful to some people.

There is, however, a point in Internet history that is generally accepted to be the birth date of spam. It's ironic, however, and particularly appropriate for this book, that the invention of this form of unsolicited mass e-mail is traced to two Arizona lawyers in 1994.

Internet lore has it that on April 12, 1994, a husband-and-wife pair of immigration lawyers sent a solicitation regarding the INS "green-card lottery" to thousands of Usenet newsgroups. One of the lawyers, Laurence Canter, created a small computer program that automatically sent their message with the subject line "Green Card Lottery—Final One?" to as many of the groups as the program could find. The posting was indiscriminate—targeted groups included rec.music.makers.bass, comp.programming.literate, and sci.physics.electromag, among hundreds of others.

Response from the Internet community to this blatant advertisement—a breach of their unwritten code of netiquette—was swift. Thousands of people angrily called for retribution in their own subsequent posts. One poster to sci.physics.electromag offered this advice in his April 14 post:

"Here's a suggestion. Everyone send these lawyers a note telling them what you think of their ads . . . which have appeared on *every* newsgroup. Include 10-15 copies of their original posting, just for fun . . . "

Many people had the same idea, and soon Canter and his then-wife and law partner, Martha Siegel, were indeed bombarded with angry responses.

The barrage of e-mail caused one ISP after another to drop Canter and Siegel's account. While the lawyers capitalized (quickly) on the firestorm they'd created by publishing *How to Make a Fortune on the Internet Superhighway* in 1994, by 1995 they had stopped practicing law. In 1996, the couple divorced. In 1997, Canter was disbarred by the Tennessee Supreme Court. This e-mail campaign was cited as one of the reasons for that action. (Canter is now a software developer in San Francisco. Siegel died in 2000.)

TIP: You can use the information in this story to locate the actual e-mail Canter and Siegel sent by conducting a search of the Google Group archives (**http://groups.google.com**). On the Advanced Groups Search page, enter "canter" in the Author box, "green card lottery" in the Subject box, and in Message Dates set the date range from April 12, 1994 to April 14, 1994. (For more information on conducting searches of Google Groups, see the "Search Engines" section of Chapter 4, "Search Tools.")

Internet Ethics

Basic netiquette applies as much to the legal professional as it does to a lay person. The ABA's 2001 Legal Technology Survey found that "Lawyers rely heavily on e-mail for everything from routine correspondence to client communications," with nearly three-fourths of respondents (72.9%) sending documents to clients for review as attachments to e-mail messages. This growing reliance on online communications between lawyers and clients has moved bar associations to create more specific rules to guide the online behavior of lawyers.

As early as 1996, many state bar associations began issuing opinions on Internet ethics, often focusing on law firm Web sites. The formalization of the rules of netiquette to address lawyers' behavior online varies from state to state, but most of the rules and opinions relating to online communications apply the state's existing rules for print advertising.

The State Bar of California, for example, has issued only one opinion on Web site ethics—and didn't do so until 2001. Designated Formal Opinion No. 2001-155 of the State Bar of California Standing Committee on Pro-

fessional Responsibility and Conduct (**http://www.calbar.org/2pub/
3eth/ca2001-155.htm**), the opinion deals specifically with the ethical
issues lawyers must address when creating and displaying Web sites relating to their law practices.

The specific question that the bar addressed was "What aspects of
professional responsibility and conduct must a lawyer consider when providing an Internet Web site containing information for the public about
her availability for professional employment?" In a nutshell, the opinion
views Web sites as a "communication" under the Bar rules (1-400(A) of
the California Rules of Professional Conduct) and an "advertisement"
under the state's Business and Professions Code (Sections 6157 to 6158.3),
applying those existing criteria to lawyer Web sites in the state. The principles behind the opinion, however, may be applied to all forms of online
communication, including e-mail, domain names, e-mail addresses,
online articles, discussion groups, and chat rooms, in addition to Web
sites.

California is not alone in applying existing principles of attorney-
client communication to new forms of electronic correspondence.

In Arizona, State Bar Opinion 2001-05 holds that while a firm's
domain name does not have to be identical to the firm's actual name, the
domain name must not be false or misleading. Furthermore, a law firm's
domain name cannot state or imply any special competence or unique
affiliations unless the claim is factually true (**http://www.azbar.org/
EthicsOpinions/Data/01-05.pdf**). The opinion also indicates that a for-
profit law firm domain name should not use the .org suffix or use a
domain name that implies that the law firm is affiliated with a particular
nonprofit or governmental entity. Thus, a private firm's request to call
itself "arizonalawyer.org" was rejected.

The registration of descriptive domain names, rather than domain
names that reflect the actual name of your law firm, should therefore be
examined carefully. The ABA's 2001 Legal Technology Survey found that
over half (50.1%) of the survey's respondents indicated that their law firm
Web sites utilized "their firm name or some version of it" for their
domain name. "Only 5.0% of respondents report using a generic domain
name relating to one of the firm's practice areas," the survey also noted.

For example, registering a law firm Web site with the URL "bestre-
sults.com" or "bestattorney.com" would almost certainly violate the Arizona and California rules. It is possible that a naive consumer may
assume that a lawyer with these domain names is promising to be the best
or is guaranteeing the best results.

These names might also violate ABA Model Rule 7.1, which prohibits using superlatives to distinguish one law firm from another without factual proof. A bankruptcy lawyer who uses the domain name dontpaythosebills.com might, likewise, expect to face ethical problems if, for example, the domain name misleads a client who is reorganizing rather than declaring outright bankruptcy.

ABA Model Rule 7.1 also prohibits communications that contain "guarantees, warranties, or predictions regarding the result of the representation." Thus, advertising past client successes on a lawyer's Web site or in e-mail messages could also be deemed unethical because it could indicate to a potential client that he or she can expect similar results. Personal injury lawyers who use their sites to detail past successes or advertise damage awards may therefore want to reconsider, or clearly display an appropriate disclaimer.

Lawyers should also consider the ethics of their e-mail signature line or tag line (a signature block that includes "King of Torts," for example, might not be a good idea). A lawyer's e-mail signature should not include anything that could be interpreted as false, deceptive, or tending to confuse or mislead the public.

Another ethics issue for lawyers online is giving legal advice or soliciting clients in chat rooms or discussion groups. The Florida Bar Standing Committee on Advertising held in Opinion A-00-1 (see **http://www.flabar.org**—click on Ethics Opinions) that "[a]n attorney may not solicit prospective clients through Internet chat rooms, defined as real time communications between computer users." Thankfully for lawyers who write for magazines, articles that are published online—with or without the author's knowledge—are probably protected by the First Amendment. If someone in or out of state reads the article and relies upon the information to his or her detriment, the lawyer-author may not be liable for either the unauthorized practice of law or malpractice. This ethical area becomes more problematic, however, when lawyers begin expressing their opinions in chat rooms or discussion groups that feature, as most do, two-way communication.

The ethical principles that apply to lawyer advertising and communications in older media may serve as a guide for lawyers seeking to avoid ethics difficulties online. Therefore, lawyers and firms should review their state's advertising and communication rules and determine if their Web sites meet those existing criteria. Finally, it pays to observe common netiquette. Lawyer Laurence Canter, for example, violated netiquette rules by spamming (see "The Invention of Spam" sidebar in this chapter), thus drawing complaints from offended computer users. Your online manners can matter just as much as your in-person manners.

*CHAPTER***THREE**

Search Strategies

Finding It Online

It is no longer sufficient only to understand how to use traditional print sources for secondary research. There are numerous sources that exist only on the Internet and have no counterpart in the print world. While simply knowing what types of traditional print sources contain the information that you need is a start, it's no longer enough.

There are two reasons for this: first, more and more material is being posted directly (and only) to the Internet, so there is no traditional print correlation. Examples range from electronic-only journals and newsletters, to postings made on Internet discussion groups, to the creation of personal Web logs (also known as "blogs"). To find information these days, you need to look to new developments and sources placed only on the Internet instead of just looking back to Internet versions of traditional print sources.

Second, you must truly understand the basic workings of the Internet in order to find information on it. This entails understanding the distinction between the "visible" and "invisible" Web and knowing how to find information in each. Thus, understanding the nuances of search engines that search both parts of the Web is imperative.

The Invisible Web

The information which is not readily indexed by most search engines is said to reside in the Invisible Web. (For a more detailed discussion of the Invisible Web, see the section "Search Engines" in Chapter 4, "Search Tools.")

Of the vast amount of information posted on the Internet, only a small portion is actually indexed by search engines or directories. Although Internet search engines do an amazing job of collecting and keyword searching millions of Web sites and billions of pages, some of the most valuable data is not indexed by search engines because:

- The data is in a format that the search engines do not recognize.
- The data is contained in a database that must be queried before the data can be retrieved.
- The search engine does not know that the Web site containing the data exists because the site has not been submitted to the search engine for indexing.
- The search engine has chosen not to index a particular site.

That said, there is a small group of search engines that *do* index many of the Web sites that are invisible to numerous other search engines. Currently, the most useful are Google, Alltheweb, AltaVista and FirstGov.gov (for government documents only). There are a few other ways to locate information on the Invisible Web, as noted below.

Finding Invisible Databases

To penetrate the Invisible Web for the valuable data that often lurks deep within a Web site's database, you have to know where to go by having the URL, or using some of the methods we discuss in this chapter and in Chapter 4, "Search Tools." For example, if you want to find out what a specific stock was worth on July 22, 1970, just typing that date and the stock name or ticker symbol into a search engine will *not* find the answer. The answer is on the Internet, in a database of historical stock quotes maintained by Yahoo!. The specific answer is not findable by a search engine because a search engine cannot index databases. But even though the database is invisible to a search engine, the information is still findable—but only if you know where to go.

So, using one of our invisible Web strategies for finding databases, we use a search engine, such as Google, Alltheweb, or AltaVista and type the keyword "database" plus any keywords, such as "historical stock quotes", that describe the type of database you are seeking into the search box. If using the home-page search box of any of the aforementioned databases, you can type the words in without any Boolean connectors since they default to the AND Boolean connector. (For a discussion of Boolean connectors, see the Search Strategy Checklist on pages 56-58.) The keywords "historical stock database" will lead you to a discussion of where to find this sort of information, and then provide a link to the relevant database for you to query.

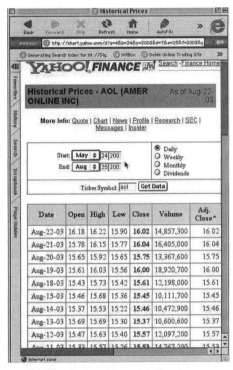

Figure 3-1. This illustrates the results of a database search of Yahoo!'s historical stock database. Enter your ticker symbol and your ending and starting dates into the blanks and then choose a daily, weekly, or monthly report (or dividends). Reproduced with permission of Yahoo! Inc. © 2003 by Yahoo! Inc. YAHOO! and the YAHOO! logo are trademarks of Yahoo! Inc.

Search Engines: Last Resort or First Resort?

While search engines have their place in the fact finders' search toolbox, their results can sometimes be too broad to be immediately useful. Using a book like this one can be a shortcut to finding relevant sites or specific search engines that might return more relevant results. For instance, if you know you are after a government document, first look at Chapter 6, "Government Resources Online," where you'll be advised to use FirstGov.gov over Google. For those times when you simply have no clue as to where to find the data, turning to a search engine—as long as you choose the right one—is your best option. (See also the section "Getting Help: Expert Research Support" later in this chapter to learn where to find an experienced law librarian who—for a fee—will cobrowse the Internet with you.)

These search tools take time and experience to master—but you've already got a head start by using this book. Refer to Chapter 4, "Search Tools," where the nuances of Google and a few other search engines are highlighted, and use some of the search tips found in the section "Cost-Effective and Time-Saving Search Tips" later in this chapter. You'll improve your search strategies tenfold and become a search-engine guru in no time. Don't try to overwhelm yourself, though; learning the nuances of two or three search engines should do it—we recommend Google, Alltheweb, and AltaVista (and for government documents, First Gov.gov).

Search Strategy Checklist

1. Peruse this book to locate a likely Web site to begin your search.
2. Review your own bookmarks (hopefully, you will add the metasites discussed later in this chapter to your bookmarks).
3. Go to Google and type your search terms into the search box and then click on **I'm Feeling Lucky**. This will bring you to the one site that Google deems the most relevant to your search terms. Very often, the site selected by Google will contain enough information to answer your question. If it does, you've just saved yourself the time you might have spent slogging through dozens of results (or even slogging through hundreds if you are one of the truly compulsive) and then deciding that the first one would have done it after all. Occasionally, the site returned by an **I'm Feeling Lucky** search may only be the most popular and not necessarily the most relevant.
4. If you don't have luck, then use your back arrow, and click on the **Google Search** button next to the **I'm Feeling Lucky** button. This will automatically run the same search through Google's entire index, and display all of the results.
5. Too many results? Add more search words to focus in on the topic. Connect the search words with Boolean connectors (AND, OR, NOT). If you need a refresher on Boolean logic and Boolean connectors, see **http://www.google.com/help/refinesearch.html**. Google supports the Boolean concepts of the connectors AND, OR, and NOT. When you are entering your search words into the search box on the Google home page, there is no need to use the AND

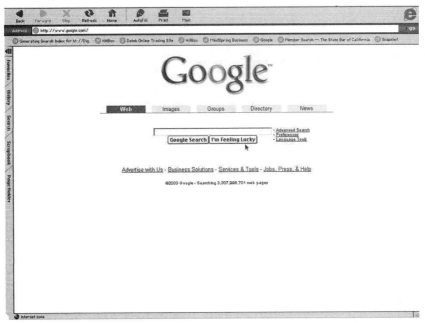

Figure 3-2. Clicking Google's "I'm Feeling Lucky" button takes you to the one site Google deems most relevant to your search. Google™ is a trademark of Google Technology, Inc.

Boolean connector at all—Google automatically defaults to it whenever there is a space between words. Use the minus (-) symbol for NOT (such as "cat -kitten" to represent "cat NOT kitten"). To search with an OR connector, you must type "OR" in uppercase (cat OR kitten). Enclose phrases in quotation marks ("contributory negligence"). For more information on how different search engines handle Boolean connectors, see the "Search Engines" section in Chapter 4, "Search Tools."

6. Not enough results? Check your spelling—is it correct? Are there multiple ways to spell the word or name? If yes, add them to your search (smith OR smyth). If there are synonyms for your original search word, you can also try adding them to the search. For example, to add the following synonyms (connected with the OR Boolean connector) to your original search for the word "car," enter "car OR auto OR automobile OR vehicle."

7. If you don't want to think too much about Boolean connectors and symbols, then select Google's Advanced Search option (see Figure 3-3), where Boolean logic search boxes are already set up for you (such as **Find results with the exact phrase**). Type your key words or phrases into the appropriate Boolean search boxes. The box labeled **Find results with all of the words** is the same as using the Boolean AND connector. The box labeled **Find results**

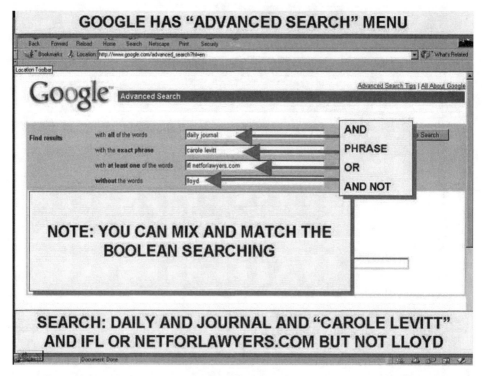

Figure 3-3. Google's Advanced Search page makes it easier to construct sophisticated searches using Boolean logic such as and, or and AND NOT. Google™ is a trademark of Google Technology Inc.

with at least one of the words is the same as using the OR connector. The box labeled **Find results without the words** is the same as using the minus (-) sign (equivalent to the Boolean NOT connector). Typing the three words "robert bob bobby" into the **Find results with at least one of the words** box is automatically interpreted by the search engine to mean "robert OR bob OR bobby" without you having to type in the ORs. It is important to note, however,that Google has a limit of ten terms per search.

8. Use the other features on the Advanced Search page to create even more complex or targeted searches, such as a file format search (see Figure 3-4), which allows you to search for specific types of data commonly found on the invisible Web (Microsoft PowerPoint presentations, PDFs, and so on).

File Format Searching

Selected search engines allow you to limit results to a specific type of file format, such as a PowerPoint presentation, Word document, Excel

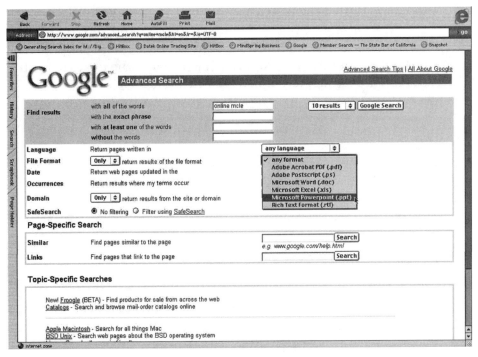

Figure 3-4. The Advanced Search page of the Google search engine allows you to select a specific file format, such as Microsoft PowerPoint (.ppt), among others. Google™ is a trademark of Google Technology Inc.

spreadsheet, or a PDF file. Most search engines do *not* index *any* of these file formats—they're simply invisible. But Google and FirstGov.gov index all of them (although FirstGov.gov is limited to government documents while Google is not). Alltheweb indexes Word, PDF, and Macromedia Flash files (but not PowerPoint or Excel), and AltaVista indexes PDFs. To conduct file format searches, you'll need to visit the Advanced Search page found on the search engine Web sites.

PowerPoint Presentation

Use Google to restrict your search to a PowerPoint presentation if you are looking for:

- Your expert witness's (or the opposition's) presentation at a conference—to see if there are any public inconsistencies in an opinion he'll be giving at your upcoming trial. Many presentations are created in PowerPoint and many people post them on the Web, so you might be in luck.
- A "hot" topic that no one has had time to write about yet. It's possible that someone may have given a recent presentation on the

topic and posted the PowerPoint slides. For example, this was the case when everyone was scrambling to understand and comply with the Sarbanes-Oxley rules spelled out in the Sarbanes-Oxley 2002 Act. There wasn't much written on the topic that you could put your hands on quickly, but there were scores of Power-Point presentations posted on the Web that you could download.

PDF File

Restrict your search to PDFs if you are looking for:

- Forms
- Newsletters
- Charts
- Graphs
- Government Documents
- Brochures

A number of the major search engines index PDF files posted on the Internet. Currently, these include Alltheweb, AltaVista, FirstGov.gov and Google.

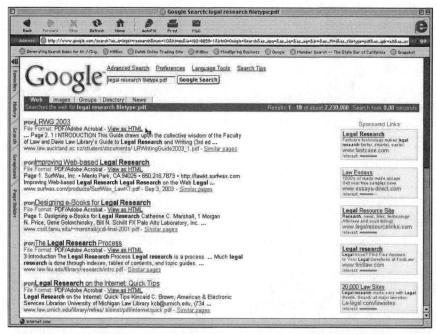

Figure 3-5. Google usually offers an alternative to viewing files with the Acrobat Reader software when PDF files are included in a list of search results. Clicking on the **View as HTML** link opens a stripped-down, text-only version of the document. Google™ is a trademark of Google Technology Inc.

PDF Search Tip

When Google returns a document in PDF in its search results list, it usually also includes an identical document in the plain text (HTML) format. (Only Google offers this option.) You'll want to click on **View as HTML** for the text version if you want to easily copy and paste any of the text into your own document. We once ran across a Federal Aviation Administration (FAA) document posted in PDF format that must have been corrupted; every time we tried to either print or download it from the FAA Web site, it crashed the firm's computer. Instead of giving up and calling the FAA for a print version, as someone suggested, a simple click on the **View as HTML** link displayed the document on the computer screen and we were able to print it without crashing the computer. Granted, the text document lacked the attractive formatting and graphics of the PDF document—but the all-important content was intact.

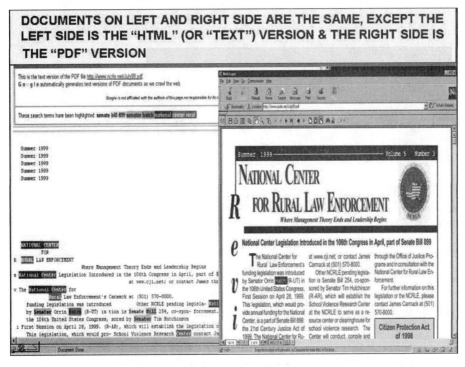

Figure 3-6. These two images illustrate the differences in the coding (the document's instructions to the computer detailing the content, layout, and so on) between a PDF and an HTML version of the same document.

Excel Spreadsheet

Restrict your search to Excel documents if you are looking for:

- Financials
- Charts
- Graphs

Word Document

Restrict your search to Word documents if you are looking for:

- Someone's resume
- A conference paper
- An agenda for a meeting
- A chart created by a committee

Word Search Tip

In the search for information on Sarbanes-Oxley mentioned earlier, we searched using the keywords "Sarbanes Oxley" and limited the search to Word file format only. We found a detailed comparison chart prepared by KPMG International for a meeting of an audit committee. The search also netted an agenda for a meeting on the same topic, to be held by the Nashville Audit Committee Institute Roundtable. It listed the place and the time of the meeting, and the speakers. Repeating the same search in AltaVista did not bring up either of these two Word documents (or anything close), which we expected since AltaVista does not index Word documents.

Domain Searching

Many search engines such as Alltheweb, AltaVista, FirstGov.gov, and Google allow you to limit a search to a specific domain. Alltheweb, Firstgov.gov, and Google also allow you to exclude a specific domain from your search. These functions are available on the Advanced Search page of each of these respective search engines. This type of search can be extremely helpful when you can't find something that you *know* is on a specific site. Sometimes the site has poor navigation, lacks a good internal search engine (or doesn't have one at all), or doesn't have a site map.

By conducting a domain search, you are more or less superimposing the search engine's capabilities onto a specific site. It is important to remember, though, that not every search engine has indexed every page of every Web site. Therefore, it may be necessary to run this type of domain search with more than one search engine to find the data you are looking for.

Domain Search Tip

We found a domain search useful in pinpointing the Minimum Legal Continuing Education (MCLE) rules for providers on a state bar Web site when it was not clear on the site where the information was located. We knew it had to be there—they were the bar's rules, after all. Google helped us locate the rules within seconds when we restricted our search to the bar's domain and used the search phrase "mcle rules" and the additional search term "provider."

If you still aren't finding what you need on the Internet, see the section "Free versus Pay Resources" in Chapter 1, "Using the Internet for Factual Research," for some pay database suggestions, and see the section "Getting Help: Expert Research Support" in this chapter.

Cost-Effective and Time-Saving Search Tips

"Time is money." "Every minute counts." Everyone in the legal profession, especially those in the billable-hour world, knows these mantras. Here are some time-saving search tips that will save you time *and* money, since time is money and every minute counts.

Look for the Free Sites!

If there is more than one site on the Internet to answer your question, use this book to identify the free site and use that first. But, read "Our View" and the "Tip" to be certain that the free site is going to meet your needs.

Save Time with an Auto-fill-in Program

With so many free sites now requiring registration, a time-saving search tip from Catherine Sanders Reach, a research specialist at the ABA's

Legal Technology Resource Center, is to use an auto-fill-in program. She suggests two different types. The first is Roboform (**http://www.robo form.com**). Reach says, "It's an automated form filler and password keeper. It automatically fills in forms with amazing accuracy and remembers all my passwords (so I can dump my cookies without having to go through them). It is free [30-day free trial], but you can get a 'professional' edition [for $29.95] and a networked edition. It saves all the information on your hard drive (passwords, etc.) so someone would have to have access to it or hack it."

The second program Reach recommends is A-fill, which you can use if you don't want to give your actual information. According to Reach, "It fills in forms with the word 'anonymous' in each blank and fills in the e-mail address as anonymous@anonymous.com and things like that. You can go in and change fields if you want to."

The only downside we experienced using A-Fill is that you do have to change some fields, like phone numbers, because sites we visited were looking for numbers, not text. So, the word "anonymous" in the phone number field didn't pass muster and those sites rejected our registration or asked us to go back and correct certain fields.

Bookmark Metasites

Bookmark subject-specific metasites instead of hundreds of individual sites for the types of sites you only use occasionally. Metasites are created to assist you in linking to hundreds or thousands of other sites. Metasites are either set up like a directory (think Yahoo!, FindLaw, or the Google directory), a simple laundry list, a site with an internal search engine, or a combination of any of these features.

For example, if you only occasionally need to search for public records, use SearchSystems.net as your metasite for public records. It's a good example of a metasite that has a directory and an internal search engine. However, if you regularly search your state's secretary of state Web site, then by all means, bookmark it individually. In each of our factual research chapters, we endeavor to list the metasites for that topic—and usually it's the first site we list.

First, You Google

Throughout this book we discuss the many useful functions of the Google search engine. Currently, it indexes more pages on the Internet and more file formats than any of its competitors. Its results are also

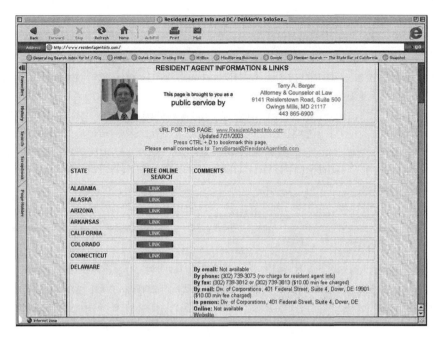

Figure 3-7. ResidentAgentInfo (**http://www.residentagentinfo.com**) is a free met-asite maintained by Maryland lawyer Terry A. Berger. The site offers a state-by-state breakdown of information regarding sources for locating information on registered agents for service of process. Information is also included on selected foreign countries, such as Canada and the United Kingdom.

extremely relevant. Even with all its strengths, Google is not perfect. There has been much debate in the online research community regarding Google's limit of ten terms per search and that it only indexes the first 101 kilobytes of information in a document. (If any of your search terms do not appear until after the first 101 kilobytes in a long document, that document is not returned in a Google search.)

So, if you don't find what you're looking for using Google, try Alltheweb and AltaVista. If you're looking for a government document, skip over Google and the rest of the engines and go directly to FirstGov.gov.

See Chapter 4, "Search Tools" and the earlier part of this chapter for more on "Googling" and other tips.

Try the Google Toolbar

A free tech tool, the Google Toolbar (**http://toolbar.google.com**), is favored by Ben M. Schorr, Director of Information Services at the law firm Damon Key in Honolulu, Hawaii (**http://www.hawaiilawyer.com**). "For folks who use Google frequently, it's a fantastic add-on. Sits quietly on your toolbar, lets you quickly search Google from anywhere, gives you quick ways to search within the page or within the site, search Google Groups and its dictionary, and just about anything else you'd want to search. It'll highlight the search terms you used . . . and you can even have it take you to the next hit or prior site in your results list." Some of the lawyers at the twenty-five-member firm probably do not even realize they are using this tool because Schorr installs it by default on all new firm machines. Schorr notes, "About two-thirds of them have it and quite a few are actually using it regularly. They rave about it, generally."

Use a Metasearch Site

Metasearch sites such as DogPile (**http://www.dogpile.com**), Teoma (**http://www.teoma.com**), and Vivisimo (**http://www.vivisimo.com**) query several different search engines at once and display the results from each on a single page (or in a series of pages or folders). Metasearch sites can be time savers, and anything that saves you time saves you money. However, most metasearch sites impose a time limit for each of the various search engines to respond. If a particular search engine takes longer to respond, the metasearch site will display zero results from that search engine— when, in fact, that particular search engine might have returned relevant results if given a few more seconds to respond. Therefore, it can sometimes be better to take your search to a search engine individually if a metasearch site shows zero results since you might find more data that way. Additionally, most of the individual search engines offer Advanced Search functions that the metasearch sites do not have access to.

Use High-Speed Internet Access on the Road

Sometimes a cost-effective tip is one that will cost you some money, but will save you time and, in the end, save you more money.

When traveling on business, obtain a local dial-up number to your Internet Service Provider (ISP) to avoid long-distance charges when dialing into the Internet. However, in some states (such as Florida), hotels meter even local phone calls to the extent that local access to the Internet can quickly become more expensive than the room. Therefore, it may be a good idea to stay at a hotel with high-speed access (for about $10 per day extra), because high-speed access will save you time while you are on the

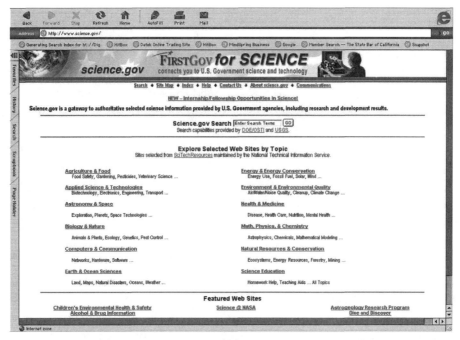

Figure 3-8. The Science.gov metasearch site allows you to query up to ten government science-related sites and databases at once (such as the EPA, Agricola, PubMed, Medline, and many more). It shows the number of results from each site, and then lists, site by site, each result with a brief abstract.

Internet and may save you money, in the long run, on your hotel phone bill. Check the following sites for information regarding hotels that offer high-speed Internet access: **http://www.wayport.net/locations** and **http://www.stsn.com**.

Some other hotels also offer wireless access to the Internet for guests who have the necessary wireless access hardware on their laptop computers or cell phones. While wireless connectivity can be convenient, it is significantly less secure than a hard-wired connection to the Internet.

Use Small Tools for Big Savings

Expensive technology, with all its bells and whistles, sometimes promises to save us time and money, increase our efficiency, and at least double our productivity.

But sometimes it's the smaller tech tools or even the free tech tools that help us save time and money and increase our efficiency and productivity. Two very small tech tools—one software and one hardware—that provide very big solutions are TinyURL and a thumb drive.

TinyURL

Anyone who has clicked on a link from an e-mail message or a posting where the URL is longer than one line soon learns that the link will not work because browsers only recognize the first line of a URL. TinyURL can solve this problem. Next time you need to post or e-mail a long URL, you can save the recipient the trouble of copying and pasting the long URL into a browser by transforming it into a much shorter (yes, tiny) URL. Visit **http://www.tinyurl.com**, and type the long URL into the Make TinyURL box. Voila! It is transformed into a much shorter URL for you to e-mail or post. Die-hard TinyURL users can add it to their browser toolbar to automatically create a TinyURL for any page they are viewing by using a single click on their toolbar. And TinyURL is free.

Thumb Drive

The second small tool that packs a large punch is a mini USB drive, also knows as a thumb drive. When asked for her favorite tech tool, Cindy Chick, manager of Latham & Watkins' Information Services Department, literally whipped out her thumb drive. The drives, used for document storage, are actually about the size of a thumb (with a capacity of up to 1 gigabyte). For lawyers who transport documents between office and home PCs, these USB drives offer extreme portability. For those who travel with a laptop and worry about having it stolen before arrival, loading documents onto the thumb drive adds security since it can be placed in a pocket or hung around the neck with a lanyard (usually included with the drive). To use a thumb drive, simply plug it into the USB port of almost any computer (newer operating systems do not require a driver). The thumb drive is a good alternative to storing files on either Zip disks or CDs. Prices vary (a 64-megabyte thumb drive was recently advertised for $9.99 after rebates).

Switch Browsers If You Need To

If you're having trouble using a site (perhaps parts of it are obscured, you click and nothing happens, or a site won't even open), chances are you're using Netscape Navigator. Some sites tell you up front that they only work (or work better) with Internet Explorer. However, some don't mention it at all, leaving you to figure it out. The solution? Use IE for those sites. You can install both browsers for free on your desktop for easy access to either one. You don't have to use the browser that was the default when you purchased your PC.

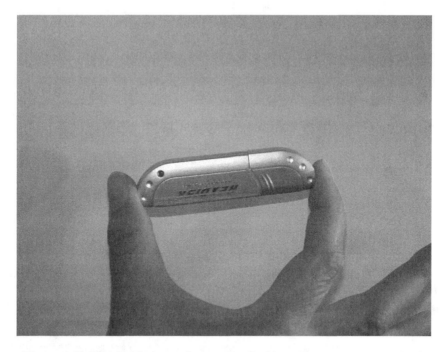

Figure 3-9. Despite their small size, thumb drives can store up to 1 gigabyte of data. Their size makes them extremely portable.

To install IE, go to **http://www.microsoft.com/windows/ie/enthusiast/default.asp**. To install Netscape, go to **http://channels.netscape.com/ns/browsers/download.jsp**.

Tracking Changes Automatically and Setting Up Alerts

Are you spending money on a pay database to track or set up alerts about a specific company, individual, case, event, or product? Since there may be information unique to the Web (such as blogs, forums, mailing lists, and auctions), you might also want to track the same data on free sites that you're currently tracking on a pay site. Or you may be able to discontinue the pay alert altogether if you can locate the same service on the Web for free. For example, some legislatures and some courts allow you to sign up for an e-mail alert every time there is any action affecting a pending bill or taken in a case. Just visit the site and see if they offer the service, then specify what to track (such as senate bill 213 or docket number 2002-98). If you're paying for an alert like this, consider canceling it. Or, you might want to track a specific page on a Web site, such as a client's company site or the opposition's company site. You decide how often you want to be alerted to changes. You also decide whether you want an e-mail alert or whether you want to visit the tracking service and check for changes at your convenience. Chris Sherman of SearchEngineWatch (**http://www.searchenginewatch.com**) recommends the following trackers:

- WebSite-Watcher (**http://www.aignes.com**): It's powerful and highlights all changes, but is desktop-based. A free thirty-day trial is offered. Thereafter, the cost is $29.95 for personal use and $99.00 for corporate use.
- WatchThatPage (**http://www.watchthatpage.com**): It's Web-based, so you can access it from anywhere and it's free to individuals. (It requires registration.)
- InfoMinder (**http://www.infominder.com**): It highlights changes, and is Web-based, but only allows you to track up to 100 Web pages. The subscription is $24.95 annually.

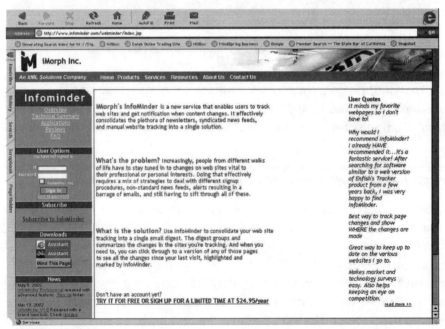

Figure 3-10. Infominder allows subscribers to track changes made on up to 100 Web pages at a time.

Find, Find, Find!

This tip can't be emphasized enough: Use your browser's Find function to quickly scan through long documents. For more detailed information on this helpful hint, see the "Browsers and Favorites" section in Chapter 2, "Internet Tools and Protocol."

Keeping Informed About Internet Research Resources

The best way to begin educating yourself about the vast resources available on the Internet is to purchase a comprehensive research reference book like this one. This book is designed to give you a definitive overview of research resources available across a broad collection of factual research categories—and some guidance in using those sites.

As with any reference book, this one offers a snapshot of the available resources as they appeared at the time of publication. Because new sites are added to the Internet with startling regularity, and existing sites can add or delete features just as quickly, it is also important to keep up to date with the sites with which you are already familiar. To help keep you informed, the authors and the ABA offer a monthly e-mail companion newsletter to this book that highlights the changes that can impact your research needs. More information on that newsletter is available at **www.lawpractice.org/factfinder**.

There are also a variety of Web sites and Web-based Internet newsletters, magazines, and e-mail alerts to update you about the Internet and technology in general, Internet legal research, and Internet legal issues.

Pay Resources

The Internet Lawyer

http://www.internetlawyer.com **$**

Purpose: To keep up to date with research resources.

Content: This print newsletter reviews free law-related Web sites, books, and paid (online) research services.

Our View: Internet resources are only a small part of what this newsletter covers. Its content is well written and insightful. Subscriptions are $179 for ten print issues.

Tip: The site includes a search engine for the newsletter's archives. Returned results include the title, publication date, and abstract of the article. Online access to the full text of the newsletter's articles is available only to print subscribers.

Legal Information Alert

http://alertpub.com/contents_lia.html   **$**

Purpose: To keep up to date with research resources.

Content: This print newsletter reviews law-related Web sites, books and paid (online) research services.

Our View: Internet resources are only a small part of what this newsletter covers. While targeted primarily at librarians, this newsletter is valuable to lawyers who conduct research on a regular basis. Subscriptions are $149 for twelve issues.

Tip: The site offers free online access to its article index only. No online access is available to the full text of the newsletter's articles.

Internet Connection

http://www.glwinternetconnection.com   **$**

Purpose: To keep up to date with government resources on the Internet.

Content: The articles in this print newsletter review the contents of government Web sites at the federal and state level. It also includes discussions of the policy and legal issues surrounding government information on the Internet.

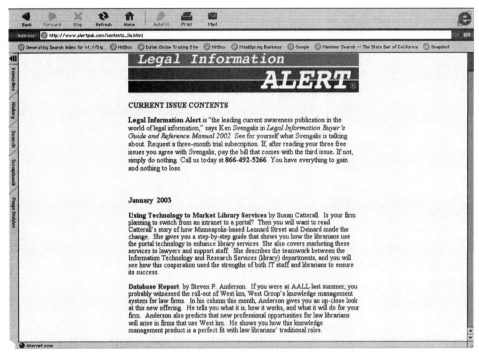

Figure 3-11. Legal Information Alert is a newsletter that reviews law-related Web sites, books, and paid (online) research services.

Our View: If you use a lot of government resources on the Internet, this newsletter can help you stay on top of new developments. Subscriptions are $119 for ten issues.

Tip: Subscribers can also access online versions of the newsletter's articles.

Internet Law Researcher

http://www.internetlawresearcher.com $

Purpose: To keep up to date with research resources on the Intenet.

Content: This print newsletter discusses the content of law-related Web sites, and important Internet-related court decisions. Additionally, it covers technical issues impor tant to the lawyer computer user.

Our View   The newsletter covers Internet resources for a wide variety of legal areas, including bankruptcy, legislative research, litigation, and intellectual property, among others. Subscriptions are $200 for eleven issues.

Tip: Subscribers can also access online versions of the newsletter's articles.

Free Resources

The Virtual Chase (TVC)

http://www.virtualchase.com

Purpose: To keep up to date regarding online research sites and resources.

Content: The Virtual Chase (TVC) offers articles about the most useful Internet research sites. It covers various areas of factual and legal research, as well as offering articles about Internet law and technology.

Our View: This site is sponsored by a Philadelphia law firm and run, full time, by the firm's former librarian. News and articles are added to the site daily. The content is presented in a very useful and practical manner.

Tip: Sign up for the editor's free daily e-mail alert with headlines of the day's Internet-related new stories.

LLRX (Law Library Resource Xchange)

http://www.llrx.com

Purpose: To keep up to date regarding online research sites and resources.

Content: LLRX provides up-to-date information on a wide range of Internet research and technology-related issues, applications, resources, and tools.

Our View: Since its inception in 1996, LLRX has consistently provided some of the most useful, in-depth coverage on the subjects of conducting legal and law-related research online.

Tips: Sign up for the site's free e-mail alert with headlines of the newest articles added to the site. For daily updates covering copyright, privacy, censorship, the Patriot Act, identity theft, and freedom of information issues, also check out the editor's Web log (**http://www.bespacific .com**).

SearchDay

http://www.searchenginewatch.com/searchday/index.php

Purpose: To keep up to date regarding search engine features and functions.

Content: SearchDay is the daily publication of SearchEngineWatch.com. The site provides tips and information about using search engines effectively, and analysis of the search engine industry.

Our View: An excellent resource for anyone conducting research on the Internet. While extremely informative, the daily e-mail update might be overwhelming to all but the most devoted Web researchers(**http:// e-newsletters.internet.com/searchday .html**).

Tip: If the daily update is too much for you, sign up for the editor's free monthly newsletter Search Engine Report

(**http://e-newsletters.internet.com/searchengine.html**).
Also, this site can be very useful if you are trying to learn
how to improve your own Web site's placement in
search engines.

Search Engine Showdown

http://www.searchengineshowdown.com

Purpose: To keep up to date with search engine nuances.

Content: Search Engine Showdown contains in-depth examina-
tions of the search functions of various search engines.
The site owner, Greg Notess, has also compiled detailed
comparisons of search engine features and functions,
including sizes of results lists, freshness of data, and
database overlap.

Our View: The site's easy-to-read search-engine news feature is
updated regularly, with the most recent entries at the
top of the list.

Tip: Check out the search engine comparison chart at
**http://www.searchengineshowdown.com/
features.** (A screen shot is included in Chapter 4,
"Search Engines.")

Site-tation

http://www.lawtechnology.org/site-tation/home.html

Purpose: To keep up to date regarding Internet resources.

Content: The site covers all angles of law office technology, not
just research resources. This includes practice-related

software, search-engine optimization, and computer security. Each issue includes brief descriptions of useful online resources for lawyers, and even includes a few entries on subjects like travel and gardening.

Our View: "Site-tation" is just one resource of the ABA's Legal Tech-nology Resource Center (LTRC). By their own description, "The ABA's Legal Technology Resource Center is the starting point for lawyers seeking information about implementing and understanding technology."

Tip: Sign up for the LTRC's free monthly e-mail newsletter by clicking the link on the Site-tation (**http://www.law technology.org/site-tation/home.html**) home page. Check out the LTRC's other online technology features at **http://www.lawtechnology.org/home.html**.

Law Technology News

http://www.lawtechnologynews.com

Purpose: To keep up to date regarding Internet resources.

Content: This monthly magazine covers a wide range of technol-ogy subjects applicable to lawyers in any size practice.

Our View: The Web Watch column specifically devoted to Internet research and practice-related resources is particularly useful for keeping up with Internet resources.

Tip: You can either register for a free print subscription or access the columns and news online (it requires registration).

There are a number of other free newsletters and discussion lists that also include information on Internet research resources in the course of their discussions of practice-related technology, including TechnoLawyer Community (**http://www.technolawyer.com**), ABA's Solosez list (**http://www.abanet.org/solo/solosez.html**), and ABA's LawTech (**http://mail.abanet.org/archives/lawtech.html**).

Getting Help: Expert Research Support

At the end of an Internet research seminar, we often hear the following comment: "That was a great seminar. I really understand the Web now and everything I can find on it. *But,* where do I go now to find someone to do it for me?" The goal of our seminars is twofold: (1) to teach lawyers how they can use the Web for research on their own, and (2) for those lawyers who don't have the time (or inclination) to use the Web on their own, to inform them of what's available on the Web so they know what to ask for when handing a research assignment over to an associate, librarian, or paralegal.

When There's No One to Help You, Think Virtual

However, for many of you in a small or solo practice, there is no one else to take over the research task! Or maybe you have an assistant, but in certain instances the subject matter is beyond that person's knowledge base. In both cases, this is the time to seek expert research support.

If you need expert help, but you also want to stay involved in the research process, consider working with a virtual law librarian over the Internet. This is one of the newest means of interaction between an experienced law librarian and a lawyer. Legal Reference Service Inc. (LRSI) is the innovator of this type of service (**http://www.lrsionline.net**. See Figure 3-12.

Imagine the benefit of being able to ask a law librarian to assist you the minute you're in crisis mode—whether you need help finding an answer from a free Web site, from a pay database, or even from a print resource. Simply by clicking on an icon on your desktop, you are able to interact with a librarian as if the two of you were on the phone or face to face. The online librarian simply picks up the "call" when you click on the icon, and begins working on the query with you over the Internet in a cobrowsing mode.

Let a Librarian Take Control of Your Browser

In cobrowsing, the librarian takes control of your browser and brings you to the same free Web sites or pay databases she is using to research

Figure 3-12. LRSI offers online access to experienced law librarians who can assist you with your research.

your query. All along, you are viewing the results live and chatting over the Internet as the search session is in progress. You can make comments or suggestions or ask questions while the search is going on. This gives you not only an element of control over the research, but can also serve as a training tool so you can do the same type of search on your own, if you choose, the next time. This service is available on a 24-7 basis.

After each interactive session is completed, a transcript is immediately produced and e-mailed to both the lawyer and the virtual librarian for follow-up on either side. The transcript, which contains live links to all the sites visited during the reference session, is extremely valuable for both sides. It shows exactly what was done, and can serve as a refresher, be a springboard to continue the research, or allow viewing of the results again by clicking on the live links (See Figure 3-13).

The service is available as a subscription service (ten hours minimum), based on a fee of $50 per hour.

To summarize, a virtual law librarian service offers:

- A law librarian available on your desktop or from anywhere you have access to a computer and Internet connection
- Advanced search strategies that are more easily communicated and understood via cobrowsing and chatting online
- URLs that are easy to share, with cobrowsing and transcript documentation of every session
- Easy integration with e-mail and telephone reference already being used

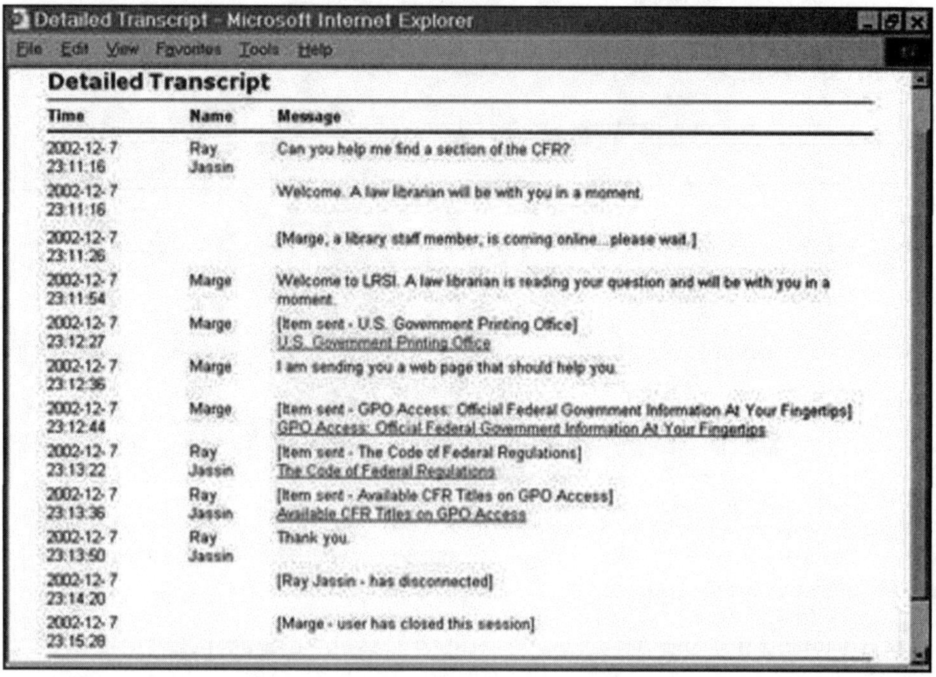

Figure 3-13. At the end of an online reference session with one of LRSI's online librarians, users receive a transcript of the entire session, including clickable links to any Web sites visited as part of the session.

For those who don't want an interactive experience, or don't have the time, LRSI will also handle e-mailed reference requests where a librarian works on a project on her own and e-mails back the results. What kinds of subject matter can LRSI handle? Just about anything you need researched, or, if the scope is beyond a law librarian's knowledge base, they can refer you to librarians who are subject specialists in other fields.

If you need public record retrieval, LRSI may be able to handle this too. But another option is to visit the BRB Public Record Retriever Network site (see Figure 3-14) and contact one of their recommended retrievers (**http://brbpub.com/PRRN**).

Free Local Library Reference Services

Many local libraries offer free chat reference services (but not to the extent of a commercial service like LRSI). For example, the New York Public

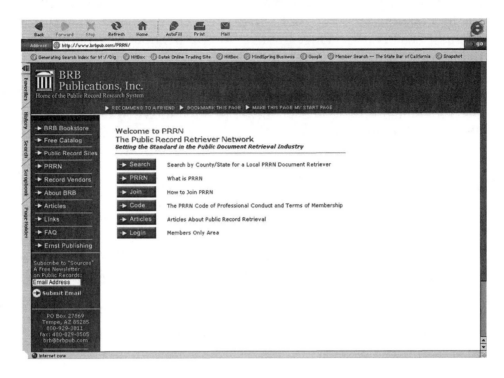

Figure 3-14. Research book publisher BRB Publications maintains a searchable database of members of the Public Record Retrieval Network (PRRN), a trade organization for contractors who retrieve documents from local government agencies in over two thousand counties in all fifty states.

Library hosts a chat at **http://ask.nypl.org**. At Asknow.org (**http://www.asknow.org**), public-library patrons can chat 24-7 with a librarian. A patron can also choose to chat with a Spanish-speaking librarian, a law librarian, or a medical librarian. Locate your local public library's Web site at the LibWeb site to find out if they offer a similar service (**http://sunsite.berkeley.edu/Libweb**). Use the LiveRef directory to link to various types of libraries (government, university, or special libraries) that offer free chat reference services (**http://www.public.iastate.edu/~CYBERSTACKS/LiveRef.htm**). An example of a special library offering this service is the Illinois CPA Society (**http://www.icpas.org/icpas/library/library.asp**).

Pay Library Chat Reference Services

Many libraries also offer pay reference services. With the advent of the Web, you don't even need to be restricted to your *local* library, but can make use of any library's services remotely. For example, the New York Public Library's pay reference service can assist you in "locating a discrete fact to compiling a report." See NYPL Express at **http://www.nypl.org/express/fees.html**. Fees range from $75 to $125 per hour, depending on the turnaround time requested. The Los Angeles County Library hosts FYI Research Services (**http://www.colapublib.org/fyi.html**). They are strong in business references (among other subjects). These pay services use both electronic and print resources to answer your questions. Academic libraries and county law libraries also may offer pay reference services.

Other Reference Assistance

The Association of Independent Information Professionals offers a free referral service at their site to obtain contact information for fee-based reference assistance (**http://www.aiip.org/AboutAIIP/referral.html**). Finally, take a look at the Chapter 9, "Finding and Backgrounding Expert Witnesses," for ideas on where else to find subject specialists. Often, a professional or trade association has a staff person (or even a library) where you can make inquiries about research assistance.

*CHAPTER***FOUR**

Search Tools

Search Engines

Search Engines: A Quick View

- Not all information is available on the Internet.
- Not all the information on the Internet is findable via a search engine.
- No search engine can actually search the entire Web, no matter what the propaganda says. Among the places no public search engine can search are sites requiring passwords, and the content of sites that can only be viewed by searching a database contained at the site.
- Google, AltaVista, and Alltheweb are the best search-engine starting points.
- Take advantage of advanced search options. Very often, you'll get different results over using the "plain vanilla" search offered on the opening page.
- Use more than one search engine per search.
- Metasearch sites use multiple engines for each search.
- If you plan to rerun a search at a later date, consider bookmarking the search results page.
- If you want to refer to a search throughout your browsing session, you can leave the search open in its own browser window, and open subsequent Web pages in new browser windows.

The majority of this book is designed to steer the researcher toward specific resources that contain information directly related to their search topic, thereby skipping an initial visit to a search engine to (hopefully) locate those resources. Because of the volume of results returned by search engines, and the invariable questions of the relevance and credibility of those results, it is preferable to use a resource that has already been tested and evaluated by a reputable reviewer. Search engines, however, can be useful for general Internet searching, particularly if you are not familiar with the subject area in which you're searching. Some of the most well-known of these include Google, AltaVista, and Yahoo!.

One of the frequent complaints concerning search engines is that they return too much irrelevant information in response to search requests. Admittedly, at times when the researcher has no clue what he is really looking for, and needs the search software to make suggestions in the form of a variety of Internet destinations, this search engine flaw is a good thing. But the more common and disappointing experience is to receive two million responses to a simple request, which then need to be reviewed, page by page, until the most worthwhile and informative sites are found. Even though the experienced researcher can sense right away whether the responses are relevant and likely to lead to an appropriate site, it would, obviously, be a poor use of time to scroll through those two million responses. Additionally, the highest-rated results are most likely to be the most relevant to the search request. Ordinarily, the relevance of the search results (as determined by the engine's search algorithms) diminishes the further down the list you look. If the first few hits are irrelevant, the best thing to do is to review the original search and construct a new search to produce more pointed results.

Search Engines' Limitations

The first thing to remember about search engines is that no single search engine has indexed the contents of every Web site on the Internet. Recent reports estimate that there are 550 billion pages on the World Wide Web. Of those, it is estimated that only 5 billion have been indexed by search engines. And there is not a single search engine that covers even those 5 billion. Google (3.3 billion pages), Alltheweb (2.1 billion pages), and Teoma (1 billion pages) currently search the largest chunk of the Internet. While the total number of pages indexed by these three search engines (6.4 billion) adds up to more than the 5 billion pages estimated on the "visible" portion of the Internet, don't assume that a search using these three search engines amounts to a search of all the available information. There is overlap in the Web sites searched by each of those search engines. If you conduct similar searches at each of these three, you will notice that a number of results turn up on more than one of the search engines.

That part of the Web that is not indexed by search engines is referred to as the "Invisible Web." (Other terms used to describe this segment of the Internet include Hidden Web, Deep Web, and Dark Web.) These pages might be invisible for any number of reasons. They may be protected by a firewall or password, be contained in a database, be in a format other than HyperText Markup Language (HTML), such as Adobe Acrobat Portable Document Format (.pdf files) or Microsoft Word (.doc files), or be information maintained in a searchable database (such as membership records).

To their credit, despite this large quantity of un-indexed material, the major search engines generally do a fairly good job of returning something useful in the first few hits. You will often retrieve different results even if you conduct the same search using different search engines. For example, if a search engine is designed to only look for your search terms in the document's title, but the terms for which you're searching are only in the document's abstract, the search engine will not return results. However, engines that search through abstracts or, better yet, do full-text searches of pages, tend to find more documents.

Because no search engine has catalogued the entire contents of the Internet, for more in-depth results it is advisable to conduct the same search on two or three of the most comprehensive search engines in order to retrieve the highest volume of useful information.

The quality of search results is dependent on choosing the right search engine and creating the best search. A lousy search strategy will be unsuccessful no matter what search engine is used, and a precise search string will generate better results, even with the weakest search tool. But the optimal situation is for the researcher to understand the nuances of each engine, and to submit focused search requests that take advantage of such nuances. This takes practice, but is possible. It also requires keeping on top of the all-too-frequent enhancements made to search engines' functionality. This book's companion e-letter is a valuable resource for the researcher who wishes to keep up with these enhancements (**http://www.lawpractice.org/factfinder**). On the Web, Search Engine Report (**http://www.searchenginewatch.com/sereport**), SearchEngineWatch (**http://www.searchenginewatch.com**), and Search Engine Showdown (**http://www.searchengineshowdown.com**) are good sources for new developments regarding search engines.

All search engines provide some limited Boolean logic capabilities (meaning the ability to use logical operators to connect words and phrases, such as AND, OR, NOT, and so on). Most free Internet search engines do not reach the level of Boolean search sophistication that online researchers have come to expect from pay services like Lexis and Westlaw. Most free search engines also lack the proximity connectors (such as "within two words") that lawyers use in pay databases. With enough practice and training, you could one day be certain that you could extract any piece of information contained in these pay services' databases. Unfortunately, there are no such certainties on the free Internet.

That's where this book comes in. It is designed to be a researcher's user manual for the Internet, a tool that has not existed before.

Learning How to Search

The best way to learn how each search engine works is to read the instructions and tips found in the Help or Tips pages offered by each of the respective search engines. Such instructions demonstrate how the designers recommend using the engine. What the Help pages don't usually tell you is exactly how the engine was built, or how the search algorithms weight the search-string elements you submit. These are the main criteria that determine how the engines work, why they return some pages instead of others, and why they rank certain pages higher than others. Search engines usually do not divulge this information in an effort to keep unscrupulous Web developers from exploiting their index and ranking systems.

After reading the Help pages, the next best way to learn how to use search engines effectively is simply to use them. Familiarity leads to expertise. By trying out various engines, and using them frequently, you'll get a sense of the strengths and weaknesses of each. We recommend Google, AltaVista, and Alltheweb, for reasons we explain below.

If you take the time to read the instructions and suggestions at each of the individual search engines, your searches will be more accurate. One thing you'll find, however, if you study the various engines, is that each search engine indexes the Internet differently, and that each offers different search functions. What works well on Google may not work at all on AltaVista. Some vary slightly from one to the next, and some vary a lot. With so many available search engine options, remembering what search strategies to use at which site can be a challenge. Therefore, it might be more realistic to become familiar with two or three of the most comprehensive search engines—and stick with them.

When switching between search engines, it's important to remember that different search engines recognize different connectors. For example, AltaVista allows you to use the "near" proximity connector (which to AltaVista means within ten words). Google does not recognize this connector, and will search for the word "near," including it as a search term in your results.

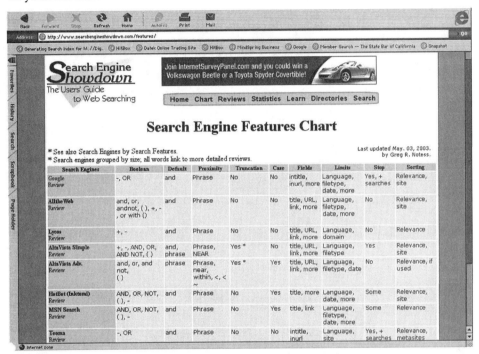

Figure 4-1. It is important to know what Boolean connectors are recognized by the search engine you are using. It is equally important to know what the search engine you're using automatically adds as a default Boolean connector. Search Engine Showdown offers a comprehensive chart of the features of numerous search engines (arranged by search engine) at **http://www.searchengineshowdown.com/features.** © 1999-2003 by Greg R. Notess. All rights reserved. Reprinted with permission.

Common words (also called "noise" or "stop words"), such as "of," "the," "an," or numbers are ignored by most search engines. Some search engines, such as Google, can be forced to include these terms if it is important to your search. For example, to force Google to search for the phrase "to be or not to be," put the phrase in quotation marks. To search for "Star Wars Episode I," place a plus sign (+) before the word you want to force it to search for (Star Wars Episode +I). Each of these strategies returns different results. It might be useful to try both for a tricky set of search terms.

For more information about effective searching than the search engine Help screens offer, try using a tutorial, such as the "Guide to Effective Searching of the Internet" at **http://www.brightplanet.com/deepcon tent/tutorials/search/index.asp**, which compares search strategies of different search engines, and more.

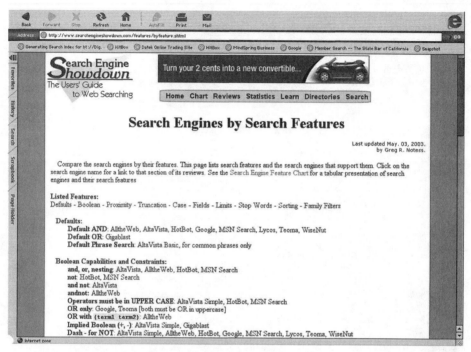

Figure 4-2. Search Engine Showdown also provides an excellent comparison review of the major engines' features (arranged by feature) at **http://www.searchengineshowdown.com/features/byfeature.shtml**.
© 1999-2003 by Greg R. Notess. All rights reserved. Reprinted with permission.

Who Owns What?

In recent years, the search engine industry has undergone a major ownership shuffle, leading to greater ownership consolidation among major search engines. The chart below offers a snapshot of some of the biggest deals. With Yahoo!'s recent purchase of Overture, Yahoo! now owns Inktomi, Overture, AltaVista, and Alltheweb.

	Ask Jeeves	Yahoo!	Overture	Overture	Yahoo!
Date of Purchase	October 2001	December 2002	February 2003	February 2003	July 2003
What It Purchased	Teoma	Inktomi	AltaVista	Alltheweb	Overture
Reported Purchase Price	$4 million	$235 million	$140 million	$100 million	$1.6 billion

How Search Engines Work

No search engine is comprehensive in scope or time. When you enter your search terms into the search box of any search engine, you are not searching the entire Internet. You are only searching those pages that a particular search engine has previously found ("visited") and added to its index. Additionally, depending on the frequency with which the search engine revisits pages, search result lists might be based on Web page content that is one week to many months old.

Search engines are essentially large, automatic classifiers. To gather information about the content of various Web pages, the search engines send out robots (also known as spiders) that automatically add information from Web pages to the search engine's index. This process is known as indexing or spidering. It is from this index that the search engine returns its list of results when you enter your search terms into the search box.

After completing the search, the search engine displays a list of links to sites that include your search terms. This is your list of results or hits. Sometimes the results will be right on target and other times completely irrelevant, even though they contain your search terms. Ordinarily, the results that the search engine deems to be the most relevant to your search terms will be at the top of the list.

Sponsored Links

Most search engines place links labeled Sponsored or Partner above the results generated from their own index. These types of links are advertisements generated to correspond to your search terms. These sites may or may not be the most relevant to your search, but they have paid to appear at the top of the list for certain search terms. There is no harm in clicking to see if those sites are useful to you. Very often, though, the best results are found below in the regular Web search results.

One of the leading suppliers of paid placement search results is Overture (**http://www.overture.com**). Overture supplies its paid placement search to numerous other search engines, including Yahoo!, MSN, and CNN.

Advanced Searches

Most search engines offer an advanced search capability. *Find it and use it!* The advanced search gives you significantly more options for conducting your search. These might include sophisticated Boolean-connector searching or limiting the search to a certain Internet domain or specific file format (such as PDF) that is not available to you if you use the "plain vanilla" search box offered on the search engine's home page. A

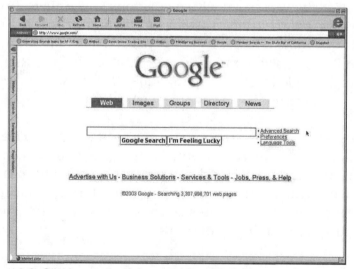

Figure 4-3. Clicking on the **Advanced Search** link opens the Advanced Search page. Google™ is a trademark of Google Technology Inc.

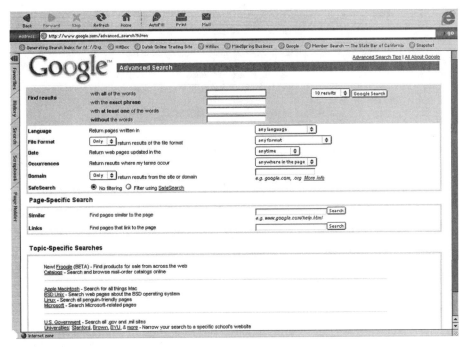

Figure 4-4. Google's Advanced Search page offers greater search strategy options. Google™ is a trademark of Google Technology Inc.

link to the advanced search functions is often on the right-hand side of a search engine's opening screen.

Indices and Directories Versus Search Engines

While search engines operate off a large index of automatically spidered pages, directories and indices contain fewer links that have been hand-selected by humans who are (usually) subject specialists. These directories divide sites into increasingly more-narrow subjects based on their content (such as Government > Law > Legal Research > Libraries). Yahoo! started out life as the personal directory site of two Stanford grad students before growing into the media titan it is today. Google, the search engine that started out as a project of two other Stanford grad students, later added a directory (see Figure 4-5).

Some directories only allow users to click through the categories until they come to the level that holds the information they're looking for. This practice is often referred to as drilling down. Others add the ability to search through the index with an internal search engine that points the user to the category where he'll find the information he needs.

Figure 4-5. In addition to its search engine, Google also offers a directory of topics that include Internet resources reviewed and selected by human editors. Google™ is a trademark of Google Technology Inc.

Our Favorite Search Engines

The following is a list that includes some of the most comprehensive search engines and directories (beginning with our most favorite to least favorite). Google is our top pick; of law-related sites, our favorite is Lawcrawler.com.

- **Google at http://www.google.com.** Google spiders over 3 million pages daily, indexes nearly 3.3 billion pages of the Internet (as of August 2003), searches more of the invisible Web than other engines, and updates its index every twenty-eight days. Some Web sites are spidered more often. Google utilizes its proprietary page-rank technology to determine a Web page's relevance and importance based on the number and types of other Web pages that link to it, among other criteria.
- **Alltheweb at http://www.alltheweb.com.** Alltheweb indexes over 2.1 billion pages as of July 2003. It returns results based on analyzing the language patterns and common phrases of your search words; it updates every eleven days.

- **LawCrawler at http://lawcrawler.lp.findlaw.com.** Law Crawler searches the World Wide Web, but only sites that contain law-related information. You can limit LawCrawler to a specific state, to federal legal sites, or to international legal sites. Because this search engine is powered by Google, it returns very relevant results.

- **AltaVista at http://www.altavista.com.** AltaVista's Prisma technology is designed to help searchers narrow down their search results by suggesting more specific terms to search within the search results. AltaVista is also useful for finding images and current news.

- **Yahoo! at http://www.yahoo.com.** A manually created, browsable (and searchable) directory of sites. Web search results also come from Google's index.

Spotlight on Google

There are a number of reasons to make Google your first choice. Google:

- Has the largest index of Internet pages (3.3 billion)
- Searches files on the Internet that many other search engines do not
- Offers a robust Advanced Search page
- Returns the most relevant results
- Searches various file formats
- Can perform a newsgroup search (of Google Groups)
- Can conduct an image search
- Has a browsable directory

The opening screen features four tabs, two buttons, and a search box for entering search terms. There are no flashy ad banners. In fact, there's no advertising at all on the home page. The gaudiest thing on the page is the site's multicolored logo.

The site's clean, uncluttered opening screen indicates that Google is ready to get down to the business of searching.

As an antidote to the multitude of results returned for a search, more adventurous researchers can try Google's **I'm Feeling Lucky** button. This search returns just one site—and the searcher is taken directly to it. No list of results is presented. That site is the one deemed most relevant by Google's search algorithm and relevance weighting system.

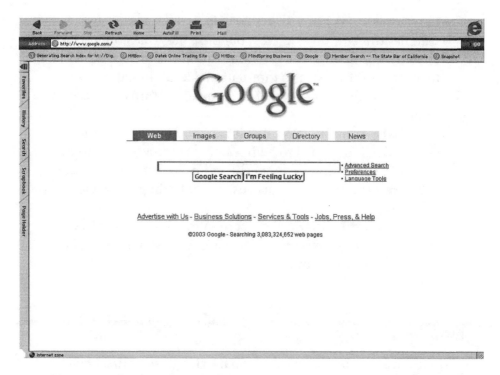

Figure 4-6. Beneath its minimalist home page, Google hides a powerful search engine. Google™ is a trademark of Google Technology Inc.

As part of its quest to deliver relevant search results, Google employs a proprietary page-rank system to determine a Web site's value in relation to other pages. Similar to a lawyer using *Shepards* or *Key Cite* to determine which other cases have relied on a case they are reading, the page-rank system weighs the number and quality of other Web sites that link to the site being ranked. As explained on its Web site, "Google interprets a link from page A to page B as a vote, by page A, for page B. But, Google looks at more than the sheer volume of votes, or links a page receives; it also analyzes the page that casts the vote. Votes cast by pages that are themselves 'important' weigh more heavily and help to make other pages 'important.'" To return the most useful and relevant search results, Google considers this page rank as it matches the keywords of a search query with the text contained in Web pages its spiders have added to its index.

Search within Results

Like the Focus feature on the pay version of LexisNexis and the Locate feature of Westlaw, Google also allows users to narrow down their list of results. By selecting the **Search within results** link at the bottom of the first page of results, Google searchers can add additional keywords to their search, instructing the search engine to search for those keywords only within the list of sites included in the results list currently being displayed.

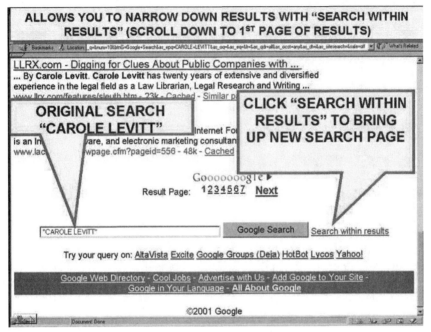

Figure 4-7. Google allows you to narrow your search by adding additional search terms and clicking the **Search within results** link on the bottom of the first page of your results. Google™ is a trademark of Google Technology Inc.

Cache Is King

As stated earlier, no search engine offers a complete picture of all the content that is on the Web. Depending on how often a Web site is updated, or how often a search engine revisits the sites in its index, the information on which a search engine bases its results may be many weeks or months old.

For example, if a client wanted to sue for libel, based on a libelous statement posted on a Web site, the site owner could remove the libelous statement by the time a lawyer visited the site to view the statement. Clicking on the **Cached** link might return Google's saved version of the page before it was altered—the one that contained the allegedly libelous statement in question. (There is a chance however, that the cached page may still be displaying "live" information from a Web site. For more information on locating archival information on Internet sites, see the section on "Finding Extinct Pages and Archived Material" later in this chapter.)

Figure 4-8. Google offers a **Cached** link accompanying nearly all of its returned results. **Cached** links to a saved version of the returned Web site as it appeared on the day that the Google search engine last visited the site. Google™ is a trademark of Google Technology Inc.

Google People Finder

Google, which claims "the largest index of Web sites available on the World Wide Web and the industry's most advanced search technology," has made it easier to retrieve phone numbers and addresses from its database.

The search engine has added street address and phone number information for residences and businesses to the results returned by a standard Google search. Results are limited to published, United States phone listings.

To find listings for a business, you only need to type the business name, city and state into the Google search box. The business's ZIP code can be substituted for the city and state if you know it. Conversely, you can conduct a reverse search to retrieve a complete listing for a business by entering only the area code and phone number.

To retrieve residential listings, users can type any of the following combinations into the Google search box:

- First name (or first initial), last name, city (state is optional)
- First name (or first initial), last name, state
- First name (or first initial), last name, area code
- First name (or first initial), last name, zip code

- Phone number, including area code
- Last name, city, state
- Last name, ZIP code

Phone number and address results are displayed at the top of results pages. Residential results have a House icon to the left, while business results feature a Skyscraper icon to their left.

In addition to the phone number results, if any, these searches will retrieve HTML documents on the Internet that contain the keywords included in the query.

Individuals can have their contact information removed from the Google database by filling in the form found at **http://www.google.com/help/pbremoval.html.**

Google Uses Wildcards

Like many online pay databases, Google offers the ability to incorporate variables into Google phrase searching through the use of wild cards. (A wild card is a placeholder used to represent a variable, so phrases with any text in the position of the wildcard may be returned in search results.) The placeholder is represented by an asterisk (*) and can take the place of a single word. For example, a search for "John * Jones" would return results including the names John Paul Jones, John Howard Jones, John W. Jones, and so on.

Additional File Formats

For more sophisticated search options, click on **Advanced Search** to search a variety of non-HTML file formats Google includes in its index. The most useful of these may be the Microsoft Office files, including Word, Excel, and PowerPoint, as well as Adobe PDF.

For example, a regular Google search for "accounting expense report forms" returns results that include Word, Excel, and PDF files, with each file type clearly labeled, as noted above. Clicking on the document's title downloads the file to your computer and automatically opens it in the corresponding software. As mentioned earlier, Google only indexes the first 101 kilobytes of information in a document. (So if any of your search terms do not appear until after the first 101 kilobytes in a long document, that document would not be returned in a Google search.)

To save download time, and to lessen the possibility of downloading a virus or worm along with the file, you should take advantage of the **View as HTML** link Google provides. Clicking this link displays a stripped-down version of the file (in plain text) in the Web browser rather than downloading it to your hard drive. You can save the lengthier

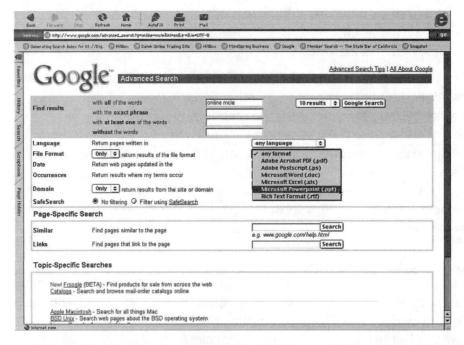

Figure 4-9. Because Google is able to index many files types, such as Microsoft Word, Microsoft Excel, Microsoft PowerPoint, and Adobe Acrobat, a search for "accounting expense report forms" returns results in all of those file formats. Google™ is a trademark of Google Technology Inc.

process of downloading (and scanning for viruses) for only the most important or relevant files.

Google was the first major search engine to move beyond indexing just the traditional HTML format by indexing documents in Adobe's popular PDF format, adding them to its search results in 2001. This marked a significant advance in searching the Invisible Web. Other search engines that have since added PDF files to their search results include Alltheweb, AltaVista, Adobe's specialty PDF search at **http://searchpdf.adobe.com**, and FirstGov.gov (for government documents).

Since many researchers and universities utilize the PDF format for their papers, theses, and other research results, the availability of PDF files in the Google index is a boon to all researchers. Many government documents are also created in the PDF format, especially forms.

Because the PDF format requires users to download the Adobe Acrobat Reader software before viewing, Google clearly highlights any PDF document returned in a search with a blue **[PDF]** next to the returned item. For those who do not have the Acrobat Reader software, you can also utilize the **View as HTML** option to view a text version of the document (with the formatting and special fonts removed).

You can use Google's Advanced Search page to limit your results to one of the specific popular Microsoft Office file formats the search engine indexes. The file format is noted by an abbreviation (the same as the file extension the programs use when saving a file on a user's hard drive) in blue and in brackets to the left of the document's title. They are

- [DOC] for Word files
- [XLS] for Excel files
- [PPT] for PowerPoint files
- [RTF] for Rich Text Format files
- [PS] for PostScript files

The ability to search various formats is very useful in locating memos, tables, or other documents published on the Internet that might not be easily accessible or indexed by most search engines.

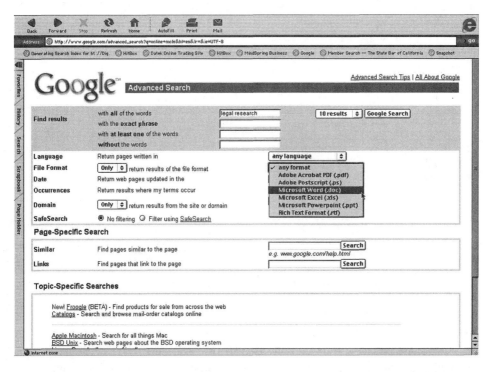

Figure 4-10. You can also use Google's Advanced Search page to limit your search to specific file formats. For example, entering the search terms **legal research** and selecting **File Format: Only return results of the file format Microsoft Word (.doc)** returns only Word documents containing the keywords "legal" and "research." Google™ is a trademark of Google Technology Inc.

Usenet Postings

Google offers a searchable archive of 800 million messages posted to public Usenet news groups back to 1981 at **http://groups.google.com**.

Utilizing the Advanced Groups Search, you can perform full-text searches or narrow the results down to a specific newsgroup or author. Locating postings by a specific author assumes that the author used their real name, or that the researcher knows the e-mail address or online alias of the individual for whose messages they are searching.

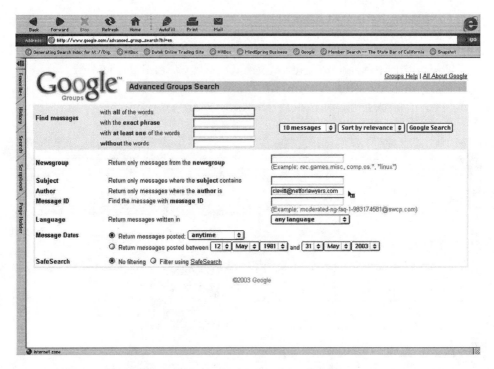

Figure 4-11. Google Groups Advanced Groups Search allows you to search for Usenet postings by a specific author using the person's name or e-mail address. Google™ is a trademark of Google Technology Inc.

Google News Search

Google's News Search collects recent news stories from sources around the world, updating them continuously throughout the day. Google retains news stories in its index at **http://news.google.com** for approximately four weeks.

A recent search for "iraqi oil" returned over six thousand results. The first result included a story from the BBC that carried the qualifier "less than 11 hours ago." (Using the Advanced Search page, you can sort your results list by date or by relevance.) Other stories listed the time they were collected as "less than 30 minutes ago," indicating the up-to-date nature of the search results. Under the first result were related news stories from other publications around the world.

A sampling of some of the sources from which Google indexes news stories include:

- Islamic Republic (of Iran) News Agency
- *Washington Post*
- News24 (South Africa)
- *Melbourne Herald Sun* (Australia)
- *Taipei Times*
- MSNBC
- Al-Jazeera (Qatar)
- *San Jose Mercury News*
- *Christian Science Monitor*

You can also browse the latest news headlines. The Google News home page lists news in a variety of categories (including Top Stories, World, U.S., Business, Entertainment, and so on) in a directory style. Within those categories, stories are grouped together by subject, with stories from multiple sources that cover the same news subject arranged in subgroups.

In the summer of 2003, Google also added the ability to limit news searches by country or state, or to a specific publication.

For more information on locating news resources on the Internet, see Chapter 5, "General Factual Research."

Google Image Search

To build its index of images, Google looks at the text on the Web page surrounding an image, the accompanying caption, and other elements to determine the content and context of the 425 million images (as of March 2003) in its searchable database at **http://images.google.com**.

Image search results are displayed as thumbnail images, up to twenty per page. Each thumbnail lists the size (in bytes and pixels), file type, and URL of the image. Clicking on the thumbnail displays two frames. The top frame displays a larger view of the image. The lower frame shows the picture in context on the Web page where it resides. The images can also be viewed alone.

The image searches can be very effective. A search for "Carole Levitt" resulted in two hits, one of which was a photo of this book's coauthor.

The Google Image Search Frequently Asked Questions page claims that "Google also uses sophisticated algorithms to remove duplicates," but a search for images of Hillary Clinton yielded a number of duplicate images (granted, they were located at different sources on the Web).

For more information on locating images on the Internet, see the section "Finding Video, Audio, and Images" later in this chapter.

Metasearch Sites

Another variety of Internet search engine is the metasearch site, which enables simultaneous searching using several individual search engines—a search engine of search engines. Metasearch sites are good for searching for very obscure subjects or for searching the most Internet space possible. The downside of these tools is that they are generally less precise and accurate than an individual search using each search engine. They also do not include results from the most comprehensive search engines (including Google) or those that (usually) return the most relevant results. Some of the more popular metasearch sites are

- Vivisimo at **http://www.vivisimo.com**
- Teoma at **http://www.teoma.com**
- Copernic at **http://www.copernic.com**
- Dogpile at **http://www.dogpile.com**
- HotBot at **http://www.hotbot.com**
- Ixquick at **http://www.ixquick.com**
- Metacrawler at **http://www.metacrawler.com/**
- Surfwax at **http://www.surfwax.com**
- Webcrawler at **http://www.webcrawler.com/**

For more information on using metasearch sites in your searching, see the "Cost-Effective and Time-Saving Search Tips" section in Chapter 3, "Search Strategies."

Finding Video, Audio, and Images

More and more each day, the Internet-age axiom "you can find anything online" becomes truer. It is especially true of multimedia content. Whether you're looking for audio clips from famous films (at **http:// www.moderntimes.com/palace/audio.htm** or **http://www .moviesounds.com**), from the Kennedy White House (**www.gwu.edu/ ~nsarchiv/nsa/cuba_mis_cri/audio.htm**), of aviator Charles Lindbergh (**www.charleslindbergh.com/audio/index.asp**), or of the U.S. Supreme Court's "Greatest Hits" (oral arguments at **http://www.oyez .org/oyez/frontpage**), it's all available online for free.

When preparing client presentations, or multimedia arguments for arbitration or mediation, the addition of video news coverage, stock photos, sound effects, and clip art can make your compelling argument even more memorable. Additionally, photos, diagrams, or videos of a product from a manufacturer's Web site might be useful in a product liability case.

Finding the video, audio, or image files is just half the battle. If you want to use them you have to download them to your own computer; and they can be *very large*. If you do not have a high-speed connection to the Internet, it can take a very long time for the files to download to your computer. If you are using a dial-up connection to the Internet, there is also the possibility that you could get disconnected before the file has downloaded completely.

Once you have the files on your own computer, you'll find that the audio and video files come in a variety of file formats. The different formats are distinguishable by the three-letter extension that follows the file-name (such as .wav, .ram, .asf, .mov, and so on). To see and or hear these clips, it is necessary to have the appropriate media player software installed on your computer. The three major media player programs are available as free downloads. Versions are available for Windows and Mac operating systems. (Paid versions with more features are also available.)

The major media players are

- Quicktime, at **http://www.apple.com/quicktime/download**
- RealOne Player, at **http://www.real.com**
- Windows Media Player, at **http://www.windowsmedia.com/download**

Not all media players play all types of files. Therefore it is advisable to have more than one player installed.

With any online audio or video resource, be sure to check the source Web site for any usage requirements or restrictions, or copyright information. When necessary, be certain to obtain permission to use the audio or video element in your own work.

Finding Video

For news coverage, check your local TV stations' sites for footage of local events. Internet For Lawyers maintains a page linking to major market and network news gathering organizations at **http://www.netfor lawyers.com/TVlinks.htm**. Also see Chapter 5, "General Factual Research," for more information on locating news sources online.

AltaVista

http://www.altavista.com/video

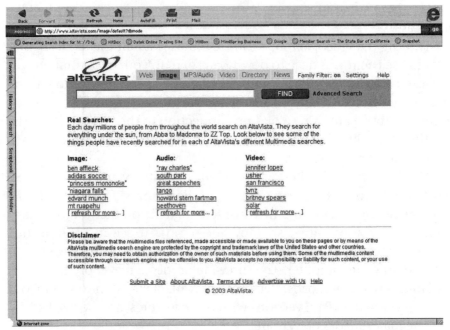

Figure 4-12. The AltaVista search engine is an excellent resource to search for multimedia content. In early 2003, the company expanded its index of multimedia files to encompass over 240 million unique media files, including images, video clips, MP3s, and other audio files. Reproduced with permission of AltaVista Company. All rights reserved.

Purpose: To locate video clips on the Internet for download.

Content: AltaVista offers the ability to limit your search results to video files. The results are returned with small still images from the videos (called thumbnails), as well as links to the full video on the Internet.

Our View: By using the drop-down menu and check boxes under the search box, you can specify file types (AVI, MPEG, Quicktime, Windows Media, Real, and Other), as well as selecting the duration of the audio clips returned. Additionally, you can choose to limit your search to include content from AltaVista partner sites, which include

MSNBC and RollingStone.com. (Content from the partner sites is copyrighted material.)

Tip: The Advanced Search also allows you to filter out so-called "noise" images such as buttons and banners that might be included on a Web site.

Alltheweb

http://www.alltheweb.com

Purpose: To locate streaming video and video clips on the Internet for download.

Content: Alltheweb claims to have "hundreds of millions" of multimedia files in its index. To search for video, click the **Video** tab at the top of the home page.

Our View: To conduct the most targeted search, click the **advanced search** option next to the search box. This allows you to specify file types (such as AVI, MPEG, Real, Quicktime, and so on), as well as giving you the option to view results from static downloadable files, or from streaming video sources.

Tip: For the greatest number of results, select **All** formats and **Both** streams or downloads.

Prelinger Video Archive at Archive.org

http://www.archive.org (click on **Moving Images**)

Content: The archive contains links to more than twelve hundred films digitized by the Prelinger Archive. The collection

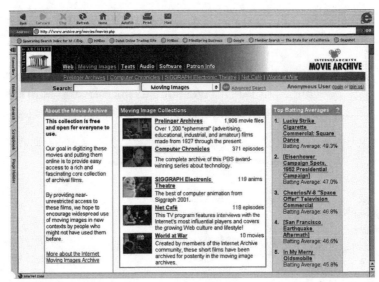

Figure 4-13. The Prelinger Archive presents a browsable database of over 1,200 advertising, educational, industrial, and amateur films dating back to 1903.

consists primarily of instructional, educational, advertising, and documentary films (in a mixture of AVI and MPG file formats), as well as home movies dating from 1903 through the 1980s. Most films can be viewed as streaming media or be downloaded. All material is in the public domain.

Our View: This offbeat collection of films includes cigarette commercials from the 1950s, Civil Defense films regarding preparation for a nuclear attack, and other items that might prove worthwhile in certain class action suits.

Tip: The Prelinger Archive is just one of many video collections accessible from the Archive.org site.

Finding Audio

FindSounds.com

http://www.findsounds.com

Purpose: To locate various sounds on the Internet for download.

Content: FindSounds doesn't have content of its own, *per se*. It is an Internet search engine, like Google and AltaVista, that searches only for sound effects and musical instrument samples on the Internet. Clicking on any of the results usually opens or plays the sound automatically. You can usually save the sound to your computer to use in your own work.

Our View: You can choose three types of sound files (WAV, AIFF, and AU) for which to search. You can also dictate the quality of the sound returned by selecting the minimum resolution (8-bit or 16-bit) and minimum sample rates (8,000 to 44,100 Hertz).

 If you are making a presentation to a claims adjuster about your client's accident, the addition of screeching tires, crashing glass, or an ambulance siren coupled with pictures from the accident scene or of the client's injuries could help punctuate the seriousness of the accident.

Tip: To return the largest number of sound results, select all three sound file types, 8-bit minimum resolution, and 8,000 Hertz as the minimum sample rate. Also, the site claims to filter out audio files containing obscenities, claiming " . . . this site is safe for children."

AltaVista

http://www.altavista.com/audio

Purpose: To locate various sounds on the Internet for download.

Content: AltaVista is a general-purpose search engine that offers you the ability to limit your search results to just audio files. Clicking on any of the results takes you to the Web page where the sound file can be accessed.

Our View: You can specify file types (WAV, MP3, Windows Media, Real), as well as selecting the duration of the audio clips returned.

Tip: AltaVista includes copyright information in its results. You should note, however, that lack of information in the copyright field does not mean it is in the public domain.

Alltheweb

http://www.alltheweb.com

Purpose: To locate various types of audio clips and sound on the Internet for download.

Content: Alltheweb boasts "hundreds of millions" of multimedia files in its index. To search for audio, click the **Audio** tab at the top of the home page.

Our View: Alltheweb's audio search is the weakest of its multimedia search functions. It currently offers no Advanced Search options. While the search results include only MP3 files (primarily songs), Alltheweb offers a unique **see other files in this folder** link under each of the results. Clicking it returns a new page of results that lists other audio files stored in the same location on the Internet.

Finding Images

Google

http://www.images.google.com

Purpose: To locate various types of images on the Internet for download.

Content: In mid-2003, Google boasted that it had indexed nearly a half-million images.

Our View: To return the images most relevant to your search terms, Google looks at the text on the Web page around the image and the accompanying caption, among other elements, to help determine an image's content. The Advanced Search page offers sophisticated search combinations, including:

- Boolean logic
- Phrase searching
- File type limitation
- File size limitation
- Color or black and white

Results are displayed as thumbnail images, up to twenty per page. Below each thumbnail is the file name showing the file type (such as JPG or GIF), image resolution (in pixels), file size (in bytes), and the URL of the image. Clicking on a thumbnail brings a larger view of the image in the upper frame of the page, and a view of the picture in context on the Web page where it resides in the lower frame. The images can also be viewed alone.

Tip: Use the Advanced Image Search page. There, you can also limit your search to a single domain (such as www.netforlawyers.com). This can be extremely useful if you are looking for photos of executives or products from a particular company. Using the **Return images from the site or domain** option, you can search only that company's Web site.

AltaVista

http://www.altavista.com/image

Purpose: To locate various types of images on the Internet for download.

Content: AltaVista also offers the ability to limit your search results to image files. Like AltaVista's video search, results are returned with thumbnails, as well as a link to the original image on the Internet.

Our View: You can choose to search for either photos or graphics (or both), as well as designating color or black and white (or both). Additionally, you can choose to search the Web only, or also include content from AltaVista partner sites that include Corbis.com and Rolling-Stone.com. (Content from the partner sites is copyrighted material.)

Tip: You can filter out "noise" images such as buttons and banners by not selecting the **Buttons/Banners** check box.

Alltheweb

http://www.alltheweb.com

Purpose: To locate various types of images on the Internet for download.

Content: Alltheweb boasts "hundreds of millions" of multimedia files in its index. To search for images, click the **Pictures** tab at the top of the home page.

Our View: To conduct the most targeted search, click the **advanced search** option next to the search box. This allows you to use check boxes to specify file types (.JPEG, .GIF, .BMP), color (color, grayscale [black and white and shades of gray], line art (black and white only), and background transparency (transparent, nontransparent)

Tip:　　　For the greatest number of results, select these check boxes: for files types, **All formats;** for color, **All types;** and for background, **Both types.**

Corbis Archive

To search: 　　To license:

http://www.corbis.com

Purpose:　　To locate professional and news photos.

Content:　　Founded in 1989 by Microsoft's Bill Gates, the Corbis collection is made up of more than 65 million images, 2.1 million of which are online. The collection includes the holdings of the former Bettman and United Press International photo archives and contains images that date back (at least) to the Civil War.

Search the database by entering keywords or phrases into the image search box on the home page. Thumbnail versions of corresponding images are returned in the results list. Clicking on a thumbnail opens a larger version of the image (with a Corbis "watermark"). Click the **Information** tab above the image for more information on the photo and its per-mitted uses. Usage restrictions and licensing fees vary from image to image.

Our View:　　The famous images and news photographs available from the Corbis Archive can be very persuasive to mediators, arbitrators, and jurors, or in business presentations. Images include asbestos cleanups, lung cancer effects, car crashes, cigarette ads with celebrities, among many other subjects.

Tip: Be certain the image you select is available for the use for which you want it. Also see Corbis's business presentation site at **http://bizpresenter.corbis.com** to license business-themed photos, cartoons, and illustrations for inclusion in presentations.

Finding Extinct Pages and Archived Material
Isn't the Most Current Information Better?

You might wonder why you'd want to find old information that has been altered or removed from the Internet completely. After all, aren't we supposed to be looking for the most current information?

- What if your client claims to have been libeled on a competitor's Web site? Your client swears the offending comments were posted, but when you visit the site, the offending statements are nowhere to be found.
- What if your client is being sued for theft of trade secrets by a competitor? Your client swears he got the information off their Web site, but when you visit the site, the information is nowhere to be found.
- What if you'd read an article on opposing counsel's Web site that ends up contradicting a point they made later in arbitration, but the other firm has taken it down from the site when you go back to look for it?

There may still be a way to find the information you need!

War Story: Using the Wayback Machine

Marcia Burris, library manager at Ogletree, Deakins, Nash, Smoak & Stewart, P.C., in Greenville, South Carolina, tells this story:

"I needed to confirm the contents of a two-year-old news article that appeared on the Internet. The story was about a mugging and was needed to verify an individual's date of injury in a litigation matter our firm was involved in. The story had appeared in the *Daily Star,* 'The First Bangladeshi Daily Newspaper on the Internet,' but the archives from that year were no longer online.

"My e-mail to the editor may have gone through, but I got no response. My e-mail to the Webmaster bounced back.

"I also tried looking in other sources on Westlaw and Lexis for coverage of the same story, but found nothing.

"After posing the question on a research LISTERV, a number of people suggested the Wayback Machine. I was able to find the archived version of the online paper for the date I was looking for and printed out the article I needed."

As we have mentioned many times in this book, material on the Internet changes constantly. This can be a boon or bane to a lawyer searching for information. While Web page changes usually result in more information being available, the opposite can also be true.

For a variety of reasons, a Web site owner might remove information from a Web site. Just because information has been removed from a site does not (necessarily) mean that it is gone forever. Here are two ways you might be able to retrieve that information after it has been deleted from the site owner's Web server.

Internet Archive (the Wayback Machine)

http://www.archive.org

Purpose:	To retrieve older versions of Web pages.
Content:	In 1996, the Internet Archive set about building a permanent historical record of that ephemeral new medium, the World Wide Web. Since then, the Internet Archive has been collaborating with the Library of Congress, the Smithsonian Institution, and others to store and record Web pages. The Internet Archive made its collection available to the public via its Wayback Machine

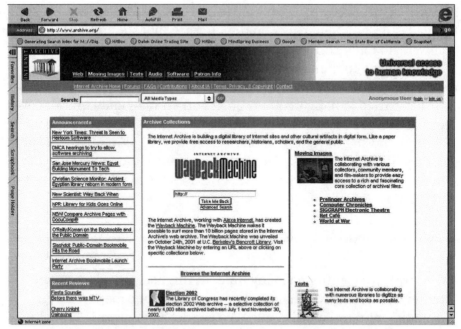

Figure 4-14. The Wayback Machine at Archive.org has archived versions of many Web sites dating back to 1996. Its Advanced Search allows you to see side-by-side comparisons of current and archived versions of a particular Web site.

Web site in October 2001. In August 2003, the site boasted more than ten billion Web pages in its archive.

Our View: While the Wayback Machine's archive is not complete, it does offer a rare opportunity to view Web site content that has been changed or removed from the Internet. Type the URL of any site you are interested in viewing into the search box on the Archive.org home page to comb the archive's hundreds of terabytes of data. Results are returned in a table listing the target site's stored pages by the date they were modified and added to the archive. Clicking on any of the returned links brings up the stored version of that page as it appeared on the date indicated.

Clicking on the **Advanced Search** option underneath the **Take Me Back** button on the site's home page gives you additional options for homing in on the pages you want from the target Web site. You can request results be returned only within a specific date range. (If you don't select a date range, the results will include links to all of the versions of your target site in the Wayback Machine's archive.) You can also request that the results show check boxes to allow comparison of two versions of a page.

Tip:
- The archive has seemingly stored complete versions of the Web sites for that particular date. For example, if you were to view the Internet For Lawyers Web site as it appeared in May of 2000, you would be able to click through all the various pages then available.
- If available, a side-by-side comparison of the opposition's Web site, showing changes detrimental to your client, can be very persuasive in an arbitration, mediation, or trial.
- Selecting a date range in the Advanced Search results in the first instance of an archived page for the target site within the specified range. Not specifying a range and using the comparison feature will give you a better sense of the changes made to the site over time.

Google

http://www.google.com

Purpose:　To retrieve older versions of Web pages.

Content:　When Google adds most pages to its index, it also takes a snapshot of the page, adding it to Google's cache of stored Web pages. This allows Google to show you where your keywords appear in the returned page, or to display the page in the event that it later becomes unavailable. It also creates a viewable record of the page before it changed or became unavailable.

Our View:　If a page is changed (or removed from the Internet) after it was added to the Google index and before your search, you may still be able to access an earlier version by clicking on the **Cached** link, if one accompanies your search result (see Figure 4-8 in Chapter 4). When the cached page is displayed, your search terms are highlighted on the page.

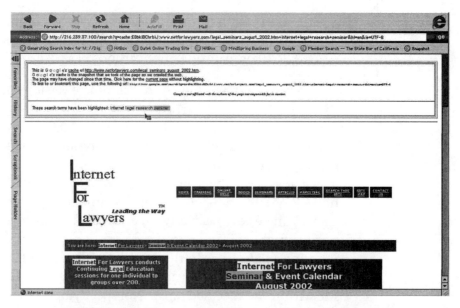

Figure 4-15. Clicking on the **Cached** page link returns a snapshot of the text of the target Web page on the day that Google's robots last visited it. Nontext elements such as images or movies seen in a cached page are not actually cached on the Google servers, but are fed live from the target Web page's server if still loaded there.

Tip: • We can't really be certain how long an archived version of a Web page will remain in the Google cache. On average, Google revisits Web pages once a month (though some are visited on a significantly more frequent basis). The older cached version is replaced by a newer cached version after Google revisits the page.

• Additionally, the **Cached** link is not available for all results. Web site owners can request that Google not cache their pages.

The Google cache stores only the HTML content of the first 101KB of a Web page on Google's servers (the actual HTML code that makes up the page, including any text visible on the page). One major drawback of the Google cache is that it *does not* store non-HTML information such as images (photos, buttons, banners, and so on), video, audio, or multimedia files (such as Macromedia Flash files). When displaying the cached page, Google's server retrieves this non-HTML content from its original location on the Web server where the cached page was originally stored. Therefore you might find large empty spaces with little red X's in place of the non-HMTL content if those files have been removed from their original locations; or you might be viewing more current, live graphics or video content from the current version of a page along with the archived text content stored in the Google cache.

Archive.org also stores primarily the HTML content of the pages it archives, but in many instances, it does also store non-HTML content associated with the pages stored in its archive, but not all of the images, and not for all of the pages. Therefore, you may or may not get to see the full view of the old version of the Web page when using the Google cache or Archive.org.

Web Logs

Web logs, known as "blogs" for short, are the Internet's version of personal journals or diaries—but with an attitude. Their ease of development and updating make it extremely easy for anyone, even those with limited technical ability, to create, host, and update a personal Web site.

Blogs are usually made up of short, frequently updated posts. The posts are ordinarily arranged chronologically, with the newest posts at the top of the page. The contents and purposes of blogs vary with the personalities of the people who create them, who are known as "bloggers." Blogs contain everything from links and commentary about current events, to news about a specific topic or company. More personal blogs might constitute online diaries, and include photos, poetry, mini-essays, project updates, or fiction. Often blogs are no more than a chronicle of what's on the mind of the blogger at any given time.

Blogs give their owners an unfettered opportunity to express themselves, vent frustrations, espouse a particular point of view, discuss important issues, or spread rumors for their own purposes. Blogs can range from the off-beat humor of Davezilla (**http://www.davezilla.com**) to Stanford Law School Professor Lawrence Lessig's discussion of Internet law (**http://cyberlaw.stanford.edu/lessig/blog**), and everything in between. For lawyers who represent companies that manufacture products or provide services to the public, periodic checking of blogs can provide early warnings of product liability issues or shareholder unrest that could later lead to individual or class action lawsuits.

You can sample some of the most popular law-related blogs (also known as "blawgs") by visiting the Daily Whirl at **http://www.dailywhirl.com** and Detod at **http://my.detod.com**. (Detod also offers a search engine to locate information in blawgs at **http://blawgs.detod.com**).

Why Use Blogs for Research?

"So, how do blogs fit into my search for facts on the Internet?" you might be asking yourself.

Many bloggers include links to breaking news, magazine stories, or other Web sites that interest them. Because blogs are updated often (often daily), they can be rich sources of current news or information on a specific topic.

A more personal blog might give you valuable information about the opposition or one of their witnesses. Have a look at a few of the diary-style blogs available at some of the sites mentioned below. You will probably be surprised at the volume and kinds of information people post about themselves on the Internet.

For the office, one provider of blogging tools, Blogger.com, suggests that "blogs are also excellent team/department/company/family communication tools. They help small groups communicate in a way that is simpler and easier to follow than email or discussion forums. Use a private blog on an intranet to allow team members to post related links, files, quotes, or commentary."

There are a number of companies that provide creation tools and Web-hosting space for bloggers. They are

- Blogger at **http://www.blogger.com**
- Journalspace at **http://www.journalspace.com**
- Moveable Type at **http://www.movabletype.org**
- Trellix at **http://www.trellix.com** (business web hosting provider Interland [**http://www.interland.com**] acquired Trellix in December 2002, but Trellix continues to operate under the Trellix name)
- UserLand at **http://www.userland.com**

Searching Blogs

Searching blogs is almost like listening in on someone's phone conversation, except the blogger expects people to be listening. Blogs can be an excellent way to gauge consumers' perception of a client company or product. If bloggers are unhappy with a company, its financial performance, or the performance of its products, they may discuss it in their blogs. Additionally, if someone were particularly upset, he might set up a blog devoted to bashing the company. Conversely, a blogger might offer praise for a company (it could happen!). Regardless, numerous blog posts about a company or product could be a harbinger of greater unrest, or legal action, in the future. Knowing about it early can help you advise your client about steps to help minimize the damage, or to avoid the confrontation altogether.

As of this writing, only Journalspace offers a search engine function to search across all of the blogs created through its service. With their increased popularity and numbers, blogs have found their way into general purpose search engines' results such as Google. In February 2003, blogs' popularity and the sheer volume of information they contain led Google to buy blog publishing pioneer Blogger.com. There are some search engines that focus primarily on returning results from blogs. Some of these are listed below.

Daypop

http://www.daypop.com

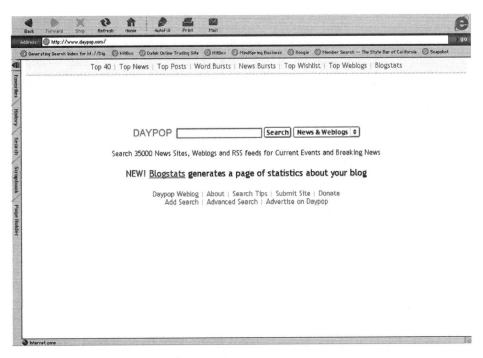

Figure 4-16. Daypop offers a search engine covering nearly thirty-two thousand blogs and almost eight thousand other news and current events Web sites.

Purpose: A search engine for blogs and traditional news sources.

Content: Daypop offers a search engine covering nearly forty thousand blogs, news, and other current-events Web sites (about thirty-two thousand of these are blogs). Daypop allows you to perform keyword and phrase searching of all of these sites at once. You can also use Daypop to track specific words or phrases that are currently appearing in many blogs (click on the **Word Bursts** option at the top of the home page), a list of the most-linked-to Web sites from the blogs that Daypop monitors (click on **Top 40**), and the most-linked-to news stories from the blogs that Daypop monitors (click on **Top News**), among other features.

Our View: Even though you never know what you may or may not find when searching for information from blogs, Daypop offers a number of powerful tools to make the search process more effective.

Tip:
- Search for your clients' names and product names regularly to see what people are saying about them.
- Use **Advanced Search** (**http://www.daypop.com/ advanced**) to limit your searches to a particular country or language. You can also use **Advanced Search** to specify a time range for the creation date of blog posts you are searching.

BlogStreet

http://www.blogstreet.com

Purpose: A search engine for blogs.

Content: The BlogStreet search tool is a very straightforward query box for keyword searching blogs. (See the Tip below for information on its Advanced Search.) Once you get your results list, each result is followed by a **BlogRank** link. You can click on the main link and visit the blog page that contains your search terms, or you can click the **BlogRank** link to learn more information about the blog that contains the search result. This information includes **BlogBack** (a list of other blogs that highly recommend the site containing your search terms) and **Neighborhood** (a list of other blogs that BlogStreet deems similar to the blog containing your search terms).

Our View: In addition to returning relevant results, the site's **Blog-Back** and **Neighborhood** information can help lead you to other blogs that might contain more information on the subject for which you're searching.

Tip: Use the site's Advanced Search to limit your search to a specific date range or to one particular blog.

CHAPTER*FIVE*

General Factual Research

Standard Reference Resources

From elementary school through college, we've been trained that the solutions to all of our research questions can be found by going to the library. While this is still true, the Internet now brings much of the library to us, allowing us to access a great amount of information from the comfort and convenience of our home or office.

Many tried and true resources that we are used to using in print form, such as the *Merriam-Webster Collegiate Dictionary* and the *Encyclopedia Britannica*, are now available online, along with a host of other resources.

Don't Count Out the Library Yet!

In addition to the sites included here, many public libraries offer their patrons access to some of the online pay databases used by the libraries' reference staffs. Ordinarily, all you need to access these normally expensive resources on your home computer is a library card and an Internet connection. Some of these include:

- Selected news, periodical indices, and full-text articles
- Gale's Biography Resource Center
- Oxford English Dictionary
- Physician's Desk Reference (PDR)
- Reference USA
- Standard & Poor's

Starting-Point Web Sites for General Research

Figure 5-1. Bartleby.com links to numerous general reference resources, including dictionaries, encyclopedias, and thesauri of all types.

Bartleby.com

http://www.bartleby.com

Purpose: To locate general information from various references.

Content: Bartleby.com offers a wide range of reference resources searchable online, including the CIA's *World Fact Book,* dictionaries, encyclopedias, Gray's *Anatomy of the Human Body,* the *King James Bible,* and various thesauri.

Our View: Bartleby is a good place to start when looking for various types of general information. The site allows you to keyword search through all of the site's five dozen reference works (a sampling of which are noted above) all at once or individually.

Selecting the **All Reference** option in the search box returns a list of suggested resources in which to search for information on your keyword, including dictionaries, thesauri, encyclopedias, quotations, and nine other subcategories, rather than returning the actual definition or synonyms. To retrieve definitions or synonyms, select **Dictionary** or one of the thesauri names and search those resources directly.

Tip: The site also features a searchable and browsable version of Strunk's English language usage guide, *The Elements of Style*.

Refdesk.com

http://www.refdesk.com

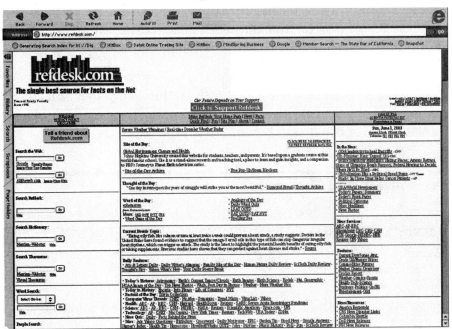

Figure 5-2. Access to the Refdesk site is like having your own virtual reference collection right at your fingertips.

Purpose: To locate general information and reference material on various subjects.

Content: The site links to more than twenty thousand other resources in numerous categories, including news, weather, sports, reference, dictionaries, encyclopedias, and search engines, among others. Among its many **Reference Resources** (scroll down on the home page to locate this category) are a **Facts Subject Index** and **Facts Encyclopedia** that include links to nearly ten thousand different sites, arranged by category. The home page also includes news headlines from sources such as ABC News, CNN, and Reuters.

Our View: A good site to bookmark for links to all sorts of useful general information. Making all of this information accessible from the home page gives it a cluttered look, but it's well worth scrolling through the page for pointers to resources on the subject you need.

Tip: Cut your book budget by asking every lawyer and staff person in the office to bookmark this site. That way you won't have to buy each person their own standard dictionary and legal dictionary!

Interesting side note: the Refdesk creator and Webmaster, Robert Drudge, is the father of Internet muckraker Matt Drudge, the creator and "citizen reporter" behind the *Drudge Report* Web site.

Dictionaries and Thesauri

Merriam Webster

http://www.m-w.com

Purpose: To locate definitions and synonyms for common (and not-so-common) words.

Content: The site offers a searchable version of *Merriam-Webster's Collegiate Dictionary, Tenth Edition*. Access to a larger, unabridged Webster's dictionary is available for $29.95 annually, or $4.95 per month. (A fourteen-day free trial is available for the unabridged version subscription.)

Dictionary and thesaurus search boxes are available at the top of the home page. If you're not certain of the spelling of the word you're looking up, you can use wild card characters. A question mark (?) can be used to take the place of one letter and an asterisk (*) can be used to take the place of more than one letter. For example, a search for "m?n" will find "man" and "men," as well as the abbreviations "min," "mon," "mtn," and "mun." A search for "m*n" will find those entries, as well as entries for "macaroon," "magnification," "maiden," "maintain," and many other words that begin with "m" and end with "n."

Our View: The site is fairly straightforward and easy to use. The wild card capabilities of its searches are especially helpful. The results can be inconsistent, though. For example, the synonyms returned as part of a dictionary search may not correlate to the results of a thesaurus search for the same word. A sample dictionary search for the word "scion" included two synonyms along with the definition. Clicking the **Thesaurus** tab revealed that the site had no thesaurus entries for the word scion, but on the list of similar words were entries like "chain" and "gum." Apparently including consonants and vowels is enough to be considered similar! Therefore, if you do not find a thesaurus listing for the word you're seeking, try clicking the **Dictionary** tab to see if there are any synonyms listed along with the definition.

Tip: ● Definitions also include audio pronunciations of the word. Clicking on the Speaker icon next to the main entry plays a recording of the proper pronunciation of the word you've looked up.
     ● Based on sample searches, such as this "scion" search, this thesaurus is not as comprehensive as the *Roget's Thesaurus* discussed below.

The American Heritage Dictionary

http://www.bartleby.com/61

Purpose: To search for definitions and meanings.

Content: Based on the *American Heritage Dictionary of the English Language,* Fourth Edition, this site offers ninety thousand entries and audio pronunciations for seventy thousand words. This dictionary does not offer a direct link to a thesaurus entry, although many entries do include synonyms.

Our View: The site's search options can be a bit confusing. To locate the definition of a word, you must select **Entry Word** from the pull-down menu located next to the search box. Selecting **Definition** from the pull-down menu instructs the dictionary to look for the word you input in the definitions of other words. For example, an Entry Word search for "scan" returns one result—the definition of that word. A Definition search for the word "scan" returns twenty results, nineteen of which are for the definitions of other words where the word "scan" appears in the definition.

Tip: Included with the dictionary definitions are notes regarding the word's history and information regarding the etymological origins of the word.

OneLook Dictionary Search

http://www.onelook.com

Purpose: To search for definitions and translations of words and phrases.

Content: With a single search, the OneLook dictionary search engine can return the definition of one of more than five million words from its database of over nine hundred dictionaries, broken down into a dozen categories.

Our View: The site can be particularly helpful if you are not sure of the correct spelling. OneLook offers the asterisk (*) and question mark (?) wild card search options to fill in the blanks when you're not sure how the word you're looking for is spelled. (See the entry above on the **Merriam-Webster** dictionary for more information on searching with these wild cards.)

To help narrow down your search, click the **Browse Dictionaries** link on the upper right-hand side of the home page to see the list of available dictionaries by category. For example, clicking **Browse Dictionaries** and then selecting **Science** brings up a list of over one hundred dictionaries on scientific topics, from a dictionary of scientific units to an online browsable version of the periodic table of the elements. From these pages, you can also see the date when each particular dictionary was indexed by the OneLook directory.

Tip: You can also use wild cards to search for words (if you aren't sure how to spell them) in a particular category. For example, searching for "f*:construction" will return all words that start with the letter F that are related to the topic of construction. This can be especially helpful in deciphering terms of art from other industries heard in meetings or in conversation.

Google Glossary

http://labs1.google.com/glossary

Purose: To find definitions, meanings of words, phrases, and acronyms.

Content: Google uses its powerful search algorithm to locate definitions in the Web pages it indexes. Type any word or phrase into the search box, click the **Google Glossary Search** button, and you'll get several links to Web pages that give you a definition of the word or phrase, often using the word or phrase in context.

Our View: An excellent quick reference guide. Like a huge, multi-subject glossary, this site can return definitions for concepts and phrases as well as for individual words.

LookWAYup

http://lookwayup.com/free/default.htm

Purpose: To find definitions, meanings of words, phrases, and acronyms.

Content: LookWAYup is a downloadable addition to your Web browser. Clicking the **LookWAYup** button that it adds to your browser pops up a search box that allows you to search for the definition of a word without leaving the Web site you're viewing.

Our View: This can be a handy tool if you often have to define words or technical terms in Web pages, but don't want to leave that site to find a dictionary. LookWAYup is available in English, German, French, Dutch, Spanish, and Portuguese. A limited version is free for individuals. Small Web sites may also install a free version, as long as the site receives no more than a thousand visits per day (for nonprofit volunteer organizations, the limit is twenty-five thousand visits).

Tip: LookWAYup works with version 4 and above of the Netscape, Internet Explorer, and Opera browsers, on Windows, Unix, and Mac operating systems.

Roget's Thesaurus

http://www.bartleby.com/thesauri

Purpose:	To find synonyms of words.
Purpose:	To find definitions, meanings of words, phrases, and acronyms.
Content:	Two editions of *Roget's Thesaurus* are available to search online (via Bartleby.com): *Roget's International Thesaurus of English Words and Phrases* (1922), and *Roget's II: The New Thesaurus, Third Edition* (1995).
Our View:	Searching is straightforward. Returned results also include thesaurus entries for synonyms of the word you've looked up. For example, a search for "scion" returned that word's entry, as well as entries for "progeny," "offspring," "descendant," and so on.
Tip:	Based on sample searches, such as this "scion" search, these thesauri are more comprehensive than the thesaurus offered at the Merriam-Webster site noted above.

Legal Dictionaries

FindLaw's Legal Dictionary

http://dictionary.lp.findlaw.com

Purpose:	To find definitions of legal words and phrases.
Content:	The dictionary at FindLaw is licensed from *Merriam-Webster's Dictionary of Law*. It is keyword searchable by words or partial words.

Our View: We prefer this to any of the other legal dictionaries because it not only provides very complete definitions, it also includes pronunciations, hyperlinks to related words or comparative words, and in some instances, citations for cases where the word has been used. (It would be even better if it then hyperlinked to those cases.)

Tip: You can search the dictionary right from FindLaw's home page (**http://www.findlaw.com**) by typing your word into the search box at the top and choosing **Legal Dictionary** from the drop-down menu.

Everybody's Legal Dictionary (NOLO's Shark Talk dictionary)

http://www.nolo.com/lawcenter/dictionary/wordindex.cfm

Purpose: We'll let NOLO tell you the purpose: it's "your life-raft in the sea of legal jargon."

Content: It has plain-English definitions for over a thousand legal terms.

Our View: We like that you can either browse alphabetically by clicking on any letter in the alphabet, or you can type a word (or partial word) into a search engine. The definitions are very thorough.

Tip: • If you don't find the word you want, check back—it's being built word-by-word.
    • You can also try NOLO's Legal Encyclopedia for a list of broad legal topics and short articles (**http://www.nolo.com/lawcenter/ency/index.cfm**).

Duhaime's Law Dictionary

http://www.duhaime.org/dictionary/diction.htm

Purpose: To find legal concepts defined in plain language, created as a public service by the Canadian law firm of Duhaime & Company.

Content: An alphabetical list of definitions of legal concepts.

Our View: It's an easy-to-use site, with easy-to-understand definitions. We'd prefer a search engine, too.

Tip: There may be one or more hyperlinks within each definition. When you click on one, it takes you to the definition of the word used in the entry you've just looked up.

Morse Code Applet (Morse Code translator)

http://www.babbage.demon.co.uk/morse.html

Purpose: To translate messages into Morse code.

Content: The site is powered by a Java applet that turns the text you type in the message box into a Morse code message that you can hear. As the audio Morse Code message is being played, the individual letters are displayed in a separate text box so you can identify the specific sound patterns associated with each letter. A translation table, listing the dot and dash patterns of each letter of the Morse Code alphabet, is also included at the site.

Our View: Morse Code decoding is one of those things that falls into the "you never know what you're going to need" category. It's included here for that reason. The applet is compatible with most current Web browsers. See the site for a current list of incompatibilities.

Acronym Finder

http://www.acronymfinder.com

Purpose: To decode acronyms and abbreviations.

Content: Acronymfinder.com offers a searchable database of over 309,000 acronyms and abbreviations. The database is limited to acronyms of up to 24 characters, and definitions are limited to a maximum length of 255 characters.

Our View: Users can search for definitions by choosing one of these from the Option drop-down menu:

- Exact acronym
- Acronym begins with
- Acronym (wild card)
- Reverse lookup (keywords)

While the first two methods are self-explanatory, the wild card search does not permit the insertion of a wild card character into the search, but rather returns multiple acronyms that include the search string you've entered. For example, a search for "FBI" returns not only Federal Bureau of Investigation, but also the acronym AAFBI (which is the Appaloosa and Foundation Breeders International), among other results.

The site also allows a reverse lookup to deter-mine any acronyms related to a specific subject by allowing users to search by keywords. For example, a search for the keywords "oil" and "drilling" returned seven oil-industry-related hits, including PHPA (Partial Hydrolytic Polyacrylamide) and ERD (Extended Reach Drilling), among other results.

Tip: The site will not return more than three hundred results for a search. If a search returns more than 500 definitions, no results are returned and an error message is displayed.

Abbreviations and Acronyms of the U.S. Government

http://www.ulib.iupui.edu/subjectareas/gov/docs_abbrev.html

Purpose: For specialized acronym decoding.

Content: The Indiana University-Purdue University Indianapolis Library offers a browsable list of nearly eight hundred U.S. government acronyms and their definitions.

Our View: The list is included on one long page, with the ability to jump to any particular letter in the alphabet from a row of alphabetical links at the top of the page. A search function would be helpful.

Tip: Use your browser's Find function to search for an acronym quickly, rather than scrolling through the list.

Military Acronyms and Glossaries

http://www.ulib.iupui.edu/subjectareas/gov/military.html

Purpose: For specialized military acronym and term decoding.

Content: The Indiana University-Purdue University Indianapolis Library also offers a metasite listing nearly twenty on-line resources for decoding military terms.

Our View: The majority of the sites are maintained by the military (.mil domain names), so you can be sure you're going right to the source.

SEARCH Publications Criminal Justice Acronyms

http://www.search.org/publications/acronyms.asp (\$)

Purpose: To decode law-enforcement-related acronyms.

Content: This site provides a list of nearly 150 selected criminal justice acronyms, their definitions, and relevant links. (For example, one entry is "NIJ, National Institute of Justice, U.S. DOJ http://www.ojp.usdoj.gov/nij.")

Our View: The list is all contained on one long page. The list is short enough that it's not a great chore to scroll through it to find the acronym you might be looking for, although a search function would still be helpful.

Tip: Use your browser's Find function to search for an acronym quickly, rather than scrolling through the list.

Encyclopedias

The Columbia Encyclopedia, Sixth Edition (2002)

http://www.bartleby.com/65 (\$)

Purpose: To search for information on a topic, person or place.

Content: The online edition of this encyclopedia includes nearly 51,000 entries. Entries can be searched full-text, or just by the entry titles. You can also browse the entries from an alphabetical table of contents.

Additionally, there is a separate index covering the encyclopedia's more than 17,000 biographical entries. They are classified into 140 subject categories.

Our View: Just like a print encyclopedia, this site offers informative entries on myriad topics. One advantage of the online format is the more than 80,000 hypertext cross-references sprinkled throughout the individual entries. For example, within the entry for Albert Einstein there are links to related topics discussed, including his special theory of relativity, the photoelectric effect, and Brownian movement, among other topics.

Calculators and Converters

Martindale's Calculators OnLine Center

http://www.martindalecenter.com/Calculators.html

Purpose: For help on calculations and conversions of various types.

Content: This site has an impressive collection of over seventeen thousand specialized online calculators from over three thousand sources. The calculators are created and maintained by a variety of public and private sources around the world. They are broken down into two main categories: Science and Math Calculators, and General. There are several subcategories for science and math, such as statistics and chemistry, and the general calculators are arranged alphabetically.

Our View: Whether you need to convert ounces to milligrams, barrels of oil to U.S. and Imperial gallons, or calculate the field of view for a particular type of camera, you're bound to find the source for your solution here.

Maps

MapQuest

http://www.mapquest.com

Purpose: To retrieve maps of various locations, as well as driving directions and other helpful information.

Content:　　The site is probably most often used for its Driving Directions feature. It also provides maps of the U.S. and of foreign countries, as well as aerial photographs of selected locations.

Our View:　　MapQuest is an easy-to-use tool for creating maps and getting driving directions. You can get (usually) clear driving directions and maps simply by putting your starting address and destination address into the appropriate boxes on the Driving Directions page.

　　　　Clicking on the Maps icon on the home page allows you to use the **Country** drop-down list in the **Map an address** window to select one of nearly three hundred countries for which the site can provide general or detailed maps. After retrieving a map for a given destination, MapQuest also gives you the option of viewing an aerial photo of the location by clicking on the **Aerial Photo** tab. (Be sure to select the **Big Photo** button on the right side of the aerial photo window to get the best view of the photo.) Maps and aerial photos can be easily printed for your later reference.

Tip:　　　• MapQuest can also be a handy way to calculate mileage between two points for expense or tax purposes.
　　　　• Additionally, you might want to include a link to a MapQuest map of your office on your Web site.

TerraFly

To search: To purchase photos (and advanced searching):

http://www.terrafly.fiu.edu

Purpose:　　To view satellite images of neighborhoods.

Content: This site allows you to search for aerial photos by address. The returned maps include labels for streets, parks, schools, restaurants, hotels, and homes listed for sale (including price), among other information. Clicking on the map takes you to a page where you can access more information, such as demographic data, EPA maps, flood zones, median household income, and population, as well as local businesses and hospitals, among other categories. Using the control panel on the left-hand side of the screen you can "fly" over the area. (Click the direction you want to fly on the red directional crosshairs to select a direction. Click in the center of the crosshairs to stop.) You can also select from several major cities (click the **Browse** button on the home page to see a list of states and cities). After selecting a city from the list, click on **Fly over aerial imagery starting at [name of city you selected]**.

Our View: This is the most flexible of the free sources for aerial photos, but also the slowest loading. The maps and Java control panel took nearly a minute to load over a standard DSL connection. Once they do load, these maps offer the most information. Clicking the **Layers** button and then checking the zip box changes the view to show ZIP codes. Click the **Mark** button to draw a box around the specific area for which you would like to order a custom map, then the **Dispense** button to order. Prices vary. This site is run by the High Performance Database Research Center (HPDRC), which is associated with the School of Computer Science at Florida International University.

Tip: Currently, the closest resolution is one mile. The site promises to add one-foot resolution for the entire country in the future. (Fort Lauderdale is the first city available for viewing at one-foot resolution.)

Terraserver

To search: To purchase images (and advanced searching): **$**

http://www.terraserver.com

Purpose: To retrieve aerial photos of selected locations.

Content: Terraserver provides satellite and aerial photographic images of selected cities around the world. The majority of coverage is in North America and Europe, with some coverage of Australia, Asia, and the Middle East.

Our View: Terraserver started as a joint research project among Terraserver.com, Microsoft, the U.S. Geological Survey (USGS), and Compaq.

You can view all imagery for free down to 8 meters of detail. As a Terraserver subscriber you can view high-resolution images of 1 or 2 meters of detail and then purchase the images immediately. Subscription fees range from $4.95 (for five days) to $99.95 (for one year). Free searches can be conducted by:

- City
- ZIP code
- USGS
- Map (this is actually only a map showing Ter raserver's coverage areas of selected cities)

Address searches are available only to subscribers. U.S. cities covered include:

- Boston
- Chicago
- Los Angeles
- Miami
- New Orlean
- New York
- San Diego
- San Francisco

Tip: This site can be useful for attorneys who need demonstrative evidence (such as for a car accident).

Microsoft also maintains a separate free service at **http://terraserver-usa.com**. Searches for U.S. addresses can be conducted for free at this site by click-ing on the **Advanced Find** option on the left navigation bar, and then selecting **Address**.

Unlike the aerial photos available at MapQuest, those available at the Microsoft site include the date the photo was taken.

Geographic Names Information System

http://geonames.usgs.gov/#db

Purpose: To locate places throughout the U.S.

Content: The U.S. Geological Service maintains this database of "almost 2 million physical and cultural geographic fea-tures in the United States" (states, territories, and protec-torates). These include airports, beaches, cemeteries, dams, lakes, military installations (historical only), parks, populated places (cities, towns, and so on), schools, and more.

Our View: This database can be extremely useful if you're trying to pinpoint a geographic landmark or location in an area you are unfamiliar with. You can enter as much or as lit-tle information as you know about a place to conduct a search. Search fields include feature name, state or terri-tory, and feature type. Returned results include the state and county where the feature is located, the type of fea-ture, its latitude and longitude, and the name of the USGS map where it can be found. Clicking on the fea-ture's name in the search results brings additional infor-mation, as well as links for maps, aerial photos (if avail-able), and other information.

Tip: The search engine also offers a **Query Variant Name** option for searching unofficial names, as well as using the percent character (%) as a wild card to replace one or more letters in your place name. For example, a search for the name "whit%", limited to airports, returned a list of sixty-two airports from White Mountain Airport in Nome County, Alaska to Whittlesey Cranberry Airport in Wood County, Wisconsin.

Phone Books

See Chapter 7, "Finding and Backgrounding People," for an in-depth discussion of phone directories available online.

Quotations

Bartleby.com

http://www.bartleby.com/quotations

Purpose: To locate famous quotes (mostly) from well-known authors.

Content: Bartleby.com offers a searchable index of over eighty-six thousand quotations from three primary sources: Bartlett's *Familiar Quotations* (10th ed., 1919), *The Columbia World of Quotations* (1996), and *Simpson's Contemporary Quotations* (1988).

Our View: Searching is fairly logical. You can either perform a keyword search, or you can select any of the three sources and browse their subject categories to find the quote that best suits your need.

Tip: A good, famous quote (when it's on point, of course) can be a good addition to a brief, opening statement, or closing argument.

Quoteland

http://www.quoteland.com

Purpose: To locate famous quotes (mostly) from well-known authors.

Content: Quoteland also offers a database of quotations searchable by keyword, or browsable by topic.

Our View: One advantage to this site is that its search engine allows for use of the percent sign (%) as a wild card to represent one or more characters. This can be extremely helpful if you know the name of an author, but are unsure of the correct spelling.

Tip: This site offers the added ability to purchase your favorite quote on a T-shirt, coffee mug, and more.

The Quotations Page

http://www.quotationspage.com

Purpose: To locate famous quotes (mostly) from well-known authors.

Content: This site offers quotations from over two thousand authors in categories ranging from Acting to Writing.

Our View: This site is also easy to use. The database is full-text searchable, or you can browse through an alphabetical list of categories or authors. Individual quotation entries include cross-references to other quotations by the same author, other quotations in the same category, and biographical information (on selected authors).

Tip: If you don't find a category in the list that matches your needs, try doing a keyword search. If those quotes don't fit the bill, use the cross-reference links to locate other related quotes that might work.

Online Translators

AltaVista's Babel Fish Translation

http://world.altavista.com

Purpose: To translate words, phrases, or Web pages.

Content: Babel Fish was one of the first online translation sites. It offers nineteen possible translation possibilities among eight different languages. They are

• English to Chinese	• Chinese to English
• English to French	• French to English
• English to German	• French to German
• English to Italian	• German to English
• English to Japanese	• German to French
• English to Korean	• Italian to English
• English to Portuguese	• Japanese to English
• English to Spanish	• Korean to English
	• Portuguese to English
	• Russian to English
	• Spanish to English

Online Translators

While useful, online translators are no substitute for a human translator. The online translations can sometimes be a bit too literal or stilted to make sense. For example, translating the sentence "Where are you going?" from English to Spanish (using both the Babel Fish and Google translation sites noted below) produces the following Spanish translation: "¿Adónde usted va?" Translating that exact phrase from Spanish back into English produced the following result: "Where you go?" While understandable, it is not exactly a proper translation. The bottom line is that online translation sites can be useful in a pinch to translate a document or website on the spot or to make yourself understood to a client. But for important case-related issues, use a qualified live interpreter or translator to ensure a proper result.

Our View: Babel Fish allows you to enter up to 150 words at a time for translation. Once your translated phrase is returned, you are offered the option of searching the Web with that translation as your keyword phrase.

The site also allows you to type in a URL to have that Web site translated into your choice of language.

Tip: • For a "quick-and-dirty" translation of a document, you can "cut and paste" or type the text into Babel Fish (150 words at a time).
    • Despite the stated 150-word limit per translation, we were able to translate a document that was 767 words in length before the site cut off words at the end of the document.

Google Translate

http://translate.google.com/translate_t

Purpose: To translate words, phrases, or Web pages.

Content: Google also offers a translation site covering twelve translation combinations of six languages.
They are

• English to French	• French to English
• English to German	• French to German
• English to Italian	• German to English
• English to Portuguese	• German to French
• English to Spanish	• Italian to English
	• Portuguese to English
	• Spanish to English

Our View: Google offers the same features and functions as Babel Fish, albeit with a shorter list of languages and combinations. Google, however, seems to have no limit on the size of document you can translate. We were able to translate a document of over twelve thousand words with no signs of rejection. The longer documents take significantly longer to translate than shorter ones.

ZIP Codes

ZIP Code Lookup

http://www.usps.com/zip4

Purpose: To search for ZIP code and related information

Content: This page is part of the U.S. Postal Service's Web site. Here you can search various ZIP code information by selecting one of the following options in the drop-down menu:

- ZIP+4 Code
- All ZIP Codes for City/Town
- All Cities/Towns in a ZIP Code
- ZIP+4 Code for a Company

Free Internet Access to Library Databases and Catalogs

Since the first edition of this book was written we've come a long way in terms of access to library resources over the Internet. In the first edition the chapter was simply called "Library Catalogs Online" and the authors lamented, "At present, however, only Gale's *Encyclopedia of Associations* is available in full text on the Internet, and, as with all of the Net-converted Gale sources, pre-payment is required."

Oh, how far we've come; libraries are now providing library patrons with *free* remote access over the Internet to selected pay databases that contain a wealth of factual information, even to the above-mentioned *Encyclopedia of Associations*. Who would have foreseen that you'd be able to have remote access for free into expensive databases such as Gale's *Encyclopedia of Associations*? Consequently, we've added "databases" to the front of this section's title and relegated "catalogs" to the end of the title. To say that the addition of free remote access to pay databases is a valuable resource is an understatement! In fact, it's invaluable. It not only saves you a commute to the library, it opens up amazing amounts of expensive and useful information to you, free—saving you from investing in database subscriptions that you might need only occasionally.

Whether a library offers remote access at all varies widely from library to library. To find out if your local public library does, visit their Web site. Don't know your public library's URL? You can locate it at the LibWeb site (**http://sunsite.berkeley.edu/Libweb**). If your library does have remote access, you'll need to have a library card. Some libraries allow you to apply online and then pick the card up in person. Once you have your card, you'll need to enter your library card number into the library's remote access database Web page. You may have to also enter a password or your ZIP code. For those libraries that offer remote access to databases, the number and type of databases vary widely. Here are links to three library remote access databases: Chicago Public Library (CPL) at **http://www.chipubweb.org/4carlweb/013databases/dbhome.html**, Los Angeles Public Library (LAPL) at **http://databases.lapl.org**, and New York Public Library (NYPL) at **http://www.nypl.org/branch/idescriptions.html**.

The following are examples of the types of databases that can be accessed at NYPL. Many of these can also be accessed at LAPL and CPL, among other libraries:

- Academic Search Premier: 3,288 scholarly publications (full text) covering social sciences, humanities, education, computer sciences, engineering, medical sciences, and more
- Biography Resource: information on over 150,000 people
- Business and Company Resource Center (Gale): subjects include finance, acquisitions & mergers, international trade, money man agement, new technologies & products, local & regional business trends, investments, and banking
- Business Source Premier: 2,470 scholarly business journals (full text) covering management, economics, finance, accounting, international business, and more
- Business Wire News
- Clinical Pharmacology
- *Encyclopedia Americana*
- Funk & Wagnalls New World Encyclopedia
- Health Source, Consumer Edition: access to nearly 300 full-text consumer health periodicals, 1,200 health-related pamphlets, and 20 health reference books
- Health Source, Nursing/Academic Edition

- *New York Times* and *New York Post* Full-text (Gale): full-text newspaper articles for one full year
- Newspaper Source: full text for 159 regional U.S. newspapers, 18 international newspapers, 6 newswires, the *Christian Science Monitor,* the *Los Angeles Times,* and more
- OCLC FirstSearch: service includes an index of articles from the contents pages of journals and, for borrowing purposes, a list of periodicals and a catalog of books held by OCLC member libraries
- Psychology and Behavioral Sciences Collection: the database has nearly 480 full-text titles

You will find that some of the databases that are available at one library on a remote basis may be completely unavailable at another library (remotely or in-person). Other times, you will find that one library's remote database is another library's in-person database only. There's no rhyme or reason. For example, at LAPL, Reference USA and the Oxford Dictionary are remote access databases, but not so at NYPL. They can be accessed only by an in-person visit to NYPL. All of the libraries in this discussion offer remote database titles that the others do not. For example, CPL has remote access to ABI Inform while the other two libraries don't carry this database at all. And the *Encyclopedia of Associations*, coveted by the prior authors, is available remotely (free) only at LAPL. This title is extremely useful for locating experts—especially those in unusual fields. See Chapter 9, "Finding and Backgrounding Expert Witnesses," for our quest for a chewing gum expert.

As you peruse the NYPL list of remote databases, you should have one foot out the door—heading over to visit your local library to pick up your library card. These databases have truly remarkable information. We'll give some detailed examples throughout this book describing situations when lawyers (or when we) made use of remote databases. They are especially useful for company research and competitive intelligence. Remote databases, particularly the full-text articles from newspapers, journals, or books, are also useful for any type of subject-specific research or for finding experts.

The convenience of being able to search remotely (and for free) through the full text of so many databases for information, and to read and print the full text of the materials from your office or home computer, surpasses anything we imagined just a few years ago. The usefulness of browsing through a library's online catalog to locate books or journals probably now pales in comparison to what you've just learned you can find in the remote databases.

News, Periodicals, and Broadcast Media

News coverage can be a valuable source of factual information on hot topics, or background information on high-profile individuals or select businesses. News sites on the Internet provide you with the unique ability to choose the topics you want to see when you want to see them. In addition, many sites provide archives that can be searched as needed.

Because news is constantly changing, it's ordinarily useless to search for the latest news with *most* search engines. There are two search engines that do a good job of keeping up with changing news (Google and AltaVista); otherwise it's best to go directly to the source.

There are many news sources on the Internet. Some are Internet versions of respected media sources such as CNN, *USA Today*, the *Wall Street Journal*, and so on. Often, content from newspapers and magazines that is available for a fee from a commercial database (such as LexisNexis or Dialog Service) might be available for free on the Internet or via a public library's remote database.

However, that doesn't necessarily imply that the content on the Internet duplicates what is found on the commercial sources, or what was originally disseminated by the media source. Some material, such as audio, is not yet compiled into searchable databases by commercial database sites. However, broadcasters such as National Public Radio (NPR) at **http://www.npr.org** offer the ability to conduct keyword searches to retrieve audio (free) of past NPR news and feature coverage, back to 1996. (Some searches may return abstracts of stories from before 1996. No audio is available for those stories, although transcripts are offered for purchase.)

In some instances there are differences between the Internet version of a story and what's been published by the same media source elsewhere. For example, there may be a limit to the number of articles displayed on the Internet from each edition of a periodical, or only headlines may be provided, or the news may be summarized. Additionally, news stories on the Internet are occasionally updated throughout the day—long after the print version of a story has been finalized.

Some news sources are exclusive to the Internet. Whenever a big news story happens, whether it's floods in the Midwest or a war in a third-world country, Web sites are set up just to give people a way to exchange information and find ways to help victims. This seems to happen spontaneously. Such is the nature of the global publishing forum available to everyone, and known as the Internet.

Everyone has their favorite local or national newspaper or magazines that they turn to for their news fix. For news of local interest, the Web sites for local newspapers, radio, and TV stations may be your best source for information. Regionally, news outlets in large, nearby cities may also yield useful information on a particular topic. When conducting research, it can be necessary to look beyond those usual sources for regional or specialty news topics.

Links to many major market newspapers, television networks, and national news magazines can also be found at the Internet For Lawyers Web site (**http://www.netforlawyers.com/news.htm**).

Don't Forget Your Local Library for Remote Access to Newspapers, Too!

Many libraries offer patrons remote access to local newspapers and other papers from major cities around the country. For example, the Beverly Hills (California) public library offers its patrons remote access to Newsbank with its full-text content of the *Los Angeles Times, Christian Science Monitor, USA Today, Orange County Register, Riverside Press-Enterprise, San Diego Union-Tribune,* and *San Francisco Chronicle.* All a patron needs is a library card. The National Newspaper Index, offered remotely by some libraries, provides access to an index of the *New York Times,* the *Wall Street Journal,* the *Christian Science Monitor,* as well as to news stories written by the staff writers of the *Los Angeles Times* and the *Washington Post.* Local libraries may also other local and regional databases that offer full-text searchable archives of various papers.

Search Engines for News

Google News

http://news.google.com

Purpose: Search engine for news.

Content: This site uses Google's search and page-ranking technologies to gather stories from over 4,500 news sources around the world, ranging from the BBC, CNN, and the Boston Globe to press releases from selected companies. News stories displayed on the Google News home page or in News search results are updated continuously

Figure 5-3. Google News home page. Google™ is a trademark of Google Technology Inc.

throughout the day. (On a recent visit to the site, the "freshest" story was only five minutes old.) Headlines and abstracts are prominently displayed on the main page under Top Stories. Users can also perform keyword searches for links to news stories on particular subjects. Returned results can include stories up to (approximately) thirty days old.

Our View: The search results page lists news in a variety of categories (including Top Stories, World, U.S., Business, Entertainment, and more) in a directory style. Within those categories, stories are grouped together by subject, with stories from multiple sources—covering the same news subject—in subgroups.

A recent search for "Fidel Castro" returned over 1,900 results. In Google's ordering of the stories by rele-vance, the first result linked to a story from Moscow's *Pravda* that was two weeks old, while the second result from the *Washington Post* was from "19 hours ago," indicating the up-to-date nature of the search results. Under the third result were related news stories from other publications around the world.

A sampling of other sources included:

- The BBC
- *Christian Science Monitor*
- CNN
- *Hindustan Times*
- *Miami Herald*
- *Jordan Times*
- *San Jose Mercury News*
- WPTV (Florida)

The oldest story in the results list was nine days old.

It is important to take note of a story's source, since Google may also include company press releases in its news search results.

Tip: Use the site's **Sort by date** function (on the right-hand side of the results page) to put the most current results at the top of the list.

AltaVista News

http://www.altavista.com/news/default

Purpose: Search engine for news.

Content: The AltaVista News search includes over four million articles from three thousand sources, worldwide. It is powered by the stand-alone news search engine More-over.

Our View: In addition to conducting standard keyword and phrase searches, you can use the AltaVista News index to search only for articles that contain images (with a check box) or to limit your search with user-definable parameters in drop-down menus. You can select:

- Date range
- Topic category
- Geographical region
- News source

Tip: While there is no Advanced Search option in the AltaVista News search, it supports all search commands also used on its Web search. If you enter multiple words, AltaVista returns only articles that have all of the words.

- To exclude words, put a minus sign (-) in front of them
- Use quotation marks for phrase searches
- Use Boolean commands including AND, OR, AND NOT, NEAR

NewsTrove

http://www.newstrove.com

Purpose: To search for news stories from publications around the world.

Content: NewsTrove is a metasearch engine that covers over seven thousand news sources from around the world.

Our View: You can also peruse the site's list of nearly four thousand links to individual publications, or browse through an ever-changing topical list of news subjects.

News Metasites

There are several metasites that link to general newspapers and magazines, business newspapers and magazines, and wire services.

Drudge Report

http://www.drudgereport.com

Purpose: To search for news and information through various links to news organizations.

Content: The Drudge Report site offers a comprehensive set of links to major news organizations around the world. The site also includes a list of American columnists (listed alphabetically), Chinese, Japanese, and English language wire services, and even the *National Enquirer*.

Our View: While best known for the "shoot-from-the-hip" muckraking style of his own reporting, Webmaster Matt Drudge provides a good list of links to more-established news organizations on this site. Along with the links comes Drudge's own (conservative) opinions on the news stories he chooses to highlight.

Tip: For links to many of the same news resources, and thousands of other resources in dozens of other categories, see the Refdesk.com site (discussed in the "Standard Reference Resources" section of this chapter) maintained by Matt Drudge's father, Robert Drudge.

BuzzFlash

http://www.buzzflash.com

Purpose: To search for news and information through various links to news organizations

Content: BuzzFlash offers a comprehensive set of links to major news organizations around the world. The list includes links to wire services and major market newspapers in the United States, as well as selected international news resources.

Our View: Many of the links to news sources at BuzzFlash are also available at other sites mentioned in this section. The site offers a decidedly more liberal view of current news than the Drudge Report. The top 80 percent of the Web site's home page contains links to current news stories, opinion, commentary, and satire from a liberal perspective.

Tip: There are media links buried near the bottom of the page.

Online Newspapers

http://www.onlinenewspapers.com/

Purpose: To search for news and newspapers from specific countries.

Content: Developed and maintained by the Australian search engine Web Wombat, Online Newspapers contains links to over thousands of newspapers around the world. (The site lists more than 100 newspapers for Japan alone.) Links to individual counties' newspapers can be accessed through the series of regional pull-down menus on the site's home page (e.g. "Central America," "Africa," West Indies," etc.), or from the alphabetical list of all countries for which links are included.

Our View: This is another good place to start a search for news sources in specific foreign countries.

Bizjournals

To search: To read articles:

http://www.bizjournals.com

Purpose: To locate business news from forty-one cities around the U.S.

Content: Bizjournals is from American City Business Journals, which publishes local business newspapers in forty-one cities across the country. Some of their major markets include Atlanta, Austin, Baltimore, Boston, Dallas, Nashville, San Francisco, and Tampa, among others. Clicking the **Archives** link (next to the search box on the home page) gives you the option to search any of their publications (or all of them at once) back to 1996.

Tip: With the free registration, you can also sign up to receive an e-mail notification whenever a company you specify is mentioned in one of their business publications. Additionally, you can sign up to receive general business news alerts via e-mail.

NewsLink

http://newslink.org

Purpose: To search for news and information through links to various news organizations.

Content: The site offers links to television and radio stations across the country, as well as to newspapers and magazines in the U.S. and around the world.

You can view lists of these sources broken down by:

- Geographical area (state for the U.S., country for foreign media)
- Daily or nondaily newspapers
- Network affiliation (TV)
- Subject matter (such as alternative, business, and so on)

Our View: NewsLink is run by University of Illinois Journalism professor Eric Meyer. He is also a research scientist at the school's National Center for Supercomputing Applications (the birthplace of the Mosaic browser that became Netscape Navigator). While it would be difficult for any worldwide database of media sources to be complete, with his credentials, it would seem that if anyone could create a comprehensive list, Meyer could.

CEOExpress

http://www.ceoexpress.com

Purpose: For information and news on business.

Content: CEOExpress contains links to hundreds of business-oriented newspaper and magazine sources arranged by subject. These include:

- Daily news
- Business news
- International news
- News feeds
- Tech news
- Lifestyle publications
- Television news

Our View: The site's layout can be a bit hard on the eyes, but the volume and quality of the links make it worth visiting.

Current News

The Web sites of the twenty-four-hour cable television news networks are all good sources for news on the Internet. Because they are constantly updating and rewriting stories to appear on TV, the news on their sites is generally very up to date. The most popular all-news network Web sites are

- CNN at **http://www.cnn.com**
- Fox News at **http://www.foxnews.com**
- MSNBC at **http://www.msnbc.com**

Current news is also available from newspapers and magazines (see above) and wire services (see below).

Wire Services

Wire services are collectives, or membership organizations, that gather and report news, distributing the resulting stories to their members. With the recent trend toward shrinking news-gathering budgets, the international wire services have become more and more important to news coverage around the world.

> *Tip:*   Use the Drudge Report for News Archives. The most con-
> venient way to search the archives of the major news
> services is via the news metasite the Drudge Report
> (**http://www.drudgereport.com**). You can search the AP
> and Reuters archives back fourteen days via search boxes
> offered on the Drudge site. (See the "News Metasites"
> section earlier in this chapter for more information on
> this site.)

The major wire services listed below (in alphabetical order) offer headlines and links to their most recent stories, as noted.

AFP (Agence France Presse)

http://www.afp.com/english/home

Purpose: For current and archived news stories from around the world.

Content: AFP is the successor of the world's first international press agency, founded in 1835. Its site offers headlines and links to select current articles.

Our View: Even though there is no search engine at the site, it is still a good source for breaking news.

Tip: Searches for current news stories from AFP can be conducted via the Yahoo! News page (**http://news.yahoo.com**).

Associated Press (AP)

http://customwire.ap.org

Purpose: To locate current and archived news stories from around the world.

Content: AP is the oldest American wire service. Its site offers access to its headlines through the Web sites of its member newspapers. From this page, you can select your local paper, or any member paper whose Web site you wish to visit. These pages usually offer headlines and abstracts of the latest stories, with links to the full articles.

Our View: The Associated Press is probably the best known wire service in the United States. Its vast resources, coupled with the resources of its member newspapers, make this wire service an excellent source of breaking news. Having to select a member paper and click through to that paper's AP search page can be cumbersome. That's why we recommend using the AP search box provided at the Drudge Report Web site (**http://www.drudgereport.com**). Drudge has tapped directly into the AP search page of the *Washington Post* to provide this service.

Bloomberg.com

http://www.bloomberg.com

Purpose: To locate news stories from around the world.

Content: Bloomberg.com presents news coverage with a heavy focus on business news coverage. Its site offers headlines and links to selected, current news stories.

Our View: Founded in 1990, Bloomberg is the newest of the wire services discussed here. Even though no archive search is available, the site is still a good source for breaking news—particularly for business and financial subjects.

Reuters

http://www.reuters.com

Purpose: To locate current and archived news stories from around the world.

Content: The site offers headlines and links to current news stories and stories from the recent past. It presents browsable headlines in over a dozen categories, ranging from **Technology** to **Oddly Enough** (strange stories), as well as a search engine to retrieve recent stories by keyword.

Our View: The easy-to-use keyword search function makes the Reuters site simple to use. The results can go back as far as five days, but are limited to the one hundred newest stories. Therefore, if there are three hundred stories on a particular subject over the course of a week, a keyword search for that subject will only show the headlines and links for the most recent one hundred, regardless of what day they appeared (even if all appeared today). You cannot see or access stories numbers 101 through 300.

With optional free registration, you can access raw news video and receive news alerts via e-mail, among other features.

United Press International (UPI)

http://www.upi.com

Purpose: To read selected current news stories.

Content: UPI offers links to only a minimal number of news stories on its home page. Currently, there is no search function or access to the archive.

Our View: Until the first quarter of 2003, UPI offered the ability to search its archive of news, feature stories, and columns, back two years. Now the site serves only as a sales tool for the packaged news products the wire offers. Without a search function or access to the wire's archive, there is little reason for researchers to use the UPI Web site.

Company Press Releases

In addition to the traditional news wires mentioned above, there are services that distribute news releases (for a fee) for the companies that issue them.

While press releases often put the most positive spin on a story, it can be extremely interesting and important to see what a company said about itself or a given situation in retrospect—especially in intellectual property, business transactional, and family law cases, and in stockholder lawsuits.

Below are the two largest such distribution services. While there may be some overlap in the companies that use these two services, it's a good idea to check both when you're looking for company news. You can also locate some company press releases by using the Google News search engine (discussed earlier in this chapter).

You should also keep in mind that not all companies utilize these types of services. An excellent source of company press releases is often the Web site of the company itself.

Business Wire

http://www.businesswire.com

Purpose: To locate business news and press releases.

Content: The site offers a full-text, searchable database of all company press releases issued through Business Wire over the past forty-eight hours.
                You can search or browse the latest headlines by:

- Industry (from Accounting to Universities)
- Subject (from Bond/Stock Ratings to Webcasts)
- Geography

Our View: If you're looking for news from a particular company or industry, the press releases they issue can be an excellent source of information. For older news, click on **Company News Archive** for an alphabetical list of companies distributing news through Business Wire and links to each of their news releases. Some companies also proffer an online media kit. Additional information can also be obtained by clicking on **Company Profiles.**

PR Newswire

http://www.prnewswire.com/news

Purpose: To locate business news and press releases.

Content: Like Business Wire, PR Newswire offers headlines and browsable lists of the most recent news releases by subject or industry. To find news released by a particular company, click on **Company News**. There you have the option of searching (by company name) for all releases sent by a company during the past thirty days. Additionally, you can browse an alphabetical listing of PR Newswire member companies to view all of the press releases sent by a particular company back to 1996.

Our View: The availability of an archive of press releases from a particular company can be a valuable tool in charting that company's history.

Locating Books and Videos

While the Internet offers ready access to millions of information sources, there are still many instances when only a hard copy of a book or video will do. For example, when you are locating or researching an expert, you may want to find a book the expert has written that relates to the testimony you need. The book can help establish expertise, and also give you an idea of the expert's perspective on the issue. (For more information on researching experts, see Chapter 9, "Finding and Backgrounding Expert Witnesses.") The Internet may come in handy in tracking down materials from experts. Here are some resources that can help.

Books

It's hard to imagine anyone with an Internet connection who has not heard of the Internet's premiere bookseller, Amazon.com (**http://www.amazon.com**). Launched in July 1995, Amazon offers what it describes as "Earth's Biggest Selection" of books (and other consumer goods). While there are any number of other traditional book retailers that have entered the online book sales fray, none has approached the notoriety of Amazon. Even book retailing giant Borders Group (owner of the Borders, Waldenbooks, and Brentano's chains) has teamed up with Amazon.com to provide online sales. Barnes & Noble online bookstore can be located at **http://www.barnesnoble.com**. Amazon and Barnes & Noble's sites both also offer videos of current and recent film releases.

Likewise, major retail video outlets have staked their claim on the Internet. New and recent releases can be purchased from Blockbuster Video (**http://www.blockbuster.com**). Other online retailers include Buy.com (**http://www.buy.com**) and Reel.com (**http://www.reel.com**), which has teamed up with Amazon to handle its sales.

It should also be noted that Amazon maintains an auction service where users can offer personal copies of books or videos for bid. (Click on the **Auctions** tab at the top of the Amazon opening screen.) Also on the auction front, you shouldn't discount the possibility that the book or video you're looking for might be available on eBay (**http://www.ebay.com**).

Hard-to-Find and Out-of-Print Books

Powell's Books

To search: ⊘$ To purchase: **$**

http://www.powells.com

Purpose: To locate new and used technical, hard-to-find, and rare books.

Content: Powell's has divided its collection into more than two hundred browsable categories and offers a sophisticated search engine. You can keyword search by author or title, among other criteria.

Our View: The site's clean design and clear navigation make it easy to go directly to the genre, author, or title you're looking for. The site also includes an incredible breadth of titles, from the latest Harry Potter release ($29.99, hardcover) to an 1853 first-edition French translation of selected works of Edgar Allan Poe ($1,550.00, paperback). Additionally, Powell's has an extensive selection of technical

books and text books if you are searching for or conducting background research on an expert.

Tip: Click on **more search options** to create the most targeted searches.

Figure 5-4. Powell's Books offers thousands of new and used books for sale in (nearly) every imaginable category.

Abebooks

To search: To purchase: **$**

http://www.abebooks.com

Purpose: To locate new and used technical, hard-to-find, and rare
books.

Content: Abebooks (from Advanced Book Exchange) has created a
searchable database of the combined inventory of a net-

work of more than ten thousand independent book-sellers. All told, these booksellers hold more than forty million books. This inventory is a mix of popular, mass-market titles; scientific and technical books; and rare, out-of-print, limited, or first-edition printings.

Our View: Returned results feature full information for the books including binding, cover type, ISBN, price, and location of the bookseller who owns each particular copy that's available. The site also features a section specifically for librarians that includes helpful recommendations geared toward library collection development. Its research and professional links can also be useful to a lawyer looking for information on specific topics.

Tip: You can search by author, title, or keywords to find the title you need. Additionally, an asterisk (*) can be used as a trailing wild card to truncate search terms ("Ste*" would stand in for "Stephen" or "Steven").

Alibris

To search: (🚫$)   To purchase: **$**

http://www.alibris.com

Purpose: To locate new, used, hard-to-find, and rare books.

Content: Like Abebooks, Alibris connects thousands of independ-ent booksellers and their thirty million new, used, and hard-to-find titles with the people who are looking for them. You can browse through the more than sixty cate-gories (and innumerable subcategories) or use the site's comprehensive search engine.

Our View: You can search by author, title, or keywords to find the title you need. Returned results indicate a book's avail-ability and pricing (new and used). Clicking on a book's title displays details for each copy of the book selected, including condition, cover type, number of pages, price, ISBN, and name of the bookseller that has the book for sale.

Tip: Alibris also utilizes the asterisk (*) as a wild card at the end of a search term.

Videos

The TV MegaSite

To search: To purchase: **$**

http://www.tvmegasite.net/prime/videostobuy.shtml

Purpose: To locate obscure or hard-to-find videos.

Content: This site's Videos to Buy page maintains a list of nearly thirty sources for all types of videotapes.

Our View: The list runs the gamut from commercial video clubs (Columbia House) offering new and recent releases, to small specialty retailers around the country. Not all of the sources listed have Web sites or e-mail addresses, so you'll have to contact those by phone or snail mail.

Tip: See the Video Trading Post at **http://tvmegasite.net/ trading** for a list of links to other trading lists and resources where specific programs might be obtained.

The Video Den Collection

To search: To purchase: **$**

http://www.rarevideo.com

Purpose: To locate obscure or hard-to-find videos.

Content: The Video Den Collection maintains a database of "tens-of thousands" of hard-to-find titles in a fully searchable database. You can search by:

- Film title
- Director's name
- Stars' names

Our View: The site contains a wide range of titles and genres, from special collector's editions of *E.T. The Extraterrestrial* to both versions of *Jacob Two Two Meets the Hooded Fang* (1979, starring Alex Karras; and 1999, starring Gary Busey). You can also browse the titles alphabetically. Prices vary (wildly).

Tip: If the Video Den does not have the title you're looking for in its collection, they can help you locate it on a "'collector-to-collector' basis with no rights given or implied." Click the **Inquiry** tab to submit information on the title you need.

Traditions Military Videos

To search: To purchase: **$**

http://www.militaryvideo.com

Purpose: To locate military-themed and military-produced videos.

Content: The site maintains a growing catalog of over six hundred training films and documentaries produced by the U.S. military dating from the 1930s through the 1980s.

Our View: You can browse the entire catalog by title, by service branch (Navy, Army, and so on), by theaters (such as

Vietnam, Korea, World War I), or perform a keyword or title search. Prices vary from title to title.

Tip: If you are looking for a particular title or subject, on return visits to the site you can use its New Videos option to see new titles added in the previous two weeks or previous month.

The Video Beat

To search: To purchase: **$**

http://www.thevideobeat.com

Purpose: To locate hard-to-find genre videos.

Content: The Video Beat specializes in video copies of 50s and 60s movies. Their genre list includes Rock 'n' Roll Movies; Teen, Beach & Hippie Movies; Rock 'n' Roll TV Shows; and more. From the 1956 "seedy art house film" *Dance Hall Racket* starring Lenny Bruce to a collection of Elvis-Presley-insider Joe Esposito's rare 8mm home movies of Presley, this site is filled with esoteric and difficult-to-locate items.

All tapes cost $25 and run two hours in length. Shorter programs are filled out with filler material of the same genre.

Our View: While the focus of the Video Beat collection is narrow, you never know what you'll need some day.

Tip: It should be noted that the site carries the following disclaimer: "All videos are VHS NTSC and for home use only. All titles are sold on a 'collector-to-collector' basis with no rights given or implied. All titles have been researched and found to be in the public domain."

A Million and One World-Wide Videos

To search: To purchase: **$**

http://www.wwvideos.com

Purpose: To locate obscure or hard to find videos.

Content: While they do not maintain a list of available titles, this site claims to have "video detectives" who locate "out-of-print videos, rare movies, and lost films." They advertise in numerous consumer and video specialty publications to locate the videos their clients are looking for. Once you have asked them to locate a video, "Your only obligation is to guarantee with your credit card, that you'll pay for it when we mail it to you," according to the site. If they do not find your video there is no charge to you.

Our View: While offering a valuable service, this Web site is difficult to navigate. To inquire about locating and purchasing a title, click on the **Get Free Information Now** link at the bottom of the home page (not the **Search** link). That takes you to a form to fill in the title and star or director, along with your name and e-mail address. The site promises an answer to queries "within minutes."

Tip: Be certain your video is really hard to find before contacting A Million and One World-Wide Videos.

For more information on locating video on the Internet, see Chapter 4, "Search Tools."

CHAPTER **SIX**

Government Resources Online

Is That Really a Government Site?

Generally, government Web sites end with the .gov (federal) or .us (state or local) domain. Military sites usually end with the .mil domain. In many instances, the government had the foresight and ability to also register .com and .org domain names for its sites; in other instances it did not. For example, **http://www.usps.com**, **http://www.senate.com**, and **http://www.culvercity.org** will take you to the Web sites of the U.S. Postal Service, the U.S. Senate, and the city of Culver City (California) respectively. But **http://www.whitehouse.com**, **http://www.house.com**, and **http://www.culvercity.com** will take you to an "adults only" site, a real estate site, and a personal Web site, respectively—rather than to the White House site (**http://www.whitehouse.gov**), the U.S. House of Representatives site (**http://www.house.gov**), and the site for the city of Culver City. Similarly, **http://www.co.bexar.tx.us** and **http://www.bexar.org** both lead to the official Web site of Bexar County, Texas, while **http://www.bexar.com** is the personal site of a former San Antonio resident.

A domain ending in .gov or .mil can almost certainly be counted on to be authentic government sites, as there is no mechanism to register those domains outside of the federal government. Some domain registrars do offer .us domains to the general public, so it's worth a second look to be certain you are visiting the "Real McCoy."

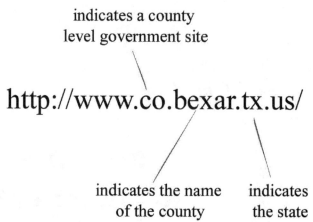

indicates a county
level government site

http://www.co.bexar.tx.us/

indicates the name   indicates
of the county   the state

Figure 6-1. In official local government sites, .us is usually preceded by a two-letter designator for a city or county (.ci and .co respectively), the name of the city or county, and a two-letter abbreviation for the state.

Federal, state, and local governments regulate, license, and collect data on a broad cross section of our professional and personal lives. More and more, government Web sites are making this information available online, but the amount and type of information varies from site to site. The George W. Bush White House has developed an action plan to create a government-wide, citizen-centered e-government program. In April 2003, the U.S. Office of Management and Budget issued its latest annual "Implementing the President's Management Agenda for E-Government" report (**http://www.whitehouse.gov/omb/egov/2003egov_strat.pdf**). The report presented an update of the plan, including a grading system for agencies that have met their implementation goals (such as the Department of Justice and the Department of Transportation) and those that still have goals to meet (such as the Small Business Administration). Additionally, almost every jurisdiction (from the state down to the city level) is implementing or planning some type of online access to its services and information.

Currently, some government sites provide only utilitarian information, such as directories of agency staff, regulations, and reports. Other sites offer juicier information like administrative decisions, background information about the industries (or individuals) they regulate, the companies within those industries, and in some instances, any action taken against those companies.

For more topic-specific government Web sites, see the following chapters in this book: Chapter 8, "Accessing Public Records;" Chapter 7, "Finding and Backgrounding People;" Chapter 10, "Company Research;" Chapter 12, "Medical Research;" Chapter 14, "Environmental Research;"

Chapter 17, "Statistical Research;" and Chapter 18, "Transportation Research."

Government Metasites

There are a number of metasites that can help you locate the federal, state, and local government resources you need.

FirstGov.gov

http://www.firstgov.gov

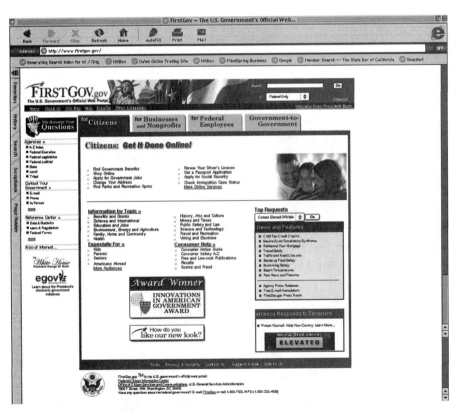

Figure 6.2. FirstGov.gov is the government portal. The site is a public-private partnership through which you can search millions of federal, state, District of Columbia, and U.S. territory government Web pages and the documents they contain.

Purpose:	To locate government documents and Web sites at all levels.
Content :	FirstGov provides a comprehensive search engine and a drill-down index covering millions of government Web pages at the federal and state level, including the District of Columbia and U.S. territories. Using the drop-down menu in the Search box, you can select **Federal Only, Federal & All States, All States, One State,** or **Federal & One State**. You can choose topics and subtopics (such as **Environment, Energy and Agriculture** or **Science and Technology**) by click-ing on **Information by Topic**. The returned results include direct links to Web pages and other documents from the resources you have selected to search. This includes PDF, Power-Point, Word, and Excel documents, in addition to HTML Web pages.

The **News and Features** section in the lower right-hand corner of the home page includes links to press releases and free e-mail newsletters from numerous federal agencies.

For an alphabetical list of federal agencies, click the **A-Z Agency Index** link (under the **Agencies** heading) in the upper left-hand corner of the home page. This list also includes links to state agencies. (Entries for the states are in alphabetical order by the name of the state.)

Our View:	This site is a good first stop when you're looking for government information on the Web. It can be especially useful if you're unsure what federal agency might oversee a particular issue, or when more than one agency might have jurisdiction. For example, a search of **Federal & All State** sites for "toxic waste" returned results from the U.S. Department of Agriculture, the Army Corps of Engineers, the Texas attorney general, and the King County (Washington) government site.

To narrow down your search results, click on **Advanced** in the upper-right corner of the home page to go to the Advanced Search page, which offers additional criteria with which you can focus your query.

Because so many government documents and forms are created for distribution in print and posted on the Web in non-HTML formats (such as PDF), it's best to start with a broad search that includes all of the file formats searchable by FirstGov.

Tip:

- To help put your search results into categories, use the Vivisimo Clustering Engine's customized FirstGov search at **http://www.vivisimo.com/firstgov**.
- For links to Native American tribal government sites, and federal government agencies dealing with the tribes, use the **Tribal** link on the left-hand side of the home page.

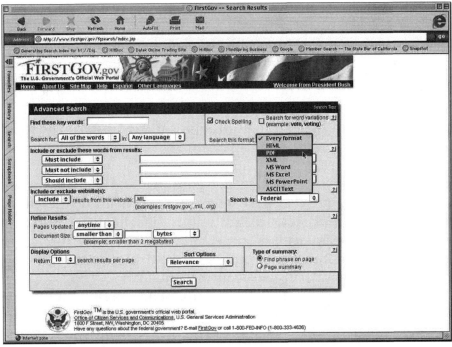

Figure 6-3. You can use FirstGov's Advanced Search to focus on only PDF or PowerPoint documents. To do this, select those options from the Advanced Search page's **Search this format** drop-down menu. Similarly, you could limit your results to only military Web sites by entering ".mil" in the **Include or exclude website(s)** box.

Three of the most oft-requested government sites are for the White House (**http://www.whitehouse.gov**), the U.S. Senate (**http://www .senate.gov**) and the U.S. House of Representatives (**http://www.house.gov**).

For links to other government sites at the federal, state, and local level, there are four metasites in particular that have each compiled hundreds of useful links to government resources at every level. While no list is complete, a combination of these four should point you to the information you're looking for:

- GovSpot at **http://www.govspot.com**
- FindLaw
  - Federal Resources at **http://www.findlaw.com/10fedgov**
  - State Resources at **http://www.findlaw.com/11stategov**
- University of Michigan Library's Government Resources on the Web at **http://www.lib.umich.edu/govdocs/govweb.html**
- LexisONE
  - Federal Resources at **http://www.lexisone.com/legalresearch/ legalguide/federal_resources/federal_resource_center_ index.htm**
  - State Resources at **http://www.lexisone.com/legalresearch/ legalguide/states/states_resources_index.htm**

These metasites offer drill-down directories to select the particular information you need. Each site organizes and presents its information differently. Your preference of one over another will depend on how you like to retrieve and review information.

GovSpot offers links to executive, legislative, and judicial resources at the federal level, as well as links to individual state and local government resources. For example, click the **Executive Branch** link on the left-hand side of the GovSpot home page to access links to cabinet-level agencies such as the Departments of State, Commerce, and so on. (Don't miss the site's list of toll-free phone numbers for a variety of federal agencies at **http://www.govspot.com/lists/800numbers.htm**.)

Similarly, clicking the **Executive Branch** link on FindLaw's federal government resource page (**http://www.findlaw.com/10fedgov**) and then clicking **Executive Agencies** returns a list of links to the same cabinet-level agencies. Also included are links to the Web sites of other government entities they supervise. For example, beneath FindLaw's link to the Department of Justice Web site are links to the Drug Enforcement Administration, the Federal Bureau of Investigation, and the Office of the Solicitor General. (FindLaw also offers links to state government information, as noted above.)

At the University of Michigan Library page, clicking the **Federal** link on the left-hand side, and then clicking **Executive Branch** returns a long list of links to other sites where you can find information and links to federal agencies, but not direct links to the agencies themselves. (This site also provides links to state and local government resources by clicking the **State** or **Local** links, respectively, on the left-hand side of the page.)

LexisONE's federal and state government resource pages are also organized similarly to GovSpot's. Clicking on the **Federal Executive Departments** link returns an annotated list of links to cabinet level agencies. Links to independent agencies such as the Central Intelligence Agency are found by clicking the page's **Federal Independent Agencies** link.

For links to historical data and documents, visit the U.S. National Archives and Records Administration site at **http://www.archives.gov**.

TRACfed

http://tracfed.syr.edu

Purpose:	To locate government regulatory data; civil, criminal, and enforcement data; judicial data; and track trends in those areas.
Content:	Syracuse University's Transactional Records Access Clearinghouse (TRAC) has compiled a massive database of information detailing how the federal government "enforces the law, where it assigns employees, and how it spends money." TRAC has developed a set of forms-driven pages to help you extract the data you need. Individual subscriptions of $50 per month allow twenty queries per month. Contact TRACfed for pricing of organizational subscriptions and site licenses.
Our View:	The pull-down menu and fill-in-the-blank forms used to generate these reports are very easy to use. The available data can be worthwhile as you formulate your strategy for a particular case. For example, you can discover the percentage of convictions in cases brought by federal

enforcement agencies in a specific district (or the entire country). A search of this data, in the Central District of California, revealed that 42.6 percent of cases filed by the Bureau of Alcohol, Tobacco and Firearms, in the most recent year for which data was available, ended in conviction of the defendant. The data also showed that the percentage had dropped steadily each year over the five years for which data was presented.

TRACfed does not require an annual subscription, so you can subscribe for just one month if you do not need continued access to this kind of information.

Tip: See Chapter 17, "Statistical Research," to locate resources on the Internet that offer free access to some of this type of information.

LSU Libraries Federal Agency List

http://origin.lib.lsu.edu/gov/fedgov.html

Purpose: To locate links to hundreds of federal government agencies, boards, commissions, committees, and so on.

Content: This site from Louisiana State University links to hundreds of federal agency, commission, board, and committee Web sites. The links are accessible either as an alphabetical list or as a hierarchical list arranged by level (such as **Boards, Commissions and Committees, Independent,** and **Quasi-Official**)

Our View: LSU's list is best suited for use when you know the name of the agency you're looking for, but don't know the URL of its Web site. It can also be useful when you have only the partial name of an agency. Unlike FirstGov, which searches the content of millions of government Web sites, this site's search box only searches within its own database of agency Web site names. For example, a search for "toxic waste" returned no results, since there is no agency with those words in its name, while a search for "energy" returned links to Web sites that contain that word in their title (such as Department of Energy and Federal Energy Regulatory Commission).

Tip:

- Note that the U.S. Government Printing Office (see below for its Web site) considers this list complete enough to supply a link to it, rather than creating its own duplicate list of agencies.
- The Chicago Kent College of Law also provides its Federal Web Locator, containing alphabetical lists of agencies, commissions, and quasi-agencies, at **http://www.infoctr.edu/fwl**.

Government Publication Sites

GPO Access

http://www.gpoaccess.gov

Purpose: To locate government publications on the Web, or for purchase in print.

Content: GPO Access is an online service of the U.S. Government Printing Office (GPO) providing free electronic access to the official, published versions of information products produced by the federal government. Available information ranges from the federal budget and the Code of Federal Regulations to topic-specific books published by the GPO. The publications are also offered for sale through their online bookstore.

Our View: Use the **GPO Access Resources by Topic** drop-down menu near the bottom of the home page to select the topic in which you're interested. Many topics include links to Congressional committees related to the topic, as well as links to regulations and pending legislation.

The GPO Access internal search engine uses the FirstGov search index. Therefore, any search results returned via GPO Access can also be located through a search at First-Gov. However, you can use the GPO Access Advanced Search options drop-down menu to further narrow your results to **All of GPO, Only GPO Access,** or **Only the U.S. Government Online Bookstore,** among other options.

Tip: Also see the site's **Finding Aids** page at **http://www.access.gpo.gov/su_docs/tools.html** for links to available materials.

Uncle Sam Migrating Government Publications

http://www.lib.memphis.edu/gpo/mig.htm

Purpose: To locate U.S. government publications on the Internet.

Content: The University of Memphis Library maintains this index of U.S. government publications available on the Internet. The site includes links to documents that have been converted from print to the online format, as well as to some that are only available on the Internet. The documents come from a wide variety of entities, from the Department of Agriculture to the (House) Committee on Ways and Means. The "Migrating" in the site's title originally referred to those documents that were being converted ("migrating") from print to electronic formats.

Our View: To locate the document you're looking for, you must know its title or its SuDoc number (similar to a library's call number). There is no keyword searching. One main advantage to the site is that it links directly to these documents, and not just to the Web sites of the agencies that authored them. While the site is extremely useful, the ability to locate documents through a topical search engine would make it more useful.

U.S. Government Manual

http://www.gpoaccess.gov/gmanual/browse-gm-02.html

Purpose: To access the official handbook of the federal government.

Content: The United States Government Manual provides comprehensive information on the agencies of the legislative, judicial, and executive branches. Each section (such as Office of National Drug Policy or Department of Commerce) is presented as a separate PDF or text document that can be read online or downloaded to your computer. From this page, you can access the current or past editions of the manual.

Our View: The Government Manual includes useful background information, such as lists of staff and office locations. The table of contents, with its descriptive chapter titles, is easy to browse. A keyword or phrase search engine for the publication would make it more useful. The inclusion of page number references to the print version of the manual is helpful if you need to later refer to or cite the print version.

Unfortunately, the text version of the 2002-2003 edition does not have any formatting—therefore all of the text is presented in line after line, with the heading and subheadings almost indecipherable. Oddly enough, the text versions do include links to the Web sites dis-cussed in the manual. The PDF versions, while signifi-cantly easier to read, do not contain links to the agency sites discussed.

Other Useful Government Sites

Google's Uncle Sam Search

http://www.google.com/unclesam

Purpose: To search only military and government Web sites.

Content: Google has created a specialty search engine that returns results only from the .gov and .mil domains reserved for government and military Web sites, respectively.

Our View: As we've mentioned a number of times throughout this book, Google is our preferred search engine. The fact that you can utilize the Advanced Search features, just as you would in a regular Google search, while limiting the search to .gov and .mil sites makes it that much easier to narrow your search for the precise government-related information you need.

Tip: See Chapter 4, "Search Tools," for more information on conducting effective Google searches.

CyberCemetery

http://govinfo.library.unt.edu

Purpose: To locate Web sites of defunct federal government entities.

Content: Maintained by the University of North Texas Libraries (in partnership with the GPO), this site offers archived versions of more than four dozen Web sites of now-defunct federal government agencies and commissions. The Web sites are stored with all of the pages that were available at the time the Web site was closed down.

Our View: While there's no search engine, it's easy enough to browse the alphabetical list of archived sites. (Click the **A to Z List of Sites** link on the left-hand side of the screen to access the list.)

Tip: Also see Chapter 4, "Search Tools," for more information regarding locating archived material no longer available in its original location on the Internet.

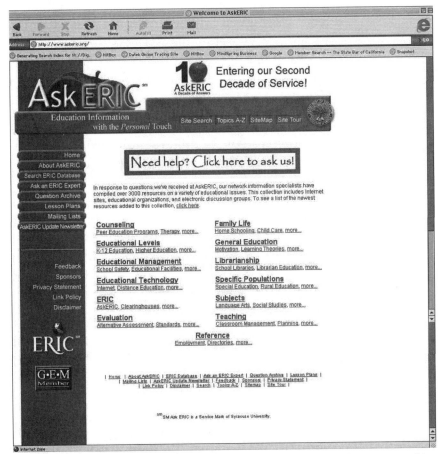

Figure 6-4. If you can't find the education-related information you need in one of ERIC's nearly four hundred subtopics, you can pose a question directly to one of ERIC's education experts.

AskERIC

http://www.askeric.org

Purpose: To locate education-related research and information.

Content: ERIC is the Educational Resources Information Center
               from the U.S. Department of Education. This site offers a
               collection of over three thousand educational resources
               organized into a Yahoo!-style directory. Within the
               directory's thirteen primary topics are nearly four hun-
               dred subtopics covering many aspects of educational
               theory and practice. Each subtopic includes links to
               Internet sites, ERIC resources, organizations, or discus-
               sion groups.

               The site also offers a keyword or phrase search engine
               that searches all of the topics simultaneously, as well as
               an archive of questions posed to the site's experts by pre-
               vious visitors.

Our View: You can access the high volume of information in what-
               ever manner suits you best: by drilling down through
               the directory, by selecting the subtopic that looks most
               relevant (click on the **Topics A-Z** button in the upper-
               right-hand corner of the home page), or by conducting
               a keyword or phrase search.

               You can also use the Advanced Search page to construct
               more sophisticated phrase searching or to limit your
               search to a particular grade level.

Tip: If you need expert information on an education-related
               topics, or pointers to research data, don't miss the site's
               AskERIC's Q&A Service. Click on the **Ask an ERIC
               Expert** link on the left-hand side of the home page.
               Questions submitted to AskERIC are answered within
               two business days via e-mail. Responses include ERIC
               database citations that deal with your question, as well
               as links to other Internet resources for additional infor-
               mation.

The Downside

Despite the explosion of the Internet in the 1990s as an information distribution platform, not all government agencies provide as much information as some of the sites discussed here. For example, it wasn't until 2002 that the U.S. Immigration and Naturalization Service (now the Bureau of Citizenship and Immigration Services) created an online database to check the status of applications made to the agency (**https://egov.immigration.gov/graphics/cris/jsps/index.jsp**).

Also, easy access to all these government computers and information via the Web isn't always a good thing. In 2001, U.S. District Court Judge Royce Lamberth ordered the U.S. Department of Interior to take down all of its Web sites. The order was part of a long-running case in which the Department was charged with mismanaging billions of dollars held in trust since the late nineteenth century for millions of Native Americans. As part of the underlying class-action suit filed in 1996, the judge hired a security expert who was able to access sensitive information regarding the Indian trust funds by entering the Department of Interior computer network through its Web site. This security breach brought about the judge's order to essentially quarantine the Department's network from any outside contact until the data in question was secured. This led to the Department closing all of its Web services, including e-mail. Though the services eventually returned to the Web, some of the agency's sites were off line well into 2002.

After the September 11, 2001 terrorist attacks on the United States, many government agencies removed some of the more sensitive information publicly available on their Web sites. For example, the U.S. National Imagery and Mapping Agency (NIMA) suspended online and off-line sales of maps of military installations; the U.S. Office of Pipeline Safety (OPS) restricted access to its Internet mapping application, pipeline data, and drinking water data; and visitors to the Nuclear Regulatory Commission (NRC) Web site were greeted with the following disclaimer: "In support of our mission to protect public health and safety, the NRC is performing a review of all material on our site. In the interim, only select content will be available. We appreciate your patience and understanding during these difficult times."

CHAPTER**SEVEN**

Finding and Backgrounding People

Finding Versus Backgrounding

Lawyers frequently have to find people, from a missing heir to an expert witness. Other times lawyers need to "background" a person. Backgrounding can be defined simply as finding information about people and about their background. It's a term commonly used by private investigators. There are two major ways to find and background people: by searching through public records and by sifting through bits and pieces of publicly available information. While public records are filed with government agencies, publicly available information is not. Publicly available information is that information that you voluntarily provide to a private entity or publish in a public place (such as the Internet). For example, you provide your phone number and address to a private entity—the telephone company. You publish information on the Internet—from postings to an online community, to the content on your own Web site, to the information you provide to Classmates.com. That information is now publicly available and may be found by anyone surfing the Internet, or sold to marketing companies or public record database companies. In a recent study, 70 percent of the respondents gave personal information to a commercial Web site to get a product or service (but only 29 percent did so to a government Web site). The fact is that information about each of us is scattered among countless computer files held by the government, by private entities, and now by the public entity known as the Internet.

This chapter focuses on using the publicly available information found on the Internet to find and background people. We'll discuss both traditional resources found on the Internet—such as phone directories, and nontraditional resources—ones that you'll need to "think outside the box" to find, such as online communities. Some of this publicly available information contained within nontraditional resources would never be found on a pay database, yet could provide you with the "smoking gun."

The next chapter, "Accessing Public Records," focuses on using public records to find and background people.

Try the Internet First

There's nothing as convenient or as cheap as using the Internet to search for people via public records or publicly available information. This is not to say that the Internet provides access to all records. For example, there is no comprehensive site on the Internet to search for all reported state or federal court decisions going back to the time when each court first began publishing its decisions. If you want to search for something like that, you'd be better off using a pay database such as Lexis or Westlaw. However, the convenience of the Internet's perpetual availability from almost any computer (or hand-held device) with an Internet connection, and the negligible cost of using the Internet, makes it a logical first choice for finding and backgrounding people, even if you end up accessing a fee-based database later.

Backgrounding People

Although we noted that the term backgrounding is one used by private investigators, which conjures up images of cloak and dagger surveillance, it actually refers to investigating a person via research instead of by surveillance. Backgrounding can be as straightforward as finding someone's biography in a *Who's Who* directory or as offbeat as finding out something mentioned about them in a posting in an online community or in an eBay feedback profile. (The eBay feedback profile includes a rating number for the bidder and the seller, as well as written comments about either. Because not everyone uses their real name in these types of communications, you might not have any luck finding information about your subject, but it's worth a try.)

eBay Feedback Profiles

A California judge cleared eBay in a libel suit brought by one of its users who asked eBay to remove a seller's negative comments about him in the feedback profile (see **http://www. usatoday.com/tech/news/ 2003-05-06-ebay-suit_x.htm**).

Backgrounding can include the following information about a person:

- Address
- Phone number
- Social Security number
- Date of birth (or death)
- Marriages and divorces
- Education
- Occupation
- Professional or occupational license
- Place of employment
- Publications by or about the subject found in books, articles, e-newsletters, blogs, and Web sites (such as an employer's site)
- Biography or profile
- Image
- Hobbies
- Interests
- Assets (assessment value of the subject's home, and whether he or she owns a plane, boat, trademarks, copyrights, patents, stocks, businesses, and so on)
- Liens, judgments, and bankruptcies
- Lawsuits
- Political party membership
- Campaign contributions
- Civic and volunteer work
- A PowerPoint presentation, Excel spreadsheet, or Word document created and posted on the Internet by the subject or about the subject
- Postings to, from, or about the subject (found in the ongoing discussions or archives of online communities)

Other Backgrounding

Much of the same data can be gathered for background information about companies, their executives, products, and experts as well. See Chapter 10, "Company Research;" Chapter 11, "Competitive Intelligence Research;" and Chapter 9, "Finding and Backgrounding Expert Witnesses."

Finding People

War Story: Finding Someone Without Having a Name

Sometimes lawyers have the name of the person they are trying to find and sometimes they don't. Even when you don't know the name of the person you seek, the Internet can be the answer to your problem. Lawyer and law librarian Cathy Pennington Paunov tells this story:

"One of my favorite examples is the case where someone in Ohio was working on a salmonella ice cream case. She was desperate. She needed additional information. We only wanted to get hold of practitioners that had worked on cases like this. So I went to AltaVista, which is my favorite search engine on the Internet, and searched the Internet for the following three words: "salmonella" and "ice cream." I got something like three hundred hits. One of them, and it was in the first batch—the nice thing about AltaVista is it ranks the stuff in order of probable relevance—the third or fourth hit down, was some law firm in Chicago. Their Web site said that one of their senior litigation partners had handled the largest salmonella ice cream case in the country. I actually picked up the phone because I knew how desperate this poor lawyer was. I picked up the phone and called the lawyer in Ohio and said, 'Listen, here's someone in Chicago.' I also called the Chicago lawyer and warned him I was doing this—and he said, 'Fine, I'd be happy to help her out.'

"I don't think I would have found the salmonella ice cream guy but for the Internet. There's no way I could have found him anywhere else.

That was the most incredible story. I've got one very happy small-town lawyer and she's got the name of the top legal expert in the field."

Free Is Sometimes Best

If Paunov had tried searching for this information before we were using the Internet for research, she might have racked up a huge bill by running a nationwide search looking for court opinions in a commercial database about salmonella ice cream cases. And to boot, she may have come up empty-handed if there were only state trial-level opinions on the topic, since trial-level cases are not usually published. The beauty of the Internet is you might find a story about an unreported trial-level case right on point on some firm's Web site as Paunov did, or in a posting in an online community—information resources that the commercial databases don't index (yet).

Search for the Expertise

When you don't have the name of an expert, you often need to search by the expertise to discover names of potential experts. See Chapter 9, "Finding and Backgrounding Expert Witnesses," for various places to find and background experts.

The Internet is an excellent source for finding people if you know something about the individual. For example, if you're looking for a lawyer, there are two comprehensive American lawyer directories available free on the Internet: the West Legal Directory found on their Find-Law site (**http://lawyers.findlaw.com**) and Martindale Hubbell (**http://www.martindale.com**). In addition, private companies, universities, government agencies, and other entities provide staff directories online, so if you know that the person you seek is on the faculty at Rutgers University, you can use the Internet to find a way to contact that person even when it's after normal business hours and nobody's answering the telephone at the university's main number. If you're looking for an

American physician, the American Medical Association provides a database that can locate over 650,000 doctors by name, specialty, and location who are licensed to practice in the U.S.

Reverse Searching

If you don't have the name of the person you are trying to locate (or if you are unsure of the spelling or there has been a name change), but you do have other clues about the person, reverse searching is a possible option. The following clues about a person can be turned into a reverse search and lead you to that person (sometimes a combination of these clues needs to be employed):

- Social Security number
- An alias
- Phone number or address (current or past)
- Date of birth
- Age range
- Occupation

Problems with Name Searching

Even if a lawyer has the name of the person he is trying to find or background, the search can prove difficult if any of the following events have occurred:

- Address or phone number change
- Name change due to marriage or divorce
- A misspelled name
- Death

Another problem with name searching is you can't always be sure that you have the right person since many people share the same name. Also, because many people refer to themselves in various ways, it's hard to be certain that you've done a thorough search. Name searching requires finding all the various names (and variations) that the subject uses and then searching using all of them. You need to discover what name your subject uses:

- First and last name only?
- First and last name, with a middle name or middle initial?
- Nickname?

- Aliases?
- Married name?
- Maiden name?

Tips for Name Searching

If you think the person uses only a first and last name, enter the name into a search engine as a phrase by surrounding it with quotation marks ("carole levitt"). This will help narrow your search.

If it's possible that the subject uses a middle name or initial (either regularly or sporadically) or if you don't know the middle name, use a Boolean connector between the first and last name (carole AND levitt) to find any document with the name "carole" and the name "levitt"—and anything in between those two names. This can give you many irrelevant results, though—you might find a Carole Brown and a Robert Levitt in the same document, which is technically a correct result but not the one you're looking for.

Or, better yet, if using Google (and we suggest you do), use a wild card (an asterisk [*]) to take the place of any middle name or initial (carole * levitt). This search will find, for example, Carole Levitt, Carole A. Levitt, Carole B. Levitt, Carole Ann Levitt, and so on. It will not return the type of irrelevant results that the above Boolean search might. Be sure to enter this search into the Advanced Search page using the **with all of the words** option.

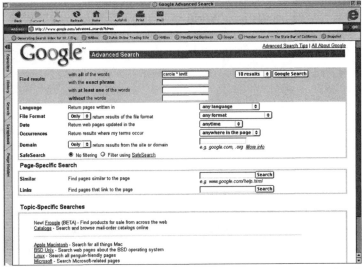

Figure 7-1. Google allows the use of a wild card (an asterisk) to take the place of any middle name or initial. Google ™ is a trademark of Google Technology Inc.

Some search engines (such as AltaVista, but not Google) allow you to use the proximity connector "near." A search for **carole near levitt** will only include documents with the names "carole" and "levitt" within ten words of each other. This avoids returning documents that discuss someone named "Carole Brown" in the first sentence of the document's first page and "Robert Levitt" several sentences later.

If a name is commonly misspelled, search for the subject by the misspelled name, too. A Lexis search for Carole Levitt's property records found she owned nothing, until we entered "Leavitt," which is the common misspelling of her last name.

Use the OR Boolean connector for names that have various spellings (Smith OR Smyth) or have nicknames (Andy OR Andrew).

Privacy Issues

Computers are incredibly useful tools if you're looking for someone or backgrounding them, and slightly scary if you're concerned about personal privacy (especially your own). After we've already disclosed personal data, it is difficult to recall it. Some sites do offer you the chance to remove your data, however. For instance, if you find your contact information available at Swithchboard.com and you want to remove it, simply click on **Update/Remove this listing.** In order to protect our personal privacy, the most useful thing we can do is to be aware of the power of digital communications, and be cautious about what personal data we release. But if you're looking for someone, maybe because they owe you money, or because an estate you're administering owes them money, or just simply to invite them to a reunion, computers make the process easy, and even fun.

Off-line Searching

Keep in mind that although the free Internet and pay databases can be useful sources for public record and publicly available information research, a comprehensive search may also involve physically traveling to court houses, government agencies, and other archives (public and private) to review paper records. It's estimated that only 20 percent of public records are online.

Using Web-Based Traditional Resources

To find and background people, researchers used to rely extensively upon print materials (such as directories and phone books), CD-ROMs, microfilm, microfiche, and proprietary databases. These resources would often be inaccessible to many researchers because they were expensive, cumbersome to use, cumbersome to store, or geographically inaccessible.

But as more and more of these traditional research resources have been converted to Web-based resources, they have become much more accessible in every way and thus much more useful for finding people. Take print phone directories that are now Web-based, for example: since many are free, the expense of buying and storing them is no longer an issue; since they are searchable in a digital format, there is no longer a need to manually search through multiple directories so they are no longer cumbersome to use; since they are stored on the Internet, they are no longer cumbersome to store; and since they can be accessed by anyone with a computer and an Internet connection, there is no longer an issue of geographical inaccessibility.

Phone Directories on the Web

The most common (though often overlooked) way to find people is to use the most common reference book there is—the telephone book, now found free in Web-based phone book directories. The thousands of U.S. regional phone directories are perfectly suited to the quick lookup speed of computer databases. Results usually include street address, telephone number, and sometimes an e-mail address and more. While some years ago a number of CD-ROM publishers seized the opportunity to issue national phone directories on disk, Internet-based phone books are a step ahead of CD-ROM phone books in some ways. The Internet makes databases easier to update and distribute, so they can be more current than a CD-ROM, although it's hard to tell how often the Web-based directories are actually updated. Using the Internet avoids the need to change disks. Internet phone books are accessible from anywhere (assuming you have an Internet connection, of course) and Internet phone books are free.

On the flip side, if you want to print large phone lists, CD-ROM is superior because Internet-based directories generally allow you to display only a few names and phone listings at a time. Karen Olson, librarian at Bryan Cave in Santa Monica, California, still finds that phone directories on CD have several advantages over the Web directories. Olson explains, "The CD has an auto-type-ahead feature, which the Web lacks. This makes it possible to see the list of query results fill in as you type the search terms. Often with both individual and business names, the searcher is trying to find a name and is handicapped with an incorrect spelling. The auto-type-ahead feature lets you see the possible answer set at each character stroke. Secondly, although it is true that the CD is not up to the minute in currency, the product at least lets the user know what release date they are working with whereas the Web directories don't provide any date information at all. Finally, the CD directories search faster. Not only does the CD have a faster search response time, but it saves you the time from going from one phone web directory to the next since the CD is more comprehensive than any one Web directory site."

Unpublished and Unlisted Phone Numbers

Many of the Web phone directories draw data from the same sources—published White Pages directories and other publicly available sources. If a phone number is unpublished, you most likely won't find it in one of these Web phone directories. But sometimes people with unpublished phone numbers do provide their phone numbers to sources other than the phone company. You might be able to find the number in those sources, especially if it's in a public record or private database. Also, if the person has a Web site, you might find the number listed on the site or in a registration application (using one of the Whois registries noted in Chapter 10, "Company Research").

More Information?

Nearly all of the phone book sites are advertiser-supported, with enticements labeled **More Info** or **Public record click here**. For example, after finding Carole Levitt's name, address, and all three phone numbers in a free Yahoo! People Search, we were offered a **More info at US Search** link. Upon clicking over we were informed that for $39.95 we could find "current and previous addresses, phone numbers (if available), possible aliases, current full names, and a deceased search." Considering that Yahoo! had already shown the current address and phone number, and that we could run a deceased search for free at Ancestry.com or Rootsweb.com (though this wasn't really necessary since we were searching for a person who was not deceased), and that we knew where to find the other information for less, we weren't willing to bite. If you need past addresses and phone numbers or possible aliases, you would be better off with a subscription to Accurint.com or Merlindata.com, where this information would cost between $0.25 and $6.50.

Traditional Directory Searching and Reverse Searching

For finding phone numbers, addresses, neighbors, maps, e-mail addresses, and so on, we prefer Infospace of all the Web phone directories because it has so many ways to locate people and businesses through both traditional searching and reverse searching.

Reverse phone number or address searching is the perfect tool when you are uncertain of someone's name (or the spelling), but you know that person's phone number or address. With a reverse phone search (or address search) the person's name (and correct spelling) should be retrieved. Reverse phone or address searching is also the perfect tool for business searching when you don't know the company name (or its correct spelling), but do have its address or phone number. Address searching is also useful when you want to be certain you are naming all relevant parties and you suspect that multiple businesses owned by the same person are operating out of one address. The reverse address search results may show you all the company names related to that one address. If Infospace doesn't bring any results, try using a phone directory metasite, such as Trackem (see below), to identify other phone directory sites.

Phone Directory Metasite

Trackem People Search

http://johnsonxdesign.tripod.com/trackem.html

Purpose:	To locate various types of people-finding and business-finding directories
Content:	This is one long laundry list of a variety of directories to choose from. The list points you to basic information like White Pages, as well as esoteric data like a college's e-mail address.
Our View:	We use this when we can't find the person we're looking for and want to view a variety of other phone directories. Scroll down the laundry list until you find one that you haven't tried yet. It would be useful if Trackem filled

in all the search boxes automatically, but then again, it might take too long.

Tip:

- This is the third URL for this site in three years, so if it doesn't work, go to Google and try typing in "Trackem." That's what we do.
- You need to fill in each database's search box and then conduct the searches one by one; you can't search the various databases simultaneously. Although The Ultimates (**http://www.theultimates.com**) and Craig Ball's Phone Finder (**http://www.craigball.com/ phonefind.html**) also do not offer simultaneous searching, they do automatically fill in the database's other search boxes once you fill in the first search box.

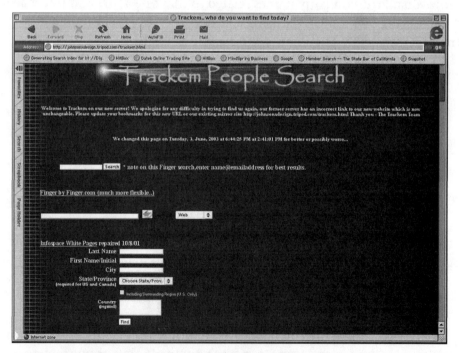

Figure 7-2. Trackem offers a laundry list of directories to search from, from phone books to e-mail directories and more.

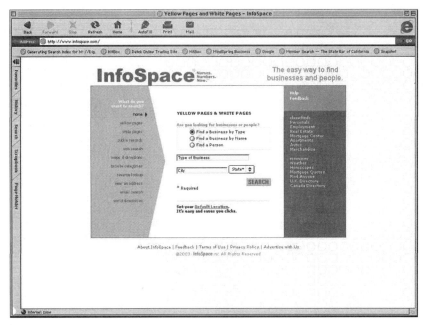

Figure 7-3. Infospace offers numerous resources to search for telephone number information, including White Pages, Yellow Pages, and a Reverse Lookup to help locate a name when you only have a phone number or address. © 2003 InfoSpace, Inc. All rights reserved. Reprinted with permission of InfoSpace, Inc.

Infospace

http://www.infospace.com

Purpose: To find people and businesses (phones numbers, addresses, and e-mail addresses) and maps to homes and businesses. Also, see the Tip below for how to find neighbors.

Content: Infospace has separate White Pages and Yellow Pages searches.
White Pages:
- Quick search: this is for searching by last name and first name (or initial), city, and state. Only the last name is a required field, but the more fields you fill-in, the more you are assured of finding the correct party.

- E-mail search: search by last name, first name, city, state, and country to find e-mail addresses of people worldwide.

Reverse lookup:
- Search by phone number to find a name and address (U.S. only). Use this to identify who called you when they failed to leave their name, but left a phone number on your voicemail (or on your caller ID).
- Search by area code to find a city (this can help trigger your memory if you're not sure how you know the person who left a voicemail message with an out-of-town phone number).
- Search by city and state to find an area code.
- Search by e-mail address to find a name and address.
- Search by address to find name and phone number:
- To search by address, enter one or more of the following: the house number, street name, city, or state (or choose **All States**).

Yellow Pages:
- Quick search: search by either a business name or category, and choose a state—this is required (there is no **All States** option). Limiting the search to a specific city is optional.
- Detailed search: to identify names of businesses in a state that fall within a certain category, search by a business category and state. You can also limit the search further to one or more of the following: an address (street number, street name, or both), a city, or a ZIP code. To find contact information for a specific business by its name, search by its exact name; if uncertain of the exact name, enter the letters you think the name begins with (in whole or partial words); or, enter any one of the words in the business name. Business name searching requires entering a state (city, ZIP code, and address are all optional). Nationwide searching by business name is also an option.

Our View: The **Near Address** search, a combination White Pages and Yellow Pages search, is also useful. Use this option when you want to find out what businesses are near a specific home or office address (from one to one hundred miles). For example, if you are meeting a client at his home or office and you will need a notary, type "notary" into the **Type of business** field and type the client's address into the **Near this address** field.

Tip: You can use reverse address searching to find a missing person—by identifying their neighbors, who may be able to give you some forwarding information. To create a list of all the neighbors of a missing person who lived at 4040 Karlov in Skokie, Illinois, for example, enter the street name, city, and state into the search boxes, but in the **House Number** field, enter only the numbers "40." This would display a list of all people on the 4000 block of Karlov. If you wanted to also find all people who lived in the 4100 to 4900 blocks, enter only the number "4" in the **House Number** field. You can also just fill in a city and state, but you'll only get up to 250 results.

There are dozens of phone directory sites that have features similar to Infospace (such as Bigfoot.com, Whitepages.com, and Switchboard.com) or are powered by other phone directory sites. For example, Bigfoot's White Pages search is powered by Whitepages.com. Each one includes traditional and reverse White Pages and Yellow Pages for phone, address, area code, and city searching. They also include maps, international calling code lookup by country, and e-mail listings (but they only found Carole Levitt's former e-mail address, which is defunct).

Other Phone Directory Features

For finding toll-free numbers, use Anywho.com's toll-free number page (**http://anywho.com/tf.html**). This free site includes many of the same searches as the other directories described above, but you can also type in a company name to discover its toll-free number.

Anywho.com can also help you find out who else lives at the address associated with a phone listing. If you click on **Try Public Records!** after finding your subject in Anywho, you are taken to KnowX.com, where you might pick up some extra information about who else resides at that same address. For example, we did a search for "Carole Levitt." After clicking on the **Try Public Records!** link, the free KnowX information showed her husband's name connected to the Levitt listing—even though his name is not listed in Anywho. Even without paying for a public record search, we obtained an extra nugget of information.

International Phone Directory

Infobel (formerly teldir)

http://www.infobel.com/teldir/default.asp

Purpose: To link to the White Pages, Yellow Pages, business directories, and other people-finding directories in more than 184 countries.

Content: Choose a country to search (listed by continent) and you will be informed of the types of phone directories available and whether any are in English.

Our View: We found this site to be a wealth of information and easy to use. For example, when we searched for a listing in Denmark and couldn't recall the exact spelling of the city we wanted, all we had to do was click on **City list** and type in part of the name ("Hel"). This brought us to a city list showing three cities beginning with "Hel" (ours was Helsingor).

Tip: You can click on Extended search to add in first names and postal codes to refine the search, and you can also click on Reverse search.

Pay Database Phone Directory

MasterFiles

http://www.masterfiles.com/index.html

Purpose: For real-time access to over 130 million listings.

Content: Listings of U.S. residences, businesses, and government agencies for the contiguous forty-eight states. Data is from Ameritech, Bell South, Cincinnati Bell, PacBell, QWEST, Southern New England Telephone, Southwestern Bell, and Verizon.

Our View: Considering you can search by name, phone, or address for $0.20 to $0.45 (based on search type and volume), and that the content is refreshed continually, this may be useful to find someone who has recently moved or who is continually on the move.

Tip: Make sure the coverage fits your needs. If you're searching for international listings or listings in Hawaii or Alaska, this won't do much good. (It's not too hard to locate Alaskans—every single Alaskan adult and child receives a tidy sum annually from the Permanent Fund—and the Fund's index is searchable. And as you can imagine, it's quite up-to-date at **http://www.pfd.state.ak.us/n&afile.htm**.)

Pay Site Directory Searching

Most of the pay public record databases we discuss in Chapter 8, "Accessing Public Records," have all sorts of traditional or reverse phone and address searching functions. Most noteworthy is that they allow you to search by an old address or phone number and get an updated result. You won't find this option at the phone directory sites noted in this chapter.

Cell Phone (Wireless) Searching

FoneFinder

http://www.primeris.com/fonefind

Purpose:	To discover if a specific phone number is for a land line or a wireless phone.
Content:	Search by the area code and prefix of a phone number. The results do not show the name of the person who owns the phone number but shows the type and name of the phone company that "owns" the prefix (a wireless company or a regional Bell operating company, like Pacific Bell or Bell Atlantic). It also displays the city and state connected to the prefix.
Our View:	This can be very useful when you're having trouble tracing a phone number, because you are tipped off right away whether it's a wireless number. And, if it's wireless, you won't be able to use the same avenues to find out who owns it as you would for a land line.
Tip:	Once you've identified the number as wireless, see the two listings below for further tips on how to identify who owns the wireless number.

MobilephoneNo.com

http://www.mobilephoneno.com

Purpose:	To discover who owns a wireless number.
Content:	This site offers free listings to people who choose to register their wireless number here. Searching (by name) is also free.

Our View: Though it's nifty to be able to find the name and address of a wireless owner, the content is very limited—to those who have chosen to self-register.

Tip: If you want others to be able to locate you by your wireless number, you might want to register it here. A cell number is kept online for one year only, so you need to remember to renew your registration (for free).

Figure 7-4. The content at Mobilephoneno.com is limited only to those who have chosen to self-register at the site.

Cell-Phone-Numbers.com

http://www.cell-phone-numbers.com

Purpose: To discover who owns a wireless number

Content: For $85 you can request a reverse wireless number search to discover the name and address of the person who owns the number.

Our View: We haven't used this service, but there was an interesting story in the *Chicago Tribune* about Eric Smith, a 21-

year-old student at the University of New Orleans who used it when he needed to find the name and address of someone who had defrauded him of $3,000 on eBay. It worked!

Tip: You wouldn't use this service until after discovering that the number is wireless and after being unable to locate it at MobilephoneNo.com.

Fax Number Searching

Finding fax numbers is not as straightforward as finding phone numbers (or even e-mail addresses). To find a fax number for a person at his place of employment, try locating the company Web site to see if it is listed there.

Thinking Outside the Box to Find and Background People

Aside from the traditional resources now available over the Internet to use for finding and backgrounding people, there are other numerous nontraditional avenues to take. Most of these resources would never be found in any of the traditional places noted earlier in this chapter, nor in public records or pay databases. We'll call our searching of these nontraditional avenues "thinking outside the box."

Thinking outside the box, however, does not entail doing anything illegal, such as obtaining a credit report without a permissible business reason or "pretexting" (see below). Let's take a look at those two issues and see why those aren't part of our thinking-outside-the box search strategy.

Consumer Credit Reports

For anyone who wants to use a consumer credit report to simply locate a person or to obtain general and financial information about a subject, beware of the Fair Credit Reporting Act (FCRA), 15 U.S.C. §§ 1681b-1681u (2000). It prohibits the disclosure of consumer credit reports by consumer credit reporting agencies, except in response to the following kinds of requests:

- Court order or subpoena, § 1681b(a)(1)
- Request authorized in writing by the consumer about whom the report is made, § 1681b(a)(2)
- Request by a person whom the reporting agency has reason to believe intends to use the consumer report for one of a number of specific, permissible business reasons, § 1681b(a)(3)
- Request by governmental agencies involved in setting or enforcing child support awards, § 1681b(a)(4) and (5)

In the case of *Phillips v. Grendahl*, a "concerned" Minnesota mother, Mary Grendahl, hired a private investigator from McDowell Investigations. She asked him to check out her daughter's fiancé, Lavon Phillips. The PI retrieved Phillips's Social Security number from a database and then contacted Econ, a company in the business of furnishing consumer reports, finder's reports, and credit scoring to creditors and PIs. Econ provided a finder's report, showing the fiancé's credit card accounts and child support obligations.

The Eighth Circuit Court held that the finder's report was actually a consumer report under FCRA and that none of the actors in this escapade had a permissible business reason under § 1681b(a)(3) for the information (*Phillips v. Grendahl*, 312 F.3d 357 [8th Cir. 2002]). The court remanded the case for trial, ruling that it was an error to grant summary judgment to the defendants (Grendahl, McDowell Investigations, and Econ) regarding Phillips's claim for wrongful disclosure of a consumer report. While the act allows access to consumer reports for decisions bearing on extending credit to, insuring, or employing someone, it does not allow access for decisions about marriage, noted the court. However, the court held that Phillips's invasion of privacy claim relating to disclosure of his child support order (noted in the finder's report) couldn't support this claim. Even though the information was sensitive, it was not considered a publication of a matter that would be "highly offensive to a reasonable person" because it already was of public record. (The daughter ended up not marrying her fiancé, by the way.)

Pretexting with Financial Institutions

We've often been asked to get information about a person's bank account balance. There is no database for this information and if anyone has obtained this information for you in the past, then it was done by "pretexting," which is illegal. Pretexting, the practice of obtaining consumers' private financial information under false pretenses, was specifically outlawed in 1999 by the Gramm-Leach-Bliley Act (GLB), 15 U.S.C. 6821 and 6822(a). Under GLB, it is also illegal to solicit others to obtain information via pretext.

In April 2001, the Federal Trade Commission (FTC) filed suit in three U. S. district courts to halt the operations of three information brokers, all of whom allegedly used false pretenses, fraudulent statements, or impersonation to illegally obtain consumers' confidential financial information—such as bank balances—and sell it. The brokers were asked to find out how much money a woman's fiancé had in his bank account. The woman (actually an FTC investigator involved in Operation Detect Pretext) supplied the brokers with her fiancé's name and the name of his bank and other "limited information," (though not stated, it was probably his Social Security number and his mother's maiden name). In each case, the broker used pretexting by posing as the fiancé to obtain the information (**http://www.ftc.gov/opa/2002/03/pretextingsettlements.htm**).

The FTC and the brokers ended up in settlement. The brokers had to forfeit any money they made while using pretexting to obtain information. Also, they were prohibited from engaging in any activity in connection with the obtaining, offering for sale, or selling of customer information of a financial institution, obtained by:

- Misrepresenting their identities or their right to receive customer information
- Using others who will obtain information using deception
- Selling or disclosing customer information obtained from a financial institution
- Making false and misleading statements

Paying for Pretexting

Since pretexting is illegal, it would be an ethical violation for a lawyer to use pretexting. It would also be an ethical violation for a lawyer to hire someone (such as a private investigator or information broker) to do the same. According to the ABA Model Rules of Professional Conduct, Rule 5.3, Responsibilities Regarding Non-lawyer Assistants, a lawyer is responsible for the conduct of non-lawyers hired to do something that would be a violation of the Rules of Professional Conduct if engaged in by the lawyer himself and if "the lawyer orders or, with the knowledge of the specific conduct, ratifies the conduct involved."

Pretexting with Other Institutions

Until recently, we've always said the jury is out on whether it's illegal to use pretexting to obtain nonfinancial information. The jury may not be out any longer on this question. In *Remsburg v. Docusearch*, 816 A.2d 1001 (N.H. 2003), Liam Youens wanted to find out Amy Boyer's work address. He paid an Internet research company, Docusearch, to find her home address, phone number, and Social Security number, but Docusearch was unable to find her work address.

Docusearch then hired an information broker who placed a pretext call to Boyer at her home. The broker lied about her identity and the purpose of her call. She convinced Boyer to reveal her work address. On October 15, 1999, Youens drove to Boyer's workplace and fatally shot her as she left work. Youens then shot and killed himself. A subsequent police investigation revealed that Youens maintained a Web site containing references to stalking and killing Boyer. The court said, "We conclude that an investigator who obtains a person's work address by means of pretextual phone calling, and then sells the information, may be liable for damages under RSA Chapter 358-A to the person deceived."

Maiden Names

As illustrated above, it wasn't too hard to find Boyer's Social Security number, so you can see how the information brokers in Operation Detect Pretext (above) could have gotten the fiancé's Social Security number if the FTC investigator hadn't provided it.

Finding someone's mother's maiden name, which the information broker in Operation Detect Pretext probably had to do to convince the bank he was the FTC investigator's fiancé, on the other hand, is tougher. We'd try various pay public record databases that link people to their relatives and associates (such as Accurint at **http://www.accurint.com**), and we'd also try a free family tree search at RootsWeb.com at **http://www.rootsweb.com** (as discussed later in this chapter).

Using a Search Engine

To locate a person and to find information about him, first enter the name into a search engine (such as Google). You never know what you're going to find on the free Internet and sometimes it's more than you would find using a pay database. The second step is to run their name through a newsgroup site (like Google Groups at **http://groups.google.com**).

War Story: A Search Engine Finds Fraud Convictions

"Not using the Internet [to find people or find out about them] is malpractice," asserts Steve Whiteside, J.D., from Sheppard, Mullin in San Diego, California. "I'm a law firm librarian . . . and an incident the other day pointed out the importance of Internet research. I was asked to find information on a person believed to be involved in tax fraud schemes. I happened to be on Westlaw at the time, so I searched their news database. Only one hit came up on the name and that was some insignificant committee the person was on. Without the Internet, the guy checked out OK. I then ran the name on the Internet and received dozens of hits on his multiple convictions for tax fraud and various news items on schemes he was involved with. The main difference was the PDF files that I could access through Google from the Treasury Department and attorneys general sites."

PDFs

Lucky that Whiteside knew to choose Google as his search engine, one of the few general-purpose search engines (aside from AltaVista) that indexes PDF files. If he hadn't, he would have missed these documents. He also may have had luck at FirstGov.gov, a government site that indexes PDFs, considering that some of the PDF documents Google found were from government sites (see Chapter 6, "Government Resources online," for more on FirstGov.gov.)

Standard of Care

Diane Karpman, a California ethics expert, asks the question, "Will the use of technology change the standard of care?" In a scenario where the average lawyer uses online resources to find the most current information, while another lawyer fails to, then "the failure to do so is below average and therefore below the ordinary standard in the community. Falling below the average, typical, ordinary standard in the community opens the door to charges of professional negligence. In this case liability would not be for failing to use technology, but for failing to find the information that other lawyers could find and use for their clients' benefit." ("Keep Up or Face Peril," 20 GPSOLO, Number 4 [June 2003]) available at **http://www.abanet.org/genpractice/magazine/ june2003/keepup.html.**)

War Story: A Search Engine Leads to a Settlement

Charlie Cochran, a lawyer in Northern California, relates this story of how thinking outside the box allowed him to settle a case the day before the trial, for a fraction of the original settlement demand: "Anyhow, after attending your seminar I tried to implement some of your research tools to a trial I had scheduled in March 2003. The Plaintiff was a well-known musician and producer who claimed he had brain injury from an auto accident and could no longer play the piano. My search began with a Google 'I'm feeling lucky' which sent me to the Plaintiff's home page. On the home page he was selling an album that he had recorded after our auto accident. The Google search naturally hit many online sites where his albums were being sold. One of the Google hits had him giving an online interview with an entertainment reporter where he discussed his auto accident, that he could not play piano for a few months but after that he was back to playing and writing with a new spirit and inspiration. Google image hits are amazing. It's fascinating what people post on the Internet. One image of the Plaintiff was a concert he did about a year after the accident where he was shown playing piano in front of a class of graduate level pianists. The look on their faces showed that they were really impressed with his abilities. We ended up issuing a trial subpoena to the woman that held the concert and interviewed the Plaintiff for the online interview. The case settled the day before the trial for a fraction of the original settlement demand because, in my opinion, we were going to confront the Plaintiff with the photo of him playing the piano, the words from his online interview, and albums that he was selling over the Internet."

I'm Feeling Lucky

The **I'm Feeling Lucky** search button returns one Web site only and, as illustrated here, often it's the most relevant. Using

Google's **I'm Feeling Lucky** search button quickly led lawyer Cochran directly to the plaintiff's own Web site. To obtain more results, Cochran returned to his original search page and merely clicked on the **Google Search** button. This search led him to an online interview of the musician and to sites selling his recent albums, information that he probably would not have found without the Internet. Finally, using Google's Images feature, Cochran proved that a picture is indeed worth a thousand words.

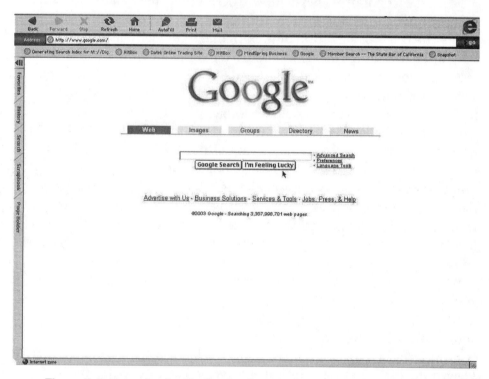

Figure 7-5. Using the I'm Feeling Lucky search button returns just one site; it's often the most relevant, especially when searching by a person or company's name. Google™ is a trademark of Google Technology Inc.

Definitions of Online Communities

- Usenet (also called newsgroups): a global online electronic bulletin board of Usenet newsgroups, covering thousands of topics. They are different from mailing lists because they do not communicate through passive e-mail. Instead, messages reside on central newsgroup servers where they can be read and commented upon like a community bulletin board.

- Mailing lists (also called LISTSERVs or discussion groups): a group discussion via e-mail. To actively participate, members first must e-mail a subscribe request to the list manager. Then, the subscriber can both post and receive messages. All messages are e-mailed to a central server where they are then distributed to each subscriber's e-mail in-box. Some lists distribute messages automatically while others are moderated. If the list is moderated, then the e-mails are reviewed by an actual person—the moderator—to be sure the discussion stays on topic, and so on, before being distributed. Some people mistakenly use LISTSERV as a generic term for all mailing lists. It's not. LISTSERV is a type of mailing list software.
- Message (or bulletin) boards: messages are posted to a Web-based bulletin board where visitors can read, comment upon, or leave new messages (or files). Requires users to visit the site.
- Forums: Same as message (or bulletin) board
- Blogs (Web logs): a Web site "light." Blogs have been compared to an online diary. They are easy to create and to update. They can be educational, entertaining, or frivolous, depending on the person who set up the blog. There are numerous sites offering tools to create blogs, such as Blogger.com (**http://www.blogger.com**) and Blogspot.com (**http://www.blogspot.com**). Blogs are indexed and searchable at such sites as Daypop.com (**http://www.daypop.com**) and Blogstreet.com (**http://www.blogstreet.com**). Google have begun to index some blogs.
- Blawgs: same as a blogs, but topics are law related only.

Searching Online Communities

The ease of communicating over the Internet has fostered the creation of a countless number of online communities (which focus on countless topics) used for the public exchange of ideas. There are various types of (and labels for) online communities, such as LISTSERV lists, mailing lists, discussion groups, Usenet newsgroups, forums, message (or bulletin) boards, and blogs, and there are various ways that people join and participate in a community on the Internet. Despite the variances, we'll discuss them generically and focus only on those that are public, have been archived, and are searchable by anyone.

There are various ways to participate in an online community:

- You can initiate the discussion
- You can respond to someone else's discussion
- You can "lurk," which means you simply read the discussions posted by others and do not join in the discussion
- You can visit the group's archives (if the group has one and it's public) and search the archived postings by keyword (or by a person's name or e-mail address) to see what has been discussed in the past (and by whom)

Some groups have strict membership rules for joining (for example, to join the Los Angeles County Bar Association's Family Law Section group you first would need to join and pay your dues to the association and the section). Some types of groups require registration before you can join (but place no restrictions on who can join), while others may not require registration at all. Some groups require you to visit the group each time you want to participate (or even to lurk) while others "visit" you via e-mail. For instance, each time you want to participate in a message board, you need to visit that board by typing its URL into your browser's address box and then either read messages, answer a message, or post your own message. On the other hand, to participate in a mailing list, you only need visit once—to subscribe. Once you've done that, you'll automatically begin receiving e-mails from other participants. You can then respond to the entire list (or just to the individual sender) if you want to join the discussion and you can also initiate a discussion by sending an e-mail to the list. Once again, for convenience's sake, we'll label any online community communication a "posting."

Why do we care about online communities? Because, from the ongoing discussions in the online community to the postings that are archived, online communities can contain a treasure trove of information. Reading a posting might help you to find someone or to find out about someone. From a person's hobbies, to opinions, to concerns, it's all available to any Internet researcher who knows where to look. Many people use their actual names and e-mail addresses when posting to an online community, failing to realize that their postings are being archived and can be searched. This is a boon to the researcher (assuming the postings have relevant information). A further boon to a researcher is when a subject has configured his e-mail with an automatic signature block (with all his contact information) that attaches to any e-mail sent.

On the other hand, online communities can be a complete black hole. For instance, in your quest to find someone (or find out about him) you may come up empty-handed if that person has joined a community using an alias or using an anonymous e-mail address. There is always the chance that even if the subject has joined an online community, he joined one that has restricted membership or one that lacks a searchable archive.

Google Groups

Google Groups (**http://groups.google.com**) is one of the best-known online communities. (Google Groups is a feature separate from Google's general-purpose search engine, Google.com.) Using Google Groups, one can anonymously search through over 850 million postings. There is no need to subscribe to a Google Group to be able to search and lurk. The postings are from the archives of thousands of Usenet newsgroups, dating back to 1981, that Google purchased from Deja.com. While the Google Groups' archive is full-text keyword searchable, there is an even more useful feature when you're looking for information about a specific individual. Google Groups provides the ability to search for a specific person's message by a name or e-mail address. (Many other community archives are not keyword or name searchable because they are only arranged in chronological date order.).

War Story: Online Community Search Finds Hobbies

If you know something about the person, add a descriptive keyword (such as the name of his city, his company, or his profession) to the name search when searching through an online community's archives (or search engine). For example, one of this book's authors, Carole Levitt, was looking for background information about the president of Elite.com because she had to introduce him at a conference. She decided to search Google Groups and because he had a very common name, she searched using his name in conjunction with the name of his company and came up with some interesting information, including his hobby—he's a Trekkie.

When else might these types of tidbits come in handy? Sometimes it's useful to find out a potential client's hobby before your first meeting. Or, according to Texas lawyer Craig Ball, he uses these tidbits of information at deposition to show the deponent that Craig Ball knows all! Ball swears deponents are more forthright when they think he already knows everything—even information about their hobbies. He also uses information found on the Internet about a deponent to "bond" with the deponent and help them feel more comfortable.

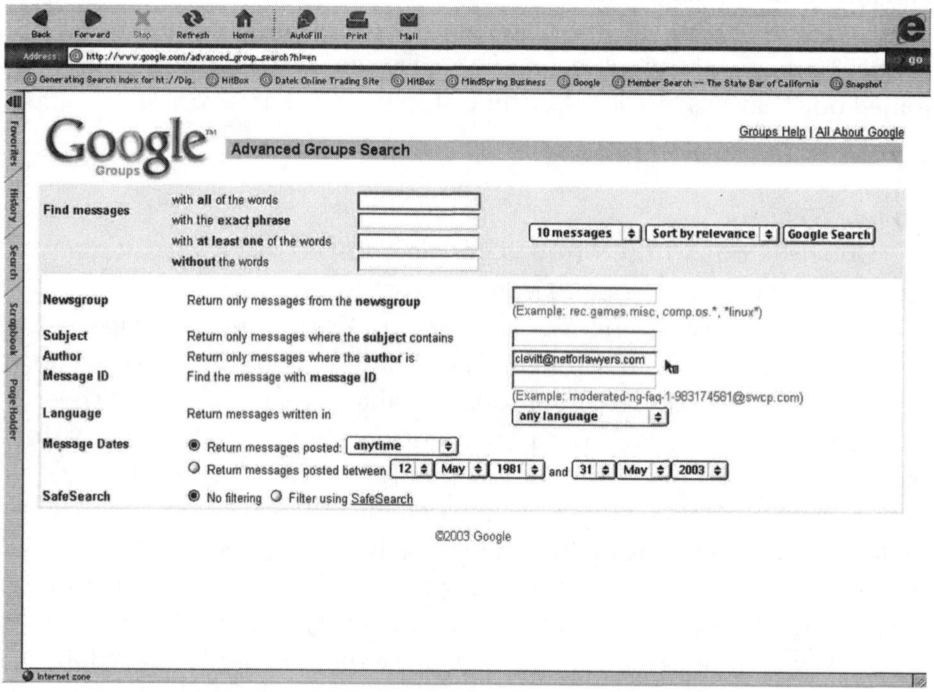

Figure 7-6. The Google Groups Advanced Groups Search allows you to search for group postings by the name or e-mail address of the person who posted the message. Google™ is a trademark of Google Technology Inc.

Google Groups Search Strategy Tips

To find a specific person's messages, users should conduct a few different types of searches on Google Group's Advanced Groups Search page (**http://groups.google.com/advanced_group_search**).

First, search the name in the **Return only messages where the author is** field. However, keep in mind that some people surf anonymously by using pseudonyms, so you may find nothing.

Second, search the specific person's e-mail address in the **Return only messages where the author is** field. After all, besides a Social Security number, what other identifier is more unique than an e-mail address? Since many people share the same name, searching by a unique e-mail address will help you verify that you've found the correct person.

Because some people have more than one e-mail address, try to discover all of them to conduct a complete search of their postings.

The third search method is to search for the specific person's name in one of the keyword fields of the Advanced Groups Search page (either in the **with all of the words** field or the **with the exact phrase** field). This may disclose other people's messages that contain your subject's name. You might learn about someone's opinion of your subject or the message may disclose some contact information about your subject. You can also attempt to e-mail the author of the message to learn more.

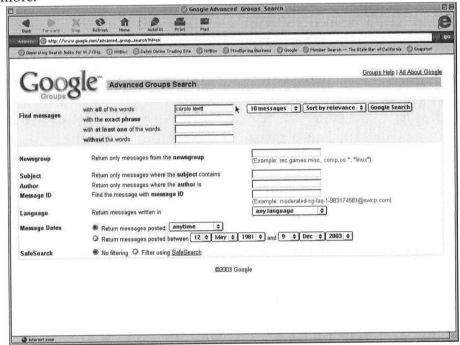

Figure 7-7. Is someone else discussing the person you're interested in finding out about? You can also use Google Group's Advanced Groups Search page to search using your target's name as a keyword (phrase). Google™ is a trademark of Google Technology Inc.

Finding Other Online Communities

To find other online communities to join or to search through aside from Google Groups, you can make use of CataList (**http://www.lsoft.com/lists/listref.html**), a catalog of LISTSERV lists, or Topica (formerly Liszt), a newsgroup directory (**http://www.liszt.com**).

CataList

http://www.lsoft.com/lists/listref.html

Purpose: To find a LISTSERV list that will meet your purposes

Content: CataList is the official catalog of LISTSERV mailing lists, covering 75,450 public lists out of 280,228 LISTSERV lists. There are several ways to use this catalog of lists: view lists by host country; view lists by number of subscribers; search the list by keyword, with the option of limiting your keyword search to list name, host name, or list title; and search lists that only have a Web archive interface.

Our View: A search for "research" returned over twelve hundred mailing lists. Results included the name of the list, a one-line description, and the number of subscribers. Clicking on the title provided additional information, including host name and some features of the lists. The amount of information in the annotation for each list varied considerably. While it was useful that some of the lists had an Eye icon indicating access to archives, some of those archive links worked and some of them didn't.

Tip: If you don't find what you need at CataList, use a search engine and type in keywords that describe the type of list you are seeking and the word "listserv" or try searching a newsgroup directory such as Topica (**http://www.liszt.com**). At Topica, you can either search by keywords or browse categories and subcategories to find the right group.

Locating a Picture of a Person

See the section "Finding Video, Audio, and Images" in Chapter 4, "Search Tools," to learn how to search the Web for someone's picture. If a person's picture is on a Web site or in a faculty directory, for instance, it can be found. We use this whenever we are meeting a new client at a public place and want to be able to readily spot the person.

Locating the Dead

People often ask us how to locate where a particular relative has been buried. This is after they have been unable to verify the death through the Social Security Death Index (SSDI). People who ask this question are always certain that the relative died, and that the relative left them a fortune, even though they'd been out of touch with the decedent for a good long time. There are some other options besides the SSDI for the hopeful heir trying to verify a death. For instance, locating the gravesite or an obituary can help establish the place of death. From there you can narrow down the search to a specific jurisdiction and begin your phone and letter inquiries.

Cemeteries and Graves

Find A Grave

http://www.findagrave.com

Purpose:	To locate gravesite locations of 4.2 million people.
Content:	The site contains information on gravesites of both the celebrity and the mere mortal. Search by name or location. It even includes noncemetery burial sites, such as cremation "sites."
Our View:	Information is provided by over 100,000 contributors.
Tip:	Another site to check is Interment.net (**http://www.interment.net**) which has about one million fewer records than Find A Grave (from 6,846 cemeteries), but a better search engine. You can search by last name and first name and, if known, add in the location. Connect search terms with either the AND Boolean connector or the "near" proximity connector. You can also

add quotation marks when a surname is two words, and you can use a wild card for prefix searching (for example, john* will find Johnson, Johnston, and so on)

If you don't find your decedent at one of these cemetery sites, try one of the obituary sites noted below.

Obituaries

Obituary Daily Times

http://obits.rootsweb.com/cgi-bin/obit.cgi

Purpose: To discover in which newspaper an obituary is published when you don't know where to begin your search.

Content: The site is an index of published obituaries. While the actual obituary is not online, the index tells you in which newspaper it was published. To learn which newspapers participate in this index, see **http://www.rootsweb.com/~obituary/publications.html**

Our View: This free index of published obituaries, which adds over twenty-five hundred entries a day, is a good place to start a search if you don't know where someone died. With so many newspapers online, it should not be too difficult to obtain an obituary from a specific newspaper.

Tip: Another obituary index is the National Obituary Archive (NOA), with almost fifty-eight million obituaries (**http://www.arrangeonline.com**). With funeral directors across North America serving as contributing members to this site, it contains very recent data. On April 28, 2003, a search for Chester Wazny at the SSDI came up empty, but his April 26, 2003 death was listed at NOA.

If you know where someone died, check the Web to see if the local library or historical society has a site because they often have local obituaries online. To find library Web sites, see **http://sunsite.berkeley.edu/Lib-web**. To find links to many local historical societies, see RootsWeb.com (**http://www.rootsweb.com**).

Searching with a Mother's Maiden Name

We know your mother's maiden name. What else can we do with this information besides something illegal, like using it for pretexting? Let's say you're searching for a missing person. If anyone knows where that person is, it would be his or her mother. You can use this information to contact her and try to find the missing person that way—but don't pretext.

Family Trees

RootsWeb

http://worldconnect.rootsweb.com

Purpose:	Primarily for genealogy research, but the family trees may be useful for finding relatives of missing witnesses, heirs, and so on, who may be willing to assist you in finding the missing person.
Content:	There are over 239 million names on file in the Family Tree database.
Our View:	You'll learn more than you can imagine. Some family trees include names, dates of births, deaths, marriages, links to the family's home page, (with pictures), e-mail address contact information—and we even found pictures of ancestor's headstones and someone's will (search for Jordan Sanders).
Tip:	Check for your own family tree in case your third cousin twice removed put one up—and it has more information than you want publicized.

Searching with a Date of Birth

Sometimes, you need to supply a date of birth along with a person's name when you search various databases. You might be able to find it at Anybirthday.com instead of having to go through the expense of using a pay database or the time and expense of ordering a birth record.

AnyBirthday.com

http://www.anybirthday.com

Purpose:	To find birthdays.
Content:	Over 135 million records gathered from public records. It displays gender and ZIP codes for each name.
Our View:	As noted above, this is a great little free service when you need to find a birthday. Although there is a link to another service, Anybirthday PLUS, where you can search using a first name only and birth date, we were unable to link to it. Check out locateme.com (**http://www.locateme.com**), which owns AnyBirthday.com (locateme.com is a public record database that costs $99 per year).
Tip:	Since so many people share the same name, it's best to add in the person's ZIP code if you know it—this will improve your chances of finding the correct person.
	Yes, AnyBirthday.com will e-mail you a reminder of your spouse's birthday (click on **Remind** to sign up for this service).

Searching for Classmates (and More)

Classmates

http://www.classmates.com

Purpose:	Multipurpose—everyone has a reason . . . but let's just say for finding people.
Content:	Classmates includes 130,000 schools located in the United States and Canada, and also American and Canadian schools located overseas. Thirty-five million people are listed. Use the **Advanced Search** to refine your search by searching by one or more of the following: person's name, school name, city, state, or graduation year.
Our View:	You'll need to at least register to use most of this site. As a registered (nonpaying) user you can search by a person's name and if she supplied this information you can learn where she went to school before high school, where she works or worked, and her married name. To see more information, you'll need to pay $36 to join as a Gold member. Lots of private investigators have joined and claim they successfully locate people on this site. As a paid member, you can send e-mail, read profiles and biographies, post to message boards, and post photos. The search functions need improvement—you must know someone's exact name. Partial name searching would be useful.
Tip:	Some people are now adding information about their workplace, military background, or college. If you are adverse to pop-up ads and spam, you'll want to avoid registering.

Validating Social Security Numbers

U.S. InfoSearch

http://www.free-ssn-id-verification.usinfosearch.com

Purpose: For Social Security number validation.

Content: This search shows whether a Social Security number is valid, and whether it belongs to someone alive or deceased.

Our View: This site's service is limited because it does not tell you who is linked to the number. Nevertheless, it has some value because it does tell you if someone is using a deceased person's Social Security number or an invalid (made-up) number, indicating that someone is concealing his true identity. But, if someone is misusing a live person's actual number, then this site if of little value since it doesn't show names.

Tip: Since this service is free, it's useful as a preliminary check because it can show that the Social Security number is invalid or belongs to a deceased person. If the number is valid, you'll need to search a pay database sooner or later to verify that the Social Security number belongs to the person who is claiming it.

After you've exhausted your thinking-outside-the-box avenues, try searching public records and pay databases (see the Chapter 8, "Accessing Public Records"). There are also many other techniques for finding and backgrounding people that you can learn about in Chapter 9, "Finding and Backgrounding Expert Witnesses;" Chapter 10, "Company Research;" and Chapter 11, "Competitive Intelligence Research."

*CHAPTER*EIGHT

Accessing Public Records

Using Public Records for Factual Research

Public records are chock-full of facts. Because of their content, they can be used for all kinds of fact-finding research, from finding and back-grounding people and companies, to locating patents and trademarks. The original purpose of public records, of course, was not for fact finding, but very often that's what legal professionals use them for. For example, the original purpose for maintaining real estate records was to enable the free transfer of property and to protect property owner's rights. But these very same records are also useful to lawyers for fact finding, clearly not the intended purpose of the records. For example, you can use real estate records to locate someone or to find and determine a person's assets.

These are some of the purposes for which lawyers use other public records (some fall within their intended purpose and some do not):

- Skip-trace, whether it's to find a missing child, witness, or heir, or to serve a complaint
- Find assets
- Conduct due diligence (on a person or a company)
- Identify registered agents for service of process
- Locate liens, judgments, and Uniform Commercial Code (UCC) Filings
- Unearth criminal records
- Access court dockets and pleadings
- Obtain vital records (birth, marriage, divorce, and death)

- Verify or find Social Security numbers
- Uncover bankruptcies
- Find terrorists (government lawyers might use the records for this purpose)

What Are Public Records?

Public records can be loosely defined as anything filed with a government agency, and are typically open for public inspection. The records can vary from someone's divorce decree filed at the courthouse to their property records filed at the assessor's office. These treasure troves of government-held data must be made available to the public in order to advance commerce, give notice to the public, and to protect the public. For example, let's look at why bankruptcy records have been deemed to be public records. First, making them public gives notice to the public that someone they are dealing with may be financially unreliable and this protects the public (from extending credit to the person or going into business with him). Second, making the records public also advances commerce by offering some protection to the claimants.

Simply because a record is filed with a government agency does not necessarily mean the record is always subject to public scrutiny. Even though federal agencies are required under the Freedom of Information Act (FOIA) "to make their records promptly available to any person who makes a proper request for them," many records are exempted or excluded from provisions of the Act (**http://www.usdoj.gov/oip/foi-act.htm**). Thus, many records are not open to public scrutiny (or not to be shared between government agencies). Examples of such records are an individual's tax return or the FBI's National Crime Information Center's database. Obviously, these types of records would be rich sources of data that could be used to find people and find out about people—if they were available to the public.

For copies of FOIA request forms, see **http://www.usdoj.gov/04foia/att_d.htm**. Because FOIA only applies to federal agencies, different procedures must be followed for state FOIA requests. The National Freedom of Information site provides links to state FOIA information (**http://www.nfoic.org/web/index.htm**).

Public Records Vary with Jurisdictions

Every jurisdiction has its own definition of public record, and what's public today may be private tomorrow (and vice-versa). State, local, and federal governments differ greatly on what is and is not considered public. The meaning of public can also shift over time. Some states used to consider driver's license records to be public, while others, over time, shifted to deeming them to be private records. The federal government considered them private (pursuant to the Driver's Privacy Protection Act of 1994). The U.S. Supreme Court settled the controversy between the state law and the federal law, declaring drivers license records to be private records (*Reno v. Condon* at **http://caselaw.lp.findlaw.com/scripts/getcase.pl?court=us&vol=000&invol=98-1464**).

What was private before (such as a record of the books you have checked out from your public library) may be considered public (to the government) today, due to the 2001 U.S.A. Patriot Act (Public Law No. 107-56).

Every jurisdiction also has its own definition of access. Sometimes access to online public records is free, making them more accessible to more people. Other times, there is a fee for access, making the public record less accessible to fewer people. Some public records have not been digitized, so they are only accessible by in-person public inspection of the print record. For those public records that have been placed on the Web, access to the amount of information displayed may be limited. The limitations are based upon privacy concerns. However, if a record found on the Internet only displays part of the information, it is likely that the print version would show the excluded information. Thus, there are varying levels of access to the amount of information in a public record, depending on whether the record is found on the Internet or in-person at a government agency.

Public Records Are Now More Public

It's been accepted that public records are available to anyone who takes the time to go to the appropriate venue to ask for them (or resorts to a FOIA request if needed), or who has a paid subscription to commercial public records databases. However, when the very same records are being made publicly accessible (for free or for a low cost) over the Internet, privacy advocates (and even some non-advocates) are not so accepting. With this ease of access from the comfort of home or the workplace, public records have truly become public, and so has the personal, private, and sensitive information found within the public record. This concern about privacy has been referred to as the doctrine of "practical obscurity," a term the U.S. Supreme Court used in 1989 when it held that a person's rap sheet was not subject to a FOIA request and should remain in practical obscurity (*U.S. Dept. of Justice v. Reporters Committee*, 489 U.S. 749 1989). As more and more courts are requiring electronic filing and more and more court files are thus becoming accessible over the Internet, it is becoming more difficult for the government to ensure that certain records remain in practical obscurity. Chief Judge D. Brock Hornby, chair of the Judicial Conference Committee on Court Administration and Case Management, to the Conference for Chief District Judges, commented, "This 'practical obscurity' ends when the court records become easily accessible and searchable electronically from remote locations—anywhere in the world and at any time of the day or night. This end of 'practical obscurity' for court records raises a number of policy issues . . . One policy issue is created by the very nature of the Internet." (See **http://www.uscourts.gov/ttb/june00ttb/internet.html**.) With the demise of practical obscurity, lawyers need to carefully consider what, if anything, needs to be redacted from court records.

For those who advocate for access to public records as part of our open, democratic tradition and our free speech rights, nothing short of full access to public records via the Internet (public, personal, and sensitive information included), is acceptable. On the other hand, those in favor of the right to privacy want all of the information (public, personal and sensitive) taken off the Internet, especially in light of the ever-growing identify theft and stalking cases.

What's in a Public Record?

Public records can include personal, private, or sensitive information. Often these labels overlap, but we'll try to draw some distinctions.

Personal Information

Personal information can be found in public and private records. Personal information is that which personally identifies you—such as your Social Security number, your address, your phone number, and so on. This is also sometimes referred to as sensitive information.

Sensitive Information

Sensitive information can be found in public and private records. Sensitive information can be that which personally identifies you as noted above under **personal information**. There are also two other definitions of sensitive information: (1) information found in a public record that is personal or private, and if released could cause harm, bias, or embarrassment (for example, a medical disability listed on your driver's license); (2) information that is private, or personal information found in a public record about a person who is in a protected group and if released could cause harm, bias, or embarrassment. For example, minor children are a protected group—even their names are protected. If their names (or anything about them) can be gleaned from a public record (such as a divorce decree), this information is considered sensitive and might be redacted from an online record (where anyone could easily access it). An adult's name found in the same divorce decree would not be considered sensitive because they are not in a protected group. The minor's name might or might not be redacted in the paper record.

Private Information and Private Records

Private information is what you consider to be for your eyes only—and for those you've given permission to view it. Your medical records contain private information, but you have given your doctor permission to view them (and if you want to be reimbursed by your health insurance company, you've given them permission too). Your private information in your private records is not subject to general public inspection or a FOIA request.

Although you probably consider what you paid for your house to be private information, the information is considered public nevertheless. The information is found in real estate records, and real estate records are deemed to be public records, as noted earlier.

Public Records May Contain Personal, Sensitive, and Private Information

In a public divorce decree, personal and private information can also be found. Personal information such as the Social Security numbers of the divorcing couple may appear. Private information, such as tax information or their yearly income, might appear in the public record. Bankruptcy filings also include personal and private information, such as the debtor's Social Security number, credit card numbers, bank name and account numbers, and so on. Some of this personal and private information found in court records is now being protected from public scrutiny. For instance, according to new federal bankruptcy court guidelines, only the last four digits of an individual's Social Security number is displayed. Recent federal and state legislation and court opinions have also limited the access to personal and private information found in public records.

"Publicly Available" Information

"Publicly available" information must be distinguished from public records. Publicly available information does not come from a government agency. It is that information (whether it be private, personal, or sensitive) that you voluntarily provide to a private entity. For example, you provide your phone number and address to the telephone company or your ZIP code to the person who checks you out at a department store register. That information is now publicly available and may be (and usually is) sold to marketing companies or public record database companies (whose databases also include a mix of public records and publicly available information). As noted in Chapter 7, "Finding and Backgrounding People," the Internet contains loads of publicly available information such as anything you say in an online community, on your own Web site, or the information you provide to a site like Classmates.com.

Privacy and Information on the Internet

Right-to-privacy advocates and right-to-access advocates have always been at loggerheads over access to public records, but even more so after two unrelated events: the advent of the Internet and the aftermath of September 11, 2001.

With the advent of the Internet came easy, anonymous, and often free access to public records. The Internet made public records, in essence, even more public. The Internet also made access to publicly available information easy. With easy access to both came the problem of identity theft, which is now growing at an unprecedented rate.

In the aftermath of September 11, the right-to-privacy versus the right-to-access debate is taking another direction. While the privacy concerns centering around the advent of the Internet focused more on individuals invading other individuals' privacy (and stealing their identity or stalking them, for example), now the privacy concerns have shifted to the government invading an individual's privacy. The government, in a quest to ferret out terrorists, is looking more closely at background information about people. They are doing this in two ways: (1) more searching of commercial databases that contain public records and publicly available information (such as ChoicePoint at **http://www .choicepointonline.com**); and (2) passing legislation, such as the U.S.A. Patriot Act, Public Law No. 107-56 (2001) (**http://frwebgate.access gpo.gov/cgi-bin/getdoc.cgi?dbname=107_cong_public_laws&docid= f:publ056.107**) that allows the government to obtain private information about people from private and public entities.

The U.S.A. Patriot Act and Privacy

The U.S.A. Patriot Act's full title (believe it or not) is the "Uniting and Strengthening America by Providing Appropriate Tools Required to Intercept and Obstruct Terrorism Act of 2001." The law is broad enough that the FBI could demand to see records about an individual from private and public entities, such as video rental stores or even libraries to discover an individual's video viewing, Web-surfing, and reading habits. In fact, the government (primarily the FBI) has already been visiting libraries requesting to see patron's circulation and Internet records (see **http://alexia.lis .uiuc.edu/gslis/research/civil_liberties.html**). Some libraries are complying with FBI requests, some are not, and some are shredding the records in order to avoid the issue (such as the Santa Cruz Public Library in California).

The Video Privacy Protection Act

In the first edition of this book, the authors stated, "Although there is legislation protecting privately held data in random niches, including the Robert Bork-inspired Video Privacy Protection Act [18 U.S.C. 2710], which protects from public scrutiny the lists of videotapes we rent, most private data is protected only by the discretion of the private entities which possess it." While the Video Privacy Protection Act also shielded the public from government scrutiny of our video rental list (with some exceptions) and still shields us from the general public's scrutiny of that list, those very same lists are now more open to government scrutiny as a result of the U.S.A. Patriot Act.

The Privacy Act of 1974

The Privacy Act, 5 U.S.C.§ 552a, was enacted to protect against the disclosure of information that government agencies keep about individuals. The fear was that without this act, there was nothing to prevent the government from compiling dossiers about a person—going from agency to agency to collect the data. Recently, the government has reportedly paid $50 million annually to the commercial database company Choice-Point (also marketed as AutoTrack, KnowX, and ScreenNow) to search through what amounts to data that can be used to create dossiers about individuals—from both public records and publicly available information. ChoicePoint's records can vary (depending on each state's policies), but often include motor vehicle records, automobile and boat registrations, liens, deeds, military records, bankruptcies, UCCs, judgments, Social Security numbers, phone numbers, and addresses, and so on. Another commercial database company also used by the government, Accurint, has records that show the following about a person: relatives and associates, past work and home addresses, phone numbers (from up to twenty years back), Social Security numbers, and so on. Privacy advocates are up in arms regarding the government's heavy reliance upon commercial companies' databases to access the very types of information that the Privacy Act of 1974 seemingly prohibited.

Public Records Web Sites

Public Records Metasites

Access to federal, state and local agencies' public records varies from jurisdiction to jurisdiction and agency to agency. Some don't place them on the Web at all, some place them on the Web for free, and some charge a fee.

There are several excellent free metasites that link to those agencies that do place their public records on the Web. While the links on these metasites point primarily to free government sites, they also point to non-government sites that have created searchable databases from public records derived from (or purchased from) the government. Examples are universities, nonprofits, and commercial database companies. Some of the links may also point to publicly available data and not just public records per se. The following are the top metasites for beginning your public record quest:

- Search Systems at **http://www.searchsystems.net**
- Portico at **http://indorgs.virginia.edu/portico**
- BRB Publications at **http://www.brbpub.com/pubrecsites.asp**
- State and Local Government on the Net at **http://www.statelocal gov.net**

Search Systems

http://www.searchsystems.net

Purpose: To link to free and pay sites with public records and publicly available data.

Content: Search Systems links to over 13,310 free searchable public record databases covering U.S. federal (or nationwide), state, and local records; U.S. territories; Canada (nationwide and provinces); foreign countries, and Outer Space (current news from NASA).

At the state level, links point to databases that provide public record information about businesses (such as secretary of state corporate records), licensing (such as dentists), criminal records, inmates and offenders, missing children, unclaimed property, trade names and trademarks, state employee and department lookups, UCC filings, and state codes.

At the city and county levels, links are provided to local civil, criminal, probate, family, and traffic court records; birth, death, and marriage records; assumed and fictitious business name filings; recorded documents; county and city inmates; and tax information.

Our View: We can't say enough good things about this site. It keeps on getting bigger and better. An example of better: next to each link you now find a **description** pop-up to inform you about what the site contains to help determine if it's worth a visit, and also a notation of **free** or **pay**, warning you in advance if you need to get your credit card out.

Tip: Instead of browsing by jurisdiction, use the **Public Record Locator** feature at the top of the home page to search by keywords that describe the type of public record sought (such as marriage records) or to search by jurisdiction (such as Cook County) or to search by a combination of the two types of keywords. To search by jurisdiction, type in the name of a city for links to that jurisdiction's Web public records. To search by type of public record, type in a category of records (such as death records) and a list of death and cemetery records in various jurisdictions is displayed. Or, type in the name of a county (Cook County) and the category of public records you are seeking (death records) to discover if Cook County has their death records free on the Web. Use the **Advanced Search** option for more search functions.

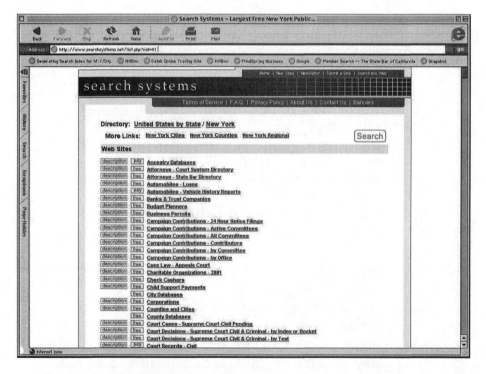

Figure 8-1. Search Systems lists thousands of public records sites, notes if they are free or pay, and offers a detailed description of the site before you link to it. This is a screen shot of their New York state page.

Portico

http://indorgs.virginia.edu/portico

Purpose: To provide, free of charge, links to public record and publicly available information.

Content: Portico is arranged topically, and then broken down by state. Topics covered include personal property, stocks, salaries, obituaries, occupations and more.

Our View: While we prefer Search Systems, sometimes we find a topical approach is what we need and Portico fits the bill.

Tip: If you need information other than public records, such as salary surveys, calculators, and various other reference resources, take a look at Portico's directory for links.

BRB Publications Inc.

http://www.brbpub.com/pubrecsites.asp

Purpose: To provide, free of charge, links to over 1,400 state, county, city, and federal sites where public record information is free. Also has a pay site with links to 26,000 government agencies that store public records at **http://www.publicrecordsources.com**.

Content: Unlike Search Systems and Portico, BRB does not contain links for state occupational licensing boards or registrations unless you subscribe to its online Public Records Research System (PRRS). The online system also has annotated links to over 26,000 government agencies, county courts, county recording offices, and federal courts that house public records.

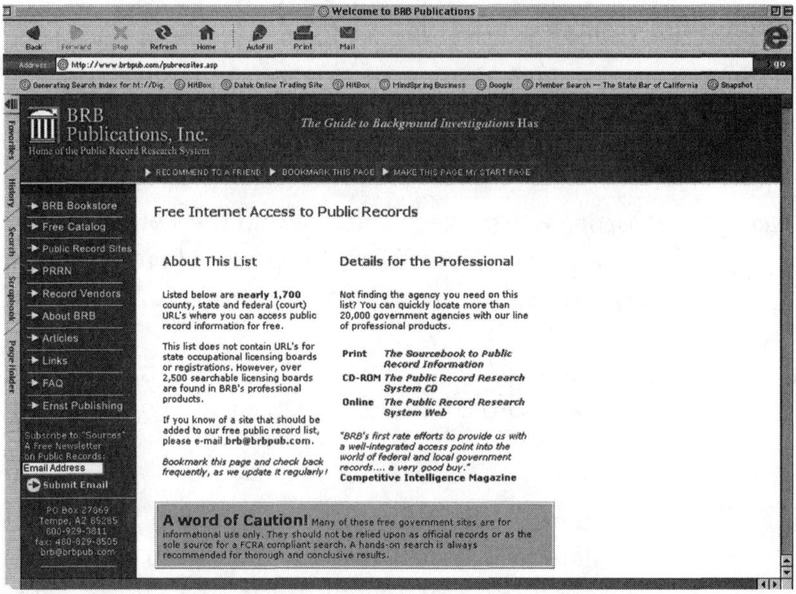

Figure 8-2. Select **Public Records Sites** from the left column to view a list of state, county, and city public records sites.

Our View: With 26,000 links, it may be worth the annual fee of $119 (for two users) to subscribe to PRRS, especially because of the detailed annotations. For instance, a search of "Anchorage accident report records" displays contact information and the following details: "Records are available from seven years. Only legal representatives and insurance agents of the participants, or the participant him/herself may obtain copies. The lawyer or legal representative must have a notarized request, an insurance agent a signed request with reason." PRRS also provides a directory of over 630 local court and county record retrievers.

Tip: For links to PRRS-approved local document retrievers, search firms, preemployment and tenant screening firms, trade associations, and PIs and process servers, see **http://www.publicrecordsources.com**. Most of these databases are searchable by state or county, and some by type of record needed or company name.

State and Local Government on the Net

http://www.statelocalgov.net

Purpose: As the name implies, to link to over eighty-five hundred official state and local government sites.

Content: First, choose a state and then browse by category to find what you need. Links are organized by jurisdiction first (state, county, city) and then within each jurisdiction by branch of government.

Our View: While browsing by jurisdiction works well, a new feature allows searching by entering terms into the **Quick Search** box on the left side. For example, for a page that lists each state's secretary of state link, type "secretary of state" into the **Quick Search** box. Don't try to choose a state from the drop-down menu and then try to enter a term into the **Quick Search** box. At first glance we thought this type of combined search would work, but they are two separate search functions. We like that a date next to each state name tells us when links were last updated.

Tip: If you don't find what you're looking for, visit the individual state's home page (as the site suggests); though their pages are updated frequently, they may not be as

Figure 8-3. Browse for government sites at State and Local Government on the Net or use a new feature that allows keyword searching by entering terms into the **Quick Search** box.

up-to-date as the various government's home pages.

Vital Statistics: Birth, Death, Marriage, and Divorce

Vital statistic records are typically found at the local level, but there are some national and statewide records. Every jurisdiction has different access policies.

Some vital statistic records are available online for free at government Web sites. Some jurisdictions offer online ordering for a fee. However, many jurisdictions, such as California, have ceased online ordering altogether because of identity theft. As of July 1, 2003, a new California law designates who is an "authorized" requestor and requires a notarized Certificate of Identity and a completed application form signed under penalty of perjury by the authorized requestor for all mail orders. Some jurisdictions sell their records outright to fee-based databases that then compile the government information and make it available for a fee. And finally, some public records may be found online at local historical societies or local library Web sites, or even at genealogy sites.

To Order Certified Copies for a Fee

If you are unable to easily find and order vital statistics, or if the jurisdiction doesn't offer online ordering, there are private companies that can expedite the process for you. For example, VitalChek (**http://www .vitalchek.com**) handles over twenty-five thousand certified vital records on a weekly basis. Their processing fees vary from state to state (and county to county) and also depend on turnaround time (for example, the cost is $18.50 for a three-to-five-business-day turnaround in Montana, but in California it is $23.50). Add to this the state or county's fees also when calculating costs. Search Systems will direct you to a similar company, CourthouseDirect.com (**http://www.courthousedirect.com**), where you can order vital statistic documents.

Though they are primarily genealogy sites, Ancestry.com and RootsWeb.com are also good starting points for locating public records, especially for vital statistic records.

RootsWeb

http://searches.rootsweb.com

Purpose: To provide links to free state and local vital statistic public records and publicly available data.

Content: RootsWeb has selected state and county vital statistics public records and publicly available data (from historical and genealogical societies and libraries). It also includes free national death records from the Social Security Death Index (SSDI). (See the separate entry below for details on SSDI searching.) RootsWeb is supported by Ancestry.com (see the next entry) and some of the data overlaps. State death records are available only for California (9,366,786 records from 1940 to 1997), Texas (death records from 1964 to 98), Kentucky (2,921,383 records from 1911 through 2000) and Maine (401,960 records from 1960 through 1997). To access those four states' death records (or the national SSDI), go to **http://searches.rootsweb.com** and scroll down to **Records from Federal and State Resources**. To view other state and county records, go to **http://www.rootsweb.com/~websites/usa/index.html** and select a state from the list. After selecting a state you can also scroll down and select a county (not all counties are included) to drill down to the county level.

Our View: This is a useful site to discover what state and county public records and publicly available records are online. It's very hit or miss, of course.

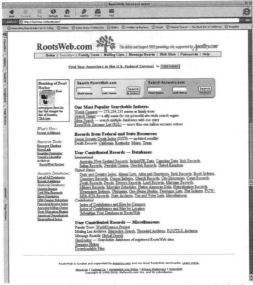

Figure 8-4. RootsWeb links to free state and local vital statistic public records (including the SSDI) and publicly available data from historical societies and libraries.

Ancestry.com

http://www.ancestry.com/search/rectype/vital/main.htm

Purpose: For genealogy research primarily, but useful for links to state and local public records and publicly available information (and other countries).

Content: Use Ancestry.com to link to a variety of U.S. state or county records or other countries' records. Go to **http://www.ancestry.com/search/rectype/vital/ main.htm**, and then scroll down until you see a list entitled **Search Individual Birth**, **Marriage & Death Databases**. Some of the same databases that are free at RootsWeb.com cost $79.95 annually to access from this site. Linking to these records used to be free.

Our View: Even though the same California, Maine, Kentucky, and Texas death records found at Ancestry.com for a fee are free at RootsWeb, we have included Ancestry.com because we wouldn't be surprised if it stopped support ing RootsWeb at some point. If that occurs, RootsWeb might cease being free (or even cease to exist), at which time you'll need to know about Ancestry.com.

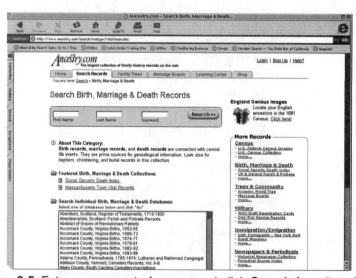

Figure 8-5. Enter your ancestor's name and click **Search** for a list of possible links. To view any of the results at Ancestry.com, though, you'll need to register.

Tip: It's going to be hard to predict whether vital statistic public records will be easy to access. After the September 11, 2001 terrorist attacks, California's governor requested that the death and birth records found at Ancestry.com and RootsWeb be taken down due to security concerns that public records were (or could be) used by terrorists to obtain new identities. That request was complied with at first. Now, however, the death records are back up. While the California birth records are still down at those two sites, they are up at others (such as Vitalsearch.com). Texas birth and death records have been taken off the Texas Department of Health page, butthey are still available at Ancestry.com and RootsWeb.

The VitalSearch Company Worldwide, Inc.

To search: To view records:

http://www.vitalsearch-worldwide.com

Purpose: To verify deaths or births by a person's last name or other criteria (such as mother's or father's last name). Discover someone's mother's maiden name (sometimes).

Content: VitalSearch has birth, death, marriage, and divorce records for nine states (including California, Oregon, and Texas); dates and types of records vary for each state.

VitalSearch contains the California birth and death databases that are no longer available for free at Ancestry.com. It has over twelve million name entries from 1905 to 2000. Searching the index and viewing the summarized results is free but for more details (such as cause of death), you must be a paid "Premium Searcher."

Our View: Though it's a useful site and most of it is free, there are innumerable ads and pop-ups that can get in the way of even beginning a search.

Tip: After just a few minutes of searching for free, the site had opened about ten new windows on the user's PC. A premium membership is worth the fee of $57.95 per year or $24.95 per quarter to avoid this. See **http://www.vital search-ca.com/gen/premregm.htm**.

On the home page, a state chart shows what records are available for various states. To utilize many of the databases, registration (free) for a "Guest Pass" is necessary.

Death Records

Lawyers often need to verify deaths for many reasons. Recently, a lawyer trying to locate an heir asked for our assistance. Before doing any extensive investigating, we first check to see if a missing heir (or witness) is deceased. National death records can be found in the Social Security Death Index (SSDI), searchable at several free sites, such as Ancestry.com (**http://www.ancestry.com**) and RootsWeb (**http://ssdi.rootsweb.com**). There are also other death indexes found at the state and local level.

RootsWeb SSDI Search

http://ssdi.rootsweb.com

Purpose: For genealogy research primarily, but useful to verify a death in the Social Security Death Index (SSDI) and to link to other public records

Content: The site contains death records for over seventy million deaths occurring after 1962 that were reported to the Social Security Administration. The index is updated monthly. The records show the decedent's name, birth and death dates; last known address; and Social Security number and place of its issuance. Beacuse RootsWeb is supported by Ancestry.com, they have some similar data. Although there are many ways to access the SSDI from the RootsWeb home page, the easiest and most direct route is to avoid going to the home page and use the URL noted above. However, if you prefer going through the home page, don't enter the decedent's name into the **Search RootsWeb.com** box on the home page; you will get too many results because you can only enter a last and first name. Also, don't enter the decedent's name into the search box that's labeled **Search Ancestry.com** because you will then be asked to register at Ancestry.com. To avoid registering, go to the **Search Engines and Databases** category on the left side of the screen, and click on **Social Security Death Index**. Once there, don't enter the decedent's name into the search box. Click on **Advanced Search** first, and then search by any of the following criteria, or combinations of them: name (for the last name you can choose exact, or if unsure of the spelling, choose **soundex**, which is the "sounds like" feature); last residence; last place benefit was sent to; Social Security number; birth date; and death date.

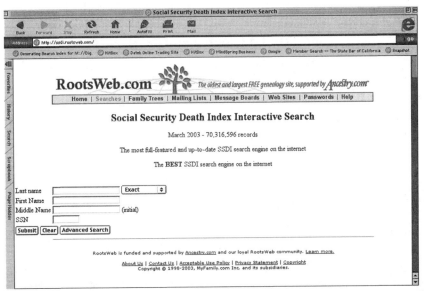

Figure 8-6. Unless you have the subject's Social Security number, be sure to click on the **Advanced Search** button on this page where more search options are provided to assist you in pinpointing the correct person.

Our View: Although RootsWeb and Ancestry.com have similar data, including the SSDI, we prefer RootsWeb because it does not require registering (Ancestry.com does) and some of the same data that is fee-based at Ancestry.com (some state public records) is free at RootsWeb.

Tip: Once you locate the record, you may decide that you want a copy of the decedent's original Social Security application for further background information. To do this, click on **Request Information (SS-5)** and then **Click here to generate letter**. The decedent's information is automatically placed into a letter to the Social Security Administration, which you can print out and mail with a $27 check to obtain a copy of the application. The following valuable information will be found once you receive the decedent's original application: full name; full name at birth (including maiden name); present mailing address and current employer's name and address (at the time of application); age at last birthday; date of birth; place of birth (city, county, state); father's full name (regardless of whether living or dead); mother's full name, including maiden name (regardless of whether living or dead); sex; race; whether the decedent ever previously applied for a Social Security number or Railroad Retirement; date signed; and the applicant's signature.

Gravesites and Obituaries

For those who haven't found the decedent's records in the SSDI, see Chapter 7, "Finding and Backgrounding People," to learn other ways to verify someone's death, such as by locating a gravesite or obituary notice.

Marriages and Divorces

Jurisdictions vary widely as to whether marriage and divorce records are online. While most counties do not provide online access, it's more likely that marriages will be online than divorces, judging by a search in Search Systems (596 results for marriage versus 43 results for divorce). In some counties, copies of marriage certificates can at least be ordered over the Internet, but in many, you have to write for the information or visit the recorder's office in person.

Marriage records are useful for skip tracing in several ways. First, the record shows a birth year of the subject and this can narrow down a search if you are given the option of adding the year of birth to a name search. With so many people sharing the same name, adding the year of birth can better target your intended subject. Also, some databases require a birth year to even conduct the search (see Rapsheets.com, where a $19.95 national search of over 140 million criminal records requires a date of birth along with the name). Second, this is another resource to discover a woman's maiden name: A maiden name can be used to try to track the subject through her relatives or to track her directly by her maiden name if she is now divorced and has gone back to using it. Third, the county where the marriage took place may also be the current location of the subject, or at least can serve as a starting point for further research. For example, searching that county's real estate assessor's records may be a good idea in case the couple settled down in the same county in which they married. Or, you might find relatives with the same name in that county who can be of assistance.

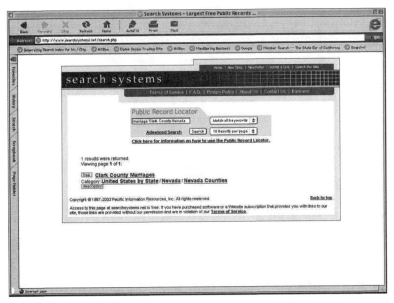

Figure 8-7. Searchsystems.net displays one result for the search "marriage Clark County Nevada."

Using Search Systems (**http://searchsystems.net**), type the word "marriage" and the name of the county and state (for example, Clark County Nevada) into the **Public Record Locator** search box or use BRB (**http://www.brbpub.com/pubrecsites.asp**) and scroll down to **County/City Sites**. The results from both BRB and Search Systems provide links to Clark County (Las Vegas) marriage records, but running a similar search at Ancestry.com does not. (But Texas marriage records up to 1850 and from 1851 to 1900 can be found at Ancestry.com for a fee and for free at RootsWeb—see the entries above). Therefore, it's always best to check a few metasites (and the jurisdiction's site too) before concluding that the records are not on the Web or are not free.

Records of all marriages taking place after 1984 in Las Vegas are freely searchable by bride's name, groom's name, or marriage certificate number at the Clark County government Web site **(http://www.co.clark.nv.us/ recorder/mar_srch.htm)**. Considering how many people get married in Las Vegas, Clark County is a good starting place to search for a marriage record when uncertain of the place of marriage. (Clark County divorce records are not online.)

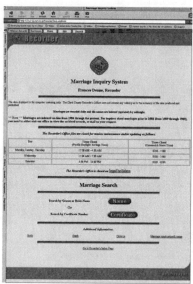

Figure 8-8. Marriages are indexed online from 1984 through the present, and are updated daily.

Professional and Trade Licensing Boards

Use a metasite, such as Search Systems or Portico, to link to national and state licensing boards.

Portico (Occupations page)

http://indorgs.virginia.edu/portico/occupations.html

Purpose: To link to various licensing boards throughout the country, arranged by occupation.

Content:	Occupations listed (with links) range from architects and brokers to lawyers, judges, doctors, and more.
Our View:	License verification for occupations such as contractors or doctors will typically be found on a government site, but we often find it quicker to search Portico or Search Systems rather than a state government's home page because most of the government pages have too much data to wade through. (And, if the licensing information is not even located on the government site, but resides at a professional association's site instead, you'll spend a lot of time spinning your wheels at the government site. For example, a lawyer license database is often found at a bar association site and not at a state site.)
Tip:	The professional association sites might also include disciplinary or biographical information, while goverment sites often do not.

Medical Doctors

There is no public access to the Practitioner Data Bank—the federal government's database of malpractice judgments and disciplinary actions taken against practicing physicians. Only hospitals, HMOs, and state medical boards can access the site. See Chapter 12, "Medical Research," for information on finding medical doctors' licenses or certifications, or search Portico's list of occupations (noted above).

Court Records and Dockets

See the separate section later in this chapter, "Court Dockets and Pleadings."

Criminal Records

There are various types of criminal records: (1) arrest records (booking logs), (2) charges filed with the court, and (3) incarceration records. There are also various entities that maintain criminal records, from the federal government, to the state, to the county, and the city. Gathering all these various records from all these various jurisdictions into one central database has not happened. The only criminal record database that even comes close to being comprehensive is the FBI's National Crime Information Center (NCIC) database, which, unfortunately, is unavailable to us mere mortals. (There are some exceptions, such as employers who send fingerprints to the FBI; see **http://www.fbi.gov/pressrel/pressrel99/ncic2000.htm**.) The FBI's database relies, in part, on the various jurisdictions to report charges and dispositions, but the system is imperfect and many charges fall through the cracks. A searcher who wants to conduct a so-called comprehensive criminal record search will find the going laborious. A mix of fee-based searching, free Web searching, and in-person searching is probably necessary. Additionally, local, state, and federal criminal records need to be searched separately.

If you plan on searching on your own, you can try using Portico or Search Systems for links to the various criminal record sites. In addition, we recommend *The Criminal Records Book* by Derek Hinton (**https://www.brbpub.com/books**), one of the best books (practical and detailed) for searching criminal records. Rapsheets.com (profiled below) might ease some of the burden of criminal record research with its low-cost state and local criminal record database, but it too is not complete. Even though some of the records found at Rapsheets.com can also be found free by visiting the specific state or county incarceration or booking log sites, or court docket sites, it might be quicker to use Rapsheets.com.

Pay Databases for Criminal Records

Rapsheets

http://www.rapsheets.com

Purpose: To find individual criminal records.

Content: Rapsheets claims to cover "almost every state" (see **http://www.rapsheets.com/about.asp**), but does not necessarily include every county in the covered states. Results typically display the defendant's name, date of birth, race, sex, offense date, offense description, case number, disposition, disposition date, county of disposition, and the sentence (these results can vary from jurisdiction to jurisdiction). Rapsheets has over 123 million records.

Our View: It's worth the monthly subscription of $14.95 plus $3.00 per search if you conduct criminal records research often. Otherwise, opt for the nonmember arrangement, but be prepared to pay more per search. Subscribers can perform a $19.95 national search of 123 million records (but must enter a date of birth along with the name) and an $8.00 regional search. The database is easy to use.

Tip: • Rapsheets also provides some noncriminal searching (click on **other searches**) to verify a name, a Social Security number, or a residential address. These searches cost from $1 to $2.
• Rapsheets doesn't work using the AOL browser.
• To find a date of birth (required for the national search above), try Anybirthday.com (see Chapter 7, "Finding and Backgrounding People").

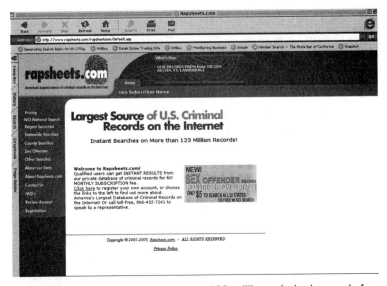

Figure 8-9. Rapsheets.com has over 123 million criminal records from various counties in 35 states.

Free State and Local Criminal Records

Some state and local law enforcement agencies have placed records of inmates, criminal docket sheets, driving-while-intoxicated (DWI) history, delinquent parents, sex offenders, and booking logs on the Web for anyone to search for free. At Corrections Connection, you can view a list of various state and local agencies that have free Web searching of booking logs or inmate records (**http://www.corrections.com/links/viewlinks.asp?Cat=20**). Some states and some counties provide free access over the Internet to criminal dockets, while others may charge a fee. For example, in California, criminal dockets are available free at the California Supreme Court and Court of Appeals Web site (**http://appellatecases.courtinfo.ca.gov**), while Los Angeles County charges a small fee ($4.00 to $4.75) to access its criminal dockets database (**https://www.lasuperiorcourt.org/criminalindex**). For more information on criminal dockets, see the section in this chapter, "Court Dockets and Pleadings."

State DWI Offender History

New Mexico recently made its DWI Offender History Application available free on the Internet. While it does not contain all DWI charges processed by the courts, searching by full name or by Social Security number for those that it does contain retrieves the full docket.

State and Local Sex Offender Registries

Wonder if your new neighbor is a sex offender? Sex offender registries have been one of the more litigated areas of free public records on the Web. A recent U.S. Supreme Court case just declared Alaska's Sex Offender Registration Act to be constitutional and compared the Web access to the registry to be "more analogous to a visit to an official archive of criminal records . . . The Internet makes the document search more efficient, cost effective, and convenient for Alaska's citizenry." (*Smith v. Doe*, No. 01-729 [U.S.], **http://supct.law.cornell.edu/supct/html/01-729.ZO.html**.)

Still, every state and county handles the logistics of access differently (for example, Alaska and Texas have statewide Web registries searchable by offender's name while California does not have a statewide Web registry). Some California counties, such as Los Angeles, provide Web access, but you cannot search by the offender's name or a specific address. You can only search by a general location—and even then no names or precise addresses are attached to the results (**http://gismap.co.la.ca.us/ sols/default.htm**). A keyword search at Search Systems (such as "sex offender clark county Nevada") might link you to your county's sex offender registry if it is online. To link to statewide sex offender databases, see the FBI's site (below).

FBI State Sex Offender Registry Websites

http://www.fbi.gov/hq/cid/cac/states.htm

Purpose: To search for state information on sex offenders.

Content: Provides links to the sex offender registry of each state that has placed records online that identify individual sex offenders. You can also locate information on crimes against children investigated by the FBI, such as kidnappings and online child pornography, on this Web site.

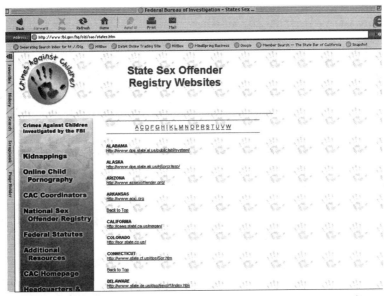

Figure 8-10. The FBI's site provides links to the sex offender registry of each state, if that state has placed the records online (**http://www.fbi.gov/hq/ cid/cac/states.htm**).

Our View: Unfortunately, the public cannot access the FBI's national database. Data in the FBI National Registry of Sex Offenders, established in 1996 under the Lychner Act, 42 U.S.C.14072, may only be released for law enforcement purposes to federal, state, and local criminal justice agencies. However, there is an exception: public notification will be made if it's necessary to protect the public.

Tip: • Merlin Information Services has created a multistate sex offender search (thirty-two states and D.C.) for $15 (**http://www.merlindata.com**).
    • Some states do not provide information on the Internet. In those states, you need to contact the local enforcement agency for such information.
    • Some state registries may require a minimum fee for every inquiry (for example, Idaho charges $1 to $2 per search), but nonprofit organizations are exempt from the fee.

Other Local Criminal Records

Booking Logs

Local law enforcement agencies vary as to whether they place booking logs or other local criminal records online. There's no central index for local booking log records. Each local entity's site must be searched. Once you're in jail, privacy, of course, goes right out the window, but in Arizona's Maricopa County privacy went right out the window and into a Web cam, until suit was brought against Sheriff Joe Arpaio. For a time, anyone could view Maricopa County inmates in holding cells, search cells, and pre-intake areas via the jail's Web cam.

The Los Angeles Sheriff's Inmate Information Center (booking log), containing six months to one year of historical data, is available free on the Internet (**http://app1.lasd.org/iic/ajis_search.cfm**). Search by an arrestee's name and the following information will unfold: full name, gender, race, age, date of birth, weight, hair color, eye color, reason for arrest, bail amount, and housing location. Placing this free on the Internet should raise some privacy concerns. Even if the arrest is later found to be unwarranted, simply being in a booking log can taint a person's reputation.

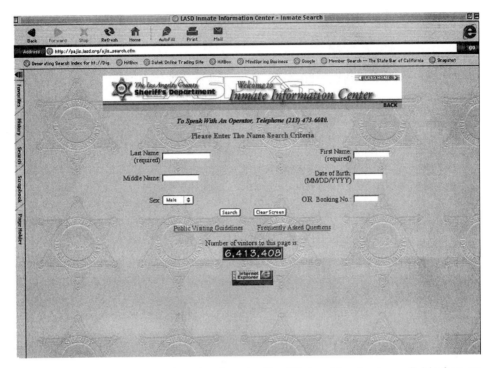

Figure 8-11. The Los Angeles County Sheriff's booking log is available free on the Internet. Visitors to the Web site can search by name for individuals who have been booked into custody.

Delinquent Parents

Access to a list (with pictures) of deadbeat dads (and moms) is available at Los Angeles County's Most Wanted Delinquent Parents site (**http://childsupport.co.la.ca.us/dlparents.htm**). This site announces to the world the name of the county's most delinquent parents, and provides the following details: amount owed, date of birth, race, height, weight, hair and eye color, number of children, and where last seen. When we visited, the most delinquent parent owed more than half a million dollars, and was last seen in Beverly Hills.

Outstanding Arrests

Florida Department of Law Enforcement Wanted Persons Search Page

http://pas.fdle.state.fl.us/wpersons_search.asp

Content: The Florida Department of Law Enforcement (FDLE) offers a free searchable database of outstanding criminal warrants in the state. Not every locale reports to the FDLE when they issue warrants, so the database is not comprehensive. Returned warrant results include full name, photo (if available), nature of offense, reporting agency, agency case number, date of warrant, warrant number, date warrant entered, date of birth, race, sex, hair and eye color, scars, marks or tattoos, occupation and last known address (at least the city and state).

Our View: Of course we'd prefer a comprehensive database. But the ability to search by so many possibilities is useful. You can search by:

- Last name
- First name
- Middle name or initial
- Nickname
- Race
- Sex
- Date of birth or age

Tip: Searches can be performed with as little information as just a last name or nickname. (A minimum of the first two characters of the last name or the exact nickname must be entered.)

Federal Inmates

The Federal Bureau of Prisons maintains a free database of all federal inmates from 1982 to present.

Federal Bureau of Prisons Inmate Locator

http://www.bop.gov

Purpose: To locate federal inmates.

Content: Contains all federal inmates from 1982 to present. The record shows name, age, race, sex, and date released.

Our View: Click on **Inmate Locator** listed in the left column. This is an easy-to-use database, with many search options. You can search the database using the inmate's register number, Detailed Case Data Component (DCDC) number, FBI number, immigration number, or just by using the inmate's first and last name.

Tip: You can't search by last name only. A first name is required.

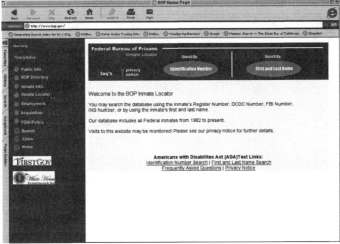

Figure 8-12. The BOP site contains all federal inmates from 1982 to the present.

Liens, Judgments, and UCCs

Besides providing information about a person's background (such as whether he failed to pay taxes, has had a judgment entered against him, and so on), these documents are also just one more place to find someone—because most of the documents include addresses.

There are two categories of liens: voluntary and involuntary. Voluntary liens are placed against a property or a person when the owner voluntarily pledges property (real or personal) as consideration for a mortgage or other obligation. Examples of voluntary liens are

- Deeds of trust or mortgage liens
- Notes
- Builder's or mechanic's liens
- Contracts for sale
- UCCs (usually UCC-1 Financing Statements—see **http://www .skipease.com/ucc.html** for a list of state UCC sites)

Involuntary liens are referred to as adverse filings. In this case, the person or company did not pledge something as consideration. Instead, there has been an adverse judgment filed against the person or his property if (1) he defaulted on an obligation to pay a lender or a governmental entity, such as a failure to pay taxes, or (2) he was on the losing side of a lawsuit and a judgment was filed against him. Examples of involuntary liens are

- Federal or state tax liens
- Mechanic's and materialman's liens
- Abstracts of judgment

Liens, judgments, and UCCs can be filed at the federal, state, or county level, so you need to search in many different places. For example, there are both federal tax liens and state tax liens, and county judgments and state judgments. Using SearchSystems.net, you can type in the word "liens" or "UCC" or "judgment," for example, and get a list of Web sites where you find documentation. Another search strategy is to use Search Systems' directory and view by state or county to discover whether liens, judgments, or UCCs are online at a particular jurisdiction. Some of the sites listed are free and some are pay. Some are searchable by document number only, while others allow for name searching (or other search criteria). Some provide limited information, while others provide the image of the original filing. Lexis, Westlaw, and other pay databases allow you to search liens, judgments, and UCCs in one fell swoop and across jurisdictions using the subject's name.

By using Search Systems' directory, we clicked on **Florida** and were pointed to the Sunbiz government site (**http://www.sunbiz.org/ corpweb/inquiry/search.html**), where we learned that the following documents can be searched in Florida at the state level: federal liens, UCCs, and judgment liens (we also learned that we could search trademarks, corporations, limited liability and general partnerships, limited partnerships, limited liability companies, and fictitious names). You can view summaries of the documents and the actual images of the original filings. Searching was very flexible and could be done by name or docket number. We searched the Judgment Lien database by debtor name and found the following information about a specific lien: (1) name and address of judgment creditor and debtor, (2) amount of lien, (3) amount of interest, (4) case number, (5) document number, (6) name of court, and (7) dates relating to the file date, date of entry, and expiration date. To determine if a writ of execution on a final judgment was docketed with a sheriff, you are instructed to click on the docket number to view the filing image.

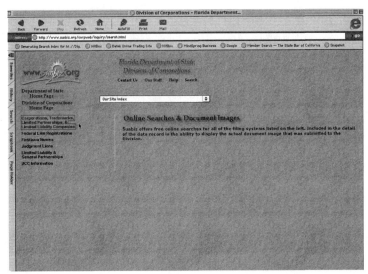

Figure 8-13. Users can search federal liens, UCCs, judgment liens, trademarks, corporate records, limited liability and general partnerships, limited partnerships, limited liability companies, and fictitious names at Florida's Sunbiz portal.

Bankruptcies

See the section "Court Dockets and Pleadings" later in this chapter.

Locating Assets

Real Property Records

When lawyers need to discover who owns a certain property, or discover its assessed value, or simply use the record to locate someone's address, Portico (**http://indorgs.virginia.edu/portico/personalproperty .html**), Search Systems (**http://www.searchsystems.net**), or the Tax Assessor Database (**http://www.pulawski.com**) can be used to quickly locate links to county assessors' offices that are free on the Web. The Tax Assessor Database site provides ratios of assessed value to market value by state and county as well as a phone number for each assessor's office.

There is no consistency in the varying states' and counties' policies regarding free access to real property records or the amount of information listed on the record once it's been found. Most free sites only permit address searches, but some do permit owner name searches. As an example of the varying policies between counties within one state, we'll use California; and as an example of a standard policy among all counties, we'll use Tennessee. In California, all but seven county assessor offices have placed some information on the Web (**http://www.pulawski.com/california .html**), and in Tennessee (**http://170.142.31.248**), ninety of ninety-five counties have (but one must still search county by county). In Los Angeles County, free searching by an address or assessor number is possible, but searching by a person's name is not (**http://www.lacountyassessor .com/extranet/default.asp**). Even after conducting an address or assessor number search at the Los Angeles County Assessor's site, the property owner's name is still not shown. In sharp contrast to California, Tennessee permits free searching by owner name. For prices of home sales (some back to 1987), see Domania.com (**http://www.domania.com**). Searching is by address only. Not all states and not all counties are in the database. Owner names are not shown.

Searching Pay Databases for Real Estate Records

Go directly to a pay site for real estate records in the following situations:

- After checking one or more of the sites that link to real estate assessor's offices (noted above), you learn that the jurisdiction does not have its real estate assessors' records online free
- When a county or state's free database only permits address searching but you only have a name
- When a county or state's free database permits address searching and you have the address, but the record does not display the owner—which is what you are seeking
- When you need to conduct a statewide (more than one county) or multistate real property search to marshal someone's real estate holdings

The cost to search property records in a pay database varies from database to database and the pricing even within one database can vary, depending on the type of search (for example, a search through a single state's records will cost less than multistate searching in some of the databases). So, do some comparison-shopping first. While all fifty states are represented in most of these databases, not every county is represented for each state. Some counties also include tax assessor deed transfer records in addition to mortgage records.

We've provided a list of pay databases that include real estate records online. The first four listed below are probably the least costly to search—but this could vary depending on individual contracts. We'll discuss two as examples: Lexis (**http://www.lexis.com**) and LexisONE (**http://www.lexisone.com**).

To use Lexis you must first have a subscription. Property records can be searched in a variety of ways—by county, by state, or by all states. You can also search by the property owner's name or address, and if you only know a partial name or address, you can use all of the special Lexis search features (Boolean connectors and wild cards) to try to find the record. For those who do not have an annual subscription to Lexis (or a subscription to the other databases), LexisONE is one of the few databases where you can access real property records on an as-needed basis by using your credit card. Unfortunately, you cannot conduct nationwide or multistate searches as annual Lexis subscribers can.

LexisONE is state-by-state searching only. Prices vary by state, but to use the public record database for one day can cost from $20 to $48. FlatRateInfo.com, as the name implies, offers a flat rate (as do some of the other databases listed below), so depending on the level of your use, it may cost less than going with a database that charges per search. The other databases below are priced at $1 per search and up.

- Accurint at **http://www.accurint.com**
- Merlin at **http://www.merlindata.com**
- ChoicePoint at **http://www.choicepoint.net**
- FlatRateInfo.com at **http://www.flatrateinfo.com**
- LexisONE at **http://www.lexisone.com**
- Lexis at **http://www.lexis.com**
- Westlaw at **http://www.westlaw.com**

Personal Property

In a search for assets, lawyers should not overlook assets that the subject himself has overlooked, such as unclaimed personal property. A lawyer who was owed money by a client (a lot of money!) found $32,000 by running the client's name through the California unclaimed personal property database. You can guess what the lawyer's next step was . . .

Unclaimed Property

Unclaimed.org

http://www.unclaimed.org

Purpose: To link to each state's unclaimed property database.

Content: Provides links to each state's unclaimed property database. Each state's database differs from the next. In some states the database record shows the amount of unclaimed property that the state is holding and in other states you'll need to contact the state by mail to find out. The property is usually money left in an old bank account, but it could be stocks, bonds, or safe-deposit contents. The site is sponsored by NAUPA (National Association of Unclaimed Property Administrators).

Our View: Searching for unclaimed money can be a laborious search if the person left a trail of unclaimed property throughout the U.S.—because you must search state by state in the free databases. On the other hand, every time we offer hands-on seminars, one or more people in the class find money they forgot they had by just searching one or two states (usually just where they have lived in the past) to hit pay dirt.

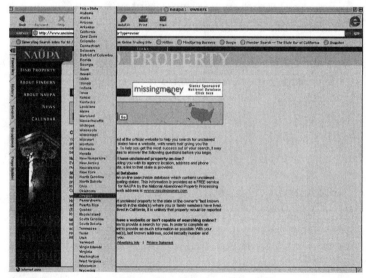

Figure 8-14. Search for money you (or your clients) forgot about. Unclaimed.org links to the custodian of unclaimed property in all fifty states.

Tip: • NAUPA also sponsors a free multistate searching database, MissingMoney.com, but it covers only about twelve states (For a list of states covered by Missing Money.com, see **http://www.missingmoney .com/Search/State_links.cfm**.) The pay database FlatRateInfo.com covers twenty-one states.
  • Ignore those e-mail messages offering to search

through unclaimed personal property databases in exchange for a percentage of anything found. The databases are public record, freely accessible on the Internet.

Boats and Airplanes

See Chapter 18, "Transportation Research," for public record information about boats and airplanes.

Drivers License Records and Driving History Records

The personal information about a driver (what is found on a driver's license) is not available free over the Web. While there are pay databases that have motor vehicle records, there are limitations to who can subscribe. In 1994, the Driver's Privacy Protection Act (DPPA), 18 U. S. C. 2725(3), placed many restrictions upon states' right to disclose or resell a driver's personal information without the driver's consent. Personal information under the DPPA is defined at 18 U. S. C. §2721(a) as "an individual's photograph, Social Security number, driver identification number, name, address (but not the 5-digit ZIP code), telephone number, and medical or disability information" but does not include "information on vehicular accidents, driving violations and driver's status." (As noted earlier in the "Criminal Records" section of this chapter, New Mexico, for instance, has placed DWI history for free on the Internet.) Consent by the driver for personal information is not required when the requestor falls within various exceptions (such as an insurer who needs the information for claims, rating, or underwriting, or for use in conjunction with a court or administrative proceeding).

Despite the passage of the DPPA in 1994, the state of South Carolina, up until the year 2000, considered driver's license records to be public and would hand them over the counter, for a fee, to anyone who wanted to see someone else's record. The only restriction was that the information could not be used for telephone solicitation. Selling motor vehicle information was big business for states; the state of Wisconsin used to receive approximately $8 million annually from the sale of motor vehicle information. During this same time frame, the state of California considered driver's license records to be private records. Finally, in 2000, the U.S. Supreme Court (*Reno v. Condon* at **http://caselaw.lp.findlaw.com/ scripts/getcase.pl?court=us&vol=000&invol=98-1464**) deemed them to be private under the DPPA, but as noted above, the DPPA does allow access to driver's license information, in specified instances, without the consumer's consent.

E-InfoData.com's e-DriverData.com database contains driving records from thirty-eight states and links directly to those states' motor vehicle records. But access is available only to members of the Association of Consumer Reporting Agencies (ACRA), a consortium of pre-employment screening companies. E-InfoData.com makes its Colorado motor vehicle and driver information records available to lawyers in a database called FastMVR.com (**http://www.e-infodata.com/fmvr.html**). Records are updated daily.

For more information about automobiles, see Chapter 18, "Transportation Research."

Other Assets

For the following public records that can be used to marshal assets or to locate people, see Chapter 19, "Entertainment Industry Research and Intellectual Property":

- Trademarks
- Patents
- Copyrights

For the following public records that can be used to marshal assets or to locate people, see Chapter 10, "Company Research":

- Stocks
- Security and Exchange Commission filings
- Corporate filings (registered agents)
- Fictitious business names

What's Your Political Persuasion (and Where Do You Work)?

An example of a database created by a nongovernment sponsor who uses data derived from government public records is Politicalmoneyline.com.

Political Money Line

http://www.politicalmoneyline.com

Purpose: Jury consultants use this database to determine potential jurors' political persuasions (assuming they have made contributions to candidates in the past twenty-three years and haven't changed their political allegiance). This site also works for finding people, especially work addresses or employer names.

Content: This site has gathered political contribution public records (from individuals who contribute over $200) back to 1980 and created a free searchable database for the public to search by donors' names. You can also search by ZIP code, employer, or occupation, and for out-of-state donors. There are various additional services for subscribers, such as enhanced searching and down loading capabilities ($99 to $2,500 annually).

Our View: Up until recently, it was a bit laborious to search each election year separately. We're happy to report that a combined search, which does take longer, is now available for election years 2004, 2002, and 2000.

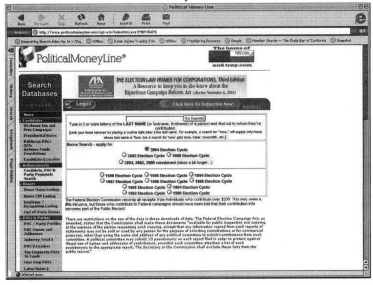

Figure 8-15. Search PoliticalMoneyLine.com to determine someone's political persuasion—if they've made a political contribution.

Tip: • If you have been unable to serve someone at a home address, this is a great place to identify someone's workplace because donors are supposed to list a mailing address and an employer and occupation. To reach this information, click on the **Image** link after pulling up a subject's record.

- To search by partial names, type in three or more letters of the last name (or last name, first name). This won't work with the first name. To limit your search to the exact name as typed, place a comma after it. For example, a search for "gold," will rule out "Goldstein," while a search for "gold" will include it.

- Some states have state political contribution records online. Check your state's home page to see if the state's election board has a database available. In Alaska, this data is searchable at the Alaska Public Offices Commission (**https://webapp.state.ak.us/ apoc/index.jsp**).

Court Dockets and Pleadings

When you think about uses for court dockets and pleadings, you probably think about their use as legal research tools. But, they also can be used for all types of factual research by lawyers, legal administrators, law librarians, paralegals, or members of the firm's marketing or recruiting departments. What used to require a trip to the courthouse to retrieve the docket sheet (and then usually a return trip to copy the chosen pleadings off the docket sheet) now has become an easier task because of Internet access to docket sheets and in some cases even the full text of some of the pleadings. The following are some of the uses of dockets for factual research.

Using Dockets for Research

Using Dockets for Backgrounding

Dockets are useful for backgrounding people. Enter the name of a prospective client (or the opposing party, and so on) to learn

- How litigious the person is
- What type of suits the prospective client been involved in
- Which lawyers the person has retained in the past
- Whether a prospective client has filed any lawyer malpractice lawsuits
- Whether a prospective client has been sued for lawyer's fees

Although this only works with docket databases that have a field for searching by judge, enter the name of a judge to learn

- What types of cases he or she typically hears
- How the judge typically ruled in the past on specific matters or issues (such as summary judgment motions, motion for new trials, and so on)

Although this only works with docket databases that have a field for searching by lawyer, enter the name of an opposing lawyer (or even a lawyer you want to recruit) to learn

- What types of cases the lawyer typically handles
- Who the lawyer typically represents

Using Dockets for Conducting Due Diligence

Protect yourself by discovering if a prospective client or partner has been involved in a bankruptcy or any type of fraud. Also, protect a current client who seeks your advice about whether to go into business with someone—by backgrounding the potential business partner. Search bankruptcy dockets in particular.

Using Dockets for Current Awareness and Client Development and Retention

Dockets can help you answer the following questions:

- Who is suing whom?
- Who is representing whom?
- Is it time to shift your area of practice to the hot practice areas? Review the types of cases being filed to figure this out. Learn which lawyers are handling the hot practice areas (for recruiting purposes).
- Is a current or former client being sued and doesn't know it? Review local dockets regularly to keep clients apprised.

Using Dockets to Locate Pleadings

Dockets can be used to help you draft pleadings by providing sample pleadings from cases similar to yours. For example, in a recent instance, a firm needed to file a motion to freeze assets (the day before the New Year's Eve holiday). Since time was of the essence, the firm wanted to locate a similar motion to pattern theirs after instead of drafting one from scratch.

Knowing of a similar case, the firm was able to pinpoint a useful motion with a quick check of that case's docket online. A messenger was then sent to the courthouse to make a copy of the motion for use as a sample.

Search docket sheets online to identify a pleading missing from your file. If the court has placed the pleading on the Internet for immediate download, you can even avoid sending a messenger to the courthouse to retrieve it.

Which Courts Have Placed Dockets on the Internet?

First of all, no blanket statement can be made as to the ready availability of dockets on the Internet. Every court is different and the rules are constantly changing. Some courts are currently:

- Providing free access
- Providing free access, but requiring a password
- Charging a fee for access
- Providing no electronic access at all
- Allowing access to both civil and criminal dockets
- Limiting access to civil dockets only
- Placing images of the pleadings online for immediate download

Privacy Concerns

Courts limiting the type of dockets and pleadings placed on the Internet are basing their decision on the need to protect a litigant's privacy in general, to protect privacy in specific types of cases such as family law where minors' names are given, or to comply with confidentiality laws (for example, in juvenile law cases). Courts are also concerned with identity theft. The federal and state courts are each drafting their own access rules, typically differentiating between the three access points to court records: (1) in-person access to the paper copy at the courthouse; (2) in-person access to the digital records via public computers located at the courthouse; and (3) remote access to digital records via the Internet.

While some courts place documents online that others would not, they might attempt to at least insure privacy for the more sensitive information found in the documents by allowing the litigants to redact the information (but in the electronic file *only*). Sensitive information (which the federal courts label as personal data identifiers) refers to Social Security numbers, dates of birth, financial account numbers, and names of minor children. This is the policy the federal courts are following for civil and bankruptcy cases.

Federal Court Privacy Policy on Case Files

In 2001, the Judicial Conference of the United States' Committee on Court Administration and Case Management recommended that the personal identifier data be redacted from any federal case files to which the public has remote electronic access, and that criminal case files not be placed on the Internet at all. As for Social Security numbers, only the last four digits could remain on the documents. The policy is not retroactive, so you will see personal identifier data in older electronic case files. The Committee explained that a "case file" (whether electronic or paper) means the collection of documents officially filed by the litigants or the court in the context of litigation, the docket entries that catalog such filings, and transcripts of judicial proceedings" (**http://www.privacy .uscourts.gov/Policy.htm**). In March 2002, the Judicial Conference adopted two modifications to the prohibition on remote public access to electronic criminal case files: (1) allowing high-profile cases to be remotely accessed by the public where demand for copies of documents places an undue burden on the clerk's office, and if the parties have consented and the judge finds access is warranted; and (2) creating a pilot project to allow some courts to return to the level of remote public access that they provided prior to the Conference adoption of the policy restricting access.

Finding Dockets and Pleadings

To discover which courts' docket sheets, pleadings, and case records are available online, use docket metasites such as the free LLRX.com site or the fee-based Legal Dockets Online (LDO) site.

LLRX Court Rules, Forms and Dockets

http://www.llrx.com/courtrules

Purpose: To discover which courts' dockets are available on the Internet.

Content: Search and link to all federal, state, and local dockets
                available on the Internet either by using keyword
                searching or browsing by court type (such as tax court),
                by jurisdiction (federal or state) or by state (choose a spe-
                cific state to view a list of all fed-eral and state courts
                located in that state). Links are annotated with useful
                information. For example, for federal courts you are told
                which docket system each uses (Web PACER, RACER,
                CM/ECF) and for state courts you are told if document
                images are available for immediate downloading.

Our View: We find the annotations useful, such as "Search by case
                number only." We also like the various search functions
                and the price: free.

Tip: This court docket database also includes links to court
                rules and court forms available on the Internet (for a
                total of over fourteen hundred sources).

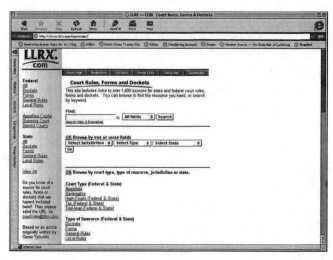

Figure 8-16. You can search or browse for court rules in a variety of ways, such
as by jurisdiction or court type **http://www.llrx.com/courtrules/.**
© **Law Library Resource Xchange, LLC**.

Legal Dockets Online (LDO)

http://www.legaldockets.com

Purpose: To discover which courts' dockets are available on the Internet.

Content: While LDO's links are browsable by state only, they also include the same types of annotations as LLRX (such as noting the type of docket system each federal court uses, and if state court dockets provide images for immediate downloading). Individual subscribers are charged $120 per year, while an entire firm is charged $1,200 per year. (A free one-week trial is available.)

Our View: Although LDO is a pay site and LLRX is free, there are two functions we like about LDO that may prompt you to subscribe: (1) subscribers receive an e-mail alert each time LDO finds a new online docket site, and (2) LDO immediately alerts you to the free sites (saving time and money) by its **FREE** notation in the left margin, in all caps and red type.

Tip: LDO also links to case information, calendars, new filings, inmate databases, and Stanford University's Securities Law database.

Between LLRX and LDO, which of these sources would we use? We'd probably use both since each one offers some information that the other doesn't. However, even taken together, neither one is 100 percent comprehensive. For instance, we did not find the Los Angeles County Bar Association Civil Register database at either site.

Federal Dockets and Case Records

PACER (Public Access to Court Electronic Records) is the federal government's pay docket site. Not all federal courts participate in the PACER program. Some federal courts still offer free dockets, and according to LDO, these include:

- U.S. Bankruptcy Court for the District of Delaware (documents before July 28, 2001)
- U.S. District and Bankruptcy Courts for the District of Idaho
- U.S. District Court for the Southern District of Indiana (civil cases filed before June 1, 2002, and all criminal cases)
- U.S. Bankruptcy Court for the District of Minnesota

- U.S. Bankruptcy Court for the Eastern District of North Carolina
- U.S. Bankruptcy Court for the Western District of Oklahoma
- U.S. Bankruptcy Court for the Eastern District of Washington
- U.S. Court of Appeals, Seventh Circuit
- U.S. Supreme Court
- U.S. Court of Appeals for Veterans Claims
- U.S. Tax Court

PACER (Public Access to Court Electronic Records)

http://pacer.psc.uscourts.gov
(PACER home page; use this to register)

http://pacer.psc.uscourts.gov/cgi-bin/links.pl (the list of Web PACER courts, what system they use, and whether they have images for immediate download)

Purpose: To allow access to federal case and docket information (and sometimes images of the documents themselves) in all approved federal judiciary electronic public access programs (PACER, RACER, CM/ECF, and the U.S. Party Case Index). Covers U.S. district, appellate, and bankruptcy court dockets.

Content: The PACER Service Center serves only as the judiciary's centralized registration, billing, and technical support center, which you need to contact for a login name and password (issued free). There is no annual charge; you are billed quarterly for your transactions, but no fee is owed until a user accrues more than $10.00 worth of charges in a calendar year. The charges are $0.07 per page for Internet PACER or $0.60 per minute for direct dial-in access.

Our View: PACER is the most economical, but can sometimes be cumbersome because each court maintains its own internal electronic case management system and its own

unique URL (or in some unfortunate cases, a modem
number for dial-in access only).

Tip:
- For those who bill their clients, a client code of your choosing can be entered each time you log intoPACER.
- At $0.07 per page, you can't beat the price of PACER, so you might start your search here before using any pay databases.
- Use pay databases when you need more user-friendly search options and to set up automatic alerts. (Information about fee-based databases is discussed later in this section).
- Because some courts do provide case information on the Internet without support by PACER, check the individual court's home page at **http://www.uscourts .gov/links.html**.
- Aside from each individual court's docket database, PACER also includes the U.S. Party Case Index, which might be your first step if you want to do a broad search to find a party's dockets in more than one court.

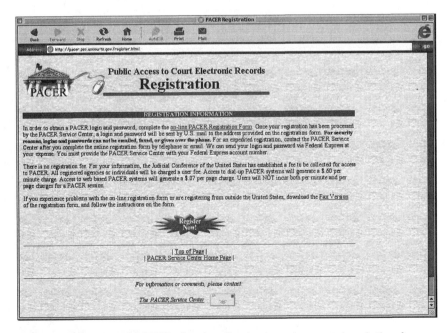

Figure 8-17. Visit PACER's Service Center to set up a subscription for access to federal court dockets.

PACER U.S. Party Case Index

http://pacer.uspci.uscourts.gov   **$**

> (Log on to the index by clicking on the large blue box that says **U.S. Party/Case Index** or by clicking on the very small **Enter U.S. Party/Case Index** link directly under the blue box.)

Purpose: To search federal filings "nationwide" and to link to . various types of courts.

Content: The Index displays the party name, court, case number, and filing date.

> You can search all courts by an individual's name (enter the last name first and the first name second (Brown, David) or by a business name (David Brown Engraving). You can also limit the all-courts search by date filed or you can change the all-courts search to search by a region or state.

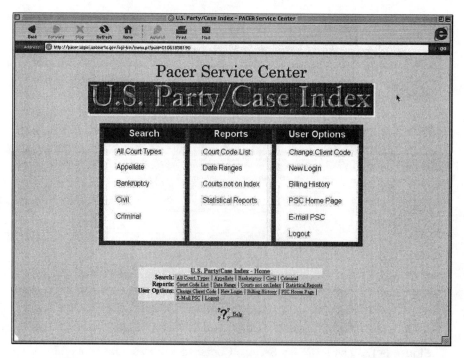

Figure 8-18. Search all court types or select a specific type, such as bankruptcy.

Our View:	Though the Index is labeled a "nationwide" locator index of federal filings, we place nationwide in quotation marks because, as noted above, not all courts participate. Although it's not a truly national index, it's the best we've got.
Tip:	For a list of nonparticipating courts, see **http://pacer.psc.uscourts.gov/cgi-bin/miss-court.pl**. In some states, all federal courts participate in the Index (California, for example).

Federal Dockets: Bankruptcy Courts

PACER Bankruptcy Case Information

http://pacer.uspci.uscourts.gov (select Bankruptcy) **$**

Purpose:	To find out if a prospective client, prospective partner, or the opposing party has filed for bankruptcy in the past, and to monitor the progress of a bankruptcy.
Content:	Search the "nationwide" bankruptcy index by party name (person or company), Social Security number, case number, or tax identification number (TIN). You will be able to view case information; names of parties, lawyers, and judges; claims; schedules and deadline information; and docket entries. Personal data identifiers (Social Security numbers, dates of birth, financial account numbers, and names of minor children) can be modified or partially redacted by the litigants.
Our View:	Though useful, there are still six bankruptcy courts that do not participate (for a list see **http://pacer.pcc.uscourts.gov/cgi-bin/miss-cart.pl puid=01049751733**).
Tip:	There are sample PACER Bankruptcy Case Information dockets to view at **http://pacer.psc.uscourts.gov/ksamples/bkcase.html**.

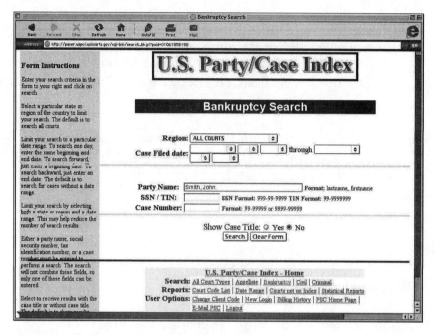

Figure 8-19. Search by a name, Social Security number, or docket number to discover bankruptcies in any bankruptcy court.

Federal Dockets: Appellate and District Courts

PACER Appellate Courts and District Courts

http://pacer.uspci.uscourts.gov

(Select **Appellate** to search the circuit courts, select **Civil** to search the civil district courts, select **Criminal** to search the criminal district courts.)

Purpose: To find U.S. appellate or district cases and dockets by party name or docket number. The appellate and civil - district courts are searchable by NOS (nature of the suit) while the criminal district cases are not. The NOS search can be useful for client development and current awareness.

Content: You can search **all circuits** (which actually includes only the First, Third, Sixth, Eighth, Ninth, Tenth, and District of Columbia Circuits) or you can search an individual circuit. For district courts, you can search a specific state or its individual districts within the state (if that state has more than one district court). You can search by name or case number, and you can also limit the search by date filed. For the appellate and civil district courts only, you can conduct a NOS search or combined party name-NOS search.

Our View:	It may be hard to know if you have the correct party since so many people share the same name. Therefore, if you have the docket number, search by number rather than party name. If you don't have a docket number, try to limit the party search by selecting a specific circuit or a date.
Tip:	• There is a detailed NOS listing on the search screen (see below) for you to review and select one NOS, a NOS range, or more than one NOS.
	• There are five district courts in five states that do not participate (for a list see **http://pacer.uspci.uscourts .gov/cgi-bin/crtmiss.pl?puid=01049751733**).

Federal Dockets: NOS Searching

PACER Nature of Suit Codes

http://pacer.psc.uscourts.gov/natsuit.html

Purpose:	For topical current awareness or to find other cases like yours for sample pleadings—for instance, a personal injury lawyer specializing in airline crashes can search NOS code 310 (airplane) to keep abreast of every personal injury suit filed involving airplanes or to locate samples of pleadings for a current lawsuit.
Content:	PACER allows you to search for cases by the NOS code, a subject matter categorization of federal civil cases. Categories and codes are listed at the above URL.

Our View: The site is easy to use, but not all lawsuits are categorized the way you might think they should be, so you might miss something useful.

Tip: While NOS searches must be conducted manually at the government's free PACER site, they can be set up to run automatically at some of the pay sites such as CourtEX-PRESS (**http://www.courtexpress.com**) or CourtLink, which is accessible through LexisNexis (see **http://www.lexisnexis.com/courtlink/online/default .asp**).

By 2005, CM/ECF (Case Management/Electronic Case Files) will replace each federal court's internal electronic case management system (and will also provide for electronic filing). At that time, assuming all courts participate, we will have a national docket lookup. See **http://www.uscourts.gov/Press_Releases/pacer.html** for details.

U.S. Supreme Court Dockets

U.S. Supreme Court Dockets

http://www.supremecourtus.gov/docket/docket.html

Purpose: To retrieve current Supreme Court dockets.

Content: The U.S. Supreme Court is not part of the PACER system. Only the current and prior term dockets are archived.

Our View: The database has good search functionality. Search by docket number (the Supreme Court or lower court), by case name, or by any word or phrase (such as a lawyer's name).

Tip: For more background information about the facts of a case or the parties, see FindLaw's Supreme Court Center

to view briefs back to 1999 (**http://supreme.lp
.findlaw.com/supremecourt/resources.html**).

Commercial Docket Databases

Why use a commercial service if you have free or low-cost access to
federal and state court dockets at some of the courts' Web sites or on
PACER? Although the commercial databases obtain the dockets from the
courts, they then create user-friendly searchable databases, with extra
functions, instead of merely providing a gateway to the court site. (Note
that these searchable databases are typically available only for federal
dockets). This allows you to search by more options than the official court
sites, which usually allow searching only by docket number (although
some do allow party name or lawyer name searching). Some of the major
commercial docket vendors are CourtLink (Lexis), CourtEXPRESS, West
Dockets, and Courthouse News Service.

The following are some of the reasons to use pay docket sites:

- Better search functions: besides party name and docket number,
  search by lawyer name, judge name, subject or keyword
- Alert functions: set up automated case tracking of a specific case or
  any case involving a specific party, lawyer, judge, NOS, and so on
- Older archives: at some time of the commercial sites, dockets are
  not taken off line, so you may be able to find a docket that has
  already been taken off of the courts' official site and archived off
  line by the court
- Document ordering: you can order copies of documents from commercial sites (they can be mailed, sent by Federal Express, e-mailed,
  or faxed)

Using the Alert Function on Commercial Docket Sites

Setting up an automatic alert with a commercial docket vendor to
track specific cases, clients, types of cases (using the NOS), or all new complaints filed in specific courts can assist you with your business development efforts and in maintaining ongoing client relations. For example, a
NOS alert can help you with your business development efforts by alert-
ing you to who is being sued in specific practice areas or to alert you to
hot practice areas that the firm might want to develop. Setting up a new
complaints alert allows you to warn ongoing clients about any complaints
filed against them—but not yet served. Alerts can be set up with the various pay docket vendors profiled below.

Commercial Docket Vendors

Courthouse News Service

http://www.courthousenews.com

Purpose: To track newly filed complaints for business and client development and to maintain ongoing client relations. Lawyers can warn ongoing clients about any complaints filed against the client, but not yet served.

Content: This fee-based site e-mails a daily summary of new cases filed in several federal and state courts. The summary includes the case caption, a brief description of the issues and facts involved, and the name of each party's lawyer. Courthouse News Service covers various state and federal courts in the following jurisdictions: Arizona, California (Los Angeles County Superior Court), Connecticut, Delaware, Florida, Illinois, Massachusetts, North Carolina, New Jersey, New York, Nevada (federal and state courts in Las Vegas), Pennsylvania, Texas, and Washington. For a complete list of specific courts covered by Courthouse News see **http://www.courthouse news.com/subinfo.html**.

Our View: If your court is one of those included, you'll find this a useful service. Many large law firms use this service.

Tip: If the complaint is available for immediate download, this will be indicated; otherwise, phone Courthouse News to request a fax of the complaint.

CourtLink (part of LexisNexis)

https://courtlink.lexisnexis.com
(for those with a Lexis account, use **http://www.lexis.com**)

Purpose: To access dockets for current awareness, business and client development, client retention, backgrounding people (judges, lawyers, clients, opposition), conducting due diligence (in particular to search for past bankruptcies), and to put your hands on missing pleadings or locate sample pleadings in similar cases.

Content: The site provides online access to dockets in over forty-five hundred courts, covering ten to twenty years' worth of cases, from federal district courts (civil and criminal) and bankruptcy courts, U.S. Courts of Appeals, and U.S. Claims Court; and online real-time access to all or parts of nineteen states. The federal district dockets (including bankruptcy) are in a searchable database. (CourtLink does not offer online access to U.S. Supreme Court dockets or the U.S. Tax Court). CourtLink claims to go back further in time than other services and to have more state and local coverage. CourtLink offers transactional and subscription pricing. There are two types of searches: (1) **Advanced Database Searching** covering federal district courts (including bankruptcy) and the Delaware Chancery Court, and (2) **Direct Access** covering state and local dockets (other than Delaware). For courts that fall within the **Advanced Database Searching** system, CourtLink downloads dockets each evening and creates a searchable database, so the searcher is not using CourtLink as a gateway to PACER. For the state and local courts that are accessible through the **Direct Access** system, no searchable database has been created. Instead, CourtLink dials into the courts and users can search only by docket number (or party name, depending on how the court has set up their database). You can also set up **Alerts** and **Tracks** to receive an e-mail message anytime a filing matches your search criteria. Create an alert for federal district courts, bankruptcy courts, and Delaware Chancery based on the following criteria: (1) all new filings in selected courts (or further limit by subject in the selected court); (2) lawsuits involving a specific practice area, litigant name, lawyer name, judge name, or debtor name; (3) class actions (all, or limit by court or subject); or (4) bankruptcy chapters (such as a search for all Chapter 7 filings). Create a **track** to watch specific cases by docket number in nineteen states in federal district courts, bankruptcy courts, U.S. Claims Court, U.S. Courts of Appeals, and selected state courts. In Connecticut and New Jersey you can track all superior courts, but in California, you can track only five of the fifty-eight county superior courts. Choose daily, weekly, or monthly notification. Pricing varies on the frequency of notification and the court chosen. For example, tracking on a daily basis in federal district court costs $5.00 per day, while the cost is $12.50 for a New Jersey state case. A monthly notification is $10.00 for a federal district court, and $18.50 for New Jersey.

Another search function in CourtLink is **Docket Smart**, which allows you to search for a name (of a party, lawyer, or judge) through all federal civil courts.

Our View: The site is not always intuitive. Some of the navigation could be clearer. For example, to search the federal case docket database, you must know to select **Search** from the home page. For the courts that are only searchable by docket number or party name (mostly state and local), researchers must know to select **Retrieve**. An infrequent user may not know to do this and may make the mistake (as we did) of clicking on **Search** and then selecting **State**, and then wondering why a local state court did not appear in the state's drop down menu. Another example of the site not always being intuitive is that in order to view the full bankruptcy docket, you need to click on **Update Full Docket** (for $9) and then **Case Results**. Since we knew that the case we were searching for had been closed in 2000, we didn't think that we needed to "update" the case so we ignored the **Update Full Docket** option and missed viewing the full docket.

Tip: • Of the major federal docket databases, only CourtLink includes bankruptcy dockets in its searchable database.
       • To retrieve any of the documents from the docket

sheet, users used to be referred to outside vendors but now you can order directly from CourtLink.

- More courts are added all the time, so check back frequently (for a full list of state courts, see **http://www .lexisnexis.com/literature/pdfs/CourtsFullState.pdf**; for a full list of federal courts, see **http://www.lexis nexis.com/literature/pdfs/CourtsFullFederal.pdf**).

CourtEXPRESS

http://www.courtexpress.com

Purpose: To access dockets for current awareness, business and client development, client retention, or backgrounding people (judges, lawyers, clients, opposition); to conduct due diligence; to put your hands on missing pleadings; or to locate sample pleadings in similar cases.

Content: CourtEXPRESS has docket content and services somewhat similar to CourtLink in that they have dockets from the following courts: federal district courts (civil and criminal) in a searchable database, gateways to the bankruptcy courts (note that CourtLink has a database for the bankruptcy courts), U.S. Courts of Appeals, and U.S. Claims Court. In addition, CourtEXPRESS also searches a few courts that CourtLink does not: the U.S. Supreme Court (by docket number only) and the U.S. Tax Court. Aside from the federal courts, CourtEXPRESS has direct or indirect access to thirty-five hundred state and local courts. For indirect access, although the searcher enters the search online, a CourtEXPRESS help desk employee actually runs the search by dialing into the court. After you enter a search, you can continue on with your usual multitasking and you will be notified by e-mail when the search is complete. Document delivery and research are also available. After selecting a court to search for dockets, enter a case name or docket number.

You also have the option of limiting your search to specific keywords that might appear in the docket when searching the U.S. District Courts and U.S. Courts of Appeals. The cost to search is $8 and up. Dates of coverage vary from court to court but may go back as far as the 1980s. Select **Clear Case** to search the federal district court docket database. There are many more search parameters in this database than in any of the other services of CourtEXPRESS. For instance, you can search by litigant, lawyer, firm, judge, keywords, phrases, case number, and case status (to limit the search to open or closed cases).

The following CourtEXPRESS alert and monitoring services are available for various federal courts, as noted:

- **Case Tracker** allows you to track specific cases by court and case number (courts that can be searched are the U.S. Supreme Court, U.S. Circuit Courts of Appeals, U.S. District Courts, U.S. Bankruptcy Courts, and selected state courts).
- **Due Diligence** (priced at $25) provides a historic federal litigation report about any individual or company and searches the U.S. Circuit Courts of Appeals, U.S. District Courts (civil and criminal), and U.S. Bankruptcy Courts; a recurring alert may also be set up.
- **Rain Maker** allows you to search federal civil dockets (U.S. Circuit Courts of Appeals and U.S. District Courts) by NOS to prospect for clients in your practice area.

The following watches and alerts are for federal district courts only:

- **Client Watch** allows you to learn about newly filed federal civil complaints relating to existing or prospective clients by party name or NOS searching.
- **Criminal Alert** alerts you to newly filed federal criminal dockets by party name.
- **Antitrust Alert** allows you to monitor, by party name, recently filed federal antitrust cases.

- **Class Action Alerts** notifies you of class action case.
- **Attorney/Firm Alert** alerts you when a lawyer or firm files a new federal court case; it can also be narrowed down to searching for a specific NOS connected to a specific lawyer or firm name.

Our View: We agree with Chuck Chandler, Vice President of Sales & Marketing for CourtEXPRESS, that searching for dockets online, and then being able to order the underlying documents online from the same company is convenient to rushed researchers and also to their billing departments, since the charge is bundled in one invoice. Another added convenience is being able to track the order online much like you can track the status of a UPS delivery. Order directly from CourtEXPRESS's **One-Source/OrderTrack** document ordering and online tracking order service. The document will be e-mailed as a PDF or delivered by Federal Express, fax, or messenger (usually within one day), or you can request a phone call first before deciding on the delivery method. The cost is $79.00 per document plus $0.75 per page for photocopying. About 30 of the 130 courts on CourtEXPRESS make PDFs of their documents available online for immediate download. In that case, CourtEXPRESS informs you of this capability and you can immediately download the document via CourtEXPRESS for $0.25 per page instead of ordering a hard copy of the document.

Tip: Do the math! For those who wonder how this fee compares to working directly with a local retrieval service, everyone needs to do their own math. Barry Berkowitz, president of Now Legal Services in Los Angeles, reported that the cost to retrieve a document from the downtown Los Angeles courthouse is $35.00 per hour, plus $0.57 per page to copy, plus $1.00 per mile to deliver the document. For delivery via fax or e-mail, the charge is $1.00 per page. Thus, the cost could fluctuate widely each time you need a document, depending on the length of the document, the degree of difficulty in obtaining the document (fifteen minutes is the usual time frame, but it could be more if the document is not yet available), and where the document needs to be delivered.

WestDockets

http://www.westlaw.com

Purpose: To access dockets for current awareness, business and client development, client retention, or backgrounding people (judges, lawyers, clients, opposition); to conduct due diligence; to put your hands on missing pleadings; or to locate sample pleadings in similar cases.

Content: The site covers the U.S. Courts of Appeals, U.S. District Courts, U.S. Bankruptcy Courts, U.S. Court of Federal Claims and various states (such as New York Supreme Court civil cases, Riverside County in California, and more). It does not cover the U.S. Supreme Court and the U.S. Tax Court.

Our View: WestDockets is a fairly new system. Westlaw subscribers used to access dockets by using the Westlaw gateway to CourtLink until CourtLink was purchased by Lexis. At first, WestDockets was simply a gateway to PACER. Now, WestDockets has added more courts and is more than a gateway to PACER. West developed a searchable dockets database (based upon the Westlaw platform) for the following courts: U.S. District Courts, the Federal Court of Claims, and New York courts. If you are paying by the transaction, the cost is $30 per search, plus $5 per docket sheet and $5 to update the docket (if necessary). WestDockets does not yet offer some of the services that the other docket databases offer, such as access to downloadable pleadings and document delivery. However, if you're interested in setting up alerts or being able, in selected courts, to keyword search with Westlaw terms and connectors (which also include field restrictors), then WestDockets is useful. The docket searching should be very easy for long-term Westlaw users (or really for anyone; we found the searching very easy). For example, to locate all negligence cases where Michael Pressman was the attorney of record, click on **Terms and Connectors** and search for the name "Pressman" in the attorney field and the term "Negligence" in the case type field. The search would look like this: at(pressman) & ctp(negligence), with "at" standing for the attorney field and "ctp" standing for case type. There are twenty-one fields to choose from.

Here is how each court's dockets can be searched:

- Federal District Court cases: party, docket number, lawyer, judge (plus terms and connectors)
- Federal Courts of Appeals: name, docket number
- Court of Claims: party, docket number, lawyer, judge (plus terms and connectors)
- New York County Clerk Civil Cases and New York Supreme Court Civil Cases: name (plaintiff, defendant, or judge), index or docket number (plus terms and connectors)
- New York Judgment and Lien Book Records: debtor, creditor, docket (plus terms and connectors)
- Riverside County, California (civil and criminal): name, docket number
- Florida, Miami-Dade County: party, plaintiff, defendant, docket number, county (plus terms and connectors)
- Florida, Brevard County (civil and criminal): party, docket number
- U.S. Bankruptcy Courts: party name, Social Security number, docket number

The alert function is called **West Dockets Alert** (found in the **More** drop-down menu on the right side of the screen). Alerts can be set up in some of the federal courts (civil and criminal cases) and in the New York state supreme courts (for civil cases). There are two types of alerts: the first type of alert can be set up for a specific case (by its docket number) in the U.S. District

Courts, U.S. Bankruptcy Courts, or U.S. Courts of Appeals; the second type of alert can be set up for new cases (by party, judge, lawyer, or NOS) in federal district courts, federal claims court, or New York state courts.

Tip:
- We had a hard time figuring out how to bring up the **Terms and Connectors** template. At the bottom of the main docket search template, there is a note that says, "Full text searching is now available through the **Terms and Connectors** Query Editor" but there was no link there or explanation as to what a query editor was. But, if you scroll back up to the top you'll see a Terms and Connectors link. Once you've learned how to bring this template up on your screen, it's simple to use.
- If you only need to pull a known docket, it's less expensive to use PACER. You also will need to use PACER (or the other docket databases) if you want to investigate whether a certain pleading is available for immediate download. If you want to order any of the underlying pleadings, the other docket databases will need to be used.
- WestDockets is a work in progress. Look for future improvements, says Marc Luther, Product Manager of WestDockets.

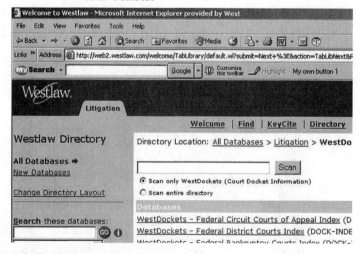

Figure 8-20. West Dockets offers many Federal Court Dockets and is continually adding State Court dockets.

Do You Need Access to All the Docket Databases?

In a recent law library online community posting, it was made apparent that we still need access to all the docket databases out there. Case in point: in a search to download a bankruptcy court pleading from the Delaware bankruptcy court, a librarian found the docket on PACER, but could not (for unknown technical reasons) download one of the pleadings listed on the docket sheet. Every time she clicked on the hypertext document number she was rewarded with only a blank page. She then proceeded to CourtEXPRESS, found the docket, but did not see any indication that she could download the pleadings. Finally, she proceeded to CourtLink and had success. Why? The answer is that CourtLink downloads dockets and pleadings every evening to create a searchable database, and is not dependent on PACER (except for same-day dockets and pleadings); thus, even though PACER was not working correctly, CourtLink came through since their system didn't have to dial in to PACER. Had the librarian needed a docket or pleading filed that day, she would not have succeeded at CourtLink either. The reason she had no luck at CourtEXPRESS is because CourtEXPRESS does not download bankruptcy dockets and pleadings into a searchable database—only federal district dockets and pleadings. So, if the PACER bankruptcy court system is not working correctly, then neither would CourtEXPRESS. This is not to say that CourtLink always comes through and CourtEXPRESS never does! The librarian stated that in similar situations she has found that sometimes PACER is the winner, other times CourtEXPRESS is the winner, and other times CourtLink is. In the final words of the librarian, "It seems you have to maintain all three so they can back up one another." And, a final word of caution: most courts have disclaimers on their docket databases that the database is "for information purposes only" and that only the clerk's transcript is the official transcript.

State and Local Court Dockets

Many state and local courts are placing their dockets on line. For example, the California Supreme Court and Appellate Court have free access to their dockets, and the New York trial-level courts also provide free access. Some courts provide docket number searching only, while others are more flexible and allow for searching by lawyer name and party name, for example.

The state courts are not bound by the rules and policies promulgated by the Judicial Conference of the United States' Committee on Court

Administration and Case Management regarding access to electronic court documents discussed earlier. Instead, the National Center for State Courts and the Justice Management Institute (at the behest of the Conference of Chief Justices and the Conference of State Court Administrators [CCJ/COSCA]) produced a model policy, "Developing CCJ/COSCA Guidelines for Public Access to Court Records: A National Project to Assist State Courts" (see **http://www.courtaccess.org/modelpolicy/18Oct2002Final Report.pdf**). The policy, which seeks to provide a consistent way to access electronic court documents in each state, advocates access to electronic court records. However, it seeks to limit access to any information in court documents that is not already accessible to the public pursuant to federal or state law, court rule, or case law. The policy was endorsed by CCJ/COSCA on August 1, 2002.

For individual state courts' public access policies, see **http://www.courtaccess.org/states.htm**. To ascertain whether a court has its dockets online, use LLRX.com or Legal Dockets Online (both described above) or FindLaw's state directory (go to **http://www.findlaw.com/11stategov**, choose a state, and then click on **Courts**).

While all sixty-two counties in New York have online dockets searchable from a unified system for free (see the New York E.Courts site described below), Texas has the opposite. First, not all Texas county courts are even online, and second, some counties that are online charge a fee to search dockets (such as Dallas County). In California, it's every county court for itself—there's no unified docket site, so the parameters of docket searching vary from county to county. For instance, in Los Angeles County the court does not permit anything but docket number searching, while some of the other counties in California allow party name searching. In addition to New York, the following states have a unified docket system that can be searched on the Internet: Alabama, Arizona, Colorado, Connecticut, Iowa, Missouri, Oklahoma, Rhode Island, Utah, Virginia, Washington, and Wisconsin.

New York E.Courts

http://e.courts.state.ny.us

Purpose: To background judges, lawyers, and parties by searching dockets (and online decisions) using names as your search terms.

Content: At the New York E.Courts site, you can look up Supreme Court civil court case information in all sixty-two counties, search the Supreme Court calendars, and search for the next court appearance in a criminal case. You can also track specific cases online and be automatically notified of any change in a case. Case information is updated four times daily and is searchable by:

- Firm or lawyer name
- Index number
- Plaintiff
- Defendant
- Supreme court calendars (by justice)
- Supreme court calendars (by part—choose a county first)

The following is just some of the data displayed once a case is selected to view:

- Names of lawyer or firm (and contact information), justice, plaintiff, and defendant
- County
- Index number
- Appearance date
- Activity count

In some counties, cases can even be filed on the Internet.

Our View: We're impressed by a unified system like this where all counties in the state are participating. Although we are also impressed with the robust search engine, better examples are needed to explain search parameters. For instance, there is no information as to how proper names should be searched (last name first and first name last, or vice-versa?). We had better luck searching last name first and first name last for plaintiff and defendant, and just the opposite for a lawyer name search.

Tip: Over 115,930 decisions from 16 counties are online (indicated by a Book icon when viewing the case information) and are full-text searchable by clicking on **On-Line Decisions**.

Pay Databases for Public Records and Publicly Available Information

While most of the data in this book is about information found at free sites, we are including this chapter on pay sites because, as we noted earlier in Chapter 1, pay databases have their place in research. Aside from this chapter, we also refer to commercial databases throughout the book in the chapters where they logically fit in. For example, in Chapter 10, "Company Research," when we discuss how to conduct a multistate registered agent search, we refer to several pay databases instead of free sites, since this type of search can only be done in a pay database.

Many commercial database companies have compiled public records and publicly available information into searchable databases. Some of these database companies are the ones lawyers are already familiar with because they use them for legal research, such as Lexis and Westlaw, while others may not be as familiar, such as ChoicePoint, Accurint, Merlin, FlatRateInfo, Knowx.com, and Rapsheets.com, to name a few. Lexis and Westlaw probably have the most diverse and broadest compilation of public records and publicly available information. Some of the others have chosen to cover a narrower compilation of records, or have chosen to focus more on publicly available information than public records or vice-versa. For example, Rapsheets.com focuses almost completely on criminal public records, while Accurint.com does not include criminal records. Instead, Accurint.com focuses more on publicly available information (current and past addresses, phone numbers, relatives and associates, and so on) and some public records, such as real property and bankruptcy records.

Where Do Pay Databases Get Their Data?

Before we examine some of these databases, a word about where they get their information. While much of it obviously comes from public records or publicly available information (such as phone directories), some of the information used to come from credit bureaus, who sold the "top" portion of the credit report (also referred to as a consumer report). This top portion contains personal identifier information, such as the creditor's name, address, phone number, date of birth, and Social Security number. (This information at the top of the report is commonly referred to as credit headers.) While the financial information in a credit report was never divulged to public record database companies, the information in the credit headers was sold to them. Only those who could prove they had a legitimate business purpose were supposed to have online access to databases that contained the personal information that had been cherry-picked from the credit report headers. Lawyers and law enforcement were two of the several groups considered to have a legitimate business purpose, and they used the information to locate and background people. Information from credit headers comprised a large part of the commercial databases and provided one of the best sources for locating and backgrounding people . . . up until July 2001.

Credit Headers, Then and Now

In 2001, after a nearly ten-year battle, the court denied Trans Union's (one of the three main credit bureaus) petition to review the Federal Trade Commission's (FTC) decision that credit headers constituted a credit report for purposes of the Fair Credit Reporting Act (FCRA). And, as such, that Trans Union violated the privacy provisions of the Gramm-Leach-Bliley Act (GLBA) by selling credit headers to commercial database companies. Trans Union v. FTC, 295 F.3d 42 (D.C. Cir. 2002), cert. denied, 536 U. S. 915 (2002). Section 6801 of the GLBA, titled "Protection of Nonpublic Personal Information," was passed in 1999 to protect against the unauthorized sales of personal information by financial institutions (which included credit bureaus).

Although credit header information could no longer be sold after *Trans Union v. FTC* was decided, credit header information already loaded into the pay databases did not get purged; it was allowed to be kept online and searched. Still, pay database companies are continuing to build their databases by finding the same or similar information (that they once found in credit headers) by obtaining information from other sources that do not come within the GLBA. Only records that emanate from financial institutions fall within GLBA. Thus, information gathered from public records and publicly available information sources is being added to these pay databases instead.

Using Fee-Based Databases for Public Records Research

If you have a lot of clues about a person or if the person has a unique name, you can probably begin your research with free public record databases. If this is not the case, it's best to begin with a pay database. Beginning your search with a pay database is also best when you need to conduct a national or multistate search, or gather records across the board and not just from one agency. Another reason you might use pay databases over free public record databases is to have access to the extra data they have compiled from publicly available information. See the section "Free versus Pay Resources" in Chapter 1, "Using the Internet for Factual Research," for more information on when to turn to a pay database.

The databases described below are geared to collection agencies, lawyers, and law enforcement agencies who are involved in skip-tracing (whether to locate a missing witness, heir, debtor, or criminal suspect), and backgrounding and marshalling assets (such as a divorce attorney who needs to search for real property records, boats, planes, patents, trademarks, and so on).

Accurint

http://www.accurint.com

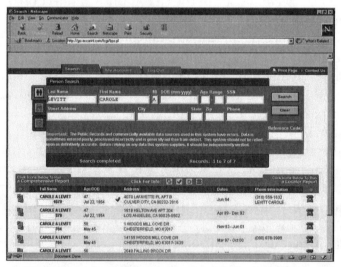

Figure 8-21. Accurint is one of the few databases that allows you to narrow a search by adding in the subject's age range. This is useful if you don't have a birth date or enough other clues about the subject.

Purpose: To search using more-sophisticated search techniques than the free public records sites offer. Accurint is useful for skip-tracing, marshalling assets, linking people together (by viewing the Associates listed in a full report), and to discover aliases.

Content: Accurint is one of the least expensive pay sites to use, with a basic search costing $0.25 and a full report about $6.50. Its database has more than twenty billion records from four hundred sources. Search with any clues you have about the person such as last name, first name, middle name, current address or phone number, old address or phone number, Social Security number, or any combination of these. The **Comprehensive Report** displays a person's current name (or names), any aliases (AKAs), property ownership, date of birth, Social Security number, current and historical addresses dating back twenty to thirty years, current telephone number, date of death, names of others living at the subject's current address, associates, and relatives. Property and bankruptcy records are also included.

Our View: We assume that Accurint stands for "accurate" and "current. " Is it accurate and current? According to a librarian at Bryan Cave, the answer is "yes" as to whether it is current; she finds it's the most up-to-date people-finding site. As to accurate, we'd say "yes and no." It is as accurate as the public records and other sources upon which it depends. (A search of Carole Levitt's record linked her to her current husband (though it labeled him a mere "associate"!), linked her to her former husband and his entire family, but then missed her parents and brothers entirely. (You can link directly to another person's report when it is noted in your subject's report.) A search by one of her old phone numbers did not work; however, searching an old address worked like a charm, as did searching by Social Security number. Users must subscribe and be approved in advance. The subscriber application requires such information as your bank name and account number, your business license, your law license, and so on. Expect a phone call (or two) to verify your information.

Tips: • When dealing with a common name, it helps to have a date of birth. If you don't have that, but are able to estimate the subject's age range, add this information into the **Age Range** field to narrow down the search.

- Besides home addresses, Accurint will sometimes display work addresses—always a difficult bit of data to locate.
- If you're looking to find all types of assets (airplanes, boats, and so on) in one search, use one of the other databases such as Lexis, Westlaw, FlatRateInfo, or ChoicePoint.

Lexis

http://www.lexis.com

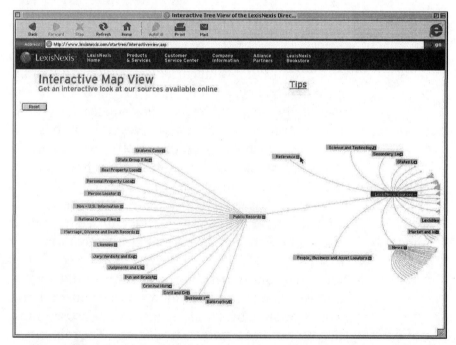

Figure 8-22. The Lexis Web Site offers the ability to search numerous different types of public records. Reprinted with the permission of LexisNexis.

Purpose: To search using more sophisticated search techniques than the free public records sites offer. Lexis is useful for skip-tracing, marshalling assets, and backgrounding people. It, along with Westlaw, has more types of public records than most of the other databases listed here.

Content: From assets to verdicts, the Lexis database contains information garnered from public records, publicly available information, and proprietary sources (for example, D & B credit reports for companies). For a complete list, see **http://www.lexisnexis.com/sourcelists** and click on the Public Records drop-down menu. For non-U.S. public record data (Argentina, Brazil, Canada, Mexico, UK, and Russia), see **http://www.lexisnexis .com/sourcelists/pdfs/nonus.pdf**.

Our View: The major advantage of Lexis is the ability to conduct multistate and nationwide public record searching and **All Records** searching (searching through a diverse group of records).

Tip: If you want to find as much information as possible about an individual, it may be worth the money to run an **All Records-All States** type of search instead of running several individual searches in selected states or agencies. Lexis also has all types of **People Finder** databases covering 146 million individuals. The data varies from state to state but could include driver's license information, marriage, divorce and death records, voter registration records, and more.

LexisONE.com

http://www.lexisone.com

Purpose: To allow Lexis nonsubscribers to access Lexis public records databases on an *ad hoc* basis by using a credit card

Content: The following types of the public records are found in LexisONE: UCC filings, tax assessor deed transfer, mortgage records, state judgments, lien filings, business locator, dockets, and more, for all states. Prices range from $20 to $48 per day, $30 to $72 per week and $66 to $165 per month.

Our View: While it is commendable that Lexis now provides the *ad hoc* user with access to their public records (something Westlaw has yet to do), being a Lexis subscriber still has a major advantage. Lexis subscribers have access to more types of public records and to sophisticated search features (such as multistate and nationwide public record searching and **All Records** searching through numerous record types). LexisONE users are limited to searching one jurisdiction at a time and one record type at a time.

Tip: • Even though some of the information can be found free on the Web, it's sometimes still worth your money to use a fee-based database to save you the time and trouble of hunting through the Web.
     • Since there is no option to pay for just one search, batch your public record searching and sign up for the daily or weekly rate.

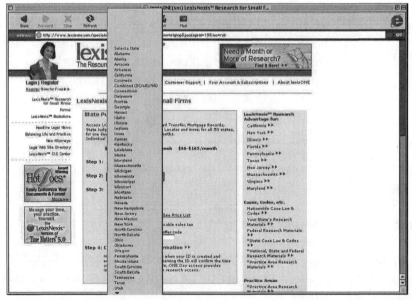

Figure 8-23. Review the Content Listing first to be sure LexisONE has the public records you are seeking, then select a state and a duration for the amount of time you want to search. The one-day access provides twenty-four hours of continuous access. Reprinted with permission of LexisNexis.

FlatRateInfo.com
(owned by e-InfoData.com)

http://www.flatrateinfo.com

Purpose: To search using more-sophisticated search techniques than the free public records sites offer. FlatRateInfo is useful for skip-tracing, marshalling assets, and backgrounding people. Directed at those who do a high volume of people searching and prefer a flat rate.

Content: After your application is approved, you can access:

- Two national people locators, including the **QI National People Locator** containing over 600 million records from most U.S. residents, including Social Security numbers, current and previous addresses, dates of birth, and aliases
- National bankruptcies, judgments, and liens
- National property records
- National fictitious business names
- Social Security Death Index (SSDI)

Our View: For those who do a high volume of people searching, such as collection laywers, FlatRateInfo may be the way to go. Contact the company for pricing.

Tip: • See the parent company site, e-InfoData.com, for access to other databases such as a multistate unclaimed property database for about twenty-one states.
- Colorado lawyers should also take a close look at e-InfoData.com—they have several Colorado specific databases, such as a real-time court records databases and a Colorado Department of Motor Vehicles database that is updated daily.
- Although some of FlatRateInfo's databases, such as the SSDI, can be accessed free at Ancestry.com or RootsWeb.com, they have been placed here simply for the customer's convenience (with the flat rate, in essence, it is free).

Merlin Information Services

http://www.merlindata.com

Purpose: Useful for skip-tracing, marshalling assets, and back-grounding people.

Content: Merlin has public information and publicly available data. It covers national data and all states. In addition, it has a heavy California emphasis.

Our View: Merlin has long been the private investigator's database of choice for investigative searching, but for some unknown reason has not been the law librarian's first choice. Law librarians typically use Lexis, Westlaw, ChoicePoint, KnowX, or Accurint. We think Merlin is worth a shot because it doesn't require a subscription or any monthly minimum usage. However, you do have to fill out a detailed seven-page application and make an initial deposit of $100 to open a debit account.

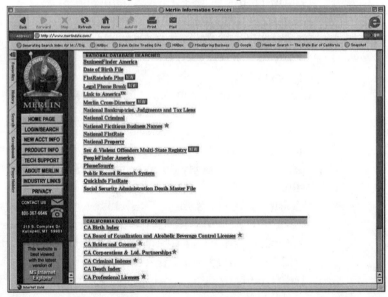

Figure 8-24. Merlin charges only per-search fees, with no monthly subscription fee, for access to all its skip-tracing, assets searching, and people back-grounding search tools.

Tip: Merlin has some proprietary databases that others may not have (especially for California). For instance, California marriage records from 1960-85 are online at Merlin—records that the State of California no longer sells. Merlin has created a National Fictitious Business Name search with over ten million records—saving you the time of a county-by-county search in each state. Link to America, a skip-tracing tool that costs 25¢ per search, is highly touted by Merlin users.

Westlaw

http://www.westlaw.com **$**

Purpose: To search using more-sophisticated search techniques than the free public records sites offer. Westlaw is useful for skip-tracing, marshalling assets, and backgrounding people. Westlaw (and Lexis) have more types of public records than the other databases listed here.

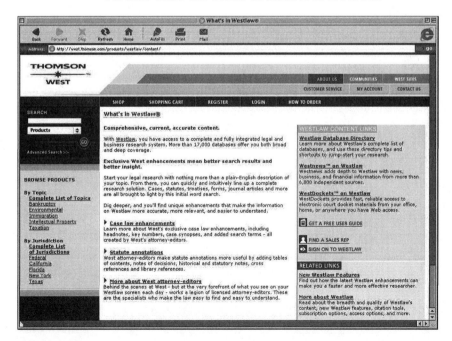

Figure 8-25. Only Westlaw subscribers can access the searchable multijurisdictional and multiagency databases available through the Westlaw.com Web site.

Content: Westlaw offers online access to national and state public records, from courthouses to government agencies and more. Records relate to searching for people, assets, and adverse filings. Search for executive affiliations, environmental records, and more.

Our View: For those who have a flat-rate Westlaw contract (and if access to public records is part of it), it may be cost effective to use Westlaw. Like Lexis, Westlaw offers multijurisdictional and multiagency searching, and many people and business finder and locator databases.

Tip: Nonsubscribers cannot use Westlaw for public record searching. Use any one of the other fee-based databases in this section if you are an occasional public record searcher.

ChoicePoint

(formerly CDB Infotek; also marketed as KnowX, Auto-Track, and ScreenNow)

http://www.choicepoint.net

Purpose: To search public records using more-sophisticated search techniques than the free sites offer; useful for skip-tracing, marshalling assets, and backgrounding people

Content: ChoicePoint provides Internet access to over seventeen billion records on individuals and businesses, by way of public and proprietary records. Information includes relatives and associates, corporate information, real property records, and deed transfers. Users must subscribe and be approved in advance. The subscriber application requires such information as your bank name and account number, Social Security number, two credit references, your business license, your law license, and so on.

Our View: Aside from individual records, one can also retrieve comprehensive reports about people by using the **Info-Probe** or **Discovery PLUS** features. The **Discovery PLUS** report shows an individual's current and previous addresses, relatives, assets, corporate involvement, derogatory information, and vehicle identification number. The **InfoProbe** report searches millions of records simultaneously and shows a list of databases containing records matching your search criteria. From the list, you choose which databases to view and regardless of the number of records viewed, the charge will never exceed $100 per search.

Tip: If you anticipate that there could be reams of information about your subject, consider an InfoProbe search instead of conducting various individual searches; it might save you time and money.

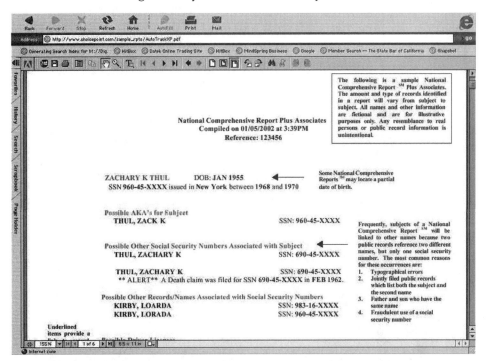

Figure 8-26. Combined, ChoicePoint's databases contain over seventeen billion records. The site's InfoProbe search allows you to choose multiple databases to search at once. ChoicePoint and the ChoicePoint logo are registered trademarks of ChoicePoint Asset Company.

KnowX

(launched in February of 1997 as Information America, and merge with ChoicePoint Inc. in May 2000)

http://www.knowx.com **$**

Purpose: To search public records using more-sophisticated search techniques than the free sites offer; useful for skip-tracing, marshalling assets, and backgrounding people

Content: KnowX searches national and state databases for a summary of assets, driver's licenses, professional licenses, real property, vehicles, liens, business entity filings, lawsuit information, marriage records, birth and death records, and more (associates, relatives and others linked to the same addresses as the subject and neighbors). Registration with a credit card is required and searches cost anywhere from $1.50 to $123.00 (for the full price list see **http://www.knowx.com/statmnts.exe?form= statmnts/priceinfo.htm**).

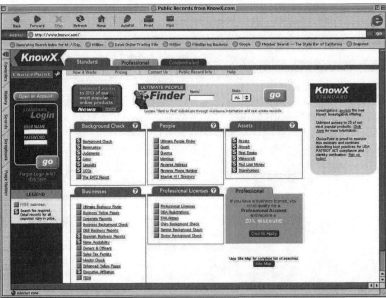

Figure 8-27. KnowX offers links to some useful free searches. The most detailed information, however, is reserved for the service's paid searches.

Our View: For the occasional user, this may be a better choice than ChoicePoint because you need not fill out such a personal application and wait to be approved. Also, you can save some money by purchasing multiple records from a search instead of an individual record.

Tip: Some KnowX searches are free (but the results are very summarized). Check the price list noted above to discover which ones are free.

Even though the free results are very summarized, sometimes that's all you need! For example, a free corporate record search for "Coastal Printworks" returns the result "COASTAL PRINTWORKS, INC. is a business entity in CA." That summarized result just might be good enough if you only wanted to know whether they were registered to do business in California. Those in need of a mailing address and registered agent, however, will need to pay for a more detailed record.

CHAPTER**NINE**

Finding and Backgrounding Expert Witnesses

There are plenty of low-tech traditional ways to find experts, such as telephoning colleagues or one of the numerous brokerages (not unlike Hollywood talent agencies) that represent experts. These companies can pump résumés and curriculum vitaes (CVs) through your fax machine to satisfy every esoteric expert need you can think of. They also often charge fees in advance of providing any expertise. You'll find scads of ads for these companies, as well as for individual experts in the back pages of most legal periodicals, especially those targeted at trial lawyers. Usually, these companies charge a representation fee in addition to the fee you'll pay to the expert. Other low-tech ways of searching are to look through an expert witness directory (in print). This is time consuming and often means a trip to a library. Also, the print directory's arrangement is not always helpful to you. If you want to search for an expert by both location and expertise, but the directory is only arranged by expertise, or only by location, or only by expert's name, you'll be out of luck.

The Internet, however, has expedited the traditional searching for expert witnesses by providing easy and free access to so many resources, from online expert witness directories, to the ability to access online library catalogs, periodical indexes, and databases that contain full-text articles (to satisfy your search for articles or books relevant to the subject or authored by the expert).

The Internet also lends itself to creative ways to find experts (and to help you learn enough about the subject matter and the expert to be able to make an informed decision about the qualifications of a potential expert). These creative ways vary from taking advantage of the professional association community, to reviewing jury verdicts, to finding mailing-list postings and the like, to searching through the expert's own site. Many of the traditional searches and creative searches can be done on the Web and usually for free.

War Story: Enhanced Collaboration

Insurance defense lawyer Jim Walter relates this collaborative use he made of a free online expert witness directory, JurisPro:

"In one case, we needed to find an expert witness who could testify regarding premises liability issues. From the JurisPro Web site, I downloaded the expert's full curriculum vitae, reviewed the expert's background as a witness, (including the number of times they have testified, and whether it was for the plaintiff or defense), and read their articles that discussed their expertise. Most impressively, I was able to get an idea how the various experts *presented* themselves—by viewing their photos and hearing them speak through streaming audio on the site. I then got on the phone with the insurance adjustor and we simultaneously reviewed the qualifications of potential experts online on JurisPro. JurisPro allowed my firm and the company to agree to hire an expert witness in one telephone call. We did not have to fax resumes back and forth, play 'phone tag' for several hours or days on potential hires, or have an adjustor simply rely on my judgment in hiring a witness. The hiring process was easy and fast, allowing both of us to make a decision swiftly and move on to other cases."

Checklist for Finding and Verifying Experts

❑   1.   Develop a working knowledge of the expertise by reading books and articles. This can also lead you to the experts in the field or help verify credentials for the experts you already have.

❑   2.   Review the expert's writings.

❑   3.   Search free expert witness directories.

❑   4.   Use online directories to find trade or professional associations.

❑   5.   Find the expert's conference presentations.

❑   6.   Join an online community to find experts' postings or to learn about the topic.

❑   7.   Review the expert's own Web site.

❑   8.   Determine if the expert has ever been disciplined.

❑   9.   Find experts via jury verdict reporter databases.

❑ 10. Find the expert's deposition testimony.
❑ 11. Find briefs and cases that refer to the expert.
❑ 12. Locate academic experts through university sites.
❑ 13. Find government experts through government reports.
❑ 14. Use pay referral sites.

Checklist Item 1: Develop a Working Knowledge of the Expertise by Reading Books and Articles

Before seeking an expert, it's useful to first familiarize yourself with the area of expertise by reading an article or two, or scanning a book on the topic. Searching a library's catalog (via the Internet, of course) by subject can lead you to some of the literature in that area of expertise. A comprehensive listing of public library Web sites can be found at Libweb (**http://sunsite.berkeley.edu/Libweb**). As you browse through the book titles, you may spot certain authors who have written several books on that specialty and this may assist you in identifying some of the top experts in the field to contact. In addition to sifting through online card catalogs for books, you should also conduct an online search for articles; articles tend to be more current than books and are certainly easier to digest than a lengthy book. This search for books and articles can also assist you in finding materials authored by an expert you have already been referred to.

Online Library Catalogs

Libweb

http://sunsite.berkeley.edu/Libweb

Purpose: To find library URLs to search their online catalogs.

Content: Use Libweb to link to all types of libraries' homepages in 115 countries by browsing by location or type of library, or by keyword searching using the library name, a location, a type of library, or a combination of these. From the library's home page, link to the catalog and search by author, subject, or title.

Our View: It's useful to begin with your public library in case you want to borrow the book or have them arrange an inter-library loan for you.

Tip: However you do a thorough search, don't overlook the mother of library online catalogs—the Library of Congress (**http://catalog.loc.gov**). Finally , don't discount online bookstore catalogs such as Amazon (**http://www.amazon.com**) or Barnes & Noble (**http://www.barnesandnoble.com**) to find leading authors in a subject area. Results at those retail sites may include a synopsis, the author's name, table of contents, a note from the publisher about the work, and, in many cases, reviews of the book.

Has the Expert Been Published?

Although someone may have provided you with a name of an expert, it's your job to independently verify the expert's expertise. One way to do this is to discover if the expert has published in his or her area of expertise. You will need to uncover the expert's authored materials (and not by just by reading the materials featured on the expert's own Web site). Reading authored material will also show you the expert's opinions and help you to discover any inconsistencies. Uncovering the opposition's expert's authored materials is also in order—for the very same reasons. This research will assist you to better prepare for direct or cross-examination.

Checklist Item 2: Review the Expert's Writings

You cannot depend on experts to have posted all of their published works on their Web sites, and therefore an independent literature search is in order. To conduct a nationwide search of newspaper or periodical articles written by (or about) your expert, pay databases such as Lexis, Westlaw, or Ingenta are best, especially for scholarly articles. Ingenta is useful for those who do not have a subscription to Lexis or Westlaw because you can search, at no cost, the summaries of articles from over twenty-five thousand publications and purchase the full text online. To obtain consumer magazine articles, at no cost, use FindArticles.com, where you can search a database of full-text articles from over three hundred magazines and journals back to 1998. For more specialized topics, such as toxic mold and stachybotrys, a search through medical literature at the government's National Library of Medicine (NLM) gateway site is in order (**http://gateway.nlm.nih.gov/gw/Cmd**). See Chapter 12, "Medical Research," for more information on the NLM.

Online Periodical Indexes and Full-Text Articles

FindArticles.com

http://www.FindArticles.com

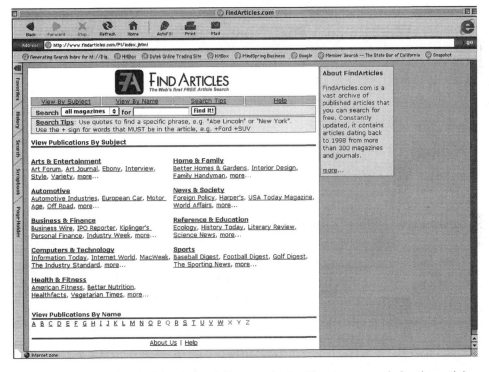

Figure 9-1. FindArticles is useful to conduct a literature search for the articles written by (or about) an expert, or to search by expertise to learn about the subject or to identify leading experts in the field.

Purpose: To conduct a literature search for the articles written by (or about) an expert to ascertain their expertise and their opinions; to obtain basic knowledge about the subject before hiring an expert.

Content: FindArticles.com is a database of published articles that can be searched for free. It is continually updated, and contains articles back to 1998 from over three hundred magazines and journals.

Our View: Being able to read and print the full text of an article at no cost is very useful, especially if you need an overview of a topic or need to find an expert. Many of the articles contain quotes by experts.

Tip: Search by keywords and Boolean connectors (use the plus sign [+] and the minus sign [-]) or phrases (use quotation marks). You can limit your search to a particular magazine by selecting the **View By Name** tab or limit your search to a specific subject by selecting the **View By Subject** tab (both tabs are at the top of the screen).

Ingenta

To search: To view and print full text:

http://www.ingenta.com

Purpose: To conduct a literature search for the articles written by (or about) an expert to ascertain expertise and opinions; to obtain basic knowledge about the subject before hiring an expert.

Content: Search 14,526,603 articles from 27,778 academic and professional publications and read the abstracts—for free.

Our View: Being able to read abstracts and purchase the full text of the articles online without having to figure out which library may carry a specified article is very useful when time is of the essence. If time is not important, you might be able to locate the article for free at a local library because Ingenta provides the complete citation.

Tip:
- Be sure to click on **advanced search** to refine or narrow your search.
- You can e-mail the entire list of results to someone so he can choose the articles he wants.

Check the Library

Before paying for an article, check your library's online databases to see if the full text of the article is offered there for free (see the section "Free Internet Access to Library Databases and Catalogs" in Chapter 5, "General Factual Research"). Also, run the article title through a search engine in case it has been posted free on someone's Web site (such as the author's).

If you need to only access an individual newspaper or magazine, the Internet is a perfect source. For information about sites that link to thousands of publications from around the world, such as NewsTrove (**http://www.newstrove.com**), see the section "News, Periodicals, and Broadcast Media" in Chapter 5, "General Factual Research."

Many trade associations publish online newsletters, and some provide either full-text articles or extracts. For example, the Accident Reconstruction (ARC) Network (**http://www.accidentreconstruction.com**), a professional organization for those in the accident reconstruction industry, has a monthly newsletter with expert's articles. This site also has an active discussion forum that includes opinions posted by various accident reconstructionists.

Use Dictionaries and Encyclopedias

Sometimes you just need a brief introduction to a subject area and an encyclopedia article or dictionary will do the trick instead of a book or journal article. Check out Refdesk.com for links to medical and drug dictionaries, technology encyclopedias, and more (**http://www.refdesk.com**). There's even an Ask an Expert section.

War Story: Finding an Expert—Fast

Ben Wright (Ben_Wright@compuserve.com) is a lawyer in Dallas, Texas and an expert on digital signatures and electronic contracts. He described how Julian Ding, a lawyer in Malaysia, arranged for his expert services.

Julian Ding needed to find an electronic commerce expert—fast. Julian is a partner in Zaid Ibrahim & Co., a large law firm in Malaysia, a developing country determined to leapfrog itself into leadership on the information highway. The Malaysian Parliament was in the process of adopting digital signature legislation, and Julian's firm wanted to convene a public seminar to examine the topic. To add the requisite cachet, the firm invited the Minister of Energy, Telecommunications and Post to open the seminar.

Unfortunately, the Minister could only confirm the invitation rather late due to his busy schedule. That left Julian in a bind. He was forced to organize the seminar in thirty days, and he needed to find, among other experts, a foreign lawyer having special experience with digital signatures. So, he turned to Yahoo! (**http://www.yahoo.com**) and searched for "digital signature," which yielded the Web page for Ben Wright's book, *The Law of Electronic Commerce* (**http://wright.safeshopper.com**). Ben obviously knew the skinny on digital signatures because his Web site contained several articles about it. Julian dashed off an e-mail invitation to Ben, and the two soon negotiated an arrangement for Ben to be present at the event.

Finding an Expert's Book

Had Ding searched Barnesandnoble.com for the key words "electronic and commerce and law," Wright's book would have come up as the first result if sorted by best match. Tip: to find the most recent books, sort results by date. Wright's book showed up as the eighth-most recently published book on the topic (out of 186 books). You can also search by the best-selling books, but you might not see the best matches (those most closely related to your search words) listed at the beginning.

Checklist Item 3: Search Free Expert Witness Directories

There are many expert directories on the Internet. While most of them charge experts to be listed, they provide free search access to everyone. All the directories are searchable by expertise, while many are also searchable by expert name, geographic location, and a few other methods. The directories that offer geographic searching are useful, especially when a lawyer wants to hold down travel expenses by finding a local expert. The directory listings vary from the very brief to the very complete.

Lawyer Jim Robinson founded the JurisPro Expert Witness Directory (**http://www.JurisPro.com**) after being frustrated about locating expert witnesses for his cases. "There are a lot of 'white page telephone' types of expert witness directories that just include an expert's contact information, with very little information about their background, noted Robinson. Attorneys rely on experts to make them look good to the client; therefore, attorneys want to be as comfortable with that expert as possible. We have not met an attorney yet who said they want to know *less* about the expert they were going to hire. We designed the features of JurisPro from an attorney's point of view. Attorneys want to know the expert's full range of experience within their field of expertise, and their background as an expert witness. They want to be able to read the expert's actual résumé (not just some blurb), and know how the expert presents him or herself. They also wanted to be able to find out this information from a place that was free and convenient to use, Robinson explained. With this in mind, we set up JurisPro as a free, content-based directory for finding and researching expert witnesses."

Free Expert Witness Directories, Searchable by Keyword, Name, and Location

Jurispro.com

http://www.jurispro.com

Purpose: To find experts, view their pictures, listen to their audio, and read their CVs and articles.

Content: Search for an expert witness by name or area of expertise, or by selecting from a list of expert categories. As each expert is displayed, you will first see a narrative summary of the expert's background, contact information, photo, and an audio clip to listen to his or her voice. Then, select any of these tabs for more data: **Background** (in the form of questions and answers), **CV, Articles, References, Web Page,** and **E-mail.**

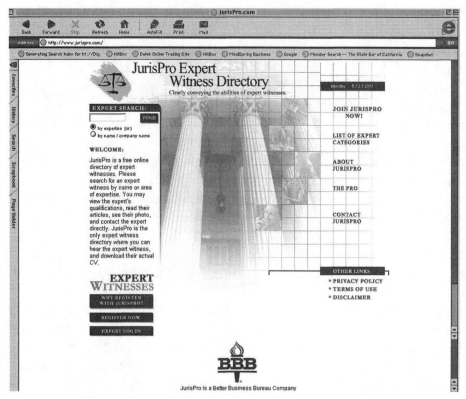

Figure 9-2. JurisPro provides lawyers with an invaluable tool by allowing them to see the experts' pictures and listen to their audio clips.

Our View: A jury survey found that jurors sided with one expert over another because one expert more clearly communicated her expertise. JurisPro provides lawyers with an invaluable tool by allowing them to see the experts' pictures and listen to their audio clips. If it sounds like the expert can clearly communicate his expertise on the audio clip, this helps lawyers decide whether to even bother phoning the expert in the first place.

Tip: Once you pull up a list of results, you can further refine the search by selecting a state.

Experts.com

http://www.experts.com

Purpose: To find experts and consultants.

Content: Search by clicking on the **search** tab at the top and then search by keywords, category, name, company, address, or a combination. You can also search by clicking on the **directory** tab and then choosing a category (some will have subcategories). To refine the directory search, choose **Categories** or **Experts** from the pull-down menu on the Directory page, then type in a keyword and click on one of the directory categories. Results will display a summary of the expert's background and a link to the expert's e-mail and Web site. Some experts have their picture displayed.

Our View: An interesting feature is the ability for the lawyer to let the experts know he's interested in hearing from them by placing check marks next to the experts' names and clicking on **SynapsUS** at the bottom of the page.

Tip:
- You have a choice of refining your search on the Search page by choosing **all words**, **sounds like**, **is exactly** or **contains**.
- Experts.com members are entitled to a discount at the MDEX Daubert Tracker database (**http://www.mdex online.com**).

NLJ (National Law Journal) Experts

http://www.nljexperts.com or **http://experts.law.com**

Purpose: To find experts and consultants.

Content: NLJ has a directory with over fifteen thousand experts, expert witnesses, investigators, court reporters, and consultants. Search by area of expertise or by name of expert or company. While free to users, experts who wish to list themselves in the database pay $495 per year for a national listing and $295 per year for a single state listing. After searching by an area of expertise, the user can find a list of national experts along with a menu that allows the user to limit the search to a specific state.

Our View: A very useful feature is the link that allows you to check **Verdict Search** for cases involving this expert. A summary of the verdicts is displayed, and you can buy them for $9.95 each (see Verdict Search later in this chapter or at **http://www.verdictsearch.com** for more information). We like the handy chart that appears with the resulting list of experts. If you can't figure out what the icons stand for, just hover over them—they indicate whether the expert has an on-line profile, photograph, or CV; a Web site; or an e-mail address.

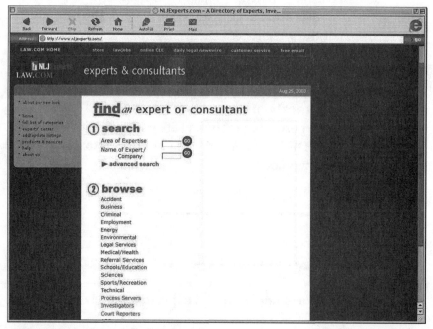

Figure 9-3. Search the National Law Journal's Expert Witness directory by area of expertise or by name of expert or company.

Tip: If you click on the **Advanced Search** button you can
               further refine your search by state, keywords, and wild
               cards (for example, "%Stein" will find "Goldstein" and
               will also find "Stein & Smith").

See Expert's Prior Cases

The NLJ Experts directory provides a useful feature: links to a
pay site that displays the expert's prior cases.

The National Directory of Expert Witnesses is a very extensive book
and a free searchable online database of fifteen hundred technical, scientific, and medical experts arranged into four hundred categories
(**http://www.claims.com**). It is published by the Claims Providers of
America and is designed to be used by law firms and insurance professionals. Search by keywords (partial or complete), phrases, category, name of
expert, or name of company. To limit the search to a certain state, use its
postal abbreviation, followed by an ampersand (for example, "IL&"). You
can also e-mail this site and ask for a referral (for free) to an expert in a
specified field.

Hieros Gamos's database is searchable by company name, city, state
or province, country, or firm's description (**http://www.hg.org**). Even
though there is no expert-name field, you can search for an expert's name
in the description field. The database is also browsable by subject.

Free Expert Witness Directories, Searchable by Category Only

Yearbook.com
(formerly Yearbook of Experts, Authorities and Spokespersons)

http://www.expertclick.com

Purpose: A very extensive searchable database of experts designed
               primarily for journalists, but anyone can search it for
               free.

Content: Once a search is conducted for a particular area of
expertise, you can read a summary about the expert,
link to the expert's site, and link to press releases posted
by the expert.

Our View: If you click on **Contact this expert** you will be
informed that you must be a registered journalist. However, you can easily contact the expert on your own—
from the information listed on the profile or by linking
to the expert's site.

Tip: • By clicking on **View Releases** you can read the
expert's press releases. But remember—this is what the
expert wrote, not what an objective third party wrote.
• Click on **View Daybook** to view the expert's calendar
of events (such as seminars).

Free Expert Witness Directories, Searchable by Category and Location

Expert Pages ⑤ is one of the oldest online directories of expert witnesses (**http://www.expertpages.com**). Experts are arranged
by hierarchical categories and subcategories of expertise. The
information for each listing is very brief, but includes links to the
expert's site.

Findlaw ⑤ , like Expert Pages, has an online directory searchable by
category, but unlike Expert Pages, there are no subcategories (**http://
marketcenter.findlaw.com/expert_witnesses.html**). The results might
include listings of individual experts or links to some of the referral sites
we note below. The expert listings are much longer than those at Expert
Pages, and include descriptions of services offered, biographical information, and full contact information.

Finding an Expert in Your State

Although several sites allow the user to narrow down the
expert witness search to a particular state, it should be noted that
no matter what state is chosen, the results may still include
experts from outside your requested state. This is because experts
can ask to be listed in states other than the one in which they
reside.

Pay Directory of Expert Witness CVs with Free Links to Experts' Sites

The Expert Witness Network **$** allows lawyers to access a database that includes two thousand CVs for $99 per year, or $25 per session (**http://www.witness.net**). Also on this site is a free Expert Witness Links database, where you can search by keyword for an expert, view a brief directory listing, and then link to the expert's own Web site. Experts pay to be included in the Expert Witness Network.

Does Your Bar Association Have an Expert Witness Database?

When you need to keep expenses to a minimum, but still need an expert, it's helpful if you can target local experts. To do this, consider turning to your local bar association's Web site to see if they have created an expert witness directory. For instance, in Los Angeles, lawyers can consult the Los Angeles County Bar Association's online expert database, Expert4law.org (**http://www.expert4law.org**), and lawyers in the Bay area can consult the Bar Association of San Francisco's online directory of expert witnesses (**http://www.sfbar.org/cgi/experts/exp.cgi**).

Checklist Item 4: Use Online Directories to Find Trade or Professional Associations

Lawyers who need an expert in an uncommon field or who simply do not know where to begin their search for an expert should consider consulting with an association that deals with that particular field. According to the American Society of Association Executives, there are over 147,000 associations in the United States (127,340 local, state, or regional; 20,285 national; and 2,409 international associations headquartered in the United States). One easy way to find an association's Web site is to simply enter its name into a Web search engine (like Google); however, this assumes you know the name of the association. If you don't know the name, you can enter a descriptive keyword and the word "association." Another easy way to find an association's Web site is to access one of the free online association indicies or directories.

Lawyers very often need to find translators or interpreters. A useful site for finding one is the American Translators Association's site (**http://www.atanet.org**). Like many association sites, it includes an on-line directory searchable by name, language, location, and various other criteria.

War Story: Chewing Gum Expert

There are associations for nearly every profession and interest group, as we learned when recently asked to find a chewing gum expert (for a personal injury case). The case involved a plaintiff who slipped and fell on a hard piece of chewing gum and the issue was one of notice, which could only be answered by figuring out how long that piece of chewing gum was on the floor. This, in turn, called for a chewing gum expert who could tell us how long it takes chewing gum to become hard. We knew it would be a waste of time to search a traditional expert witness directory and immediately thought of the Encyclopedia of Associations (also called Associations Unlimited). Seconds after logging into my public library's Web site, and locating the free Associations Unlimited remote database, we found the Association of Chewing Gum Manufacturers. We turned the contact over to the lawyers.

The Encyclopedia of Associations is only free to use if your public library provides remote access to it (otherwise, it is a pay database). If your library does provide access, you are in particular luck because it is one of the largest of the association directories. It indexes and provides detailed information for more than 155,000 organizations worldwide, and has Internal Revenue Service (IRS) data on 300,000 nonprofit organizations with 501(c) status. The Encyclopedia provides numerous search functions—keyword, acronyms, location, subject, and more. If the Encyclopedia entry for the association has a URL listed, go there to scour the site for a list of research links to learn more about the topic. Also, take note of the executive director's name or the names of any of the association's officers. Typically, their e-mail addresses or a link to them will be included. Lawyers can then contact the director or one of the officers for a referral to an expert. If you don't have access to the Encyclopedia of Associations, see below for some free alternatives. For more information on remote online resources offered by public libraries, see the "Free Internet Access to Library Databases and Catalogs" section of Chapter 5, "General Factual Research."

Online Indexes of Associations

American Society of Association Executives (ASAE)

http://info.asaenet.org/gateway/onlineassocslist.html

Purpose: To search an index of 6,589 associations.

Content: The index links you to each association's Web site.

Our View: The index offers a variety of ways to search and allows
you to use multiple criteria such as association name (or
partial name), category (all, or choose preselected categories), city, or state. For example, you can search for all
associations in Skokie, Illinois or search for all accounting associations in one state (or in all states, or in a specific city).

Tip: Bookmark this exact URL; it's hard to find this index
from the ASAE home page.

Online Directories of Associations

The Internet Public Library Associations on the Net

http://www.ipl.org/ref/AON

Purpose: To search for information about prominent organizations and associations.

Content: The Internet Public Library provides this collection of
over five hundred links to associations on the Internet.
Categories include arts, business, computers,
entertainment, health, industry, labor, law, and
science.

Our View: This site provides a description of the association and a
link to its home page.

Tip: You can search by the title of the association, a keyword
             or words describing it, or category.

GuideStar

http://www.guidestar.org/search

Purpose: To search for data on nonprofits; geared to donors,
             grantors, and nonprofits.

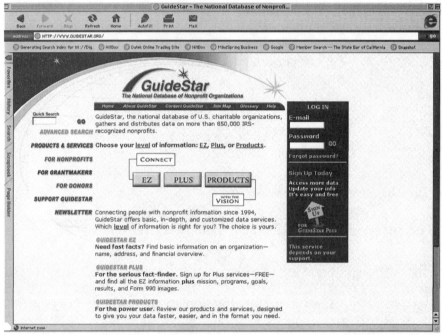

Figure 9-4. GuideStar provides annual reports and IRS 990 forms filed by
about 850,000 nonprofit organizations, and also provides direct links to the
nonprofits' Web sites.

Content: GuideStar provides annual reports and IRS Form 990s
             filed by about 850,000 nonprofit organizations, and
             also provides direct links to nonprofits' Web sites.

Our View: Those who register (it's free), can view more financial
             information (and other detailed information) about

organizations than can nonregistered users (who can only view a financial snapshot). There are also analyst reports and other customized data available for a fee.

Tip: If you don't find the charitable organization that you are looking for, check the list of charitable organizations in IRS Publication 78, Cumulative List of Organizations, and its Addendum. To visit this list, type "Publication 78" into the **Search Forms and Publications for** query box at **http://www.irs.gov**, or go to **http://www.irs.gov/charities/page/0,,id=15053,00.html**. You will find only the name of the charity, its city and state, and the percentage of its deductibility limitation.

The Foundation Finder

http://lnp.fdncenter.org/finder.html

Purpose: To search for information about nonprofits.

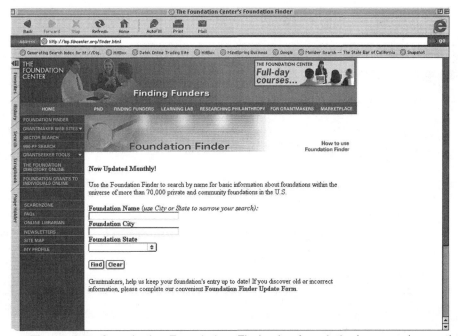

Figure 9-5. Search the Foundation Finder by foundation's name (or partial name) and add a city or state to narrow the search.

Content: Search the Foundation Finder—a listing of seventy thousand private and community foundations in the U.S. Other information on this site includes a list of the top one hundred foundations (by assets) and statistics about foundations and their funding patterns.

Our View: It's an easy-to-use directory, and also has a link to a PDF of each organization's filled-in and filed IRS Form 990.

Tip: Lawyers looking for grants need to subscribe.

Specialized Association Directories

While the above directories cover a wide spectrum of areas, there are directories that are more specialized. For example, in the health care industry, the Joint Commission on Accreditation of Healthcare Organizations has a site that includes a directory of nearly eighteen thousand health care organizations. It includes ambulatory care facilities, assisted living facilities, behavioral health care facilities (such as chemical dependency centers and developmental disabilities organizations), HMOs, home care organizations, hospitals, laboratories, and long-term care facilities, and office-based surgeons can be found here (**http://www.jcaho.org/ qualitycheck/directry/directry.asp**).

Reliability and Relevance of Experts

Harold J. Bursztajn, MD, is an Associate Clinical Professor of Psychiatry at Harvard Medical School. He also has broad courtroom experience as an expert witness in civil and criminal litigation. In his forensic practice, he has consulted to plaintiff and defense counsel and to state and federal agencies as an expert in medical-legal decision-making and forensic psychiatry. Dr. Bursztajn's Web site (**http://www.forensic-psych.com**) focuses on the nexus of forensic psychiatry, medicine, and the law. He offered the following insights regarding using the Internet to find medical experts:

"With its emphasis on judicial discretion, and the judge as 'gatekeeper' for admitting expert testimony, Daubert v. Merrel Dow Pharmaceuticals, Inc. 509 U.S. 579 (1993), has been slowly but steadily transforming how lawyers seek experts. With the increasing likelihood that an expert's testimony will face judicial scrutiny, the reliability and relevance of an expert's analysis and evaluation needs to be established long before trial, ideally prior to retaining an expert. While the specific guidelines enumerated by the Supreme Court for scientific testimony are most often used to evaluate the quantitative sciences, the more general criteria of reliability and relevance are increasingly used by judges to evaluate the admissibility of applied science-based expert medical opinion. One of my most common forensic consultations is to evaluate another 'expert's' opinion. When I analyze it as unreliable or irrelevant on medical-decision analytic grounds, the lawyer or court which has retained me can rapidly move to dismiss either the questionable testimony or the claim or defense as a whole which is founded on such testimony (*Mayotte M. Jones v. Metrowest Medical Inc.* [CA-96-10860-WD]).

"By researching via the Internet, a lawyer seeking an expert can avoid both false starts and subsequent disappointments. The Internet offers the following advantages for evaluating the potential usefulness of a medical expert in light of the general principles of Daubert:

"1. Reliability: The medical expert needs to be both a practicing physician who consults to other physicians and patients, and well published in refereed medical journals. This information can be gleaned from the expert's Web page more easily than from the CV alone. The Web page will often include not only a complete CV, but also selected case citations and authored publications. Moreover, the expert with a resource page on the Web is more likely to be able to do computer-aided literature searches. Such research can provide the foundation for the reviews and analysis needed to corroborate the reliability of another expert's opinion. In addition, such research can identify alternative opinions in the medical community.

"2. Relevance: The medical expert needs to show ability to teach not only other medical professionals but also an ability to teach other professionals and educated laypersons, e.g. judges, lawyers and jurors. The lawyer can have some sense of how the expert teaches in a public context by reviewing the expert's Web page. The fact that an expert has a content-filled, yet user-friendly Web page, can itself be an indication that an expert has the competence, confidence, and sensitivity to present work in a public context with authority rather than arrogance, and in a relevant and meaningful manner."

Daubert on the Web

See Peter Nordberg's site, Daubert on the Web, to read the Daubert decision and hundreds of post-Daubert cases—indexed by circuit and by area of expertise (**http://daubertontheweb.com**).

Checklist Item 5: Find the Expert's Conference Presentations

To locate an expert in a specific area of expertise, enter the search term "expert witness" (in quotation marks) along with any other search criteria, such as "child custody," into a search engine. Searching a known expert's name through a search engine is a way to capture any extra nuggets of information—such as links to the expert's personal Web site, discussion group messages sent by the expert, or any references to the expert on a discussion group or a Web site other than his or her own.

It is often important to learn if an expert's opinion has been consistent in public forums, such as conferences. An expert's conference papers can sometimes be found on the Web by typing the expert's name into Google. Very often, experts post their own papers, or the conference host might post them. To limit your search to an expert's PowerPoint presentations only, go to Google and click on **Advanced Search**. Enter your search term (the expert's name) and then select **Microsoft PowerPoint (.ppt)** as the file format.

PowerPoint Presentations

FirstGov.gov also indexes PowerPoint presentations, but they are limited to presentations on government Web sites only.

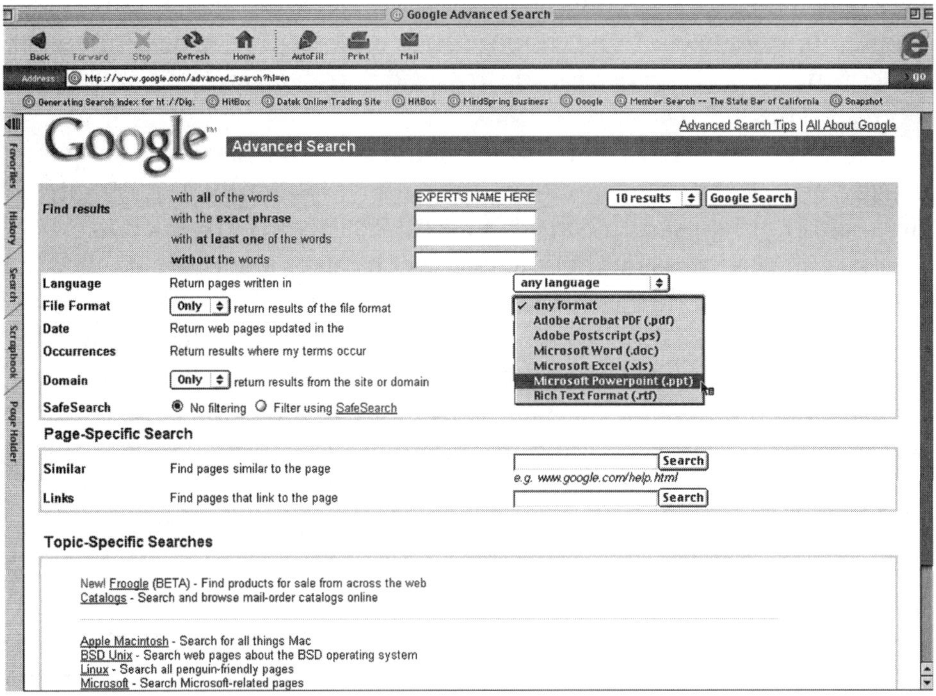

Figure 9-6. Using Google's Advanced Search page, you can limit a search to a PowerPoint presentation by clicking in the file format drop-down menu. Google™ is a trademark of Google Technology Inc.

Checklist Item 6: Join an Online Community to Find Experts' Postings or to Learn about the Topic

As noted in the "Thinking Outside the Box" section found in Chapter 7, "Finding and Backgrounding People," online discussions can take place in a variety of places on the Internet: in Usenet newsgroups, mailing lists, forums, blogs, and message boards. Though very hit and miss, searching through online communities' current discussions and archives can sometimes be excellent tools for identifying and contacting experts. For any topic you can imagine, there is an online community discussing it.

Some online communities require that you subscribe in order to participate, and some limit their subscribers to those with particular credentials. But many lists have no subscriber limitations at all. Once you locate an appropriate community, the best thing to do is lurk around a bit. In other words, read the postings prior to submitting your own, or simply browse through the archives. In this way, you may come across an expert or another lawyer you wish to correspond with. You can then send private e-mail messages to individuals, rather than letting all subscribers know your intentions. If the community has an archive, search it for your expert's name or the expertise you are seeking (not all archives are key-word searchable, however).

To determine whether an online community in a particular subject area exists, or to find out about any subscriber limitations, or to simply find out how to subscribe, consult a LISTSERV list directory such as CataList (**http://www.lsoft.com/lists/listref.html**) or a newsgroup direc-tory such as Topica (formerly Liszt) (**http://www.liszt.com**). At Topica, you can either search by keywords or browse categories and subcategories to find the right group. Browsing through the category Health & Fitness, we found many subcategories and chose Diseases & Conditions, then Autoimmune & Immune Disorders, and then CFS (Chronic Fatigue Syn-drome). Just by reading some of the current posts, we found one that included the name, e-mail address, and mailing address of a staff member of the National CFIDS Foundation, Inc., and a reference to a case involv-ing long-term disability benefits for a plaintiff suffering from chronic fatigue syndrome. It would be easy to contact her for follow-up.

The PSYLAW-L mailing list is a well-trafficked and excellent place to post a request for psychological experts. You can join this group by send-ing an e-mail message to listserv@unl.edu and by typing "SUBSCRIBE PSYLAW-L" (without quotation marks) into the Message field (not the Subject field). To review some of the archived postings, go to **http://crcvms.unl.edu/htbin/wa?A0=PSYLAW-L** and click on any of the months and years listed.

EXPERT-L is an Internet mailing list for those individuals engaged in expert witness activities associated with litigation. It was inspired by the need for experts to communicate with each other about issues related to the expert witness profession and for networking between experts and lawyers. For example, a search in the archives (where you can search with-out subscribing) found a request from a lawyer for an "expert in tensile strength and fractile characteristics of cast metal machinery components" (**http://lists.digilogic.com/archives/expert-l.html**). To subscribe, send an e-mail message to **http://lists.digilogic.com/cgi-bin/wa.exe?SUBED1= expert-l&A=1**.

Using Google Groups to Find or Background an Expert

As discussed earlier, Google Groups (**http://groups.google.com**) allows for anonymous searching through over 850 million postings of the archives of thousands of Usenet newsgroups dating back to 1981. For a thorough discussion on how to use Google Groups, see the "Thinking Outside the Box" section in Chapter 7, "Finding and Backgrounding People." Searching Google Groups by keyword, you may come across an expert who is relevant to the matter at hand. Searching by an expert's name, you may come across a posting made by your own expert or your opponent's expert. This is an excellent way to attempt to undermine the opponent's expert and to evaluate your own expert.

To find the expert's postings, users should conduct a few different types of searches on Google Group's Advanced Groups Search page (**http://groups.google.com/advanced_group_search**). First, search for the expert's name in the **Return only messages where the author is** field. However, keep in mind that some people surf anonymously by using pseudonyms, so you may find nothing.

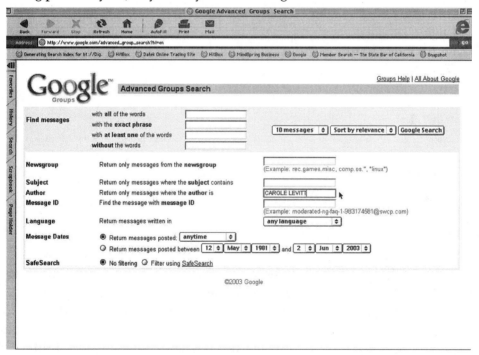

Figure 9-7. Search for the expert's name in the **Return only messages where the author is** field in Google Groups. Google™ is a trademark of Google Technology Inc.

Second, search for the expert's e-mail address in the **Return only messages where the author is** field. Since many people share the same name, searching by a unique e-mail address will help you verify that you've found the correct person. Because some people have more than one e-mail address, try to discover all of them to conduct a complete search of a person's postings.

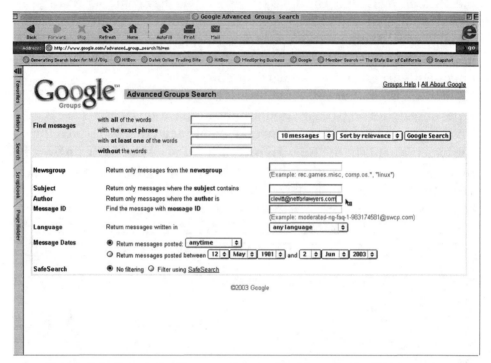

Figure 9-8. Search for the expert's e-mail address in the **Return only messages where the author is** field. Google™ is a trademark of Google Technology Inc.

The third search method is to search for the expert's name in one of the keyword fields of the Advanced Groups Search page (either in the **with all of the words** field or **with the exact phrase** field). This may disclose other people's postings that contain their opinions about the expert.

Fourth, Google Groups can also be used to search by topic to find experts in a certain specialty when you don't already have a name of an expert. For example, if you are representing a client who was seriously injured when the treads of his Firestone tires separated, causing his vehicle to overturn, entering "Firestone tires" into Google Groups as a search phrase might lead you to an expert who has testified in prior tread-separation lawsuits. Also, the same search may identify people who have also been seriously injured when the tire treads on their vehicles separated. They might mention their expert's name or their lawyer's name (which can be a lead for you), or they may express their opinion about the expert.

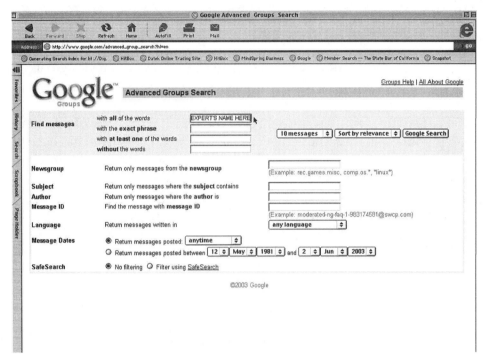

Figure 9-9. Search for the expert's name in one of the keyword fields of the Advanced Search page. Google™ is a trademark of Google Technology Inc.

Checklist Item 7: Review the Expert's Own Web Site

An expert's own Web site should be carefully reviewed prior to retaining him or her. If a search engine did not locate the expert's Web site, try simply entering the expert's name or company name followed by .com (expertname.com). Many experts post their full CV, prior litigation experience, speaking engagements, references, memberships and professional organization affiliations, and articles and newsletters on their Web sites. When reviewing an expert's Web site, keep in mind that opposing counsel can do so as well. Be aware that experts' Web sites are sometimes little more than self-promotion, so tread carefully. Is there anything embarrassing or contradictory on the site? Does the expert pronounce that he or she "is the leader in the industry" or put forth similar bravado that could affect how the jury perceives the expert? Imagine how the jury would react if the pages of the expert's Web site were displayed as exhibits at trial—because they very well could be.

Checklist Item 8: Determine If the Expert Has Ever Been Disciplined

It is also important to determine if an expert has been reviewed or disciplined by their jurisdiction's licensing boards. You may be able to find this discipline information by conducting a free public records search (See Chapter 8, "Accessing Public Records") if this type of information is public record. Although not a free search site, Idex.com has created a searchable database of experts who have been reviewed or disciplined by their jurisdiction's licensing boards (**http://www.Idex.com/about/ index.html#discipline**). To access this database, you must be an Idex member and a defense lawyer (or work on behalf of a defense lawyer). It is also worthwhile to check with any voluntary or mandatory membership professional organizations of which the expert is a member to gather this information.

Checklist Item 9: Find Experts via Jury Verdict Reporter Databases

Another way to find experts is by way of jury verdict reporters. While most lawyers search jury verdicts to assess the worth of a case, the astute lawyer knows that jury verdicts are useful in finding experts who testified in specific types of cases. By searching for an expert's name in a jury verdict reporter, you may discover whether the expert has given opposing opinions in similar cases, appears more often as a defense witness, or has usually testified for the winning side. The lawyers involved in the cases are also listed in the jury verdict database. You might consider contacting them for information about their experience with their own expert or the opposition's expert (for example, how the opposition's expert came across during cross-examination). Free online jury verdicts (and settlements) can be found at MoreLaw.com. Lexis and Westlaw offer pay jury verdict databases, as do NASJVP and VerdictSearch.com.

Free Jury Verdict Reporter Databases

MoreLaw.com

http://www.morelaw.com

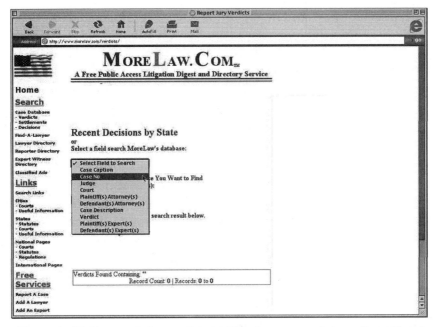

Figure 9-10. To search for verdicts at MoreLaw.com, click on **Case Database** on the top left side of the site's pages. Click on the **Select Field to Search** drop-down menu, and enter your keywords or a person's name into the search box.

Purpose: To find experts by way of jury verdict reports.

Content: MoreLaw.com is a free online legal information resource with a jury verdict reports database (where experts can be found), a lawyer directory, and an expert witness database. MoreLaw.com's verdict database has over 25,000 verdicts, all hand selected and summarized by Tulsa, Oklahoma lawyer Kent Morlan who reviews verdicts by searching Google, legal newspapers, and 125 appellate court Web sites. The database is searchable by keywords describing the expertise involved, by the facts of the case, or by lawyer, expert, or party name.

Our View: This might be the only free verdict site you'll find. It's a useful site for searching for experts; you may discover whether the expert has given opposing opinions in similar cases, appears more often as a defense witness, or has usually testified for the winning side. The lawyers involved in the cases are also listed in the verdict database and may provide you with information about their experience with the expert if you contact them directly.

Tip:

- We have found experts through MoreLaw.com's jury verdict database who did not list themselves on the expert witness database. Check both.
- To begin searching verdicts, first click on **Case Database**, then click on the drop-down menu titled **Select Field to Search**. Select **Case Description** as the field to search if looking for a case similar to your case and then enter your keywords. If you are looking only for cases where a specific expert served as a plaintiff's expert (or defendant's expert), select the **Plaintiff(s) Expert(s)** or **Defendant(s) Expert(s)** field and enter the expert's name into the search box.

Pay Jury Verdict Reporter Databases

VerdictSearch.com

http://www.verdictsearch.com **$**

Purpose: To find verdicts and settlements in order to identify experts.

Content: VerdictSearch is a product of the *National Law Journal's* Litigation Services Network and its database includes jury verdicts from the National Law Journal, California Jury Verdicts Weekly, DC Metro Verdict Reporter, Georgia Trial Reporter, Massachusetts, Connecticut, and Rhode Island Verdict Reporter, Michigan Trial Reporter, Ohio Trial Reporter, National Jury Verdict Reporter, New York Jury Verdict Reporter, and Texas Blue Sheet.

Our View: This is a useful service for those who frequently need to find experts and want to read about the cases that the experts were involved in. The cost is $2,795 for an annual subscription.

Tip: Instead of subscribing to VerdictSearch, the occasional user might try searching the expert or expertise at the

NLJ Expert Directory site (**http://www.nljexperts.com**). Then, from the NLJ Expert Directory, a user can link to that expert's list of cases at VerdictSearch and purchase a single verdict for $9.95. (See the above section, "Free Expert Witness Directories," for more information about NLJ).

National Association of State Jury Verdict Publishers (NASJVP)

http://www.juryverdicts.com

Purpose:	To find experts via jury verdict or case testified.
Content:	The NASJVP site offers an alphabetical listing of forty thousand experts. It includes their expertise and the name of the jury verdict publication where they are referenced.
Our View:	Although users can search free at NASJVP, after clicking on the expert's name, they are simply referred to the publisher where they can obtain detailed information about the verdict, for a fee.
Tip:	If you don't have the luxury of time, you'll probably be better off using one of the pay databases where the verdicts are readily available online and full text.

Checklist Item 10: Find the Expert's Deposition Testimony

Reading an expert's deposition testimony can provide an abundance of information about how the expert may perform. Currently there is no free, centralized database for expert witness transcripts, but there are several commercial sites and professional association sites that gather this information for members.

Deposition Testimony Databases

TrialSmith

http://www.trialsmith.com (formerly known as DepoConnect)   **$**

Purpose: For plaintiff lawyers only—to find expert's deposition testimony to determine possible performance

Content: TrialSmith is an online database with more than 137,000 depositions, and other documents that include briefs, pleadings, seminar papers, verdicts, and settlements. It also includes an expert witness database and e-mail discussion lists where lawyers discuss and recommend experts.

Our View: The annual subscription of $195 per year and $30 per document seems reasonable. Lawyers may find the private discussion groups useful for sharing information about experts.

Tip: Subscribers can instantly view or download any transcript.

ATLA

Also see the Association of Trial Lawyers of America (ATLA) site at **http://www.atla.org**, which makes available to its members a database of over ten thousand expert witnesses, and over fifteen thousand searchable transcripts. This database is developed by submission from its members. ATLA posts the contact information for the member who provided information about that expert.

While TrialSmith is for the plaintiff's bar, the Defense Research Institute (DRI) site, as its name implies, is only for defense lawyers who are DRI members. Also for defense lawyers is Idex (www.Idex.com). Idex has built its database of deposition transcripts (and trial testimony by experts) by submissions from its own members. Electronic versions of some documents can be viewed and downloaded directly from this site at a reduced price. According to its Web site, 6,000 records are added each month to Idex's database of over 800,000 records of expert involvement.

Defense Research Institute (DRI)

http://www.dri.org

Purpose:	To find expert's deposition testimony to determine possible performance.
Content:	DRI offers a searchable database to the complete text of expert witness testimony from trial courts around the country (and briefs, pleadings, motions, affidavits, orders, verdicts, judgments, and jury instructions). The DRI Expert Witness Database includes over fifty thousand plaintiff and defense experts and CVs for selected experts.
Our View:	The annual subscription of $195 a year is the same as TrialSmith, but for further details about pricing per document, you'll need to join DRI or e-mail them.
Tip:	The DRI has other member benefits, such as a magazine, a newsletter, and seminars.

Checklist Item 11: Find Briefs and Cases That Refer to the Expert

Briefs

Experts may also be referred to in briefs. All types of briefs can be found at Brief Reporter (**http://www.briefreporter.com**). Searching (by keywords) is free and so is viewing an abstract of the brief (which includes the case name, court, and docket number). A search for "tires" resulted in seventy-five briefs. Subscribers who pay a $35-per-month access fee can download documents for $10 each. Nonsubscribers can download briefs for $40 per brief.

BriefServe.com has searchable briefs from 30,739 cases from all United States Courts of Appeals from 1981 to the present, the U.S. Supreme Court from 1984 to the present, New York appellate courts, and California Supreme Court and appellate courts (**http://www.brief serve.com/home.asp**). Pennsylvania state court briefs are promised soon. Briefs cost $25 to download. Briefs for some courts are free at other sites (such as U.S. Supreme Court briefs at FindLaw), but they are not keyword searchable. You must search by year and party name.

Ask a Lawyer for Help

An alternative to joining one of these associations in order to search their deposition transcripts would be to contact lawyers directly to see if they will supply you with transcripts of the experts. You would either have to know of a case similar to yours to do this (which you might through your case law or jury verdict research), or you might find that the experts themselves have listed, on their Web sites, the names of the lawyers with whom they have worked in the past. Of course, you can simply ask the expert for a list of lawyer references and case names. Most lawyers keep their own expert witness transcripts, and would be willing to share (provided, of course, the favor is returned some day).

Case Law

An expert's name may also appear in a reported opinion. Fortunately, many reported opinions can be searched for free (see LexisOne at **http://www.lexisone.com** or FindLaw at **http://www.findlaw.com**). To conduct retrospective or nationwide searches, you'll usually need to use a pay database such as major players Lexis or Westlaw (which both also have a variety of other tools for finding experts, including expert witness directories and jury verdicts), or some of the newer case law sites such as LoisLaw or VersusLaw. Searching for experts in reported decisions is similar to the technique used in a general search-engine search for experts as noted above. To find cases using a known expert's name, type in the name alone; if their name is common, add keywords that describe the expertise. If trying to locate an expert in a specific area of expertise, type the word "expert" along with the expertise sought, using relevant keywords.

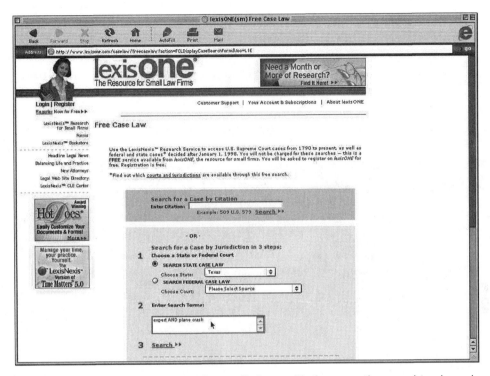

Figure 9-11. Type the word "expert" along with the expertise sought using relevant keywords that describe the expertise (e.g. plane crash). Reprinted with permission of LexisNexis.

Checklist Item 12: Locate Academic Experts Through University Sites

If you plan to hire or depose experts who happen to be professors, go to the university's Web site for a look at their CV, courses they've taught, and articles or books they have published. Links to college and university home pages can be found at the American Universities site, described below.

American Universities

http://www.clas.ufl.edu/CLAS/american-universities.html

Purpose: To search for academic experts who are teaching in universities and colleges.

Content: The site provides links to Web sites of universities and colleges in the Unites States.

Our View: You have to search college by college, which can be time consuming.

Tip: Start out with institutions nearby.

USC Experts

USC Experts Directory is a directory provided by the University of Southern California of over a thousand USC scientists, scholars, administrators, and physicians who are able and willing to comment on issues in the news. Although primarily for the media, this could be another avenue to find academic experts. See **http://uscnews3.usc.edu/experts/index.html**.

Checklist Item 13: Find Government Experts Through Government Reports

Former government employees may make good experts and so may nongovernment experts who have testified before a Senate or House committee hearing, or have been quoted in a Senate or House report. Current government employees may be able to answer your questions or point you to a former government expert. But, it can take time to cut through the layers of government to find the right person. If you persevere, you're likely to be rewarded with someone who understands exactly what you're talking about. A good starting place to locate potential experts is at a government agency's Web site because it often includes personnel directories. To find a specific state government agency's Web site, see State and Local Government on the Net (**http://www.statelocalgov.net**). To search through the alphabetical list of all federal agencies, a visit to FirstGov.gov is in order (**http://www.firstgov.gov/Agencies/Federal/All_Agencies/index.shtml**).

FirstGov.gov can also be searched using keywords to locate testifying experts by name or by the specialty you are interested in (**http://www.firstgov.gov**). FirstGov.gov indexes millions Web pages from federal and state governments, the District of Columbia, and U.S. territories.

Most of these pages are not be available on any commercial Web site.

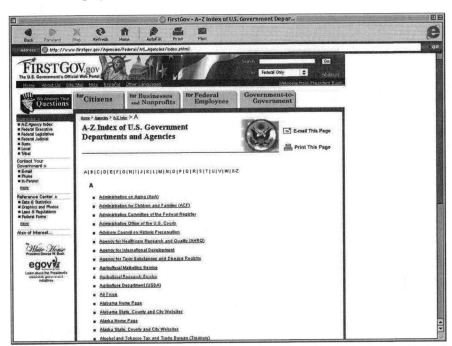

Figure 9-12. Search through FirstGov.gov's alphabetical list of agencies to link to one that deals with the subject area for which you are seeking an expert.

To search House and Senate committee reports, full text back to 1995, use Thomas (**http://thomas.loc.gov/home/thomas.html**). At the state level, the legislative history of a bill may include references to government and nongovernment experts. Use FindLaw (**http://www.findlaw .com/casecode/#statelaw**) to link to any state's legislative information.

Here is an example of how we found experts by searching California legislative history. We searched the bills for the keywords "seat belt and school bus and safety and children. " This led to a 1999 bill requiring seat belts to be installed in school buses by 2002 (**http://www.leginfo.ca.gov/ bilinfo.html**). The Analyses (California's equivalent of legislative history) section of the bill listed several committee reports. We reviewed the Senate committee report from July 12, 1999 and its staff comments and learned that "this bill is the latest in a series of efforts . . . [that] have been largely unsuccessful . . . [A] study to determine the appropriateness of requiring lap belts . . . determined that the existing research . . . weigh(ed) *against* new lap belt policies for . . . school buses." Listed in these staff comments were specific references to several studies, the names of associations in opposition to the bill, the name of the chair of the committee, and the name of the consultant for the study. Contacting any of these people or groups could be fruitful in finding an expert to testify that requiring lap belts in school buses is unsafe.

Checklist Item 14: Use Pay Referral Sites

If you haven't had luck finding the appropriate expert with any of the above sources (or if you want someone else to do the legwork for you), consult a referral site.

The California-based ForensisGroup (**http://www.forensisgroup .com**) provides referrals to five hundred technical, engineering, medical, scientific, and environmental experts. While you can view short blurbs about selected experts (by clicking on **Expert Profiles**), you'll need to contact this referral company to retain that expert or to learn of other experts in that field.

For referrals to medical experts who will review a case or testify in all types of health-care related malpractice, personal injury, and other tort litigation cases (and criminal law), go to medQuest (**http://www.med questltd.com**). It provides referrals to testifying medical experts (physicians, dentists, osteopaths, podiatrists, chiropractors, optometrists, nurses, pharmacists, therapists, and others) in every region of the country. There are no profiles for you to preview as there are at ForensisGroup.

TASA (**http://www.tasanet.com**), a site with 9,400 areas of expertise represented, is one of the best known of the expert witness referral companies. When you search TASA's online Directory of Expertise you are offered many categories to choose from, plus subcategories. Once you make your selection, the number of experts in the selected field and their geographic locations are shown. Users are then required to call or e-mail TASA for the experts' names and contact information. If an expert is engaged, there is a one-time (per-case) $100 fee payable to TASA (in addition to the expert's fee).

*CHAPTER***TEN**

Company Research

Company research is one of the subjects that ought to be taught in law school. There are endless bits of information that lawyers need to know about companies in order to serve clients. Understanding what information is available and how to access it efficiently can make all the difference, whether you're bringing suit, seeking to help your client acquire a company, or representing shareholders. Competitive Intelligence, a close relative of company research, is another subject they should teach in law school. (See Chapter 11, "Competitive Intelligence Research," for more information.)

Company research can help both litigators and transactional lawyers. For example, in a litigation matter, where your client has been injured by an improperly designed garage door, you need to do company research to learn more about the manufacturer of the door in order to answer the following questions:

- Who is the proper defendant: the manufacturer, the installer, the retailer, or all of them?
- Is your target the manufacturer who is identified on the product (the door)?
- Is the manufacturer the parent corporation, or merely a subsidiary?
- Where is the company headquarters? In Delaware or the UK?
- Who's the registered agent for service of process?

You also need to learn more about the product, so you continue on with your company research by visiting the manufacturer's Web site or even competitors' sites to find out

- If the specs for the door are listed on any of the Web sites so you (or your expert) can:
  1. Compare their designs
  2. Ascertain whether they were manufactured in a like or different manner
- If there are any claims, warranties, or admissions on the company site

Transactional lawyers, such as counsel to shareholder groups or a business lawyer counseling a client who is seeking to acquire a business, may use company research to:

- Access corporate press releases
- Locate all of the target's recent Securities and Exchange Commission (SEC) filings
- Locate corporate annual reports
- Locate sales figures
- Conduct due diligence

The Internet can help with all these tasks.

Checklist for Finding Company Information

- ❑ 1. Review the company's Web site. Use the site to discover the company structure, find specs for products, and so on. To review the site, you'll need to locate the company's URL—see Checklist Item 2.)
- ❑ 2. Locate the Web site's URL.
- ❑ 3. Google the company using both the Google search engine and Google Groups.
- ❑ 4. Use company directories (covering public and private companies) for third-party opinions.
- ❑ 5. Use Web-based phone directories to locate the company.
- ❑ 6. Use product directories to learn about the company and its products.
- ❑ 7. Locate public-company financial information, such as SEC filings, annual reports, and stock prices.

❑   8. Locate private-company information in directories and credit reports.

❑   9. Search for current and archived news about the company, its executives, and products.

❑ 10. Review secretary of state records to find registered agents and fictitious business names.

❑ 11. Consider using pay databases to find information about the company.

❑ 12. Find reported decisions, dockets, verdicts, and settlements involving the company, its executives, and products.

❑ 13. Ascertain which federal or state agencies regulate the company's products or industry. Search government Web sites for any mention of the company or products.

❑ 14. Think outside the box. (See Chapter 11, "Competitive Intelligence Research"; Chapter 7, "Finding and Backgrounding People"; and Chapter 8, "Accessing Public Records.")

Checklist Item 1: Review the Company's Web Site

Company Web sites are often the simplest starting points for company research. In addition, company Web sites often begin where a com-

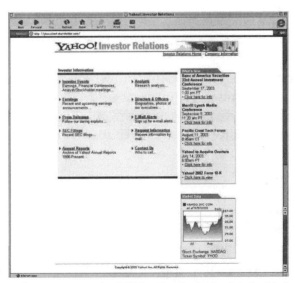

Figure 10-1. Some companies' Web sites include detailed information regarding their stock. Reproduced with permission of Yahoo! Inc. © 2003 by Yahoo! Inc. YAHOO! and the YAHOO! logo are trademarks of Yahoo! Inc.

pany's printed literature leaves off. Companies may take the printed literature and transform it into an expanded electronic dossier, offering more insight into products and activities. Thus, locating a company's Web site should be the first step you take to learn about the company. By using a company's own site, you'll be able to obtain information that you would normally have to spend hours compiling from other sources. Company sites may provide their SEC filings, press releases, background information about company executives, other financial information (stock quotes and history), and even some information not available anywhere else on the Internet (such as job openings and salaries). Some of this information will only be found if the company is public (such as SEC filings). After discovering what the company has to say about itself, you can then search the Internet for outside information about the company in order to compare the data and draw your own conclusions.

Checklist Item 2: Locate the Web Site's URL

If you do not know the company's URL and have not been able to guess it by adding .com to the company name (such as Nike.com), there are many ways to find a public or private company's URL. You can search a company directory Web site (see below) by company name. Often the URL will be noted in the directory's company profile.

If you know part of the URL, search the partial URL at Domainsurfer to try to discover the full URL (**http://www.domainsurfer.com**). See the section "Internet Source Credibility" in Chapter 1, "Using the Internet for Factual Research," to learn how to find out who owns a Web site.

You can also type the company name into any search engine (the best choice is Google—see below). If you search a company name using Google.com, typically the company's Web site will often be the first one in the results list.

Checklist Item 3: Google the Company

Enter the company name into the search box on Google's home page and click on the **I'm Feeling Lucky** or **Google Search** buttons. This will usually bring up the company's Web site. Also run the company name, executives' names, and product names through Google.com (**http://www.google.com**) and Google Groups

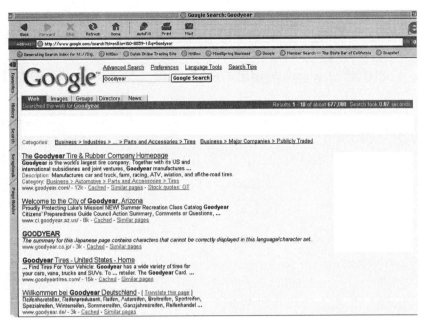

Figure 10-2. If you search a company name using Google.com, typically the company's Web site will often be the first one in the results list. Google™ is a trademark of Google Technology Inc.

(**http://groups.google.com**) just to see if you come up with any interesting nuggets of information.

For more details on Googling and searching for information in online communities, see the "Thinking Outside the Box" section in Chapter 7, "Finding and Backgrounding People."

Checklist Item 4: Use Company Directories

An important distinction to make when setting out to conduct company research is whether the target of your search is public (meaning shares in the company are traded on a public exchange) or private (meaning that shares of the firm are not publicly traded). There's significantly more credible information available about public companies. Public companies are regulated by the SEC, and are therefore required to make certain public filings, many of which are easily retrievable on the Internet for free via the EDGAR database (discussed later in this chapter—see **http://www.sec.gov/cgi-bin/srch-edgar**).

Even if you know a company is public, rather than going directly to the company's public SEC filings, we suggest going first to a company

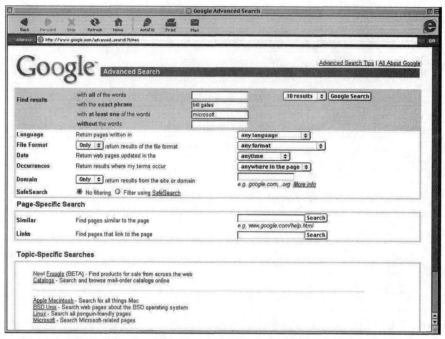

Figure 10-3. Using the Google Advanced Search page, enter both an executive's name and the company's name to search for extra nuggets of information. Google™ is a trademark of Google Technology Inc.

directory site for a more objective look at the company. And, if you don't know whether a company is public or private, these directory sites usually indicate that. (More public companies than private companies appear in these company directory sites.)

Company directory sites compile background information about companies from many sources to create a profile that gives an overview of the company. These sites also link you to secondary sources about the company (such as news articles, stock quotes, and research analyst reports), in addition to linking you to the company's Web site and its SEC filings. If you're searching for a company's address, but you're uncertain how to spell the company name, there are Internet directories that enable you to search based on the type of industry and the state where the company is headquartered. Such directories can also be used to quickly determine whether your client's proposed company name is in use anywhere in the country. Some of the company directory sites are free, and some are partially free (basic information is free, but there is a fee for detailed information). Those that charge a fee do so by subscription or on a pay-as-you-go model (or both).

The following are examples of some excellent company directory sites. Some include only public companies and some include both public and private.

Public Company Directories

Yahoo! Finance Company and Fund Index

http://biz.yahoo.com/i

Purpose:	To find public-company background and financial information.
Content:	Search 32,502 companies and funds by name or browse an alphabetical list. Your results offer you links to news, message boards, insider trading, stock quotes, and a profile (if available for the chosen company). For example, of the 32,502 companies indexed, only 9,000 have profiles (from another publication called *Market Guide*). The profile option lists the company's address, phone, fax, e-mail address, and top executives (and their pay). Links are provided to the company home page, stock price, and SEC filings.
Our View:	This is an easy-to-use site chock-full of information.
Tip:	If you click on **SEC** from the profile, you will only be shown recent filings. If you click on **More filings . . . from EDGAR Online**, you will find yourself at a pay site offering you a two-week trial. It's best to go to one of the free EDGAR sites discussed below.

Hoover's Online (a subsidiary of D & B since 2003)

http://www.hoovers.com

Purpose:	To find private and public company information and to link to their sites.

Content: The database contains twelve million companies, with
in-depth coverage of twenty-one thousand of them.
To search, enter a word or name into the search box
and then select one of the following options: Company
Name, by Ticker, Stock Quote, IPO Companies, Company Keyword (for subscribers only), Industry Keyword,
Executive Name, the News, Report Search, or D&B D-U-
N-S Number (for subscribers only). On the search results
page there are links to Fact Sheet, News, Financials, and
People (for subscribers only). There is also a link called
Related Products From Our Trusted Partners
(pay databases where you can buy information on an
ad-hoc basis with a credit card). Any links that have a
Lock icon indicate that this information is under
lock and key and is for Hoover's subscribers only. If
you click on the **Fact Sheet** link, you will find the
following free information: the company's address,
phone number, fax number, and a link to the company's Web site; key numbers (sales, growth, company
type [private or public], number of employees, and
so on); key people (names only—you must be a subscriber for biographies and for more people); rankings;
and names of a few top competitors and subsidiaries
or affiliates (for complete lists, you must be a subscriber).
If you click on the **News** link, you will find links to
very current news (for free) about the company from
various sources, including the company's press releases. If you click on the **Financials** link, you will
find that only basic information is free and that other
information is restricted to subscribers. If you click
on the **SEC** link, you will find links to the company's
filings.

Our View: When Hoover's became a subsidiary D & B, we anticipated changes, such as a reduction in the amount of free
information. It seems like there is less free information
because the results page no longer shows a company
capsule that contained a good deal of company background information (both current and historic). But it
just could be the redesign that is throwing us off—the

site is not as user-friendly as it once was (and it's less attractive). But it is a useful site for those who need basic company information and those who only occasionally need detailed information and are willing to pay for it. Some examples of available information are business and credit reports from various companies (such as D & B, from $5 to $123) and corporate hierarchy information from LexisNexis. It's also useful for heavy users of this type of information, but we can't comment on how it compares price-wise to other sites that have like information. Subscriber rates are not posted; you must make an individual inquiry. Pricing depends upon the number of users and the plan chosen.

Tip:

- A paid subscription to Hoover's is useful for gathering competitive intelligence (see Chapter 11, "Competitive Intelligence Research") because in addition to the detailed company and financial information, it offers e-mail alerts and the ability to search extensive databases and create custom reports and lists.
- Hoover's also sponsors IPO-Central; some information is free and some is restricted to subscribers only (**http://www.hoovers.com/global/ipoc/index.xhtml**).

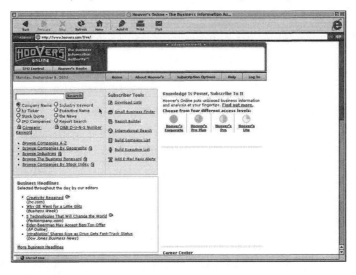

Figure 10-4. Enter a word or name into the search box and then select one of the following options: Company Name, by Ticker, Stock Quote, IPO Companies, Industry Keyword, Executive Name, the News, or Report Search.

High-Tech Company Directories

CorpTech.com

http://www.corptech.com

Purpose: To find companies that manufacture, develop, or provide services related to high-tech items.

Content: Those who register as guest members can search over fifty thousand companies by company name or ticker symbol and view a capsule profile of that company for free. The capsule includes company name, address, telephone, fax, home page, ownership, year formed, sales range, employee range, primary industry, and CEO name. Guests also can obtain up to five free standard profiles per session, which include more information than the capsule profile. For example, the standard profile also includes a list of all executives (not just the CEO) and a brief description of the company's business. Guests may purchase standard profiles for $5.00 once they have exceeded their five free ones, or extended profiles for $7.50.

Our View: Unless your clients are in the high-tech arena, you'll probably be satisfied with the free guest membership. An annual subscription, for those who want more detailed information, the ability to query by twenty search criteria (SIC code, number of employees, revenue, state, ZIP code, product line, and so on), and the ability to view and download data into lists and reports, costs $5,995 annually or $2,495 for those who don't need the download option.

Tip: • This is useful for client development since you can create all types of reports.
    • Check your local library's remote access databases (see the section "Free Internet Access to Library Databases and Catalogs" in Chapter 5, "General Factual Research") because your library may offer free access to

a database with similar information (such as Gale Business Resources or REF USA).

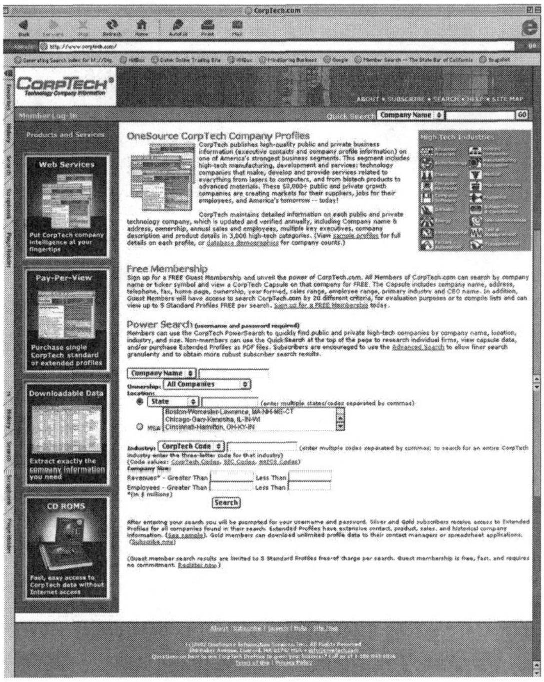

Figure 10-5. Use CorpTech to search over fifty thousand companies related to the high-tech industry and view a company profile for free.

Checklist Item 5: Use Web-Based Phone Directories

Another type of directory that shouldn't be overlooked are Web-based phone directories, both White Pages and Yellow Pages. (See Chapter 7, "Finding and Backgrounding People," for more information.) While the existence of a company with the same name your client plans to use for a new venture or product does not necessarily bar its use, a quick, free Internet search through Web-based phone directories may give you enough information to decide if an expensive trademark or trade name search is in order. Such directories also allow you to search at your own pace through the nation's business phone books, a luxury previously available only to those willing to spend time in the rare library that keeps current phone books for the nation, or those willing to pay the cost of a national phone book directory on CD-ROM.

Figure 10-6. The free Web-based phone directory InfoSpace (**http://www .infospace.com**) offers White Pages and Yellow Pages searches, as well as a reverse directory—all for free. © 2003 InfoSpace, Inc. All rights reserved. Reprinted with permission of InfoSpace, Inc.

Checklist Item 6: Use Product Directories

A products liability lawyer who needs to find out who manufactured a product that injured a client or who needs to find an expert witness about a certain product would be advised to search the Thomas Register by product name to find a list of companies that manufacture that product.

Product Directories

Thomas Register

http://www.thomasregister.com

Purpose: To search for company, product, and brand name infor- mation.

Content: The Thomas Register profiles 186,000 American and Canadian companies, with links to their Web sites and catalogs. Registration (free) is required.

Our View: This site is unique in that you can search not only by company name but also by product name, service name, or brand name.

Tip: To search for European companies by company name, product, or service, try Europages (**http://www.euro pages.net**). You can limit the search to a specific country or to a region within the country. Though not as detailed as Thomas, it provides contact information, including an e-mail address and map, and sometimes a link to a Web site.

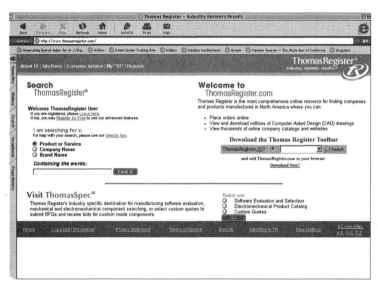

Figure 10-7. Use the Thomas Register to search by company name, product name, service name, or brand name.

Checklist Item 7: Locate Public-Company Financial Information

SEC Filings

As of May 6, 1996, all domestic public companies, with some exceptions, were required to make their SEC filings on the SEC's EDGAR (Electronic Data Gathering and Retrieval) site. Because the requirement to file electronically was on a rolling schedule, beginning in 1994, only some companies' files on EDGAR go back that far. While annual 10-Ks, 10-Qs and a variety of other filings are filed on EDGAR, annual reports to shareholders are not, since they are not required to be filed at all; however, some companies do file them (see the section on "Annual Reports" later in this chapter to learn where to obtain them). Searching for filings can be done for free at the SEC's official site, EDGAR, but other sites (some free and some fee-based) have stepped up to the plate with much better search capabilities, such as full-text searching.

War Story: Finding a Casino Deal

When Daniel T. Hardy from the Madison, Wisconsin firm of Axley Brynelson asked his law librarian, Clare L. Winkler, to find a casino management agreement between nontribal companies and Native American tribes, she found samples by using EDGAR. However, since she couldn't full-text search using EDGAR, she did some newspaper sleuthing first where she found articles that identified names of companies that had struck these kinds of deals. While surfing the Internet, she also ran into the National Indian Gaming Commission (NIGC) Web site which proved helpful as well (**http://www.nigc.gov/nigc/index.jsp**). As Winkler relates, "From here, I searched EDGAR filings [by company name] and found a contract as an exhibit in a company's 10-K. I then used the Find feature on my Internet browser to locate casino management agreements within the very large company filings." At our suggestion, Winkler tried some of the full-text SEC filings databases noted below. Although she's sure that using the full-text database would've been helpful in pinpointing an agreement by searching for the phrase "management agreement," a certain amount of sleuthing would still have been necessary in order to find the actual document because the phrase "management agreement" is mentioned quite frequently in casino management company filings. In deference to its official status, we'll look at EDGAR first and then review other sites.

EDGAR

http://www.sec.gov/edgarhp.htm

Purpose: To search for public company filings (U.S. companies as of May 6, 1996, and foreign issuers as of November 4, 2002).

Content: The content includes filings. Help aids should be
explored before beginning a search. First, look at the
tutorial for an overview of what's available on EDGAR
and for search tips. Then, click on **Descriptions of
SEC Forms** to help decide what type of form will
answer your question. Although you can search all
types, it's better to limit your search if you can. For
instance, if you only want information on material
events or corporate changes that are too recent to be in a
10-K or 10-Q, limit the search to an 8-K. Click on **About
EDGAR** to learn which forms are not required to be

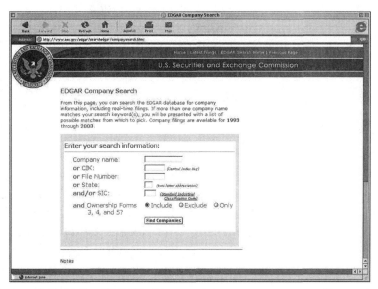

Figure 10-8. At the EDGAR site, search by company name, file number, state,
SIC code, or CIK.

filed electronically and which are optional (for example,
Form 144, notice of proposed sale of securities, is
optional). To begin searching, click on **Search for
Company Filings** (or go directly to **http://www.sec
.govedgar/searchedgar/companysearch.html**). At the
EDGAR site, you can search by company name, state,
SIC code (Standard Industrial Classification—identifying the business type), CIK (Central Index Key—a
unique number assigned by the SEC's computer system
to individuals, funds, and corporations who file), and a
very limited amount of text in the header field. You can
also search by clicking on **Latest Filings** to view the

most recent real-time filings, or on **Current Events Analysis** to view filings from the previous one to five business days.

Our View: Although EDGAR is by far one of the richest collections of information available concerning U.S. public companies, offers free access, and is now (finally) posting filings in real time, it lacks the full-text searching capability that many other free and low-cost sites offer.

Tip: • Many companies have similar names, but each one has a unique CIK. As soon as you identify the CIK (by using the CIK lookup feature at **http://www.sec.gov/edgar/searchedgar/cik.htm**) for your subject company, always search by that number to pinpoint the company.
   • Search by SIC code when you want samples of filings from specific industries.
   • If you search at a site that offers free full-text searching, but charges to view the document, you can return to EDGAR to view and print free. The downside is that you won't have your search terms (from the full-text search database) highlighted and will have to use the Find function to locate the terms. For regular SEC searchers, a subscription to a fee-based service may be a better option.

Full-Text SEC Searches

Have you ever been asked to draft an executive compensation agreement for a client? Instead of starting from scratch, use one of the full-text search SEC filing sites (such as SEC Info, 10k Wizard, FreeEdgar, Westlaw, EdgarScan, Global Securities Information's LIVEDGAR, or LexisNexis's EDGARPlus). In addition to all of EDGAR's search options, they offer searching by ticker symbol, person's name, date, type of form, and—more importantly—full-text searching with Boolean connectors. Using one of these databases, you can limit a search to your client's industry (or use the SIC code) and type in the keywords "executive compensation." You'll be rewarded with agreements that you can use as examples.

There are a variety of other ways to customize your search when using a full-text SEC database. To name just a few, you can search by a key executive's name, an insider's name, or an event such as a bankruptcy.

While some of these sites are free, the sites with the most robust search engines (as we'll point out below) are only partially free: they are free to search, but to view the filings, you must have a subscription. When FreeEdgar and 10k Wizard ceased being completely free, there was a flurry of e-mail postings on a law librarian list querying what to use now for free, full-text, real-time access to SEC filings. A law librarian answered, "No question about this one, SEC Info.com." For those who don't want to pay for a subscription, but still want to take advantage of the robust search engines of the partially free SEC databases, you can do so by using a two-step process: (1) search the more robust database (free) and make a note of the company name, the type of filing, and date of the filings that seem relevant; (2) take your results to EDGAR, where you can view and print for free.

SEC Info (registration is required)

http://www.secinfo.com

Purpose: To search for U.S. SEC filings and Canadian Securities Administrators (CSA) SEDAR (System for Electronic Document Analysis and Retrieval) databases—with more search functions than EDGAR.

Content: The following search options are provided: name, industry, business, SIC code, area code, topic, CIK, accession number, file number, date, ZIP code, and state of incorporation. There are easy-to-view lists of: most recent filings, future events, form types, insider trading, IPOs, tender offers, and so on.

Our View: There's a lot to like about how this site:

- The way it displays information (for example, it makes use of a table of contents so you can click either on the document or on any of the exhibits)
- Its useful download and print options
- It is one of the few sites to also search Canadian filings exchange

But, because SEC Info encourages searching by one or two words only, searchers can't construct as complex a search as at the other SEC filing sites. For example, there is no phrase searching or combination searches (such as company name and keyword). Finally, it is unclear how long you can use the site for free (a warning states it can be used for free "until you exceed a usage threshold") at which point you will be offered a subscription. We haven't reached our threshold yet, so we're not sure at what point you reach it or what the subscription price is.

Tip:
- Forms can be downloaded into several formats of your choice (Word, rich text, plain text, XML, and so on).
- You can print one page only.
- Once you open a document, use the internal hyper-linking (for example, if you click on the link by-laws in Exhibit 3.1, you are then taken to Exhibit 3.2, where the bylaws are found).
- There is a free e-mail alert service.

Even though it's no longer free to view or print filings, as mentioned earlier, you can still take advantage of 10k Wizard's search engine—which is still free and real time (**http://www.tenkwizard.com**).

10k Wizard

To search: To view and print: **$**

http://www.10kwizard.com

Purpose: Don't be misled by 10k Wizard's name; this site provides real-time access to all forms filed with the SEC (not just 10-Ks), and offers full-text searches.

Content: Search by any or a combination of the following: company name, ticker, CIK, industry, SIC code, date (specific, a range, or all), form group or specific form (or all forms), and keyword (words and phrases with Boolean or proximity connectors).

Our View: This site has excellent search functions but once you get your results list it's not as intuitive as we'd like it to be. For nonsubscribers, click on a company name in the results list, and then under **More Info** click on **Filing**. Clicking on any other option is reserved for subscribers only. The **Filing** page presents you with the information you need to return to the free EDGAR site to pull up the filing—the type of filing and the date filed.

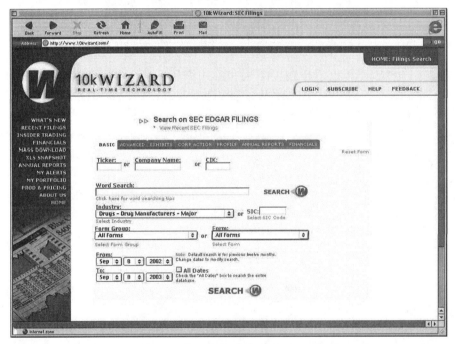

Figure 10-9. With 10k Wizard, you can search by any of the following (or a combination): company name, ticker, CIK, industry, SIC code, date, form group, and keyword (words and phrases with Boolean or proximity connectors).

Tip: For the occasional user, take advantage of its robust search engine to pinpoint the information you are seeking and then take your findings to EDGAR to view and print for free. For the more frequent user, the $99.95 per year subscription fee is well worth the cost.

Also recommended by a number of librarians as a replacement for FreeEdgar is EdgarScan, provided by the ABAS Technology Group of Pricewaterhouse.

EdgarScan

http://edgarscan.pwcglobal.com/servlets/edgarscan

Purpose: To search for company information and annual reports and to create interactive financial charts.

Content: It offers full-text searching with keywords and phrases (and Boolean connectors), and if you use the advanced search, field searching is available. There is also an IPO lookup by date, company name, and industry.

Our View: Lawyers primarily interested in the financials of a company or how its financials compare to others will like EdgarScan for the following reasons:

- When EdgarScan pulls filings from the SEC's servesit automatically locates key financial tables and creates a common format across companies
- It also has a Benchmarking Assistant to perform graphical financial benchmarking interactively
- Tables showing company comparisons can be downloaded into Microsoft Excel
- Registered users can store company portfolios for future benchmarking

Tip: Some things to be aware of:

- The site is not real-time—there is usually a twenty-four to forty-eight hour delay in adding new filings
- Only 10-Ks and 10-Qs are indexed, and only back to 1999
- The word searching function isn't as good as other SEC sites discussed—for example, a search for the word "pension" also returned filings with the word "suspension"

E-alerts $

For those who want to set up e-alerts, pay sites such as Global Securities Information's LIVEDGAR (**http://www.gsionline.com/NewsAlerts .htm**) and LexisNexis' EDGARPlus (for a sample, see **http://www.lexis-nexis.com/productsandservices/financial.asp**) are two options. Westlaw also has an SEC filings database, supplied by Disclosure Inc. It includes filings back to 1968 (pre-EDGAR).

Annual Reports

Annual reports are chock-full of interesting company information, all shaped and supplied by the companies themselves. You'll usually find a message from the chief executive, a discussion of new initiatives begun in the past year, a list of company executives, and extensive company financials. Anyone can get a copy of a company's annual report by simply calling the corporation's investor relations department. However, there are times when you might not want the company to know you're gathering information about them, in which case calling the investor relations department is out of the question. Or, there may be times when you need instant access to the report and don't have time to wait for a mailed print copy. Fortunately, there are several ways to obtain the reports via the Web.

Many companies post their annual reports on the Internet. While you can do a general search-engine search to determine whether a particular company has an annual report on the Internet, beware of too many results; a search for "Microsoft" and "annual report" returned 137,000 results. A better option is to check the company's site first.

When you need a foreign company's report or an older domestic report no longer posted on a company's Web site, you might try one of the many annual reports archival sites (see Global Reports below for both of these services). These sites might also be helpful if you need to access more than one company's report (see PRARS below), or if you want to search by industry, SIC code, or other options (see all annual report sites below, with the exception of ReportGallery).

Annual Reports for U.S. Companies

IRIN (Investor Relations Information Network)

http://www.irin.com/cgi-bin/main.cgi

Purpose: To search for recent annual reports of corporations (the past one or two years).

Content: IRIN supplies free access to over three thousand annual reports that users can download as a PDF file. In addition to the annual report, each entry includes delayed stock quotes, an image of the annual report, and links to additional company information (basic contact information, charts, and graphs).

Our View: For those who do not know a company's ticker symbol, be sure to click on the **Advanced Search/Company Listing** link to search by company name or to browse an alphabetical list. A handy feature is the ability to also search by SIC code to create a list of companies in the same industry.

Tip: Downloading the PDF of the annual report can take a bit of time unless you have a high-speed connection. Fortunately, IRIN provides an extra service so you can avoid a large download. IRIN will forward a request to the company that you would like a print copy mailed out to you. However, this may not be a good idea if you are conducting a surreptitious investigation.

Some other free sites offer different features than IRIN. If you need annual reports from many companies, and want to avoid filling out a request for each company, use PRARS (the Public Register's Annual Report Service) at **http://www.prars.com**. PRARS allows you to add multiple company-report requests to your virtual shopping cart (for free) to request that annual reports be sent to you via postal mail, anywhere in the U.S., for no charge. Also, a handy feature at PRARS (which is not available at IRIN) is a search by industry, state, or exchange. Report Gallery (**http://www.reportgallery.com**) is one more free site to check. While they focus on the Fortune 500 annual reports, the site has others, too.

Global Reports

If you don't find what you want on the free sites, or need foreign annual reports and you're willing to pay, check out Global Reports below (they recently purchased Annual Reports Library).

Annual Reports for U.S. and Foreign Companies

Global Reports

http://www.global-reports.com

To search: To view and print: **$**

Purpose:	To search for current and retrospective annual reports.
Content:	Global Reports has a collection of full-color annual reports from over seventeen thousand companies in more than sixty-five countries, going back at least five years for many, and back to 1996 for some.
Our View:	This is one of the few services where you can download more than the current annual report. The search options are very useful—search by company name, ticker country, exchange, index, report type (annual, interim, or IPO), and report year.
Tip:	You can search free, but must be a paid subscriber to download the reports. Contact the company for pricing.

Stock Quotes

Current Quotes

For a while, Yahoo! offered free real-time quotes, but it went to a pay scheme priced at $9.95 per month for streaming real-time quotes (**http://finance.yahoo.com**). Most free stock quote sites are delayed by fifteen to twenty minutes. For those that still offer free access to real-time quotes, you'll find that you typically need to register. Examples are Multex Investor, where you also have to sign three agreements before being able to access their real-time quotes database (**http://multexinvestor.com**), and ThomsonFN (**http://www.thomsonfn.com**). Most sites require you to search for quotes by ticker symbol, but they usually provide a convenient company name lookup to find the ticker.

Historical Quotes

Yahoo! Finance Historical Prices

http://chart.yahoo.com/d

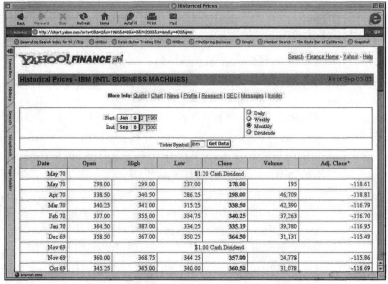

Figure 10-10. Yahoo! Finance offers access to historic stock quote information that was once only available at a (high) price.Reprinted with permission of Yahoo! Inc. © 2003 by Yahoo! Inc. YAHOO! and the YAHOO! logo are trademarks of Yahoo! Inc.

Purpose: To find historical U.S. stock quotes back to 1962.

Content: Results show the open, high, low, volume, and close, in addition to splits and dividend distributions of historical data of U.S. stock quotes.

Our View: This is great free service for those who need to know what a stock was priced at in the past. Before the Internet, access to this information was from an expensive pay database. You'll appreciate that you can create a weekly, monthly, or daily chart. Additionally, you can limit the search results to dividends only.

Tip: • Although quotes are not adjusted for splits or dividends, in the **Adjusted Close** column the close price is adjusted for all splits and dividends.
   • Click on the **Download Spreadsheet Format** link

at the end of the Historical Prices table to download into a Microsoft Excel spreadsheet.

Checklist Item 8: Locate Private-Company Information in Directories and Credit Reports

It can be very difficult to get accurate, timely information about private companies. Private firms are not bound by SEC filing requirements that result in the rich trove of public-company data available on EDGAR. One of the most common sources of private company data (and one that you must pay for), the D & B company report, is composed largely of self-reported data. This makes it hard to know whether the data is completely accurate.

Private Company Directories and Credit Reports for U.S. and Foreign Companies

Zapdata (owned by D & B)

http://www.zapdata.com

Purpose: To find private company contact information.

Content: Fourteen million private companies can be searched in the company lookup search box (**http://zapleads.zap data.com/cl/search_form.jsp**). Search nationwide by company name or refine your search by adding a state, street address, city, ZIP code, or phone number. Results include an address and type of industry, and show a company's headquarters and its branches (or whether it has a single location only).

Our View: This site is useful not only for general contact information, but also when you need to find out what type of entity the company is—in preparation for serving a complaint. For example, a search for "24 Hour Fitness" returned 150 results. Scanning the list, it was easy to separate the headquarters from the branches and single locations and to identify clubs connected to 24 Hour Fitness that used different names (for example, Scottsdale Club showed 24 Hour Fitness USA Inc. as its parent).

Tip: For $5, you can order a very basic D & B report.

Private Company Listings and Credit Reports for U.S and Foreign Companies

D & B

http://www.dnb.com/us

Purpose: To find contact information for 79 million private companies from 214 countries, and to order various business and credit reports.

Content: Search by company name and state (both are required) and the results will show a list of companies with that name. Each entry provides the company's address, phone number, and business entity type (single location, branch, or headquarters). The comprehensive report shows the background of each executive (and even includes names of their former companies), an executive summary about the company, a credit score, financials, and details about judgments, liens, UCCs, bankruptcies, suits, and so on.

Our View: This site adds one more crucial piece of contact information not available at the D & B Zapdata site: a phone number. This site also offers more-detailed reports than the $5 Zapdata report. Order a comprehensive report for $117 or a credit report for $54 (various other reports are also available).

TIP   • If you don't know in which state the company is located, use Zapdata, which allows for a nationwide search.
   • Click on **See Sample** to get a good idea of what type of information each D & B report offers.

Private Company Directories for U.S. and Foreign Companies

Corporate Information
(merged with Wright Research Center)

http://www.corporateinformation.com

Purpose: To search for information on private companies, both U.S. and foreign.

Content: This site purports to contain 20,000 company profiles and its search engine indexes 350,000 private (and public) company profiles found at other sites. Search by (1) company name (or a partial name); (2) country or a state for a list of profiled companies in that jurisdiction and for links to other sites about that jurisdiction's companies; (3) a country's industry; and (4) exchange rates.

Our View: Suddenly, you now have to register to use this site (but it's one of the quickest registration forms we've encountered lately). However, even after registering, we realized that this site is not going to be useful unless you actually subscribe. After a few searches, we were informed we had exceeded our page views and were asked to subscribe, but not given any pricing information. We're not willing to give up on this site . . . yet.

Tip: Use the Currency Converter to convert a foriegn company's financials into any currency, such as U.S. dollars, so you will be able to evaluate the company's financials.

Private Company Directories for U.S. Companies

Vault

http://www.vault.com

Purpose: To provide an insider's view of a company.

Content: This site covers three thousand public and private com-
              panies. It has some basic contact information, the name
              of the company president, and a profile of the company
              from an insider's viewpoint.

Our View: A search of E! Entertainment Television brought up a
              company profile that was very sparse but gave an idea of
              the work conditions and attitudes. There was a link to
              Vault's unofficial E! company message board where you
              could read the questions posed, but to answer or view
              answers older than sixty days, you would have to join
              (for $2.50 per month).

Tip: Search for your client companies every now and then to
              see what people are saying.

Private Company Directories for Foreign Companies

Kompass

http://www.kompass.com/kinl/index.html

Purpose: To search 1.8 million companies in 75 countries.

Content: There are three search boxes to fill in. The first box, the
              Search Text box, is for searching with words that
              describe what you will select in the second box, which is
              the **Search Type** box. In the **Search Type** box, choose
              to search by any of the following types: product name,
              services, executive name, trade name, company name,
              or keywords. The third search box, **Region**, is to select a
              region (such as Africa), or a specific country (such as
              Nigeria).

Our View: Being able to search through 1.8 million companies
              worldwide, by a wide variety of search criteria, makes
              this a good starting point even though nonsubscribers
              only get basic contact information for some of the com-

panies. For some companies, though, nonsubscribers might be able to view more information, such as company and executive name, address and phone number, number of employees, name of bank, date established, and products.

Tip:
- For more-detailed information, there is a fee-based option (e-mail Kompass for a quote regarding current pricing).
- The navigation is not the best, so here is some help: after you get a list of search results, you can mark which companies you want more information about. Then, click **View Marked** to bring up the next set of results. Look to the left once your final result is displayed, and notice you can e-mail the company or select to view parts of its profile.

Checklist Item 9: Search for Current and Archived News

Company directories can quickly get outdated, so we also recommend running the company name and its executives' names through a few major newspaper databases to verify information and to find the most current information. We've found that Hoover's is very up to date (it makes changes on the same day), while Vault is not. A few business-oriented news site are noted here, but for more information about searching newspapers, see the section "News, Periodicals, and Broadcast Media" in Chapter 5, "General Factual Research."

CEOExpress (**http://www.ceoexpress.com/default.asp#business**) has an extensive list of business news resources, arranged topically. Some of its topics are **Quotes, Banking and Finance,** and **International Business**. For local and regional business news from business journals (in over forty local markets throughout the United States), check out the American City Business Journals free (registration required) site at **http://www.bizjournals.com**. You can search current news and archives back to 1996 by headline, byline, or full text. You can also request e-mail news alerts from a list of markets or industries. Additionally, you can set up a search watch about any topic, company, or person, from any or all of the markets.

Checklist Item 10: Review Secretary of State Records for Registered Agents and Fictitious Business Names

To serve the correct party, lawyers need to discover a corporation's (or limited partnership's or limited liability company's) registered agent. If the company is not a corporation, but a sole proprietorship with a fictitious business name (FBN), then lawyers need to identify the owner to know who to serve. Many states and counties have made these business records available for free on the Internet. These records can also be used if a lawyer simply needs to know where the company is incorporated or whether the corporation is registered to do business in a particular state or states.

If you need to serve a complaint (or contact for other reasons) a general partner or an individual doing business using an FBN, this can be difficult. The difficulty of identifying general partners is that in some states they are not required to file with the secretary of state. The difficulty of identifying sole proprietors is twofold: (1) in states where they file by county, you would first have to know in which county they filed; and (2) even in states that require statewide filing, it's possible a sole proprietor has failed to file a fictitious business statement at all. InfoSpace (see Chapter 7, "Finding and Backgrounding People") may be useful if you know the business's phone number or address because you can do a reverse search on the phone number or address. The name of the person who is connected to that phone number or address may be displayed. For example, an InfoSpace reverse phone search for the phone number connected to Levitt & Levitt showed the names of both lawyers connected to that phone number.

The depth of information in a secretary of state or county clerk business record posted free on the Web varies. The record may be a full reproduction of the actual documents filed with the secretary of state (as in Florida), or merely a list of company names incorporated in the state (with no contact or registered agent information), or a mere acknowledgment that the FBN is being used (as in Los Angeles county). Some states allow you to search only by the corporation or FBN. Others also allow you to search by the name of the registered agent, an officer, or fictitious business owner. Most allow for partial company name searching.

Unfortunately, Delaware, where so many companies have incorporated, is not among the states that have placed their records free on the Web. For Delaware, you need to use a pay database (see the list of pay databases in Chapter 8, "Accessing Public Records"). Delaware doesn't allow for partial name searching either; you need to search by exact name. For a state-by-state list of where to locate registered agent information, both on the Web and off, see ResidentAgentInfo.com (**http://www.residentagentinfo.com**).

Secretary of State Sites

Resident Agent Info

http://www.residentagentinfo.com

Purpose: To link to online secretary of state sites that contain registered agent records.

Content: The site has links to states that have registered agent data online.

Our View: We like the simple straightforwardness of this site, and that is takes you directly to the page on the site that contains the database for searching the corporation records.

Tip:
- This site is also useful to get contact information for those secretaries of state that are not online. Contact information for states that don't post registered agent records online can also be found at the NASS (National Association of Secretaries of State) site (**http://www.nass.org/sos/2003roster.html**).
- To learn what other records (such as UCCs) or information are available at a secretary of state's office, you can also use the NASS Web site (**http://www.nass.org/sos/sosflags.html**), which links to the home page of every secretary of state (click on the flag of the state you want to visit).

County Fictitous Business Name Records
As noted above, if a county has placed its FBN records on the Web, you'll find that each county differs widely (even in the same state) as to how much information is included in the Web record. Also, the search functions of each county's FBN database varies. A case in point is Califor-

nia: in San Francisco, you can perform an FBN search using either the FBN or the owner's name (**http://services.sfgov.org/bns/start.asp**), but in Los Angeles county you can search only by the FBN (**http://regrec.co.la.ca .us/fbn**), and the record, once located, fails to even identify the owner.

To discover whether a county has placed its FBN records on the Web, use State and Local Government on the Net (see below) to link to all on-line counties.

State and Local Government on the Net

http://www.statelocalgov.net

Purpose: To link to FBN listings at state and county Web sites.

Content: To link to a county's FBN Web site, click first on the state in which the county is located and then scroll down to **County**.

Our View: Once you reach a county's Web site, you might need to do a lot of searching around to find the part of the site that contains the FBN records (if they are online at all). It's usually the county clerk's or the county recorder's page that you are looking for.

Tip: • If you don't know in which county (or even which state) a business has registered its FBN, use a pay data base to conduct a statewide or multistate search.
               • Don't pay for an FBN form until you verify that the county doesn't provide them online for free.

Checklist Item 11: Consider Using Pay Databases

Using a fee-based database is the better choice if you need to locate a corporation's registered agent in more than one state, or if you don't know in which state a company is registered to do business. Fee-based

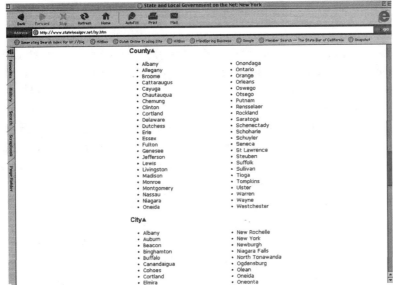

Figure 10-11. To link to a county's FBN Web site using the State and Local Government on the Net site, click first on the state in which the county is located and then scroll down to County.

sites are also useful when you need to search for an FBN but don't know the county. At the free sites, you have to search state by state (or county by county for FBNs), while at a fee-based site, you can run a single multi-jurisdictional search (such as in Lexis.com's **All States** business record database). Don't be misled by the term **All States,** though. It really means only the states that are online, and not every state is. Also, some states, such as Delaware, have opted out of the **All States** database, even though its database is online at Lexis (and in the other fee-based services). The state of Delaware requires a separate search and a separate fee of $25 to $35 to locate registered agents in Delaware. To complicate matters even further, while the **All States** database is available 24-7, Delaware limits access to its corporate records to 9:00 a.m. to 5:00 p.m. E.S.T., Monday through Friday (although they stay up late one night a week—on Monday from 7:00 p.m. to 9:00 p.m.).

Nonprofit Organizations and Associations

See Chapter 9, "Finding and Backgrounding Expert Witnesses," for information about locating nonprofit organizations and associations.

Checklist Item 12: Find Reported Decisions, Dockets, Verdicts, and Settlements

Information about companies, their executives, and their products might be found in reported case decisions. If there was no reported decision (because the case was dismissed or settled, for instance), then checking through dockets and through settlements (using jury verdict reporters) can shed some more light on a company's legal activities.

To find reported decisions about a company, it's best to use a pay database because they offer a more comprehensive search. If you only need to search one jurisdiction and primarily current years only, then try the free LexisONE (**http://www.lexisone.com**) or FindLaw (**http://www.findlaw.com**) sites. For information on how to search these sites and how to search for verdicts and settlements, see Chapter 9, "Finding and Backgrounding Expert Witnesses." For information on how to search dockets, see Chapter 8, "Accessing Public Records."

Checklist Item 13: Ascertain Which Agencies Regulate the Product or Industry

Search government Web sites for any mention of the company, its products, or the industry it falls within. Often, there will be separate Web pages on a government agency's site that gather all documents relating to a specific legal issue concerning a specific industry or company. For example, information about the Bell Atlantic/GTE Merger and various support-

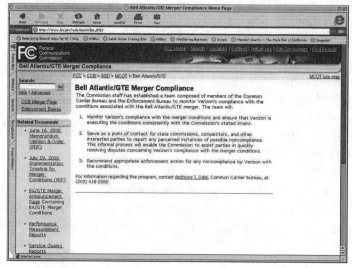

Figure 10-12. The FCC provides detailed information about the companies and industries it regulates.

ing documents can be found at the Web site of the agency that regulates telecommunications—the Federal Communications Commission (FCC) (**http://www.fcc.gov/wcb/mcot/BA_GTE**). Documents on the site range from the 226-page Memorandum Opinion and Order for approval to transfer licenses and lines from GTE to Bell, to the Performance Measurements Reports. See Chapter 9, "Finding and Backgrounding Expert Witnesses," for information about using FirstGov.gov (**http://www.firstgov.gov**) to either locate government Web sites by agency name or to use FirstGov's Advanced Search page for full-text keyword searching of company names, products, or legal issue.

Checklist Item 14: Think Outside the Box

Many of the same thinking-outside-the-box research strategies discussed in other chapters in this book also work well with company research, especially searching through postings in online community archives. See Chapter 7, "Finding and Backgrounding People"; Chapter 8, "Accessing Public Records"; Chapter 11, "Competitive Intelligence Research"; and Chapter 9, "Finding and Backgrounding Expert Witnesses."

Thinking Outside the Box with Online Communities

For example, in Chapter 9, "Finding and Backgrounding Expert Witnesses," we used a scenario where you are representing a client who was seriously injured when the treads of his Firestone tires separated, causing his vehicle to overturn. We noted that searching the online community Google Groups (**http://groups.google.com**) with the keywords "Firestone tires" might lead you to experts, lawyers, or other plaintiffs who were involved in similar lawsuits. But what if you were representing Firestone? You might also think about keyword searching Google Groups to learn what people are saying about your client and its product. A useful search might include the following keywords: "firestone tires treads accidents roll-overs or separation." Our Firestone tires search not only brought back messages from people who were having serious tire separation long before the media began reporting the problem, but also brought back a picture showing the shredded treads on someone's Firestone tire.

Also, search with company executives' names through Google Groups, just as you searched with an expert's name. If you are Firestone's in-house counsel (or their retained lawyer), you might consider doing these types of searches on a regular basis to keep apprised of any other problems concerning the company's products that are being discussed in online communities. It's better to be proactive than reactive.

Aside from searching through all postings in all groups at Google Groups, you can also try to narrow down your search to a specific group or groups. There seems to be a group for everything. There are ways to identify the most relevant group (or groups) and then either join the group or search postings only within that group. For instance, by searching with the keywords "explore tires" at Google Groups, we were able to identify the group rec.autos.4x4 as we read through many postings about Firestone tires and Fords. You can do the same thing with the companies you represent and once you find postings that are on point, you can determine what group they are coming from (by looking at the heading of the e-mail). You can then choose to follow that group's discussions by entering its name into the Google Groups search box as if it were a keyword, or entering its name into the **Return only messages from the newsgroup** search box found on the Google Groups Advanced Search page, or entering specific keywords (or names of people or companies) into the keyword search boxes on the Google Groups Advanced Search page and then entering the group's name into the **Return only messages from the newsgroup** search box.

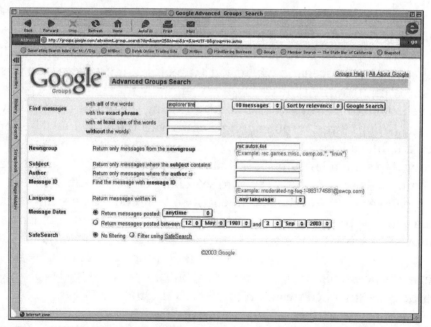

Figure 10-13. Enter keywords or names into the keyword search boxes and then enter the group's URL into the **Return only messages from the newsgroup** search box to limit your keyword search to one group. Google™ is a trademark of Google Technology, Inc.

To find other online communities to join or to search through aside from Google Groups, you can make use of CataList (**http://www.lsoft .com/lists/listref.html**), a catalog of LISTSERV lists, or Topica, a newsgroup directory (**http://www.liszt.com**). (Details about using these sites can be found in Chapter 7, "Finding and Backgrounding People.")

*CHAPTER***ELEVEN**

Competitive Intelligence Research

What Is Competitive Intelligence?

Competitive intelligence (CI) is also referred to as business intelligence or competitor intelligence. The cliché definition of competitive intelligence involves corporate spies who hoodwink rival executives into revealing trade secrets. While corporate espionage does occur, CI is not cloak and dagger. Rather, it is a recognized and growing field focused upon "the legal and ethical collection and analysis of information regarding the capabilities, vulnerabilities, and intentions of business competitors," according to the Society of Competitive Intelligence Professionals (SCIP) (**http://www.scip.org/about/index.asp**). CI is aimed at understanding the competitive environment, and as further noted by SCIP, "to help . . . companies achieve and maintain a competitive advantage." Such understanding of the competitive environment can alert you and your clients to threats and opportunities. Used wisely, CI can help you make a decision based upon your understanding of the threat or opportunity. The decisions to be made may revolve around whether a client should sell or buy a business, whether the firm should accept a new client or matter, and so on. The type of information gathered can identify new products planned, the percentage of annual revenue spent on computing, and the hiring or layoff trends of select competitors. Good competitive intelligence acts to filter through the ocean of available information to identify and analyze the most relevant facts. CI enables businesses to move beyond merely accessing information and into acting on intelligence. CI can be used not only to assist a client to make business decisions, but also to assist the firm to make internal firm-related business decisions.

Cloak-and-Dagger CI Tactics

Recently, a Swedish firm accused a Reuters reporter of using cloak-and-dagger Internet tactics when the reporter published an unreleased earnings report. The company, Intentia International, was scheduled to release its third-quarter earnings on October 24, but Reuters beat it to the punch by locating it on Intentia's Web site. Reuters asserted, "This information was not accessed from a private or password-protected site, but from the public Internet." Although Intentia had placed the report on the Internet, they had not posted a link from their home page to it. They were going to add the link to the home page when they were officially ready to release the earnings report. How did the reporter find this seemingly "inside" information? He simply took an educated guess as to the URL he thought Intentia would use to post the report. The guess was based on deciphering the naming system Intentia had used for all previous reports.

Competitive Intelligence and Knowledge Management

Competitive intelligence has traditionally focused on collecting and analyzing external data and information in order to make decisions. However, in more recent years, companies have also been focusing on collecting and analyzing their own internal data and information (and knowledge) to make decisions. This is commonly referred to as knowledge management.

CI Departments at Corporations

Of the one thousand U.S. and European companies surveyed by the CI firm of Fuld & Co. in 2002, about half had an organized CI program, and 45 percent of the U.S. firms that didn't have one said they planned to within the year. Their in-house CI departments commonly save them millions per year. But sometimes it's not just about money. For example, CI can help a company prepare for any kind of change in the marketplace by monitoring any industry or company rumors that could affect them. A case in point is Visa's quick reaction when MasterCard merged with Europay in 2001. Visa's head of market intelligence assigned one of his two staff people to troll the Internet for two hours daily to learn about MasterCard and its other competitors. When MasterCard merged with Europay, Visa had been tracking the impending merger for months. When it was finally announced, Visa already had prepared a letter to their board members on Visa's take on the situation and how it would affect them. The letter was sent within an hour of the merger announcement. Many corporate executives consider such efforts imperative to survival, especially in the global economy.

CI Departments at Law Firms

Many smaller companies either can't afford CI or, more likely, are not savvy enough to recognize its benefits. The lawyer who perceives the worth of CI and takes the time to develop CI research skills can provide immense value to clients. The even savvier lawyer recognizes that CI can benefit the firm's own business development. And the savviest lawyer recognizes the need to develop a CI department in house, just as the larger corporations have. Some firms use their marketing staff and library staff as *de facto* CI staff. The law firm of Kilpatrick Stockton, a national firm with about five hundred lawyers, designated one of their former law librarians, Donna Cavallini, as their Director of Competitive Knowledge (**http://www.kilstock.com**). Aside from providing CI to the lawyers in her firm (who then use it to assist their clients to make business decisions), she also provides CI to the firm itself to assist them to develop firm business. This can range from keeping the firm informed about competitor law firms (and the legal industry in general), to looking for new legal markets to service, to any other information that helps the firm make sound business decisions. Cavallini makes use of both external sources (such as databases, the Internet, and books) and internal sources (using the in-house knowledge management systems that might include documents and client-contact information). Thus, the title of Director of Competitive Knowledge does best describe her position since her work includes both traditional CI and the less traditional knowledge management.

Why Use the Internet for CI Research?

It is incumbent on lawyers to ensure that their business advice considers all the relevant facts, some of which are discoverable only through careful and comprehensive competitive intelligence research, including use of the Internet. The Internet has quite simply become one of the primary tools in a research strategy that aims to pull data from all relevant sources.

As those who have ventured online can attest, the Internet contains a vast collection of information, some of it fascinating and uniquely valuable, and some of it useless. But the sheer volume of data testifies to the Internet's value for competitive intelligence research. The mere size of the data collection demands attention by CI researchers. The Internet simply can't be ignored.

Emergence of the Internet as a critical business (and therefore legal) information tool parallels the rise of CI as an essential offensive as well as defensive strategic weapon. Both the Internet and CI grew from the need for the U.S. to address global issues. While the Internet was created by the U.S. Department of Defense to provide sustained communication in a catastrophic war, CI's use by domestic corporations rose in response to foreign competitive threats and the need to penetrate overseas markets. Deregulation of various industries in the U.S. and elsewhere has also increased competitive pressures and fueled the need for companies to increase their use of CI.

The parallel development of the Internet and CI suggests a certain symmetry that makes the Internet a natural CI tool. For example, due to its nonproprietary nature and widespread public accessibility, the Internet is perceived as a source of and place to provide "free" information. Perhaps because of this non-ownership, many government bodies, domestic and foreign, have chosen to use the Internet medium as a very low-cost distribution mechanism. Among the information distributed on the Internet are many national databases that are perfectly suited to investigating competitive companies. In the U.S., the Securities and Exchange Commission database known as EDGAR (Electronic Data Gathering, Analysis, and Retrieval system at **http://www.sec.gov/edgarhp.htm**) is one of the best examples of this trend. EDGAR is a source of data on domestic public companies that contains the 10-Ks, 10-Qs, and shareholder proxy statements filed by every publicly held firm. These documents provide a wealth of financial, operational, and strategic information.

As the Internet has grown up along with the discipline of CI, so has the increasing importance of technology in business. As a result, most major companies have established Web sites that are rich with all sorts of information that companies previously did not make easily accessible to the public. For example, some companies post their internal employee directories and company newsletters. Employee directories can be used to identify the caliber of competitor's staffs, while company newsletters may disclose job openings that could indicate the areas in which a competitor is planning development.

Not only does the Internet provide a wealth of CI source data, it also provides access to sources that are only available on the Internet, such as the online communities discussed in the "Thinking Outside the Box" section found in Chapter 7, "Finding and Backgrounding People." For example, if you represent a firm that plans to hire a particular acoustic engineer to develop a new technology or to serve as an expert witness, and you are charged with investigating how this individual represents herself and whether she can be trusted with trade secrets, you might search Google Groups to find a group focusing on acoustic engineering (**http://groups.google.com**). If you did this, you would find the archives of the alt.sci.physics.acoustics newsgroup (**http://groups.google.com/ groups?hl=en&lr=&ie=UTF-8&group=alt.sci.physics.acoustics**), where you could search by her name for evidence of her past online discussions and behavior. Instead of searching for a specific group, you can simply search the entire Google Groups archive using the expert's name or e-mail address. This is the type of information that is not available anywhere but on the Internet. Another reason to use the Internet for CI is that doing so can avoid data collection liability. Since the Internet is a publicly accessible source, finding information on it may defeat a claim of data theft, privacy violation, or anticompetitive behavior. For example, a company that acquired a competitor's pricing or market share data might be charged with trade-secret theft. However, if that information was found on the competitor's Web site, the defense might argue that one can't steal what's been given away for free. In fact, such a case occurred recently. Although the client insisted he obtained the pricing sheet of his former company from the company's own Web site, the lawyer was unable to locate it . . . until he searched the URL at Archive.org, where he found the pricing sheet. Indeed, it had once been posted by the company, but had been recently taken off the company's site.

Anonymous CI Researching

Your IP Address

The Internet is an almost perfect place for a CI researcher because your use of the Internet for research, in most instances, cannot easily be traced back specifically to you. Therefore, if you are viewing data on a rival's Web site, the rival would not be easily tipped off. But, every time you use your browser to visit a Web site, your browser does leave a record of your Internet Protocol (IP) address on that site's Web server. Your IP address is merely a series of numbers (like a telephone number) and is in no way connected to your e-mail address. In general, every Web site you visit can obtain the following information about you in addition to your IP address: (1) your Internet Service Provider (ISP), (2) what country you are from, (3) what Web browser you are using, (4) what operating system you are using, and (5) possibly what domain name you are using. Therefore, while it is not easy to precisely identify a specific visitor to a Web site via an IP address, if the IP address leaves behind the domain name this might give a clue that someone from your company has visited a site.

Tracking an IP Address

The Webmaster of a site you have visited could use an online IP tracker, such as VisualRoute (**http://www.visualware.com/visualroute/livedemo.html**), to determine the ISP to whom your IP address is assigned. In theory, the ISP could match that IP address to a specific user by reviewing its own log-in records. The target site could then figure out that you visited them, but it is unlikely that an ISP would turn over any identifying information without a court order. But, for researchers who want to be certain they are leaving no identifying trail at all, there are ways to do so by using third-party providers to conduct research and send e-mails anonymously.

Surfing Anonymously

A number of services exist that allow you to conduct research anonymously. By using a service such as Anonymizer (**http://www.anonymizer**

.com), you can anonymously access any Web site—leaving behind the IP address of the Anonymizer server rather than your own. To use Anonymizer's free cloaking service, just type the Web address (URL) of the site you wish to visit into the address box on the Anonymizer.com home page. The only downside is enduring the advertisement for the pay version of Anonymizer displayed at the top of each site visited while using the free service. A no-ad version, with additional security features, is available for $29.95. The Cloak (**http://www.the-cloak.com**) offers similar free and pay services.

For an example of how this all works, let's say we are conducting Internet research about IBM from a computer at our company, Internet For Lawyers. Our Internet access is provided by the ISP Earthlink, the world's second-largest ISP, and is configured much like your non-networked home (DSL or dial-up) account. If we point our Web browser to IBM's company Web site (**http://www.ibm.com**), the Webmaster at IBM can review IBM's site's traffic logs to learn that a Web user assigned our specific IP address has visited IBM.com. They cannot easily discern, however, that we specifically visited IBM.com, only that someone (or even something, since robot programs commonly visit Web sites) assigned to our specific IP address (at that precise moment) visited. With our IP address (and a court order) they could identify us.

Let's look at an example of how we can trace a domain name. The IP addresses of some corporate networks (and this includes some law firms) might broadcast more identifying information regarding their users than an ISP does, such as their domain name. We know this because when we review the traffic logs of our own Web site (**http://www.netforlawyers .com**) we readily see the domain names of specific institutions' computers whose users accessed our site. Recent examples include Gibson, Dunn & Crutcher; Pillsbury Winthrop; Jefferies & Co. (an investment bank); IBM; UCLA; and the U.S. Navy, among others. We cannot, however, determine the precise identity of the individual visitors by reviewing our traffic logs (short of that court order).

Sending E-mail Anonymously

There are also free online services that can hide your identity when sending e-mail. These free, anonymous re-mailers allow you to send anonymous messages via e-mail. Web-based versions offer you a form in which to input the destination e-mail address, subject, and message. Clicking the **Submit** button sends the message to the address you entered. The delivered message contains no information that identifies you as the sender. Additionally, most of these re-mailers claim not to retain any data regarding the IP address of the sender. One example of a re-mailer can be found at **http://www.anon-remailer.gq.nu**. Because these re-mailers can disappear from the Internet as fast as they appear, visit the Open Directory for a list of links to many such sites (**http://dmoz.org/Computers/Internet/E-mail/Anonymous_Mailers**).

Cookies Can Reveal Your Precise Identify

One way that a Web site can discover your exact identity is when another site has left a cookie on your computer and this cookie includes your identity. Basically, other sites can sneak a peek at the cookies already saved on your machine by other Web sites to determine your identity. Cookies (with such identifying information as your name, e-mail address, password, or a combination) can be accessed and deciphered by Web site servers other than the site that originally generated the specific cookie. They can then track your Internet usage—identifying sites you've visited and perhaps even your password and user name for those sites. (Newer versions of Netscape Communicator and Internet Explorer can be configured to warn you before cookies are added to your computer. This gives you the option of allowing the cookie to be placed on your computer or not.)

Protecting Yourself

There are many software programs that are cookie-killers (and more) that you can use to protect your privacy on the Internet. One of the more popular ones is called Window Washer, available from Webroot Software (**http://www.webroot.com**). The company Web site explains that Window Washer will "Wash away your online and offline tracks to protect your privacy." It also explains that the program handles both browser cleaning (it clears out your cookies, cache, history, mail trash, drop-down address bar, auto-complete forms, and downloaded program files) and PC cleaning (it clears out your recycle bin, registry streams, Windows run and find lists, history, scandisk files, recently viewed pictures, locked index.dat files, recently opened documents list, and Windows temp files folder).

ZoneAlarm (**http://www.zonelabs.com**) is a PC firewall that "keeps your personal data and privacy safe from Internet hackers and data thieves." The basic product protects against worms, Trojans, and spyware, and forty-seven types of malicious e-mail attachments, while ZoneAlarm kills cookies, and blocks ads.

Where Does CI Information Come From?

CI comes from the same Internet resources that we've already discussed for researching experts, companies, public records, and people. CI can come directly from competitors themselves (such as their Web sites and their government filings) or it can come from external sources such as industrial reports, periodical articles, directories, financial industry data, association materials, and various databases. And, we start CI research the same way we do other factual research: by gathering information from basic and traditional sources on the Internet that often have evolved from print materials (like phone and business directories) and expanding toward creative sources (such as online communities like Google Groups, eBay, blogs, and so on) that are unique to the Internet.

Web Sites for CI Research

Starting-Point Sites for CI

A useful site to get you started on the use of CI is the Web site of Fuld & Company, one of the preeminent research and consulting firms in this field (**http://www.fuld.com**). Its founder, Leonard Fuld, has placed selected chapters from his book, *The New Competitor Intelligence,* on his site for review (**http://www.fuld.com/Tindex/CIbook/chap01.html**).

To find specific URLs that will assist you in your CI endeavors, refer to Chapter 10 in this book, "Company Research." Because you often need to focus on specific industries when conducting CI, you'll find the following two sites' links useful because they are arranged by industry: (1) the Internet Intelligence Index, provided by Fuld & Company (**http://www.fuld .com/Tindex/I3.html**) and (2) Competia Express (**http://www.competia .com/express/index.html**). And, because CI has a lingo all its own, you might also find Fuld's Intelligence Dictionary of some use (**http://www.fuld.com/Tindex/IntelDict.html**).

Using Search Engines for CI Research

The first step in using the Internet for CI is to conduct a broad search to find the most obvious sources. Start with keyword searches in various search engines (Google, AltaVista, Alltheweb, FirstGov.gov, and so on) to see what turns up. Among the most obvious sources (and easiest to use) that you will find with a search engine are competitors' Web sites. The next basic source to study is company directory sites, in order to find more objective information than what's found at a company's own Web site.

News, Alerts, and E-newsletters

News is a natural place to find out what competitors are up to or what potential clients who you plan on pitching are doing. Many companies put news releases on their home pages. Read these when looking for insight about what the company has to say about new products, new hires, and so on. You can search for press releases (for free) by country, company, organization name, or keywords at PR Newswire (**http://www.prnewswire.com/news**). If you click on **advanced search** you can also tailor your search by choosing **All Releases** (in the past 30 days), **News by Company** (by company name, plus an archive search back to at least 1996) , **Topical Search** (by industry, state, company name, or subject), or **Keyword Search** (last three days or last thirty days).

But, for more current (and objective) insights, review newspaper and magazine articles about companies. For the most current news, use the News tabs on Google and AltaVista's home pages. To cast a wider net for news, try NewsDirectory (**http://www.newsdirectory.com/web**), an index of 14,500 English-language media links (from newspapers, magazines, and television stations to colleges, visitor bureaus, and governmental agencies). Also, refer to the following chapters in this book for more news and magazines sources: Chapter 5, "General Factual Research"; Chapter 9, "Finding and Backgrounding Expert Witnesses"; and Chapter 10, "Company Research."

Just as the Visa CI department relied on old-fashion manual trolling of the Web to learn about the MasterCard-Europay merger (rather than just relying upon automated alerts), so does Donna Cavallini of the law firm Kilpatrick Stockton. Her explanation is that sometimes events or concepts are stated in a much different way than she had anticipated when she originally chose the keywords for her automated alerts. However, she still uses some automated alerts, especially if they are free (Westlaw's Clips offers free alerts to headlines to its subscribers), but she manually scans about four hundred e-newsletters, most of which are free (but might require registration). Some of the newsletters that Cavallini scans relate to the firm's current clients while others may provide the firm with leads for new business, especially financial-related newsletters such as those from Financial Times (**http://news.ft.com/home/us**) or the Deal (**http://thedeal.exactis.com/cgi/subscribe.html**), which provides information about new deals, which companies are restructuring, and whose assets are available. From this information, you might be able to target potential clients. She also subscribes to newsletters offered by Forbes and Tech Wire.

Using Industry Watchdogs

Thinking like a researcher in the context of CI involves thinking about who would monitor or care about the target subject. Who would want to catalog such information? Where would they catalog it? Combine this thought process with the basic and creative sources available on the Internet and elsewhere. Industry watchdogs such as unions, government regulatory agencies, and professional or trade associations may be monitoring your target company or industry. Therefore, you might find it fruitful to search through information found on their Web sites.

Government Regulatory Agencies as Industry Watchdogs

Regulatory agencies at all levels collect information on companies. Often, vital product and plant intelligence, as well as records of complaints and investigations and any action taken as a result will be found in these Internet data warehouses. Knowing how to get around amid government data is a specialty unto itself, now made a bit easier with FirstGov.gov. It's an excellent starting point for government research because it indexes over fifty million state and federal government documents (see Chapter 6, "Government Resources Online," for more information). And, since FirstGov.gov covers all agencies, you don't need to try to figure out which agency or agencies are regulating a certain industry, company, or matter. Simply use FirstGov.gov to search with the keywords that describe the industry, company, or matter at hand, or search by a specific company or executive's name.

A potentially useful government regulatory agency site, if you are aiming to identify a competitor's weak points, is the Occupational Safety and Health Administration (OSHA) at **http://www.osha.gov**. It provides, among many other valuable free resources, Hazard Information Bulletins identifying manufacturers whose products have caused injury and death (**http://www.osha-slc.gov/dts/hib/index.html**). These monthly OSHA bulletins can make a sharp impression.

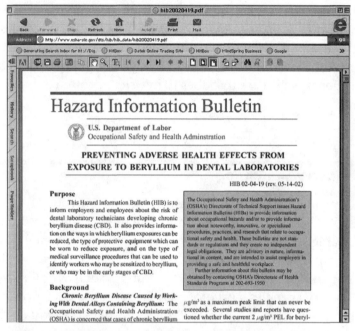

Figure 11-1. OSHA provides bulletins that are accessible on the Internet identifying products that have caused injury and death.

Finding Associations, Public Interest Groups, and Unions that Serve as Industry Watchdogs

To find associations, use Yahoo!'s extensive professional association list (**http://www.yahoo.com/Business_and_Economy/Organizations/ Professional**) and see the section on associations in Chapter 9, "Finding and Backgrounding Expert Witnesses" in this book. To find union sites, see the AFL-CIO Web site (**http://www.aflcio.org**), which provides links to numerous other unions (**http://www.aflcio.org/aboutunions/unions**) and links to sites that cover corporate accountability. Public interest groups can be found by using a search engine and searching for words that describe the industry (or situation) and adding the phrase "public interest groups" or the word "advocacy." For example, if your firm represented an oil company, you'd want to keep apprised about what the public was saying about the oil industry (or your company). To do this, we searched for "public interest groups" and oil. One of the results was a site with a list of public interest groups on the topic of oil and the environment, one of which was the Offshore Oil and Gas Environment Forum (**http://www .oilandgasforum.net**), whose mission is to "[T]o learn more about these potential impacts and what we can do [about] oil exploration and production operations [that] have the potential for a variety of impacts on the environment."

Using Government Agencies to Find Business Information

The U.S. Department of Commerce (DOC) (**http://www.doc.gov**) provides reams and reams of business-related information via the Internet. The number of bureaus and agencies that fall within the DOC's jurisdiction is staggering. There's testimony, export schedules, and regulations, and it goes on and on.

The SEC's EDGAR system (**http://www.sec.gov/edgarhp.htm**) is also among the most useful federal government sites for public company CI because a company's filings can provide significant insight into its operations. In addition, since these filings are required by law, they have a certain amount of assumed accuracy. (See Chapter 10, "Company Research," for detailed information about searching EDGAR and other SEC databases that permit full-text searching of filings.)

Researching with SIC Codes and NAICS Codes

The government's Standard Industrial Classification (SIC) system (**http://www.sec.gov/info/edgar/siccodes.htm**) and the North American Industry Classification System (NAICS) (**http://www.census.gov/ epcd/naics02/naicod02.htm**) classify all businesses into categories, from very broad categories to very narrow categories, using descriptive words and numerical codes. For example, businesses relating to the agriculture, forestry, fishing, and hunting industries are assigned the broad NAICS category code 11, while the narrow category of soybean farming is assigned code 11111. The codes can be used to search various databases that allow SIC or NAICS searching. The codes are the key for accomplishing all kinds of CI research because they allow you to create lists of specific companies within a specific industry. For instance, if you wanted to create a list of a client's competitors or you wanted to create a list of specific companies in

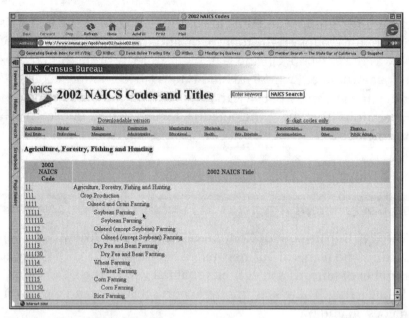

Figure 11-2. Note that agriculture, forestry, fishing, and hunting are assigned NAICS code 11, and are then broken down into more specific sectors, such as soybean farming (code 11111), wheat farming (code 11114), and so on.

an industry the firm wanted to service, you would use the SIC or NAICS codes.

NAICS was developed jointly by the U.S., Canada, and Mexico to be able to compare business activity statistics across North America. Although NAICS was to replace the SIC system, you still see references to SIC as you research. Many business directories (such as the subscriber side of Hoover's) and online databases (such as EDGAR and other SEC databases discussed in Chapter 10, "Company Research") allow searching by SIC code (and sometimes by NAICS code). Some databases also allow you to further refine the SIC and NAICS searches by geographic location, number of employees, and revenues. Gale's Company and Business Resource Center (a company directory database noted in the "Free Internet Access to Library Databases And Catalogs" section of Chapter 5, "General Factual Research") also allows for this type of refined searching (for free). Some of the databases also can generate mailing labels from your custom-designed SIC list.

The NAICS codes are found at the U.S. Census Bureau's site (**http://www.census.gov/epcd/naics02/naicod02.htm**). They can be browsed numerically or can be keyword searched. There are also tables that show how the NAICS codes correspond to the older SIC codes. There are various places to find the SIC codes, but not all have searchable keyword indexes (EDGAR has a numerical list only). For an easy-to-use searchable keyword index, see **http://www.foreign-trade.com/reference/sic.cfm**.

Locating Researchers in a Targeted Field

Another good approach for researching industry developments is to find companies and universities that conduct research in that field. For example, if you need to find chemical industry developments, use a search engine or directory to find your way to chemical companies, research organizations, and academic departments that make information available online.

Locating CI About Private Companies

Some company reports, such as D & B reports, can be purchased (**http://www.dnb.com**). (See Chapter 10, "Company Research," for a detailed profile of D & B's content.) They contain self-reported data from each company being researched (usually private companies). The information is not required to be reported by law (as public company information is). It's fair to say that a good researcher is a skeptical researcher, especially when the data is self-reported in this manner. Whenever possible, get independent verification for all information you need to depend on.

The following are some of the reasons D & B gives for ordering a comprehensive company report:

- To identify companies that have slow payment experience, which might indicate the company is undergoing financial stress
- To use business ratios to help make sure a company has enough assets to pay you
- To compare a company to others in the same industry, locally or nationally
- To background a company's owners or executives
- To discover how many times a company has moved and where— and even how well it functioned under natural disasters or fires
- To see if any suits have been brought against the target company

Using Creative Sources for CI Research

Since the Internet is a new medium, it lends itself very well to creative research or what we referred to as "thinking outside the box"in Chapter 7, "Finding and Backgrounding People." Virtually every sector of society, including government, nonprofits, public and private companies, and religious and secular organizations, are all looking for ways to take advantage of the Internet's multimedia, interactive, and international features. As a result, there's a lot of different sorts of information provided on the Internet, which you can turn to your research advantage.

For example, the many classified and job advertisement sites on the Internet are excellent places to scope out competitors. You may find that a competitor is trying to fill new positions in a brand-new business area. Alternatively, a rival might be trying to fill key positions that have recently been vacated (although no public announcement was made). To find out about job opportunities that indicate a change in a company, you can visit the following Web sites: the local newspaper, where classified are often included; a job database site such as Monster.com; or simply visit the targeted company's Web site.

Let's say you represent a telecommunications company that competes with MCI. In the course of your representation, you want to know what sort of new initiatives MCI is undertaking. While scouring the MCI site for clues, you discover the **Career Center** page that MCI uses to recruit new employees and you notice that the job openings are searchable by job category and by state (**http://careers.mci.com/careers/us/ index.phtml?pagename=jobsearch**). It so happens that your client is particularly concerned about a suspected new research and development facility being built by MCI in northern California. In your research, you discover that in fact, MCI has posted numerous ads for exotically skilled engineers in Sacramento, thereby lending credence to your client's concerns. You also notice that MCI is hiring commercial law lawyers (and you weigh the possibilities).

E-mailing the Experts

Another creative intelligence gathering technique is the use of e-mail. E-mail is an easy way to communicate with experts, reporters, analysts, insiders, educators, and players in specific industries and markets. You can use e-mail to solicit opinions, explanations, comments, and even rumors. You might use e-mail to contact journalists who are writing company profiles or researching new markets. To identify and locate experts, see Chapter 9, "Finding and Backgrounding Expert Witnesses."

Conducting a Links Search

One of the completely unique-to-the-Internet techniques you can try is to find out what Web sites link to your competitor's page. This technique may alert you to previously unknown strategic alliances or may open up a market for your client's products that hadn't been foreseen. Use the **Links Search** function at Alltheweb.com (which we explained in the section "Finding It on Line" in Chapter 3, "Search Strategies"). For example, if you type the URL of a company into the **Links** search box, you will be able to see how many pages point to your target company. This may indicate alliances or may otherwise provide you with insight about the company.

Using Online Community Postings

Another way to leverage the Internet's uniqueness is to take advantage of the "off the beaten track" information (such as rumors or public opinion) found in various online community postings about a company, product, or executive. For example, you might post a message in one of these online communities, such as ones found at Google Groups (for detailed information about using Google Groups, see the discussion on "Thinking Outside the Box with Online Communities" in Chapter 10, "Company Research"), asking a question about your client's competitor (or even about your own client) to determine what's being said about them and their products or services. You'll need to join the group to do this. Then, sit back and monitor the responses. You can join a group that is very narrow in its scope, like banking in Britain (uk.finance), or you could try broader discussion areas, like business (alt.business), import-export business (alt.business.importexport), or international marketplace (biz.marketplace.international).

The following are sites where you can locate all types of relevant on-line communities (whether you want to lurk, join, or search the archives, if available):

Figure 11-3. This is a sample of all the various science-related groups available for joining (or lurking or searching the archives) found in Google Groups. Google™ is a trademark of Google Technology Inc.

- Google Groups for Usenet postings (**http://groups.google.com**)
- Boardreader for message board postings
  (**http://www.boardreader.com**)
- CataList for LISTSERV lists (**http://www.lsoft.com/catalist.html**)
- Daypop for blogs (**http://www.daypop.com**).

For detailed information on these resources, see the section on on-line communities in Chapter 9, "Finding and Backgrounding Expert Witnesses."

Cloaking in a Group

For more clandestine research, you can search a group's archives without joining the group. If you do want to participate, however, you usually need to join. In either case, you'll probably want to mask your identity by using one of the cloaking sites discussed earlier in this chapter.

Searching Opinions, Briefs, Complaints and Settlements

Besides searching case law databases (free or pay) for lawsuit information about a company or person whom you are researching, see the Delaware Corporate Law Clearinghouse site. Posted here are selected opinions, briefs, complaints, settlements, motions, and other documents filed in business law matters in the Delaware Court of Chancery, back to March 1999 (**http://corporate-law.widener.edu/case.htm**). Caveat: the site has not been receiving new complaints and briefs from the Court of Chancery for some time now, but they are still receiving opinions. A recent addition to the site are Delaware Supreme Court opinions (corporate cases only) that have been appealed from the Court of Chancery.

Finding Confidential Company Information on the Internet

Is someone posting the "confidential" internal memos of your firm, your client's company (or the opposition's) on the Internet? InternalMemos.com offers over fifteen hundred internal memos from compa-

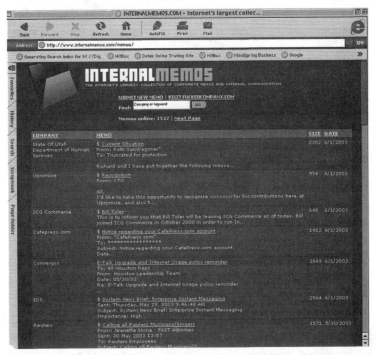

Figure 11-4. You can access the internal memos of numerous public and private companies at InternalMemos.com.

nies ranging from General Electric and WorldCom to AOL TimeWarner. It is free to browse the abstracts of available memos (in chronological order) or search by company name or keyword. However, only some memos may be viewed for free; the majority require a paid subscription to view. A $45 monthly or $180 annual subscription buys unlimited viewing of the premium memos. InternalMemos.com solicits additions to its database via a form on the site. Visitors can cut and paste the contents of internal e-mails, or type text from hard copy documents into the Internet form for posting on the InternalMemos.com site (**http://www.internalmemos.com**).

Using CI for Law Firm Business Development

To learn what your rivals are doing and saying, sign up for a trial subscription to Surfwax LawKT-Lite (**http://lawkt.surfwax.com**). This site allows you to quickly full-text search over 50,000 Web-based publications (such as client alerts, newsletters, and articles) from 220 of the world's leading firms. The annual subscription fee is $750.

Docket research is particularly useful for business development as we

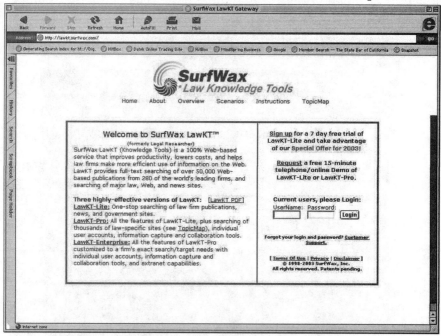

Figure 11-5. Using Surfwax's LawKT (Law Knowledge Tools), Web-based lawyers can full-text search over 50,000 publications from 220 law firms, in addition to searching major law, news, and other Web sites.

noted in the section on "Court Dockets and Pleadings" in Chapter 8, "Accessing Public Records." For example, NOS docket research can identify hot areas of practice that the firm might want to shift to. Searching dockets by a lawyer's name and a practice area might help you target someone you'd like to recruit to develop a certain practice area for the firm.

Also useful for recruiting (or for obtaining background information about specific lawyers) is Martindale-Hubbell's law directory online (**http://www.martindale.com**) or FindLaw's directory (**http://lawyers.find law.com**) because they allow for practice area searching.

Using Public Records for CI

Review Chapter 8, "Accessing Public Records," for links to public record databases. Some of the public records you might want to search for your CI endeavor are bankruptcies, liens, court dockets, real estate records, patents, trademarks, and so on.

Searching with Pay Databases

When researching CI, using pay databases is in order. Cavallini recommends VentureSource (**http://www.venturesource.com**) to track venture capital sources or find information about executives and their past affiliations, Hoover's (**http://www.hoovers.com**) when you need company executive biographies (it covers more executives than other company directories), and D & B (formerly known as Dun & Bradstreet, **http://wwwdnb.com**) for private companies (although it seems they are no longer providing annual revenues for most of the companies), to name a few.

Cookie Lewis, president of Infomania, a legal and business research company based in Los Angeles, is a proponent of using LexisNexis for CI because she believes it has the largest amount of industry-related publications. She also uses it when she needs to search nationally for public records and for docket searching (through the LexisNexis-owned CourtLink). Other databases also have industry-related publications, such as Westlaw and Dialog, and many of them have CI databases that compile company dossiers.

War Story: An Industry-Trend CI Search

Cookie Lewis relates the following CI project she recently began. A client hired her to help him decide whether to sell land to a time-share developer. The land was located in a highly desirable area—just off the Strip in Las Vegas. To assist her client, Lewis first ran a search for magazine and news articles indexed in LexisNexis, focusing her search on the time-share industry in general and also zeroing in on the time-share industry in Las Vegas. Her choice of keywords for her search, in addition to the word "time-share," are illustrative of what a typical industry-trend CI search would be. Lewis searched for the word time-share within fifteen words of the following: "forecast OR statistics OR report OR trend OR Las Vegas." (She also ran a more focused search by using the Lexis real estate articles news database.) By choosing search terms that included the word "report," Lewis would be likely to locate reports (if there were any at all) that had already been written about the time-share industry. The smart CI researcher first looks for reports that have already been written on the intended topic to save the client the expense involved in writing a new report. The next step in her CI plan was to focus on the time-share developer, to learn about his background and to ascertain his track record in time-share developments. Was he litigious? How many other time-shares had he developed? Did he have solid financial backing for his other developments? How much property did he own?

To answer these questions, Lewis knew public record searching would be in order. Lewis ran a UCC search (through Lexis) to find out who was lending the developer the money to finance his projects. The search showed her that his financers were solid. She also ran his name and the company's name through CourtLink to learn about any lawsuits filed by or against him and his company. What she found led her to ascertain that he was litigious. Putting that fact together with his financial worth (ascertained by a property record search, among other searches), it became obvious that he was willing and financially able to litigate in the face of any conflict. She alerted her client to these facts and explained that they indicated that the client might find himself being sued by the developer if he and the developer ever had a conflict over the sale or the terms. And, given the developer's worth, it might be too expensive for the client to defend himself.

Finally, as she read articles about the time-share industry in Las Vegas, she got wind that there was some Las Vegas City Council activity about it. What she learned was that the hotel industry, in their quest to fight off time-share developers from taking over the market, were getting into the time-share market themselves. The next step Lewis took was a trip to the Internet to visit the city's Web site. There, she tried to discover if the City Council's minutes were on the site (or their taped hearings). Her final step was to compile a list of time-share competitors in Las Vegas and pull their permits (approved and pending). She did this for several reasons: to benchmark the price her client should seek for his land, to identify other potential buyers to seek counter offers, and to forecast time-share development in Las Vegas for five years out.

As you can see, CI specialists like Cookie Lewis and Donna Cavallini know where to look for the information (in pay and free sites) and know how to piece the information together to assist clients to draw legally and financially sound conclusions. The clients can then take action based upon this solid information.

Parting Recommendations of a CI Expert

Cavallini recommends that you bookmark everything you find while surfing the Internet, even if you have no present use for it. She also notes, as we have earlier, that you might not find your answer on the Internet, but you may find a lead to it there. Also, she regularly takes advantage (as we do) of the remote library databases that library card holders can access for free. As a prime example of using these last two tips, Cavallini tells about the time she was searching for biographical information about an executive of a small company. She used the Master Index of Biographies (one of those valuable free, remote library databases), and although the biography was not on the Internet, the index provided a lead by showing that there was a biography of the target executive in the 1992 print edition of the Directory of Corporate Affiliations. A quick post to a mailing list resulted in someone sending the biography to her from the 1992 print edition. Finally, she recommends that you leave no stone unturned, as the following war story illustrates.

War Story: CI at Amazon.com

A client (a venture capital group) had hired a president for one of their companies. He had come from a big accounting firm. After two years of steadily losing money (and hiring his son in an executive position), the client asked the firm to do some background checking, in the hope of finding a reason to fire him. After searching the NASD database (which showed no actions had been filed against him) and finding nothing else damaging after completing a thorough search of the Internet and pay databases, Cavallini searched Amazon.com using his name. She found that he had written a book, but because it was unrelated to his profession, she nearly brushed it off. But, applying her leave-no-stone-unturned mantra, she clicked over to it, and noted that someone had left a scathing review—not of the book, but of the executive himself! It gave a long account of how the "reviewer" had been defrauded by this executive and referred to a book that had chronicled the fraud (and the pending investigation). Cavallini obtained the book and turned it over to the lawyer she was working with. It proved to be the smoking gun and gave the client grounds for firing the executive for failing to be forthcoming about his past and failing to disclose that he was currently under investigation.

Failing to conduct CI research is a mistake. To quote Cookie Lewis's mantra, "It's what you don't know that can hurt you." CI research can help you discover what you don't know. Armed with all the facts, you can then make sound business and legal decisions.

*CHAPTER*TWELVE

Medical Research

Why Do Medical Research?

Successful personal injury and medical malpractice actions usually require a fair amount of general medical information regarding the condition, in addition to the testimony of medical experts. The opinions of experts with direct clinical experience, for example, can provide invaluable perspective on the client's specific situation. However, a familiarity with the medical issues involved will help you keep in control of the case. Gathering your own medical background information can give you the edge in the case. Whether it's in cross-examining the opposition's expert, or even on redirect with your own expert, an awareness of the specific medical issues in question is essential.

Continuous change in the ever-more-complex health care industry has resulted in new sources of work for lawyers. In response to the rising cost of health care, new types of organizations, jobs, equipment, procedures, and intensified patient-privacy requirements under the Health Insurance Portability and Accountability Act (HIPAA) are changing the profession on a regular basis. These changes can result in legal disputes, for example, pitting the quality of care against health care company interests in making a profit. Recent issues include the responsibilities of managed care companies; the displacement of traditional jobs (like nurses) by new, often less-experienced workers; and pharmaceutical company liability. As the industry evolves, so will the nature of disputes and contracts handled by lawyers who practice in the health-related fields. Lawyers will need to understand the new issues and arguments relative to hospitals, physicians, corporate liability, and standard treatment guidelines for common conditions. The Internet is an excellent reference source for gathering information on these issues.

War Story: Heart Center Online

Melissa L. Gray, of Fix Spendelman Brovitz & Goldman, P.C. in Rochester, New York, tells this story:

"We had a client who suffered a heart attack while visiting his father in the hospital and underwent bypass surgery a few weeks later. We alleged that the surgery caused him to have a stroke from which he incurred permanent severe injuries.

"The defense alleged that his injuries were caused by a blood clot rather than from a blocked vein that was used in his bypass surgery. I searched the Internet to research blood clots and their effects and found www.heartcenteronline.com. That site educated me on everything from the causes of a stroke and a heart attack to the procedure for bypass surgery and even had illustrations and animated videos showing what happens to the heart and brain during both.

"The site even described different procedures that could have been used in the surgery, such as the insertion of an intra-aortic balloon, to ensure that the patient's blood would freely flow to and from the heart after surgery. HeartCenterOnline is a resource that I use every time I have a medical question about the heart and a tool that saved our firm a lot of time and money."

Starting-Point Web Sites for Medical Research

The medical research materials available for free on the Internet are both broad and deep. Available resources include the entire physician database from the American Medical Association (listing over 690,000 physicians in the United States), glossaries to help you navigate through medical jargon, and detailed collections of resources covering anatomy and medical procedure that can provide what you need to understand the facts of medically related legal matters.

There are many collections of medical information on the Internet organized by body part, disease, or area of medicine, which function quite well as introductions and as general starting points for medical research on the Internet. Listed below are some of the metasites that link you to these online resources.

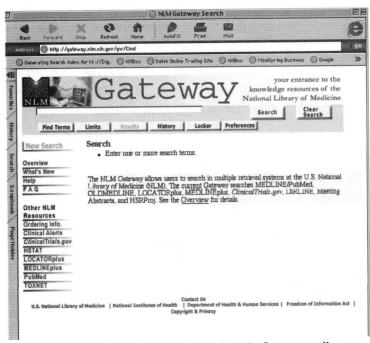

Figure 12-1. The National Library of Medicine's Gateway offers a searchable database of millions of medical journal articles, books, clinical trails, conference abstracts, and other medicine-related resources dating back to the 1950s.

NLM Gateway (National Library of Medicine)

http://gateway.nlm.nih.gov/gw/Cmd

Purpose: To locate abstracts and citations from medical journal articles, books, conference notes, and other written materials on a variety of medicine-related topics.

Content: The NLM provides this one-stop shop to search and retrieve abstract and citation information for over twelve million medical journal articles, books, conference notes, and other written materials back to the mid-

1950s, from multiple sources, including
MedLine/PubMed, OLDMedline, ClinicalTrials.gov, and
consumer health publications, among others.

Our View: Because of the breadth and the depth of the material
covered by the NLM Gateway, it is a good place to start a
search for medical-related literature. The search results
include only citation and abstract information. The full
articles can be ordered through the NLM's Loansome
Doc ordering system, by clicking the **Order Documents** button. Utilizing this service requires registration, as well as arranging a relationship with a Loansome Doc member library. (For more details, see
http://www.nlm.nih.gov/services/ldwhatis.html.) Article prices vary from library to library.

You may be able to retrieve a free copy of a journal article for which you've retrieved citation and abstract

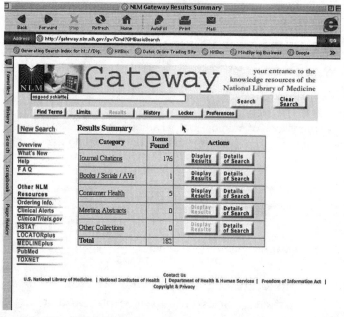

Figure 12-2. The NLM Gateway allows you to store abstract information for
articles you select, and review the searches you have conducted during your
current session.

information at PubMed Central (**http://www.pubmed central.nih.gov**). PubMed Central contains a searchable, full-text archive of more than 120 medical journals. The available date ranges vary by publication.

To locate information, enter your keywords in the search box at the top of the screen. Each result also includes a link to related articles that could lead you to additional related information regarding your search topic.

You can create a list of the citation and abstract information of the articles in your search that interest you most, using the site's **Locker** function. (Using the **Locker** requires free registration.) To hold the selected information in the **Locker**, check the box on the left-hand side of the article's title, then click the **Send to Locker** button above the list of search results. You can add as many as five hundred items to the **Locker**. Those items will remain in the **Locker** until you delete them.

To view the items in the **Locker**, select the **Locker** button near the top of the page. While viewing the list in your **Locker**, you can select individual articles for which to format information to save to a file on your computer, to print out, or to e-mail to yourself or someone else. To do so, click the check boxes next to the articles whose information you want to save and click the **Download or Display** button at the top of the list. On the next screen, you can choose the depth of the details (brief, expanded, or complete) and the destination (display in browser, display for printing, save to file, or send via e-mail), among other options. (You can also utilize the **Download** or **Display** function from your search results list.)

You can also view a history of your searches during your current session by clicking the **History** link near the top of the page. A description of each of the searches you've conducted is shown with the number of results per search and a link to get back to that search.

Tip:

- You can pay to access Medline on LexisNexis and Dialog, or you can search it for free on the Internet. The choice is yours.
- Click on **Find Terms** to use the NLM Gateway as a medical dictionary.

Virtual Naval Hospital

http://www.vnh.org

Purpose: To locate links to practice manuals and textbooks related to the prevention, detection, diagnosis, and treatment of numerous diseases and conditions.

Content: This site is arranged as an online medical library for Naval medical officers in the field. Clicking on the **Providers** link on the home page brings up a page of links to hundreds of medical resources in nearly twenty categories, ranging from **Common Medical Problems** and **Dentistry** to **Biological, Chemical and Nuclear Warfare** and **Radiation Safety**. The list also provides links to dozens more medical textbook entries in thirty-five categories from **Aerospace Medicine** to **Urology**. All entries are full-text versions of their print counterparts.

Our View: This is an excellent source of information when looking for diagnosis, treatment, and management information for a wide range of diseases, conditions, and injuries.

Tip: The site can be especially helpful in locating information for certain types of Naval-specific injuries, such as those related to deep-sea diving and high-altitude and aerospace activities.

MedWeb

http://www.medweb.emory.edu/MedWeb

Purpose: To locate links to medical information, journals, and textbooks on the Internet.

Content: The staff of Emory University's Health Sciences Library maintains this large index to biomedical and health related Web sites.

Our View: The site is set up as a drill down index, so you can select the category you're interested in and click through to the specific information you need. Some subcategories include a **Focus Further** link that lists even more subcategories from which to choose. A search engine is also available to keyword search the index. Note that the search engine supports word-stemming, so searching for "canc" would return results that include the words "cancer" and "cancerous."

Tip: Check the **New Sites!** link (on the left-hand side of the home page) that lists the newest sites added to the index in the preceding thirty days. These often reflect sites about cutting-edge, news-making medical topics. (In a recent month, they added more than two hundred new resources to the index.)

Hardin Meta Directory of Internet Health Sources

http://www.lib.uiowa.edu/hardin/md

Purpose: To locate medical sources on the Internet.

Content: This site from the University of Iowa links to thousands of other medical information sites on the Internet. The links are arranged in more than two hundred alphabetical categories (from AIDS to Yeast Infections [Male]).

Our View: This site uses a logical drill-down method to locate resources on a particular topic. First select the main category where your information is likely to be found (such as Appendicitis), then select the topic you prefer (such as Understanding Appendicitis—The Basics).

Tip: The site also contains links to pictures of medical ailments, skin lesions, and so on. Use the **Medical Pictures** link at the top of the home page.

Martindale's Health Science Guide

http://www.martindalecenter.com/Medical.html

Purpose: To locate medical sources on the Internet.

Content: Prodigious online list-maker Jim Martindale has assembled these links to more than two thousand journals, textbooks, and tutorials. This is an extremely comprehensive medical index, with links to thousands of other sites and documents. (There's even a dental and veterinary index.)

Our View: The amount of information accessible through these pages is staggering, but getting to it can be a bit trying. The site offers a long list of the sites to which it links. There's no search engine. If you scroll down four or five screens, you'll find a subject index (Anatomy to Wound Management) with internal links to the portion of the list covered by the specific subject heading you choose. It's worth clicking through to get to the large number of resources Jim Martindale has compiled on this page.

Tip: Don't miss Martindale's list of medical dictionaries online at **http://www-sci.lib.uci.edu/HSG/Medical .html#DICTION**

Other useful medical information metasites include the sites below.

U.S. Department of Health and Human Services

http://www.dhhs.gov

Content: The department oversees hundreds of programs cover-
             ing a wide spectrum of health related activities. Its site
             contains links to resources related to many of them in a
             topical index. Top-level categories include **Diseases &
             Conditions, Families & Children** (includes Vac-
             cines), and **Resource Locators** (includes a physician
             locater), among others.

U.S. Food and Drug Administration (FDA)

http://www.fda.gov

Content: The FDA provides regulatory guidance to the medical
             industry. The site includes lists of approved drugs and
             news concerning new medical procedures and devices,
             among other topics.

Tip: Note the **index, search,** and **topical** links located on
             the left-hand side of the screen.

Healthfinder

http://www.healthfinder.gov

Content: This government portal presents links to medical infor-
             mation sites in four primary categories: Health Library,
             Just for You, Health Care, and a directory to organiza-
             tions.

Our View: While much of the information available at this site is useful, the **Medical Errors** topic in the **Health Care** category will no doubt be of great interest to some lawyers.

HealthWeb

http:www.healthweb.org

Content: This site offers links to other Internet medical information resources arranged in nearly seventy browsable categories. An internal search engine allows you to search the site's collection of links.

Getting Well (also called PDRHealth)

http://www.gettingwell.com

Content: Written in plain English, this is a consumer targeted site from the publishers of the *Physicians' Desk Reference* (PDR). It offers medical-related information in four categories: **Disease Overviews, Health and Wellness, Drug Information,** and **Clinical Trials.**

Our View: Even though this site is targeted at consumers, it still contains a great deal of information—particularly in the **Disease Overviews** and **Drug Information** categories. The plain-English approach of the site can also be helpful in demystifying complicated procedures for jurors, mediators, and arbitrators. (The online version of the PDR offered only to medical professionals is available at **http://www.pdr.net** and requires registration.)

Palm Medical Dictionary

For mobile lawyers, *Dorland's Pocket Medical Dictionary,* an abridged version of the print book, is available to purchase and load onto your Palm or Pocket PC handheld computer for $39.95. For more information, see **http://www.handango.com**. A search for "dorland" will find the dictionary. (A free searchable database of medical abbreviations is also available for the Palm.)

Dictionaries and Glossaries

Health care professionals, like lawyers, have a language all their own. Some of the most respected and comprehensive medical references, such as *Dorland's Illustrated Medical Dictionary* (see **http://www.netforlawyers.com/dorland**), are available for free on the Internet. Some of the glossaries are specific to areas of medicine, and some are general. Following are a few resources to help you locate them.

General Medical Dictionaries and Glossaries

There are a number of useful metasites that will point you to many different medical dictionaries and glossaries on the Internet. One of the largest is Jim Martindale's Virtual Medical Center list of links to medical dictionaries located at **http://www-sci.lib.uci.edu/HSG/Medical.html#DICTION**.

Direct links to some of the medical dictionaries available online include the sites listed below.

Dorland's Illustrated Medical Dictionary

http://www.mercksource.com/pp/us/cns/cns_health_library_frame.jsp?pg=/pp/us/cns/cns_hl_dorlands.jsp?pg=/pp/us/common/dorlands/dorland/dmd_a-b_00.htm&cd=3d

Purpose: To define medical terms.

Content: The site contains definitions of thousands of medical and medicine-related terms. To locate the term you're looking for, navigate through the site using the links to each letter of the alphabet near the top of page. Then browse through the list of terms until you find the one you want.

MedicineNet

http://www.medterms.com/script/main/hp.asp

Purpose: To define medical terms.

Content: The doctors of MedicineNet, who also authored *Webster's New World Medical Dictionary,* Second Edition, also offer this free online medical glossary. (To access the glossary, be certain to use the **Search the Dictionary** box rather than the **Search** box, which searches the rest of the site.) Additionally, the glossary's **Advanced Search** page allows you to narrow your search by selecting a specific topic and offers tips for phrase and Boolean searching.

Medical Information Management
Approved Abbreviations for Medical Records

http://academic.med.ohio-state.edu/MIMabbrev/index.htm

Purpose: To decode medical abbreviations and symbols.

Content: This site from the Ohio State University College of
               Medicine and Public Health offers a useful glossary of
               medical abbreviations and includes a list of common
               medical symbols (the kind included in medical charts
               and prescriptions) as a PDF document.

Foreign-Language Medical Glossary

Multilingual Medical Glossary

http://allserv.rug.ac.be/~rvdstich/eugloss/language.html

Content: This site from the Heymans Institute for Pharmacology
               in Belgium offers glossaries of medical terms in seven
               European languages, in addition to English.

Medical Textbooks and Encyclopedias

Medical encyclopedias can be good sources for getting up to speed
with an unfamiliar or complex medical situation. Generally, they provide
broad (yet detailed enough) descriptions of diseases and procedures. Just
as with legal information, the more recent the book the better, but even
older books can be of value if you are able to fill in with more recent information from scholarly journals or consumer publications.

For a large list of links to medical textbooks, organized by topic, see
Emory University's MedWeb at **http://www.medweb.emory.edu/
MedWeb**. (For more information about this site, see its listing earlier in
this chapter.) Jim Martindale's Virtual Medical Center page (**http://www
.sci.lib.uci.edu/HSG/Medical.html**) also includes links to a number of online medical textbooks.

MEDLINEplus A.D.A.M. Medical Encyclopedia

http://www.nlm.nih.gov/medlineplus/encyclopedia.html

Purpose: To locate information about diseases, tests, symptoms, injuries, and surgeries.

Content: The National Library of Medicine offers the popular A.D.A.M. illustrated medical encyclopedia. The site has over four thousand articles about diseases, tests, symptoms, injuries, and surgeries, along with extensive illustrations to accompany many of them.

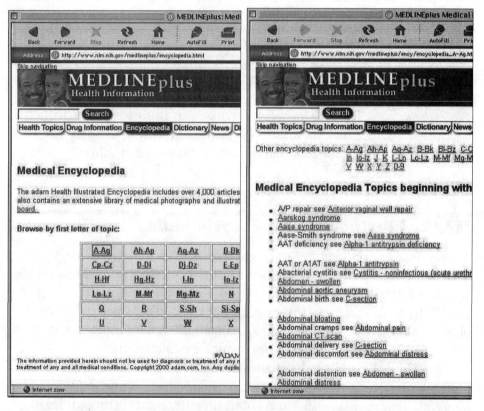

Figure 12-3. Selecting an alphabetical range from the A.D.A.M. Medical Encyclopedia (right) brings up a page of medical terms that fall within that range (left). Clicking on the name brings up a detailed entry about the term you've selected.

Our View: The site is easy to navigate, but unfortunately there's no search function for the encyclopedia. You have to browse the topic headings alphabetically, by selecting the alphabetical range in which your word or term appears, and then scrolling through the list of entries to find the one you need. Each entry includes information in a number of categories, including its definition, alternate names and terms, illustrations, causes, symptoms, tests, prevention, treatment, and so on. The entries also include cross-referenced links to associated terms.

Tip: Use your browser's **Find** function to locate the term you need in the alphabetical list of topics, rather than scrolling down the page on which it's located. (See the section "Browsers and Favorites" in Chapter 2, "Internet Tools Protocol," for more information on this browser feature.)

Anatomy Sites

Beyond Vesalius

http://www.anatomy.wright.edu/BeyondVesalius/
BeyondVesalius.html

Purpose: To view cross-sectional specimens, CT (CAT) scans, and x-rays of the human body.

Content: Anatomy professors at the Wright State University School of Medicine used images from the National Library of Medicine's Visible Human Project to create this interactive, cross-sectional view of an entire human adult male body. To access the material from this site, you must download and install a free viewer application, as well as the six modules that make up the entire human body. With this material on your computer, you can select a portion of the body from one of the modules (such as head and neck or thorax). The player and modules are available as free downloads for both Mac and Windows operating systems.

Our View: After selecting any part of the body from the six modules, you can opt to study x-ray images, cross-sections, or CT scans. Selecting one shows the first slice of that part of the body. Arrows on the left-hand side of the screen can be used to navigate down the body (one section at a time). Using the buttons at the top center of the screen, you can choose to view sections, **CT**, or **composite**, which puts the sections and CT scans side by side for comparison. Using the **Labels** button, you can turn on or off text labels identifying nearly all of the structures seen in that segment.

Tip: Be sure to select **Study**. If you select **Test**, your anatomy knowledge will be tested with on-screen questions. Remember, after all, this was developed as a teaching tool for first-year medical students.

Martindale's Anatomy & Histology Center

http://www-sci.lib.uci.edu/HSG/MedicalAnatomy.html

Content: Jim Martindale's done it again with this extensive collection of links to anatomy atlases, anatomy animation and image databases, and anatomy tutorials arranged by body parts or systems (such as cardio-pulmonary, digestive, and so on) from medical schools, associations, and other organizations from throughout the world.

Human Anatomy Online

http://www.innerbody.com

Content: This site offers interactive medical drawings and non-interactive color (drawn) animations of selected body structures and functions. The drawings feature a series of interactive identifier markers (green diamond shapes). Hovering your cursor over those points pops up the name of the structure at that point on the body (for example, hovering over a diamond on the chest might pop up the label "sternum"). If a lateral view or close-up of the body part is available, a Magnifying Glass icon accompanies the label. Click the icon to see the alternate view. Additionally, there are noninteractive drawings (click on the **Images** button at the bottom of the page) and noninteractive animated images (click **Animations**).

The Digital Anatomist Project

http://www9.biostr.washington.edu/da.html

Content: The Department of Biological Structure at the University of Washington provides two-dimensional and three-dimensional views of various organs reconstructed from cadaver sections, MRI scans, and computer reconstructions. There are also a small number of downloadable animations of some body structures available in the AVI format.

Sites About Diseases and Procedures

The Merck Manual of Diagnosis and Therapy, 17th Edition

http://www.merck.com/pubs/mmanual/sections.htm

Purpose: Locate descriptions and recommended treatments/procedures for various diseases.

Content: The Merck Manual is a primary source of information on any disease. It is available full text on the Internet. It describes symptoms, common clinical procedures, laboratory tests, and virtually all the disorders that a general internist might encounter. Current therapy is presented for each disorder and supplemented with a separate section on clinical pharmacology. You can use the search engine to locate a specific disorder (such as angina) or you can browse through topical chapters covering diseases and disorders (such as **Cardiovascular Disorders**) to find the information you need.

Our View: There are two big advantages to the online version of the Manual versus the print edition: (1) the online version is full-text searchable, and (2) the online version is more up to date than the currently circulating print version. Changes and additions (to be made in the next print version) are continually added to the online ver-

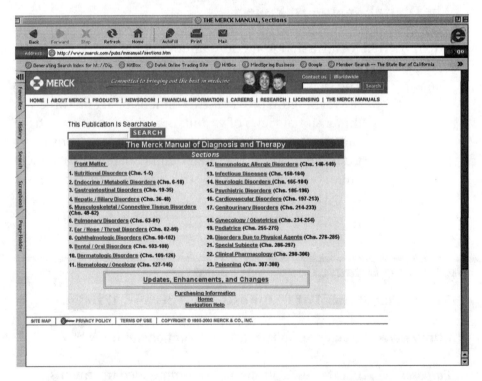

Figure 12-4. *The Merck Manual* is a trusted source for information regarding diseases and disorders. The Internet version is updated regularly, and is more up-to-date than the print version. From *The Merck Manuals*. Copyright 2003 by Merck & Co., Inc. Whitehouse Station, N.J.

sion. Therefore, an expert relying on a print copy may be using out-of-date information.

Tip: While the changes are not noted in the text of the on-line entries, you can see where changes have been made to the online version when compared to the current print edition. Click the **Updates, Enhancements, and Changes** link under the **Table of Contents** to see if there were any important changes made regarding the disorder you're researching. To compare the changed text to the original, download the PDF document found at the bottom of the **Changes** page. The dates of changes and additions are not noted on the page or in the PDF.

Centers for Disease Control and Prevention (CDC)

http://www.cdc.gov/health/default.htm

Content: The CDC provides an alphabetical list of diseases (and other health-related topics) that link to fact sheets, pro-nunciation guides (to be certain that you're pronounc-ing the terms correctly in trial, or at deposition), and other background and treatment information.

Virtual Hospital

http://www.vh.org

Content: This site, from the University of Iowa Medical School's Radiology Department, offers information in a number of categories, including **For Providers** and **For Patients,** with subcategories that include **By Topic, By Specialty,** and **By Location/Body System.** The portion of the site designated as **For Providers** includes an online multimedia textbook, offering clinical procedural guidelines and three-dimensional graphics of some body systems and structures.

Cancer and Oncology

OncoLink

http://cancer.med.upenn.edu

Content: The University of Pennsylvania Cancer Center provides a wide variety of information regarding numerous forms of cancer. The information ranges from the general to the specific. Click the **OncoLink Library** link on the left-hand side of the screen to access journal articles and additional background information on specific forms of cancer. Information is provided on pediatric and adult cancers, descriptions and stage explanations of disease, and treatment options. Click the **Clinical Trials** link for information regarding new treatments under evaluation. The site also includes a search engine.

Heart Disease and Cardiology

HeartCenterOnline

http://www.heartcenteronline.com

Content: This site contains detailed information regarding many cardiopulmonary conditions and diseases ranging from high cholesterol and high blood pressure to arrhythmia and coronary artery disease. To locate the information you need, click the **Heart Tools** link on the home page. Then you can either use the search engine to locate specific terms or diseases, or click the **Conditions & Diseases** or **Procedures & Tests** buttons at the top of the page. After clicking the entry that interests you, you'll notice many key terms are highlighted (in blue). You can click these terms for more detailed explanations.

Our View: This is a good resource for background information on heart-related medical conditions and for keeping up to date regarding those conditions. You can track news regarding a particular disease or disorder by registering (free) for the site's weekly newsletter that you can customize with up to ten cardiac related topics relevant to your cases. Registration also allows you to post questions to the site's **Ask the Cardiologist** and patient discussion boards. (See the War Story at the beginning of this chapter for one lawyer's success story using this site.)

Tip: Don't bother clicking the **Professionals Enter Here** button on the site's introduction page. That section is primarily meant as a practice management and development tool for doctors. You can access all of the disease and disorder related news and information from the **Patients** area.

Psychiatry

DSM-IV Made Easy

http://www.geocities.com/morrison94

Content: The American Psychiatric Association's *Diagnostic & Statistical Manual of Mental Disorders DSM-IV-TR* (4th Ed.), which provides diagnostic guidelines for all currently recognized psychological disorders, is not available free online. However, this free site provides "a complete set of DSM-IV criteria for all currently used mental disorders." The material was created by the site owner, James Morrison, MD (a professor of psychiatry at Oregon Health Sciences University), based on his book *DSM-IV Made Easy.*

Medical Journals and Articles

Journal articles are an excellent way to learn about current medical thinking, and possibly pick up information on more up-to-date treatment techniques than the opposition (or their experts) are aware of. One excellent source is the National Library of Medicine's MedLine databases discussed at the beginning of this chapter. Other good sources include the site listed below.

Medscape

http://www.medscape.com

Purpose: To locate abstracts and citations from selected medical journals.

Content: Medscape's online library offers full-text access to selected articles from nearly one hundred medical journals.

Our View: To search the site's collection of journal articles and news stories, click the **Advanced Search** link underneath the search box at the top of the page, and then select **Medscape Professional** from the subsequent page. The site's search recognizes the Boolean connector AND as well as the use of quotation marks for exact phrase searching.

To access the list of journal titles, click the **Library** link at the top of the home page. You can browse the journal list and tables of contents without registration, but reading the articles requires (free) registration. It's important to note that not all articles from each issue of these journals are available.

Tip: The site also has **Information Centers** focusing on the business of medicine and medical technology, as well as its **DrugInfo** database of prescription drug uses, precautions, and side effects, among other information.

DrugInfo is searchable by drug name or disease name (to find drugs recommended for use to treat that disease).

American Medical Association Journals

http://pubs.ama-assn.org

Purpose: To locate abstracts, citations, and articles from AMA medical journals.

Content: In addition to its well-known *JAMA*, the AMA also publishes a number of specialized medical journals. These include *Archives of Internal Medicine*, *Archives of General Psychiatry*, and *Archives of Facial Plastic Surgery*, among others. The AMA makes the full text of the most recent years of these available online for free (generally back to the mid-90s). For older years, only article abstracts are offered. In the instance of the oldest years (generally before 1974) only the tables of contents are available online.

Our View: From the publications page you can search a database of all the available journals, or select a specific journal and search only that one.

There are a number of other journals available online at their own Web sites (such as the *New England Journal of Medicine* at **http://www .nejm.org**), or smaller collections of journals, where they may offer full-text or partial-text access to their articles. Some may require free registration. Some of these include:

- MedWebPlus Electronic Journals metasite at **http://www.medweb plus.com/subject/Electronic_Journals.html**
- Emerging Infectious Diseases at **http://www.cdc.gov/ncidod /EID/index.htm**
- A collection of clinical nutrition articles at **http://netspace.net .au/~helmant/nut_art1.htm**

Hospital Sites

The American Hospital Directory (AHD)

http://www.ahd.com

Summary data on specific hospitals: More specific data:

Purpose: To locate hospital management and care statistics.

Content: The AHD provides select data for over six thousand U.S. hospitals online. Summary data provided free includes the following (from the American Hospital Association Annual Survey data):

- Address
- Phone
- Number of beds
- Type of business organization (for-profit, non-profit)
- General description of services offered (from the federal Centers for Medicare and Medicaid Services [CMS, formerly HCFA] data)
- Medical services provided (by category, with numbers of Medicare patients served)
- Statistics for the most common Ambulatory Patient Classification (APC) codes
- Financial data

More-detailed information in each of these categories is available to paid subscribers. Subscriptions are $395 for a single user per year. Discounts are available for additional users from the same organization.

Our View: The AHD database is a good resource to develop an overview of a particular hospital's services, caseload, and finances. It is built from Medicare claims data, cost reports, and other public use files from CMS. The directory also includes AHA Annual Survey data.

Tip: If you ever need to decode Diagnosis Related Group (DRG) codes, you can do it here. When reading a hospital report, clicking on any of the categories of service provided (such as cardiology or urology) reveals the DRG codes in that category used to identify specific diagnoses.

New Medical Development Sites

Medical Breakthroughs

http://www.ivanhoe.com

Content: This site, maintained by a news-gathering and production company that supplies medical reports to local television stations around the country, tracks medical breakthroughs in nearly two dozen categories.

               Click on any topic on the left-hand side of the home page to see the latest headlines for that topic. You can also sign up for free e-mail updates on the latest breakthroughs.

Reuters Health

http://www.reutershealth.com

Content: While this site is designed primarily as a sales tool for Reuters to offer its medical coverage to other news and Internet outlets, the wire service does present current headlines of breaking medical news and feature coverage of medical research, breakthroughs, and industry-related news.

Our View: While headlines are clickable and you can link to the full texts of the stories, there is no archive or search available. Therefore, the site is best used for keeping up to date with current information, but is not useful for historical research.

For another source of information regarding medical breakthroughs, also see the entry for GettingWell.com later in this chapter.

Medical Device Sites

The U.S. Food and Drug Administration (FDA) Center for Devices and Radiological Health (CDRH) at **http://www.fda.gov/cdrh** oversees the safety and effectiveness of medical devices as required by the Medical Device Amendments to the Federal Food, Drug and Cosmetic Act of 1976. The Center maintains a number of subsites containing information about

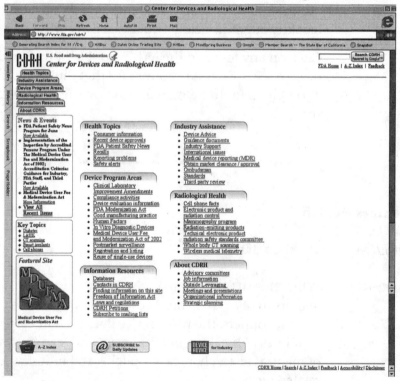

Figure 12-5. The FDA's Center for Devices and Radiological Health (CDRH) maintains numerous databases regarding medical devices and reported failures of those devices.

medical devices that have been reported to have malfunctioned, or caused serious injury or death. For example, the Center maintains a database of information regarding recalls of medical devices at **http://www .fda.gov/cdrh/recalls**.

Use the following sites maintained by the CDRH to search for other types of detailed information regarding devices and device failures.

Medical Device Reporting Database

http://www.accessdata.fda.gov/scripts/cdrh/cfdocs/ cfmdr/search.CFM

Content: This searchable database contains information regarding medical devices reported to have malfunctioned or caused a death or serious injury during the years 1988 through 1996.

Manufacturer and User Facility Device Experience Database (MAUDE)

http://www.accessdata.fda.gov/scripts/cdrh/ cfdocs/cfMAUDE/Search.cfm

Content: This searchable database contains information regarding medical devices reported to have malfunctioned or caused a death or serious injury since 1996.

Device Advice Medical Device Tracking

http://www.fda.gov/cdrh/devadvice/353.html

Content: These pages contain information regarding mandatory medical device tracking and the types of devices that require tracking.

There are also a number of nongovernmental sites that offer free information regarding medical devices and manufacturers. Some of these are listed below.

Medical DeviceLink

http://www.devicelink.com

Purpose: To locate news, and contact information regarding the medical device and pharmaceuticals industries.

Content: This site contains numerous links to medical device manufacturers and suppliers, news, and other information related to the medical device industry.

Our View: Maintained by Canon Communications, publisher of more than a half-dozen medical device and pharmaceutical industry publications, this site offers searchable databases of:

- North American medical device manufacturers
- European medical device manufacturers
- Medical electronics suppliers
- Industry consultants
- Suppliers of packaging materials
- In vitro diagnostic suppliers

Click the **Directories** link at the top of the home page to search any of these directories individually, all of them at once, or any combination of them.

On the home page, the site also features medical, pharmaceutical, and medical device news stories. Click the

All News and Categories link to view all the current headlines. Click any headline to read the full story. Near the top of the **All News** page is a pull-down menu that allows you to request the headlines that appeared on the page on any particular day of the last thirty days.

Additionally, the site also has discussion forums on a variety of industry-related topics, which are available only after (free) registration. None of the other features discussed here requires registration.

Tip: Many of the company's print magazines are available full text. Use the **Article Search** box in the upper left-hand corner of the home page to search all of their publications at once.

MDRWeb

http://www.mdrweb.com

Purpose: To locate information regarding medical devices and manufacturers.

Content: Maintained by the publishers of the *Medical Device Register*, this site offers a searchable database of nearly eighteen thousand medical device manufacturers worldwide and eighty-two thousand products. Listings include e-mail and Web site links, where available. The database costs $399 for one year of access for an individual user.

Our View: This is the *Martindale-Hubbell* of the medical device industry. Any device manufacturer can receive a free listing. You can search by more than a dozen criteria, including company or product name, geographic location, company revenue range, product keyword, registered trade name, or product distribution category, among others.

Tip: Paid subscribers also receive new product and recall alerts via e-mail.

AdvaMed (The Advanced Medical Technology Association)
(formerly the Health Industry Manufacturers Association HIMA)

http://www.advamed.com

Content: This site is maintained by the largest professional association representing the medical device industry. It includes news releases, white papers, and fact sheets addressing issues facing the industry and information regarding its lobbying activities. The organization's newsletter is also available, with archives back to 2000.

Pharmaceutical Sites

PDRhealth

http://www.gettingwell.com/drug_info

Content: This is a consumer-oriented index of drug indications, drug interactions, and other information from the publishers of the *Physician's Desk Reference* (PDR). The database includes information on prescription drugs, over-the-counter drugs, herbal medicines, and nutritional supplements. On the **Clinical Trials** page is a subtopic, New FDA Drug Approvals, that offers a year-by-year list of drugs approved. Grouped by type of disease the drug is approved to treat (such as **Neurology, Pulmonary**, and so on), lists are available back to 1995.

RxList

http://www.rxlist.com

Content: This is a consumer-oriented index with an A-to-Z list of over thirteen hundred prescription drugs. The site contains cross-referenced links to:

- Prescribing information
- Side effects
- Drug interactions

You can search for information on drugs by prescription name, generic name, imprint (on the pill or capsule), or NDC (National Drug Code) number.

The site also has a list, **Top 200 Prescriptions** of the drugs prescribed in the previous calendar year.

MedicineNet

http://www.medicinenet.com/medications/alpha_a.htm

Content: This consumer-oriented site also features an A-to-Z list of hundreds of prescription drugs. You can search by brand or generic name or browse the alphabetical list. When searching, you can use an asterisk (*) as a wild card to replace letters at the end of a drug name if you're not sure how to spell the name correctly. For example, "acet*" would return "acetaminophen," among other drugs that include that string of letters.

Tip: At the bottom of the results page is a link, **Visit eLibrary to find more information about <search term> in Newspapers and Magazines**. Clicking here takes you to an eLibrary.com (**http://www.elibrary.com**) page displaying results from its database for the drug you searched for. Even though access to eLibrary costs $19.95 per month or $99.95 per year, you can get a free seven-day trial during which you can access the full text of any articles in the site's database.

New Medicines in Development

http://www.phrma.org/newmedicines

Content: The Pharmaceutical Research and Manufacturers Association (PhRMA) provides a browsable database (by disease, indication, or drug) of new drugs in development.

Clinical Pharmacology

http://www.cponline.gsm.com

Content: Geared toward medical professionals, this site offers in-depth information regarding dosage, usage, FDA-approved off-label uses, and mechanisms of action for "all U.S. prescription drugs, hard-to-find herbal and nutritional supplements, over-the-counter products and new and investigational drugs." It also provides extensive resources for identifying drugs by size, color, markings, and ingredients, and for comparing drugs based on brand name, ingredients, and so on. A single-user annual subscription to the online service costs $435. Site licenses are also available for firm-wide access if needed.

Also see the entry on Medscape in the "Journals and Articles section earlier in this chapter for information on its **DrugInfo database**.

Health Professions Sites

Physician Directories

AMA Physician Select

http://www.ama-assn.org/aps/amahg.htm

Content: The AMA provides the primary physician directory available to the public. For information on individual doctors, choose **Search for a Physician**. All 690,000 accredited doctors (MDs and DOs) in the U.S. are represented. You can search by the doctor's name, specialty, or only for doctors available for an online consultation. Information provided includes address, phone number, specialty, where degrees were obtained, where residencies were served, and American Board of Medical Specialties certifications. No discipline information is provided.

Tip: Of course, we'd all rather have access to the government's National Doctor Index. Start lobbying.

- Use the asterisk (*) as a wild card when uncertain of a doctor's first name spelling (for example, to search for Jeffrey Smith, search for "J* Smith" in case "Jeffrey" is spelled "Jeffery" or in case the doctor goes by "Jeff").
- You can also perform a sounds-like search (click the **sounds like** box under the ZIP code entry field) if you're not sure how to spell the doctor's last name. Note that this only works for last names, not first names.
- Deceased physicians will not be found online, but contact the AMA—they keep some limited history.

---

eCare UPIN Lookup

http://upin.ecare.com

Content: Federal law provides for the creation of a Unique Physician Identification Number (UPIN) for every doctor who provides services for which payment is made under Medicare, and requires the publication of a directory of those numbers. At this site, you can search for a doctor's UPIN, or determine a doctor's name if you only know the UPIN. For each physician, the database provides medical specialty, state, ZIP code, and identification number only. For a full address, you will have to use the AMA database noted above.

Physician Licensing and Disciplinary Action Sites

Many states make their professional licensing databases available for free on the Internet. Access to these databases and the amount of information provided varies from state to state. One site that allows you to search the records of many states is the Administrators in Medicine (AIM) DocFinder (**http://www.docboard.org/docfinder.html**). DocFinder also links to discipline records, if available. New York provides both licensing and discipline information. For information on other metasites that will link you to licensing records on the Internet (if they are available), see Chapter 8, "Accessing Public Records."

New York State Department of Health

Office of Professional Medical Conduct

http://w3.health.state.ny.us/opmc/factions.nsf

Content: New York is one of the states that offers a searchable database of its physician discipline database. On the left-hand side of the page, you can choose to view lists of the disciplined doctors arranged by:

- Physician name
- License number
- License type
- Effective date

You can also search for a specific doctor by clicking the **Physician Search** button in the center of the page.

Once you've located the doctor you're looking for, clicking on the name returns an abstract about the discipline.

Tip: At the bottom of the page is the juiciest information—a link to the full **Board Order**. This order contains all of the hearing information regarding the discipline, saved as a PDF document. These can make very interesting reading.

Other Health Profession Sites

Here are some sites for more health profession associations:

- American Chiropractic Association at **http://www.amerchiro.org**
- American Dental Association at **http://www.ada.org**
- American Health Lawyers Association at **http://www.health lawyers.org**
- American Nurses Association at **http://www.ana.org**
- American Optometric Association at **http://www.aoanet.org**
- American Physical Therapy Association at **http://www.apta.org**
- American Psychiatric Association at **http://www.psych.org**
- American Academy of Nurse Practitioners at **http://www.aanp.org**

*CHAPTER*THIRTEEN

Scientific Research

While few of us are trained scientists, there are still instances when we need to find information on a science related subject. Sometimes it may be related to medicine (also see Chapter 12, "Medical Research"), while other times it might have to do with some sort of chemical reaction or an issue concerning forensic evidence. Starting your search in a consumer publication or educational resource can be a good way to locate background and introductory information before moving on to more detailed (and technical) journal articles. These introductory sources can also help you explain difficult or advanced concepts to jurors at trial.

Starting-Point Web Sites for Scientific Research

MadSci Library

http://www.madsci.org/libs/libs.html

Purpose: To locate information and resources regarding numerous scientific topics.

Content: The MadSci Library is one portion of Washington University School of Medicine's (St. Louis) Young Scientists program aimed at improving science literacy among school-aged children. It contains links to numerous articles, Web sites, and other online resources related to many different areas of science.

Our View: Don't dismiss this site just because it's geared toward helping K-12 students gain a better understanding of science. It includes introductory information on many advanced scientific principles such as biochemistry, clinical microbiology, immunology, chemistry, and physics, among other topics.

The site offers a list of topics in the left-hand frame, with the accompanying resources and links appearing in the right-hand frame after you click a topic.

The left-hand frame also has a **USENET** link pointing to specific discussion groups or forums where you can pose a question.

Tip: For hard-to-locate facts, or continually puzzling questions, click on the **Ask-A-Scientist** link to find a scientist to whom you can pose your question via e-mail.

Zeno's Forensic Site

http://forensic.to/forensic.html

Purpose: To locate links to information regarding forensic science and investigative methods, including forensic medicine, psychiatry, and psychology.

Content: The site provides an extensive collection of links to forensic science resources in nearly two dozen categories including such topics as **General Web Sites, Associations and Societies, Arson, Entomology,** and **Computer Investigation**—all in a drill-down directory. Click through the selections until you find the information you need.

Our View: Compiled and maintained since 1993 by Dr. Zeno Geradts, a forensic scientist in Amsterdam, this site covers a lot of bases. Dr. Geradts clearly knows his stuff and has taken the time to assemble a comprehensive set of links across a number of different categories. (He is employed in the Digital Evidence section of the Netherlands Forensic Institute of the Ministry of Justice where he handles forensic [video] image processing.) The site is updated regularly. (The site had last been updated less than three weeks before our most recent visit.)

Tip: The site also features a search engine (at the bottom of the page) to keyword search the links.

TNCrimLaw Forensic Science Resources

http://www.tncrimlaw.com/forensic

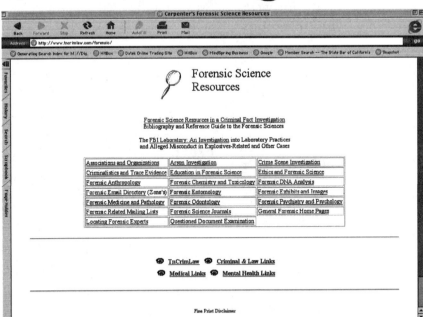

Figure 13-1. The TNCrimLaw.com Forensic Science Resources page provides links to forensic science resources valuable to lawyers in any state.

Purpose: To locate links to information regarding forensic science and investigative methods.

Content: The site provides links to forensic science resources in nearly two dozen categories including **General Forensic Home Pages, Associations and Organizations, Forensic Odontology,** and **Questioned Document Examination**.

Our View: Despite the name, this site is not just for Tennessee lawyers. The site features a drill-down directory of forensic science topics. At the top of the page is a link to **Forensic Science Resources in a Criminal Fact Investigation**, which is a bibliography of online and off-line sources for information (arranged topically). When available, the bibliography entry includes a link to the online version of the article, otherwise the print citation gives you enough information to find the book from a library or bookstore source.

Tip: Don't miss the links at the bottom of the page to other TNCrimLaw resources, including medical and mental health resources.

Scirus

http://www.scirus.com

Purpose: To locate science-related information via this science-only search engine.

Content: The site provides a free search of more than 150 million science-related pages, including text, PDF and PostScript formatted files. Scirus also claims to search "access controlled sites" and deliver "more peer-reviewed articles than any other search engine." Scirus returns both free and fee-based resources in its results.

Our View: Users are given the option of searching for information in any combination of the site's twenty-one categories ranging from **Agricultural, Biological** and **Life Sciences** to **Sociology** (or all of them).

Results are broken down into two categories, **Web** and **Journal**. While the **Web** resources are available free, the **Journal** results are available for a fee from a variety of partners including BioMedNet/MEDLINE, ChemWeb.com, and ScienceDirect, among others. Charges for these articles vary.

In a column to the right of the search results is a list of suggested words and phrases to help refine your search. If you do not want to use one of their suggestions, at the bottom of the list is a search box where you can enter your own word or phrase to refine your search.

Scirus, owned by Elsevier Science, is powered by FAST Search, a search engine from Norway-based Fast Search & Transfer, the company which originally developed the popular Alltheweb search engine.

Tip: Use **Advanced Search** to narrow down your search by time frame, information type (abstracts only, articles, books, company Web sites), file format, and more.

Refdesk's Science Information Resources page at **http://www.refdesk .com/factsci.html** contains descriptions and links to over 150 other sites containing information on scientific topics ranging from biology and chemistry to forensic science. (For more information about the Refdesk site, see its entry in Chapter 5, "General Factual Research.")

Popular Science

http://www.popsci.com

Purpose: To locate news and feature articles regarding the application of science to our everyday lives.

Content: The site features selected articles and features from the current (and past) editions of *Popular Science* magazine.

Our View: The site arranges articles into seven topical categories:

- Science
- Internet
- Medicine & Biotechnology
- Computers & Consumer Electronics
- Aviation & Space
- Home Tech
- Auto

Links to the full text of select current articles are listed on the site's home page. You can click on any of the category names (along the top of the screen) to see the available current articles from the most recent issues for that topic. A keyword search is also offered to locate available articles (see the Tip below for search techniques). An e-mail newsletter is available with (free) registration.

Tip: Make sure to add your Boolean connectors (in all caps) to your search. A search for just the words "auto" and "steering" produced no results. A search for "auto AND steering" produced twenty-four articles outlining steering technology in cars back to early 2002.

European Organization of Nuclear Research (CERN)

To search and view selected articles: To purchase articles:

http://library.cern.ch/electronic_journals/ej.html

Purpose: To locate scientific journals by topic.

Content: The CERN library provides links to nearly three thousand journals covering numerous physics, chemistry, and engineering topics.

Our View: You can view the list by subject, or as a browsable, alphabetical list. Some are available online free, in full text, while others are available only by online subscription or on a pay-per-view basis. (Some sites allow you to pay a fee to access a single article for twenty-four hours. You may or may not be able to print the pay-per-view article, depending on the site.)

Tip: Despite repeated attempts and varied search terms and syntax, we could not get any results from the "**Query online e-journal catalogue**" search engine when attempting to locate keywords that might appear in an article's abstract.

MIT Technology Review

http://www.technologyreview.com

Purpose: To locate news and feature articles regarding scientific innovations.

Content: The site features articles, columns, and features from the current (and past) editions of the *MIT Technology Review* magazine.

Our View: The site arranges articles into nine topical categories:

- Biotech
- Business
- Computing
- Energy
- Nanotech
- Security
- Software
- Telecom/Internet
- Transportation

Links to the full-text current articles are listed on the site's home page. Some are available to read for free, but most (those accompanied by a gold Key icon) are available only to paid subscribers of the magazine. (A subscription to either the digital or print version costs $28 for ten issues.) You can click on any of the category names (along the left-hand side of the screen) to see the most recent issues for that topic.

A keyword search is also offered to locate specific articles (see the Tip below for search suggestions). An e-mail newsletter is available with (free) registration.

Tip: Unfortunately, the search seems to use the Boolean connector OR as a default, so a search for the phrase "computer forensics" (without quotation marks) returns articles with the word "computer" or the word "forensics"—a pretty long list to be sure. Put search phrases in quotation marks, and add a plus sign next to search terms to force the search engine to include both of them (for example, search for "+computer +forensics"—without quotation marks—to find articles that contain both of those words).

Public Library of Science (PLoS)

http://www.plos.org/about/openaccess.html

Content: PLoS is a nonprofit organization working to create a free archive of scientific journal articles available online. Currently, the site offers links to over seventy-five journals covering biological, medical, and other scientific research that offer their full contents online for free.

Science News

http://www.sciencenews.org

Purpose: To locate news on scientific and technological advances.

Content: This site offers free access to selected articles from the print version of *Science News*, an eighty-plus-year-old weekly chronicle of scientific developments.

Our View: Published since 1922, the print magazine covers important research and development in all areas of science. The Web site provides free access to some of these articles. Recent free articles have covered carbon nano-tubes, advances in satellite mapping, and mercury fallout in earth's polar regions, among other topics. The Web site offers an online archive of back issues to 1997 and selected articles available full text back to 1994. Click **Archives** to browse the issues by date. A full-text archive of all the magazine's stories is available to paid subscribers of the print magazine (which costs $54.50 per year). Click **Search** to perform a keyword search. The site also offers a free newsletter.

Tip: For older articles, you can also contact *Science News* by e-mail to search their print archives.

Science @ NASA

http://science.nasa.gov

Purpose: To locate background information on how NASA programs and experiments affect scientific research on Earth.

Content: This site provides informative articles on NASA's scientific initiatives and how the agency's experiments can, or will, be practically applied. Articles are arranged by topic, including:

- Space Science
- Astronomy
- Earth Science
- Biological & Physical Sciences

Recent articles have discussed research on antibiotics, bone implants, and weather research, among other topics.

Our View: This is another Web site whose internal search engine apparently uses OR as a default Boolean connector (without bothering to mention it anywhere on the site). A search for the phrase "hip replacement" (even in quotation marks) nano and tube, as well as +nano+tube returned articles with the word "hip" or the word "replacement." The results list, therefore, included an interesting article about ongoing NASA research into artificial bone substitutes to replace worn human joints, but also returned a lot of off-topic results. An e-mail newsletter is available with (free) registration.

Figure 13-2. NASA provides news, updates, and explanations of how space program experiments affect scientific research on Earth.

ScienceDaily

http://www.sciencedaily.com

Purpose: To locate breaking science and research news.

Content: This site aggregates information from various academic and corporate research sources to list new announcements in scientific, medical, and technological research.

Our View: The site summarizes and posts news releases gathered from universities and other research institutions. (Contributors can actually post the news releases to the site themselves.) You can view the news either by topic, by headline, or by headlines with abstracts. The site also offers an internal search engine for its archive of news that uses OR as a default Boolean connector. Here, a search for the phrase "nano tube" (even in quotation marks) nano AND tube, as well as +nano +tube returned articles with the word "nano" or the word "tube"—ending up with a lot of off-topic results. While the site does not offer any critical analysis or peer review, it can be helpful in keeping up with new announcements.

Tip: You can also view headlines from the preceding day or week by scrolling to the bottom of the page.

Computer Forensic Resources

DFRWS (Digital Forensic Research Workshop) Links

http://www.dfrws.org/dfrws-links.html

Purpose: To locate information regarding digital evidence collection, preservation, and presentation.

Content: This site features a growing list of links to resources that can help demystify the advantages, limitations, and procedures of utilizing digital forensic evidence. Links are broken down into ten categories, including selected case law involving computer forensics, journals, white papers, and links to other lists of useful forensics links.

Our View: The Digital Forensic Research Workshop is made up of digital forensics researchers, academics, and practitioners from around the country. While they describe their list of links as "by no means complete," it is still a good place to start looking for information, as many of the sites you'll find here offer loads of useful information.

Kroll Ontrack

http://www.krollontrack.com/LawLibrary

Purpose: To locate articles, case law, and statutes related to computer forensics and electronic discovery.

Content: The lawyers of computer forensics and digital evidence consulting firm Kroll Ontrack have compiled a list of links to:

- Articles written by Kroll lawyers and consultants
- Case law (organized by jurisdiction and topic)
- Kroll newsletters (**http://www.krollontrack.com/ LawLibrary/NewsletterCenter**)
- Law review and journal articles
- Rules and statutes (federal and local, arranged by jurisdiction)

The site also contains a glossary of digital discovery and computer forensics terms.

Our View: The lawyers and consultants of Kroll Ontrack write extensively and often on the subjects of computer forensics and digital discovery. The articles included on the site are current and easy to read. (On a recent visit, the oldest article was only six weeks old.) The material accessible here can be helpful whether you're defending a client whose computer has been seized by law enforcement or has been subpoenaed, or you are working to subpoena a computer from the opposition.

A number of other practitioners also offer useful resources. The Web sites of Computer Forensics, Inc. (**http://www.forensics.com/html/resource_articles.htm**l) and Mares and Company (**http://www.dmares.com/maresware/articles.htm**) both offer numerous informative (though sometimes very technical) articles on the subject of conducting computer forensics analysis. Additionally, the U.S. Department of Justice's Cybercrime Web site (**http://www.cybercrime.gov**) offers an online version of the department's manual *Searching and Seizing Computers and Obtaining Electronic Evidence in Criminal Investigations*, located at **http://www.cybercrime.gov/s&smanual2002.htm**.

CHAPTER**FOURTEEN**

Environmental Research

Obviously, every lawyer does not have an Erin Brokovich to dig up local records regarding environmental issues. Whether it's locating facilities that use hazardous materials within a certain radius of a housing development, or identifying "brownfields" near a school, it's lucky for the rest of us that there is a wealth of sources for environmental information on the Internet.

Even though the first thing that pops into most of our minds when we think of environmental information is probably air pollution or hazardous waste, a case could be determined by an environmental condition as common as the weather. Was it really a "dark and stormy night" on the night in question? In this chapter you'll learn how you can find out for yourself.

War Story: Weather Information

Bernard P. Weisel, a lawyer in Beverly Hills, CA, tells this story:
"I represented a gentlemen who was being sued for damages based upon a contract that the plaintiff said my client signed on a February day in Los Angeles. My client denied signing that contract and claimed that the plaintiff fabricated the contract by using my client's signature from another contract that the plaintiff had access to. During discovery the plaintiff said the contract in question was signed at a meeting between he and my client on a beautiful sunny day outdoors on the patio of a coffee

shop. Prior to the arbitration hearing I researched the weather history of Los Angeles for the day in question and for two days before and two days after and discovered that it had rained all five days! Needless to say I impeached the plaintiff's testimony with this information.

"The look on the arbitrator's face was priceless! The arbitrator found for my client."

War Story: Sunset Time

Matthew J. Webb, a lawyer in Oakland, California, had this story to tell:

"I once had a case where a woman was the victim of a stray bullet, fired from across the street. The shooting took place at 7:10 p.m., in January, and the woman testified that she could see her assailant clearly. I went on line to the U.S. Naval Observatory Web site, www.usno.navy.mil, to establish that sunset occurred at 5:22 p.m., while civil twilight ended at 5:50 p.m., [and] successfully argued that the judge take judicial notice of this fact."

Starting-Point Web Sites for Environmental Research

EPA Envirofacts (Environmental Protection Agency)

http://www.epa.gov/enviro

Purpose:	To locate information about environmental activities in a particular area.
Content:	Envirofacts provides access to several EPA databases that provide information about environmental activities that can affect air, water, and soil quality anywhere in the country. You can use the **Quick Start** search (in the lower left-hand side of the home page) to enter a ZIP code, city and state, or county and state into the query box. The search returns information on facilities in the

area regulated by the EPA, including:

- Waste (hazardous waste)
- Water (water treatment)
- Toxics (chemical release)
- Air (air pollutants)
- Radiation (radiation releases)
- Land (brownfields)
- Other
- Maps (showing the locations of any facilities that fit in the above categories)

From the results page you can also access the EPA's **Windows To My Environment** service that presents federal, state, and local information about environmental conditions and features in an area you designate.

Our View: The **Envirofacts Quick Start** search and the information from the **Windows To My Environment** link

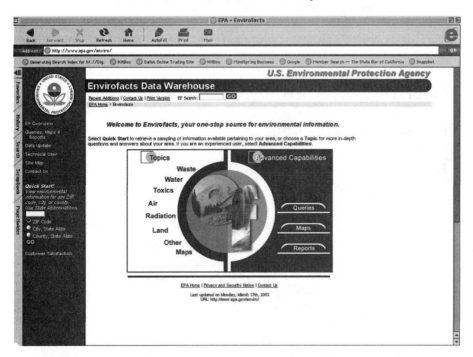

Figure 14-1. At the EPA Envirofacts site, you can search for information about environmental activities that can affect air, water, and soil quality anywhere in the country, by ZIP code or other criteria.

make for a comprehensive (quick) snapshot of the environmental state of your target area.

The date coverage is also pretty good; some of the data retrieved in a Quick Start search regarding toxic waste treatment and removal dated back to 1987.

Tip: Data from the various databases accessed by **Envirofacts** is updated regularly. Some are updated nightly. Click the **Update** link on the left-hand side to view the update schedule, and date of last update, for each database included in its searches.

To keep up to date regarding EPA activities, you can subscribe to the Agency's mailing lists to receive news and information in these categories: Compliance, Civil Enforcement, CleanupNews, Environmental Justice, Federal Facilities, and the National Agriculture Compliance Assistance Center (Ag Center) (see **http://www .epa.gov/compliance/resources/listserv.htm**).

Natural Resources Defense Council (NRDC)

http://www.nrdc.org

Purpose: To locate information on environmental issues from a protectionist point of view.

Content: The site offers concise (as well as in-depth) explanations of dangers facing the environment in nine categories:

- Clean Air & Energy
- Global Warming
- Clean Water & Oceans
- Wildlife & Fish
- Parks, Forests & Wildlands
- Toxic Chemicals & Health
- Nuclear Weapons & Waste

> • Cities & Green Living
> • Environmental Legislation

Each category offers a brief and an in-depth discussion of the topic at hand. If a topic includes subtopics, each subtopic has its own discussions. Each topic also features links to other Web sites related to that topic.

Our View: The discussions related to each topic are good starting points to learn more about topics you may not be familiar with. Even if you already have a familiarity with a topic, the accompanying links will give you additional resources to locate still more information.

Tip: To access a glossary of environmental terms, click on **Reference/Links**, in the lower left-hand side of the site's home page. Then select the letter your search term starts with under the **Glossary of Environmental Terms** near the top of the page.

Directory of Best Environmental Directories

http://www.ulb.ac.be/ceese/meta/cds.html

Purpose: To locate links to environmental resources.

Content: The site contains an alphabetical list of links to more than six hundred sources for environmental data on the Internet.

Our View: For a more worldwide view of environmental resources, see this page maintained by Bruno Kestemont, a scientific adviser and former researcher with Belgium's Centre for Economic and Social Studies on the Environment. Each entry has been descriptively categorized by subject, and those categories are listed in alphabetical order (from Accounting to World Wildlife Fund). The

setup makes it easy to find sources on the subject you
need.

Tip:　　　The site points to numerous non-English (French, German, Japanese) sites.

EarthTrends (World Research Institute)

http://www.earthtrends.wri.org　

Purpose:　To locate environmental information for countries around the world.

Content:　The World Research Institute has collected environmental data from multiple sources around the world and created a single browsable (drill-down) database offering detailed information in ten categories for countries around the world. The categories are

- Coastal and Marine Ecosystems
- Water Resources and Freshwater Ecosystems
- Climate and Atmosphere
- Population, Human Health and Well-being
- Economics, Business and the Environment
- Energy and Resources
- Biodiversity and Protected Areas
- Agriculture and Food
- Forests, Grasslands and Drylands
- Environmental Governance and Institutions

Our View:　To find the information you're looking for, select one of the categories listed above, and then drill down, selecting a more specific information topic, the country, year, and so on. The date range of available information varies from topic to topic; in some categories, the most recent data available was from 1996. While this might give you a general sense of the environmental picture, you'll find more recent domestic information from the other sites discussed in this section.

Tip: Use this site primarily for information pertaining to foreign countries.

ECHO (Enforcement and Compliance History Online)

http://www.epa.gov/echo

Purpose: To locate current and historical enforcement and compliance information about EPA-regulated facilities.

Content: The EPA's ECHO site provides compliance and enforcement information for approximately 800,000 EPA-regulated facilities around the United States. The site includes information regarding permits, inspections, violations, enforcement actions, and penalties covering the past two years. The site also includes information regarding facilities regulated as Clean Air Act stationary sources, Clean Water Act direct dischargers, and Resource Conservation and Recovery Act hazardous waste generators or handlers.

Our View: Like the Quick Start search discussed in the description of the Envirofacts site above, at ECHO you can enter a ZIP code or other location information to get a quick sketch of EPA-regulated facilities in that area. ECHO offers a more sophisticated advanced search that is not mentioned on the site's home page. It is located at **http://www.epa.gov/echo/compliance_report.html**. From here, you can sort and analyze data in many ways.

The **Advanced Search** page allows you to specify additional search criteria such as asking for information on only those facilities that have had a Formal Enforcement Action taken against them, or facilities that have had a penalty levied against them within a time frame you specify (within the last two years). You can also search for facilities with clean records—ones that have not had actions or penalties levied against them.

Clicking on the name of a facility in the search results brings up a page with more information on the facility, including compliance, enforcement, and penalty information (including dollar amount) for the past two years. Scrolling to the bottom of the page, you can click **Map Returned Facility** to render a map of the area you've searched for, with all EPA-regulated facilities marked, and the location of the one whose information you are viewing marked with a star. The data is updated monthly.

Tip: Using the ZIP code box for searching only returns larger facilities in your search results. To include smaller facilities, use the **Advanced Search** page and check the **Include Minor Facilities** box at the bottom of the form. Additionally, you can download the returned data as a comma-delimited text file which can be viewed in Microsoft Excel. (You might need to right-click and select **Save Target As** to save the data to your hard drive.)

DOE (U.S. Department of Energy) Environmental Policy & Guidance

http://www.eh.doe.gov/oepa

Purpose: To locate information regarding environmental compliance issues related specifically to DOE installations.

Content: The Office of Environmental Policy assists with environmental compliance issues for DOE installations. This Web site includes some of the environmental data and reports the Office compiles regarding DOE sites' environmental compliance.

Our View: Click on the **Env. Data & Rpts**. button to access PDF versions of some of the Office's output, including "Estimate of Potential Natural Resource Damage Liabilities at U.S. Department of Energy Sites" and "Disposal of Low-Level and Mixed Low-Level Radioactive Waste During 1990," as well as links to selected EPA online databases.

Tip: Click the **Search** button at the bottom of the home page to access a database of Federal Register notices related to the EPA, back to January 1995. Selected DOE Environmental Policy and Guidance documents are also searchable from that page.

RTK NET (Right to Know)

http://d1.rtknet.org/doc

Purpose: To locate historical docket information for civil cases filed on behalf of the EPA.

Content: The Right to Know database contains docket information for civil cases filed by the Department of Justice with regard to EPA violations. *It has not been updated, however, since October 18, 2000.*

Our View: The database is searchable by a number of criteria, including defendant or facility name, case type (such as Clean Air Act or Clean Water Act), or specific violation (such as spill or asbestos). While the data has not been updated since 2000, the search can still be worthwhile in determining if individuals or businesses have been prosecuted for violations back to 1971.

Tip: While the EPA does not have a full-text searchable database of its civil cases, it does offer information (such as complaints and consent decrees) on some of its more significant cases dating back to 1998 at

http://www.epa.gov/compliance/resources/cases/
civil/index.html.

Lawrence Berkeley National Laboratory
Air Pollution Resource

http://www.lbl.gov/Education/ELSI/pollution-main.html

Purpose:	To find background information regarding air pollution and its effects.
Content:	This site offers explanations and background information regarding the causes, types, and effects of air pollution.
Our View:	An index of topics is listed on the left-hand side of the screen. Click any topic for more information on that subject.
Tip:	While designed as a teaching module for middle school and high school teachers, the material contained in this site presents a useful basic overview.

Rainforest Web

http://www.rainforestweb.org

Purpose:	To locate rainforest related information and resources.
Content:	The site includes extensive links to other resources containing information about the world's rainforest regions.
Our View:	While this site has a conservationist bent, its links are useful for anyone. The links are classified into headings such as **What's happening in the rainforests?** and **Why are rainforests important?** Each topic has a variety of subtopics. To find the information you need, just click through the appropriate topics and subtopics.

For additional information on hazardous materials spills while the material was being transported, see the description of the Department of Transportation's TranStats site in Chapter 18, "Transportation Research."

Locating Environmental and Ecological Organizations and Agencies

National Wildlife Foundation Conservation Directory

http://www.nwf.org/conservationdirectory

Purpose:	To locate various environmental agencies and non-governmental organizations (NGOs).
Content:	This database contains contact information and links (when available) to more than four thousand federal and state government agencies, as well as national and regional environmental NGOs worldwide.
Our View:	You can search by any number of criteria, including

- Name
- Group type (such as nonprofit or local government)
- Issues addressed (air quality, oceans, forests, and so on)
- State
- ZIP code
- Country

Tip:	These organizations can be good sources of information or for locating expert witnesses.

EnviroLink

http://www.envirolink.org

Purpose: To locate regional and local environmental groups by the issues they address.

Content: This site contains an index of thousands of environmental organizations around the world, organized by the specific environment-related issue they address.

Our View: Issues range from Agriculture to Wildlife, with subcategories for each main issue. To locate the organization you want, click through the issues and subtopics until you find the ones that suit your needs. Click the **advanced search** link at the top of the home page to define numerous criteria for your search (such as ZIP code, city, topic) through the database.

Weather Information

Weather Underground

www.wunderground.com

Purpose: To locate current and historical weather information.

Content: While there are numerous sites that offer current weather conditions and forecasts of coming weather, Weather Underground is one of the few we've found that offers easily accessible historical weather information too.

Our View: Enter a city, state, ZIP code, or country name in the search box and click the **Fast Forecast** button at the top of the home page to return the usual current weather conditions and seven-day forecast.

Select a date (back to 1994) at the bottom of the list of current weather conditions to view the weather for the location you selected on that date.

Results are reported from standard weather reporting

stations (often airports). A sample search for historical weather in Culver City, California returned accurate reporting from the nearest reporting station (in Santa Monica), less than five miles away.

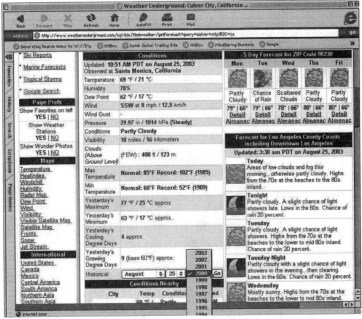

Figure 14-2. WeatherUnderground.com offers free historical weather data (accessible by zip code) back to 1994. Attorneys can also get more detailed historical weather information for a specific location for a fee. By providing a longitude, latitude, time of day and date, you can obtain weather data for three surrounding locations (including radar data). (Click on **Contact Us** for more information regarding this paid service.)

Tip: Use this site to locate historical weather data before you try to use the NOAA site listed below. For the importance of historical weather data in litigation, see "War Story: Weather Information" at the beginning of this chapter.

National Oceanic and Atmospheric Agency (NOAA)

To search: To purchase historical weather data: **$**

http://www.noaa.gov

Purpose: To locate accurate current and historical weather and other in-depth weather-related information.

Content: NOAA conducts research and gathers data about the global oceans, atmosphere, space, and sun. Its National Weather Service is the primary supplier of weather forecasts in the country. The site offers current weather conditions, twenty-four-hour satellite image loops, and historical weather information.

Our View: Current weather data from anywhere in the country is easy enough to get. The site also offers in-depth information on weather and oceanography from **Air Quality** to **Volcanoes**. Use the pull-down menu on the left-hand side of the home page to select a topic for more information and links to additional resources.

Unfortunately, there is no easy way to search or access the historical weather data available from NOAA—and it is not available for free. Historical weather data is retrievable (very easily) from the Weather Underground site listed above for the location in which you're interested. To determine if historical data is available from NOAA, visit **http://hurricane.ncdc.noaa.gov/CDO/cdo** and select a weather station from the worldwide location list. You can also select a data set (daily, monthly, annual, and so on) to narrow down your results. After selecting the precise weather station and the date range for the data you wish to retrieve, the site confirms the availability of the data and informs you of the cost. (Prices are dependent on the size of the data file you request. Data for a single month begins at $6.) Click the **Add to Shopping Cart** button to purchase the data as a downloadable text file.

Tip: The site also has a People Finder to locate NOAA employees.

Sunrise and Sunset Information

U.S. Naval Observatory

http://www.usno.navy.mil

Purpose:	To determine sunrise and sunset times for any date at any location.
Content:	Click the **Sun Rise/Set** link on the left-hand side of the screen to input a date and location for which you want to know this information. Using **Form A**, you can retrieve this information by entering a date, city or town name, and selecting the state from a pull-down menu. Using **Form B**, you can retrieve information for any point on the globe by entering latitude and longitude coordinates.
Our View:	This site allows you to easily find the sunrise, sunset, high noon, or other sun and moon information for any place and any time in the U.S. The available city and state list for the country, based on U.S. Census Bureau data, contains more than twenty-two thousand places. While the site does not list a limit as to how far back it can supply data, recent searches returned data for dates as far back as 1900.
	For the importance of this data, see "War Stories: Sunset Time" at the beginning of this chapter.
Tip:	Click **What time is it?** on the site's home page to locate a page containing the current time (wherever you are in the U.S.) according to the Observatory's atomic clock.

*CHAPTER*FIFTEEN

Foreign and International Research

Even though most of the research we do centers on information and sources from this country, there are a number of professional and personal situations where you might need information from, or about, foreign sources.

Could you ever have to solve one of these problems?

- Your client wants to open an office in Asia, and is asking your advice regarding the best markets and most stable governments.
- Your client is traveling in Eastern Europe and has scheduled a conference call for next Tuesday, at 3:00 p.m. his time. What time should you call in?
- Your client is being sued for trademark infringement in Argentina, because the Spanish-language name for his product is the same as an existing product in that country. How will you find competent local counsel?
- You're going on a tour of China and Central Asia and want to find out in advance where the U.S. Embassy is in each country you're visiting.
- You're being sent to the firm's Singapore office for a six-month project—and you don't know a yen from a yuan. Will the *per diem* they're offering be enough?

The solutions to all of these problems, and many others, can be found for free on the Internet. After all, they don't call it the *World Wide Web* for nothing . . .

For information on international news sources, see the "News, Periodicals, and Broadcast Media" section in Chapter 5, "General Factual Research." For information on online language translators, see the "Standard Reference Resources" section of that same chapter. For information on foreign companies, see Chapter 10, "Company Research."

Information About Other Countries

CIA World Factbook

http://www.cia.gov/cia/publications/factbook/index.html

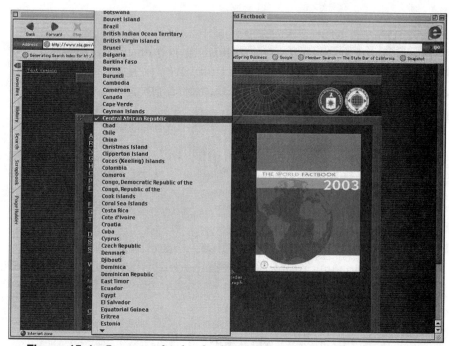

Figure 15-1. Can you think of a better source for information on foreign countries than the CIA? Its *World Factbook* contains information on over two hundred countries.

Purpose: To find facts and statistics on foreign countries.

Content: This site contains myriad facts regarding over two hundred countries around the world. Since 1975, the Central Intelligence Agency (CIA) has made its printed *World*

Factbook available for purchase by the public. It is now available for free online, or for download.

Detailed information is presented for each country in nine categories:

- Introduction
- Geography
- People
- Government
- Economy
- Communications
- Transportation
- Military
- Transnational Issues

There are numerous subcategories within each of these categories.

Our View: Who better than the CIA to ask about information regarding foreign countries, cities, and organizations? Select a country from the pull-down menu, or click on **Flags of the World** to access the core data for each country.

Appendix F is invaluable if you have a geographic name (city or town) but do not know what country it is in. This appendix offers a browsable, alphabetical list of places in all the countries covered in the book. It also includes phonetic equivalents of place names in local languages (for example, *Al Imarat al Arabiyah al Muttahidah*—the local name for the United Arab Emirates).

Tip: - Use the book online rather than downloading it. The entire book is over 80 megabytes when compressed! You shouldn't attempt to download this book unless you have a high-speed Internet connection—or you have a lot of free time. For those with lower-speed connections who must download the book, the CIA has broken it up into twenty-four smaller files that can each be downloaded separately. Also, once uncompressed, the Factbook requires over 200 megabytes of disk space on your computer. Be sure you have enough available disk space before you download it.
- Note: for some reason, in the 2002 edition's alphabetical list of countries, Taiwan is listed at the end of the list—after Zimbabwe

Infoplease

http://www.infoplease.com/countries.html

Purpose: To find information about countries.

Content: Infoplease has information on more than two hundred countries. Each profile includes information on:

- Geography
- Maps
- Flag
- History
- Current ruler
- Population
- Capitol

- Largest cities
- Languages
- Ethnicity and race
- Religion
- Literacy rate
- Economy
- Government

Our View: While much of the information is the same as is covered in the CIA *World Factbook*, some may find the layout of Information Please's Countries of the World page easier to use.

Tip: Handy lists of capitals, currency, ethnicity and race, anguages, and religions— listed alphabetically by country—are also available. Other useful information not included in the CIA site include countries with nuclear weapons, world cities' average daily temperatures, and air distance between world cities, among others.

Country Studies (Library of Congress)

http:/memory.loc/gov/frd/cs/cshome.html

Purpose: To find information on specific foreign countries.

Content: In its **Area Handbooks** program, the Library of Congress developed a set of handbooks to help inform U.S.

Army personnel about locales where they might be deployed. There are only 102 countries included. Notable countries missing include Canada, France, Great Britain, Italy, and numerous other Western and African nations.

Our View: You can keyword search on one country, or across any combination of countries. Additionally, you can browse the alphabetical list of included countries to select the region you are interested in. The individual country entries include extensive coverage of the country's history, as well as background on the social, political, and economic climates. While covering many smaller countries (for which information may be difficult to find), information in these handbooks might only be as current as 1988. (The date the data was gathered is clearly noted on each page.) However, the in-depth historical information remains valuable.

Tip: Use these handbooks for in-depth historical background on a country. Use the CIA *World Factbook* for more current demographic, political, and economic information.

Weidenbaum Center on the Economy, Government and Public Policy (Washington University, St. Louis)

http://wc.wustl.edu/parliaments.html

Purpose: To locate links to the rule-making bodies of foreign governments.

Content: The site offers links to the parliaments, national assemblies, and other legislative bodies of over 150 countries around the world—from Albania to Zimbabwe.

Our View: The site presents an alphabetical list of links all on one page. It is very easy to navigate.

Embassy World

http://www.embassyworld.com

Purpose:	To locating embassies and consulates around the world.
Content:	This site claims to have "absolutely all of the world's embassies in a searchable database." That claim is equally difficult to prove or disprove, but suffice it to say that the list seems comprehensive. (There are thirty-four pages just for the embassies of foreign countries within the United States.)

Information available includes:

- Type of office (embassy, consulate, mission, high commission, and so on.)
- Street address
- Phone number
- Web site address (if applicable)
- E-mail address

Our View:	Embassy World allows you to conduct a search in just about any combination imaginable (through a series of a browsable directory pages)

- By country (such as all embassies of Kazakhstan)
- U.S. Embassies in other countries
- Embassies of other countries in the U.S.
- Permanent Missions of the United Nation

You can also search by clicking on **Find Your Embassy** after selecting from two drop-down lists, **Whose Embassy?** and **In What Location?**

Tip:	Starting out with the search engine can save time over drilling down through the directory.

Information About Foreign Travel and Business

Travel Warnings & Consular Information Sheets from the U.S. Department of State

http://travel.state.gov/travel_warnings.html

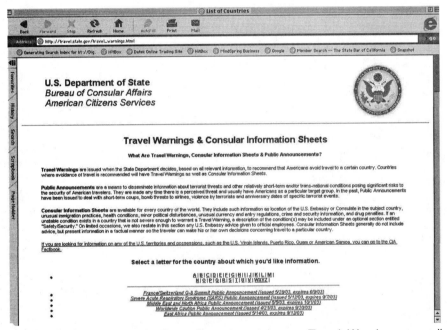

Figure 15-2. The U.S. State Department issues Travel Warnings regarding unsafe travel conditions in specific countries.

Purpose: To get current information regarding specific foreign countries.

Content: **Travel Warnings** advise U.S. citizens to avoid traveling to specific countries or regions. **Information Sheets** provide practical information regarding specific countries. This page contains an alphabetical list all of the current U.S. State Department **Travel Warnings** and up-to-date **Consular Information Sheets**.

While the content of the **Travel Warnings** is pretty self-explanatory, the **Consular Information Sheets** provide concrete information about traveling to the specific countries discussed. This includes

- Entry and exit requirements
- Safety and security
- Crime
- Medical facilities
- Medical insurance
- Traffic safety and road conditions
- Customs regulations
- Currency issues
- Photography restrictions
- Locations of embassies

Our View: Because the State Department is constantly updating its information, this is probably the best source for detailed current information on a specific country.

Tip: You can get State Department Travel Warnings e-mailed to you directly by joining their DOSTRAVEL mailing list. The online subscription form is available at **http://www.state.gov/www/listservs_cms.html**.

U.S. Government Export Portal

http://www.export.gov

Purpose: To find country and industry market research.

Content: This site presents comprehensive information on doing business with countries around the world, including:

- Broad country information
- Agricultural market research
- Market research reports (nonagricultural)
- Tariff and tax information
- Trade agreements

Our View: This is an excellent one-stop shop that aggregates content from numerous other government agency Web sites.

Consular Affairs Bureau (Canadian Department of Foreign Affairs and International Trade)

http://www.voyage.gc.ca/consular_home-en.asp

Purpose: To locate current information regarding specific foreign countries.

Content: The Consular Affairs Bureau's **Current Issues** notices advise of potentially dangerous situations when traveling to specific countries or regions; click on the **Travel Updates** link to see them. **Country Travel Reports** provide practical information regarding specific countries.

Our View: While covering much of the same ground as the U.S. State Department site, the Canadian point of view can occasionally be different enough to prove additionally enlightening.

Tip: Use this site in conjunction with the U.S. State Department Travel Warnings page.

Information from Other Countries

KillerInfo

http://www.killerinfo.com

Purpose: To locate information in foreign countries.

Content: KillerInfo is a metasearch site that you can use to limit your results to Web sites from a specific country. (On a recent visit, you could choose from thirteen countries.) Results are culled from country-specific versions of search engines such as Yahoo! and AltaVista. Webmasters also have the ability to add their Web sites (for a fee) directly to KillerInfo's own database.

You can also narrow your search to a list of topics, including business, sports, and health, among others.

Tip: While general Web searches conducted at this site can be limited to specific countries, searches in specific topics cannot.

Search Engine Colossus

http://www.searchenginecolossus.com

Purpose: To locate search engines around the world.

Content: From Afghanistan to Zimbabwe, the Search Engine Colossus offers links to hundreds of search engines from over two hundred countries and territories around the world. The list is in alphabetical order by country.

Clicking on a particular country brings up a list of search engines that index content in, or related to, that particular country. Many of these sites search and return results in English. (Instructions on the site's home page and the list of countries covered are also available in French and Spanish.)

Our View: The quality and relevance of the results can be hit or miss depending on the actual source you select. Clicking on the listing for Bangladesh brings up a list of four search engines that index information related to that country. These include the regional Asiaco search engine, as well as the Bangla version of the popular search engine Google. Although Google's search page is in the Bangla language, a search for the term government returns the same results as Google's English language search page (and none of the results listed on the first three pages was related to Bangladesh). Asiaco's search however, returned results about Bangladesh and the Central Asia region, primarily in English.

Finding Lawyers in Other Countries

Martindale-Hubbell

http://www.martindale.com

Purpose: To find lawyers in other countries.

Content: Martindale-Hubbell is arguably the world's largest lawyer directory, and the online version contains listings for untold numbers of lawyers around the world.

Our View: It's easy to find the lawyer you're looking for—wherever he or she may be located. The process of locating foreign lawyers is the same as for locating lawyers in this country. To locate a specific lawyer, click on the site's **Lawyer** tab. Then fill in the name and select the country in which the lawyer practices. Clicking the **Search** button brings up the Martindale listing for that individual.

Tip: You can also find lawyers and firms that specialize in certain practice areas. Clicking the **Location/Area of Practice** tab brings up a page with enough search criteria to allow you to search for specific listings, such as law firms with over fifty members that practice business law in Buenos Aires and have someone who speaks English (for the record, there were three).

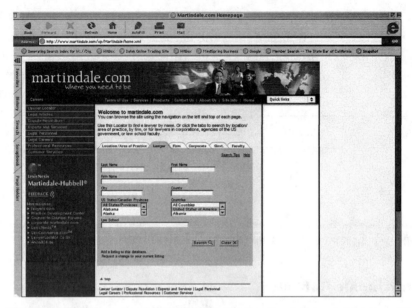

Figure 15-3. You can use Martindale-Hubbell online to search for lawyers in foreign countries.

Other Related Useful Information

The World Clock

http://www.timeanddate.com/worldclock

Purpose: To answer the question "What time is it in . . . .?"

Content: The site presents a grid of local time in (up to) 550 cities around the world.

Our View: This site is very useful whether you need to know the time in one city, or you need to track the time across an entire region.

You can choose to view the site's entire list of cities, or customize the view to only include one of the following:

- Africa
- North America
- South America
- Asia

- Australia/Pacific
- Europe

Additionally, within these custom views, you can also choose to see all of the available cities, or only the largest cities, or only the capital cities.

The **Fixed, Past, Future Time** option allows you to convert a day, date, and time for a particular location into the day, date, and time for any city in the list. This is useful for planning an upcoming event, such as a phone conversation.

Tip: The list of cities can be sorted by city, country, or time zone. Cities observing Daylight Savings Time (or Summer Time as it is known in some parts of the world) are clearly marked with an asterisk (*).

Country Calling Codes

http://www.countrycallingcodes.com

Purpose: To determine the proper telephone dialing code for a country or city.

Content: This site contains the country codes for more than 250 countries and countless more cities within countries that require additional dialing codes.

Our View: Self-explanatory drop-down menus allow you to choose where you are calling from, and where you are calling to. Clicking the **Submit** button returns a page with the proper codes to use with the phone number you wish to call. For larger countries with multiple city codes, the results page includes another drop-down menu for selecting the city you are calling. Clicking the **Submit** button on that page returns the full country and city dialing code string.

Tip: Don't be fooled by the **Quick Reference Phone Book** link on the left-hand side of the page. It is only an alphabetical list (by country) of the corresponding dialing codes. It is not an international phone directory search.

U.S. Department of the Treasury Office of Foreign Asset Control (OFAC) Specially Designated National (SDN) List and Blocked Persons List

http://www.ustreas.gov/offices/enforcement/ ofac/sdn/index.html

Purpose: To determine if the assets of potential clients or their business have been frozen or blocked by the Department of Justice (DOJ).

Content: This section of the Treasury Department site contains the (very large) list of foreign nationals and companies that have had assets frozen by the U.S. government. This nearly one-hundred-page list is provided "to assist the public in complying with the various sanctions programs administered by OFAC."

Our View: A searchable database version of the list would be useful. The easiest way to use the list is to download the PDF version, and use Acrobat Reader's search function (click on the Binocular icon in the toolbar) to search for particular individuals or companies you suspect might be on the list.

Tip: • The list is updated weekly, and actions of the OFAC are also listed in the Federal Register, so check back often.
    • The list also warns that "the latest changes may appear [on the list] prior to their publication in the Federal Register, and it is intended that users rely on changes indicated in this document that post-date the most recent Federal Register publication . . . New Federal

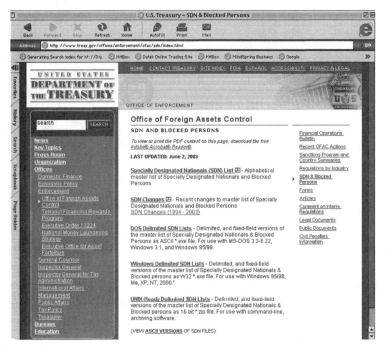

Figure 15-4. The U.S. Department of Justice's Office of Foreign Asset Control (OFAC) maintains a list of foreign nationals and companies that have had assets frozen or blocked by the DOJ.

Register notices with regard to Specially Designated Nationals or blocked entities may be published at any time. Users are advised to check the Federal Register and this electronic publication routinely for additional names or other changes to the listings."

Bloomberg.com Currency Calculator

http://www.bloomberg.com/analysis/calculators/ currency.html

Purpose: To serve as a currency converter.

Content: Select a currency to convert and a currency to change it into, enter an amount, and click **Calculate**. It's that easy.

Our View: The site offers more than two hundred currencies to choose from. Also, because Bloomberg is in the financial information industry, they update their exchange rates throughout the day.

XE Interactive Currency Table

http://www.xe.com/ict

Purpose: To obtain historical currency exchange rates.

Content: This site allows you to generate a table of exchange rates for the currency you select from a list of approximately eighty major world currencies on a specific date (back to November 16, 1995).

*CHAPTER*SIXTEEN

Law Practice Management and Professional Development

"Law practice management" is which of the following?

    A. The day-to-day management of a case load

    B. Firm calendar, docketing, and conflict management

    C. Staff management (human resource and personnel issues)

    D. Financial management (billing and receivables)

    E. Office management (physical space, equipment, and technology)

    F. Image management (marketing and networking)

    G. All of the above

Running a successful law practice means more than just doing a good job for your clients. The most successful lawyers also do a good job for themselves. In his popular *Attorney and Law Firm Guide to the Business of Law,* Second Edition (ABA General Practice, Solo and Small Firm Section, 2002), law firm management consultant Edward Poll posits that in order to survive and grow, all businesses (law firms included) must be proficient in what he has labeled "the three competencies": marketing (getting clients), technical (doing good work), and financial (getting paid).

Therefore, to insure a successful practice, lawyers must take the time to focus on the business of practicing law in addition to the mechanics of properly handling cases for their clients. The following checklist, adapted from Poll's book, outlines the principles he deems inherent to a successful law firm.

The successful law firm:

- ❏ Pays attention to the needs and desires of their clients
- ❏ Communicates their awareness of and sensitivity to the client's wishes
- ❏ Delivers their services at a price that does not offend the client
- ❏ Knows how to run the business of their practice

It is easy to see, then, that the correct answer to the question posed above is "G: All of the above."

There are a number of resources readily available online to help you focus on some of these important business aspects of practicing law.

The American Bar Association's (ABA) Law Practice Management (LPM) section (**http://www.abanet.org/lpm**) offers a wide range of resources covering all areas of running an efficient practice, including implementing technology that works, quality of life, e-lawyering, alternative billing methods, and other ways of serving your clients more effectively.

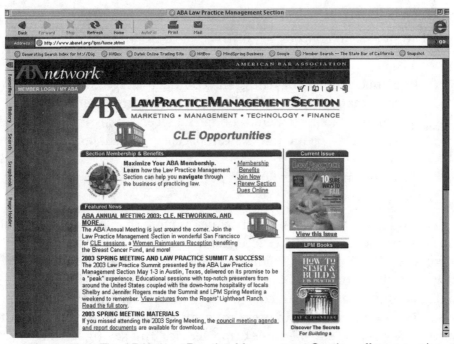

Figure 16-1. The ABA's Law Practice Management Section offers a number of free resources on its Web site to members and nonmembers alike, including *Law Practice* magazine and Law Practice Today.

Two excellent (free) resources also available to non-ABA members include the online version of the long-time favorite print publication, *Law Practice* magazine (**http://www.abanet.org/lpm/magazine**) (eight issues per year), and the new online publication *Law Practice Today* (**http://www.lawpracticetoday.org**). Full text of both publications is available online to section members and nonmembers alike.

Section members also receive discounts on registration for the ABA Techshow and LPM books (like this one), and can access special section meetings and educational programs around the country.

Another free resource that covers a wide range of law office management and technology topics is FindLaw's *Modern Practice* magazine (**http://practice.findlaw.com**). This monthly online publication's articles cover the issues of client retention, effective marketing materials, knowledge management, and software selection and use, among other subjects.

Additionally, many state bar associations have robust LPM sections. Space does not allow us to list or review all of the useful resources offered by these organizations, but a selection of those providing a broad range of information include:

- California at **http://www.calbar.org/lpmt**
- Florida at **http://www.flabar.org**
- Maryland at **http://www.msba.org/departments/loma/**
- New York City at **http://www.abcny.org/abc_small.html**
- Oklahoma at **http://www.okbar.org/map/**

If it is not listed here, also check with your state and local bar associations to see what resources they offer.

Financial Resources

As if practicing law wasn't time-consuming and difficult enough, once the work is done, lawyers must deal with getting paid. Positive cash flow is essential to any business, but the legal profession brings along its own set of difficulties tied to pricing, billing, accounts receivable, and collections. These sites offer some general (and law office specific) information on business finances.

Small Business Administration (SBA)

http://www.sba.gov/index.html

Purpose: To find information on building and maintaining a profitable business.

Content: The SBA provides information on starting, financing, and managing your business.

Our View: The site offers a plethora of information, as well as links to external sources regarding business management, finance, and accounting.

Tip: In the left-hand column of the home page, click on **Training** for links to online presentations covering cash flow, accounting, budgeting, and other finance basics.

LawBiz

http://www.lawbiz.com

Purpose: To find information on building and maintaining a profitable practice.

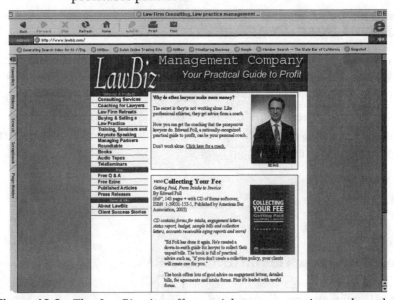

Figure 16-2. The LawBiz site offers articles on managing and marketing your practice, as well as a free e-mail newsletter.

Content: The site is a mixture of free articles, newsletters, and links to purchase law firm management consultant Ed Poll's informative books, or subscribe to his monthly (fee-based) audio CLE newsletter.

Our View: Poll, a nationally recognized law firm management consultant, covers effective methods for law firms to ensure business success, including pricing, invoicing and collection techniques, maintaining positive cash flow, reaching and maintaining profitability, and how Sarbanes-Oxley effects law firms, among other topics.

Tip: Select the **Free Ezine** or **Published Articles** links on the left-hand side to access the site's free content.

A number of other law firm management consultants also offer articles and background information on cash flow and collections, including Kohn Communications (**http://www.kohncommunications.com**—select **Articles** and then **Management Articles** at the top of the page) and the Centurion Consulting Group (**http://www.centurionconsulting.com**—select **Articles** at the top of the page).

Marketing Resources

Too often people think only about brochures, paid advertising, and (occasionally) their Web site when the topics of marketing and business development are discussed. There are a number of other online resources than can be used to develop new business, such as creating lists of targeted potential clients and dossiers about those potential clients. Additionally, you can put together fact books about your competitors to track their growth and (possibly) predict trends in your practice area.

As a brief example, you might use the Thomas Register (**http://www.thomasregister.com**) to locate information on companies that manufacture a certain type of product. You could then use Hoover's (**http://www.hoovers.com**) or Vault (**http://www.vault.com**) to find specific information (such as contacts or financials) about those individual companies. With that information you could determine if there are any potential problems with the companies' products (via complaints in newsgroups or message boards), litigation against competitors, or any other industry trends that might affect that company.

American Lawyer Media draws on its "central database of business information" to create the numerous database products and reports offered for sale on its LegalMarketInfo Web site (**http://www.legalmarket info.com**). Reports include industry rankings (by size or revenues), trends (such as revenue per partner, firm diversity, and mergers and acquisitions) and surveys (such as firm diversity, *pro bono* statistics and lateral partner surveys). Reports on individual law firms are also available. Prices vary depending on the report, but as an example, a searchable, electronic spreadsheet version of the company's AmLaw 100 is offered for $250.

For more-detailed information on conducting marketing and competitive intelligence research, see Chapter 10, "Company Research"; Chapter 11, "Competitive Intelligence Research"; Chapter 7, "Finding and Backgrounding People"; Chapter 9, "Finding and Backgrounding Expert Witnesses"; and Chapter 5, "General Factual Research."

These resources can be used to prepare presentations to potential clients or to proactively service existing clients. These techniques can also help you spot potential problems for clients and quash them before they become major, or to be prepared to deal with them when they do.

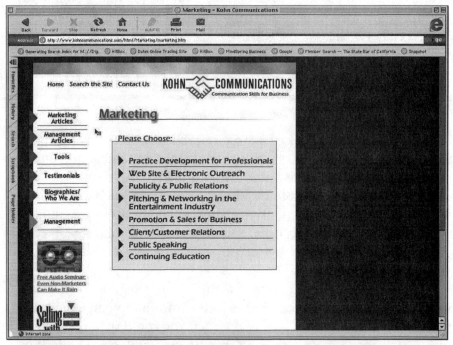

Figure 16-3. Many law firm consultants, such as Kohn Communications, offer articles and tips for marketing and developing your practice.

Additionally, there are a number of sites that focus on more traditional and Internet-based areas of law firm marketing. These include:

- Lawyer Marketing Tips at **http://www.lawyermarketing.net**
- Attorney Promote at **http://www.attorneypromote.com**
- Consultwebs at **http:www.consultwebs.com**
- FindLaw at **http://marketing.lp.findlaw.com**
- Kohn Communications at **http://www.kohncommunications.com**
- Law Biz at **http://www.lawbiz.com**
- Law Marketing Portal at **http://www.lawmarketing.com**
- Legal Marketing Association (LMA) at **http://www.legalmarket ing.org**
- LexiWebs at **http://www.lexiwebs.com**

Technology Assessment and Purchase Research

ABA Legal Technology Resource Center (LTRC)

http://www.lawtechnology.org

Purpose: To locate the latest information regarding law office hardware and software.

Content: The LTRC offers articles about, and reviews of, the latest law office hardware and software. Topics include:

- Calendaring and docketing
- Conflict checking
- Document scanning, management, and retention
- Time and billing
- Internet connectivity
- Handheld computers
- Networking (wired and wireless)

Our View: The LTRC articles vary in depth from overviews that give a sketch of available options to in-depth product reviews and comparisons. Whether you're just beginning to think about adding something new, or looking for guidance to make a final decision, the LTRC can help.

Tip: Telephone or e-mail research and assistance is available to ABA members seeking information on practice technology. Nonmembers have access to the Web site that is updated often, so check back regularly.

Law Technology News

http://www.lawtechnews.com

Purpose: To keep up to date on law office hardware and software.

Content: This monthly print magazine covers a wide range of technology subjects applicable to lawyers in any size practice.

Our View: Each issue features dozens of short items about the latest hardware and software releases. In-depth articles focus on product reviews and comparisons and technology trends.

Tip: You can either register for a free print subscription or access the articles and news online (also requires registration).

Law Office Computing

http:///www.lawofficecomputing.com

Purpose: For keeping up to date on practice management and technology tools.

Content: This bimonthly magazine offers news coverage, in-depth articles, and product reviews about the latest developments in law office hardware and software.

Our View: Online access to the articles is for paid subscribers of the print magazine only. Annual subscriptions are listed at $69.99 (by subscribing at the magazine's Web site you can get it for $59.99 if you want to be billed for the subscription, or $49.99 if you pay on the spot by credit card).

Tip: • Check out the site's free law office software tips (**http://www.lawofficecomputing.com/resources/tips.htm**) for programs such as Amicus Attorney®, HotDocs®, Time Matters®, TimeMap®, and others, as well as their links to software publishers and other resources. The tips have been submitted by the magazine's readers and site visitors, as well as by software consultants and publishers.

• You can access the magazine's product reviews for free online through LawCommerce.com's **Small Firm & Solo Center** (**http://www.lawcommerce.com/small firm**—scroll down to product reviews).

• Also, those who pay for a new subscription by credit card get instant access to the articles online.

The State Bar of California Law Practice Management & Technology Section

http://www.calbar.ca.gov/lpmt

Purpose: For keeping up to date on practice management and technology tools.

Content: The site features free access to selected articles from the section's bi-monthly print newsletter the *Bottom Line*, covering new developments in law office-related hardware and software, as well as practice management strategies.

Our View: While the newsletter is meant for section members, it is a valuable resource to lawyers anywhere. Most articles are not limited in scope to California, so they are applicable to practices just about anywhere in the country. A subscription to the print version of the newsletter is available to any legal professional for $60 per year.

Tip: Subscribe to the print version of the *Bottom Line* newsletter for useful technology and practice management tips.

ESQLawtech Weekly

http://www.mylawtips.com

Purpose: For keeping up to date on practice management and technology tools.

Content: ESQLawtech Weekly is a free weekly e-zine covering law office technology tips, tools, and tricks.

Our View: This site "comb[s] the Internet, and written publications to provide you with a consolidated view of law office technology information." Its aggregation can save you time locating the information elsewhere.

Pocket PC Legal

http://www.pocketpclegal.com

Purpose: To locate information regarding use of handheld computers in the practice of law.

Content: The site contains feature articles and news dealing specifically with the Pocket PC platform of handheld computers. The coverage focuses on how lawyers can use the handheld devices in their practice.

Our View:	The site offers a good primer on using the Pocket PC for more than a calendar and notepad. It outlines how you could (almost) replace your laptop on some trips.
Tip:	See the site's pages comparing different Pocket PC models.

Technology consultants' sites can be good sources for free information regarding hardware and software you're considering for your practice. LawCommerce.com hosts a group of Top Tier Technologists (**http://www.lawcommerce.com/t3**)—independent consultants who specialize in law office hardware and software implementation and support. Members include regular ABA TECHSHOW® presenters Ross Kodner and Andy Adkins, and other well-known law office technology consultants such as Bill Baker of Baker + Cadence Solutions. The site includes a library of articles covering hardware and software selections and recommendations, as well as information about individual products (such as TimeMatters and Amicus Attorney).

Other general-interest computer print publications also offer free online access to some (or all) of their recent articles. They are excellent sources for news of new software and hardware releases, and product reviews. See:

- *PC World* at **http://www.pcworld.com**
- *PC Magazine* at **http://www.pcmag.com**
- *Macworld* at **http://www.macworld.com**
- *pdaJD* at **http://www.pdajd.com**
- *Handheld Computing* at **http://www.pdabuzz.com**
- *Pocket PC Magazine* at **http://www.pocketpcmag.com**

Some publications (*PC World, PC Magazine, Macworld,* and others) also offer free e-mail newsletters covering some of the same topics included in their print publications.

Human Resources: Recruiting, Retention, and Personnel Management

The first step in using the Internet for recruiting lawyers and staff to join your firm should be posting information about the available positions on the firm's Web site. A recruiting section on the site can help focus potential employees' attention on the pertinent information regarding the firm and available positions.

Logically dividing available positions by category is also helpful in targeting potential hires. Categories might include

- New associates
- Laterals
- Partners
- Associates
- Summer associates
- Staff
- Paralegals
- Secretaries
- Other support

Additionally, it is helpful to potential hires for the site to include information on the firm culture, its management style, and other pertinent information regarding life at the firm.

In addition to using the firm's own Web site to recruit new hires, many job search sites allow employers to post job openings on the Internet. Each of those sites mentioned below allows firms to directly post their job openings in the sites' respective databases and browse the qualifications of available candidates who have registered at those sites. Check with each of the sites for their respective fees.

A number of law firm management consultants offer information on their Web sites regarding evaluating your firm culture and hiring and retaining the right people. Altman Weil offers downloadable PDF versions of some of its reports, including its "Special Report to Legal Management 2003" and its "Lex Mundi 2002 Corporate Counsel Survey" (see **http://www.altmanweil.com**). Older material is replaced as newer data is added. Click the **News & Events** tab at the top of the page to access these reports. Or click the **AW Articles** link on the right-hand side of the home page for access to the company's firm management articles.

Ida Abbott, author of *Developing Legal Talent: Best Practices in Professional Development for Law Firms* and other books advising firms how to attract, develop, and retain employees, offers a free newsletter and access to recent articles she has written at her Web site (**http://www.idaabbott .com**—click on the **Books and Resources** link on the left-hand side of the home page to access these). Abbott also offers free access to PDF versions of diagnostic tools (questionnaires) that you can use "to help you assess your firm's performance and identify areas where improvement is needed."

Rigorous pre-employment screening has become a regular part of doing business for many companies. Law firms (large and small) are not immune to the factors that have made pre-employment screening a fact of business life. While there are a number of companies that specialize in

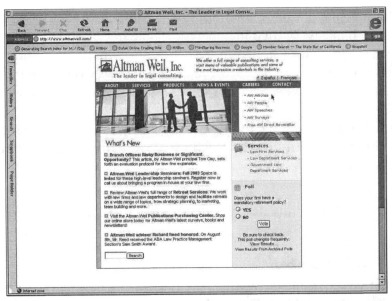

Figure 16-4. Legal consulting firm Altman Weil offers free access to some of its reports and articles on its Web site, as well as offering a free newsletter.

conducting these types of investigations, you can (depending on where you are located) find some of the same information yourself for free on the Internet.

See Chapter 7, "Finding and Backgrounding People"; Chapter 8, "Accessing Public Records"; and Chapter 4, "Search Tools" for detailed information on the types of information available, including:

- Current and previous employment
- Licensure
- Education
- Criminal background
- Civil litigation
- Other public records
- Select online activities (such as personal Web sites, blogs, and on-line discussion groups)

Not all of this information is available in every jurisdiction. For example, Texas (**http://records.txdps.state.tx.us**) and Florida (**http://pas.fdle.state.fl.us/wpersons_search.asp**) provide free access via the Internet to searchable databases of outstanding warrants, while most other states do not.

Additionally, some lawyer oversight organizations such as the Illinois Attorney Registration & Disciplinary Committee (**http://www.iardc.org**)

and the State Bar of California (**http://www.calbar.ca.gov**) have a fully searchable database of their members available free on the Internet. These sites can be very handy in helping to determine whether a candidate has ever lost the privilege of practicing law or been otherwise disciplined. Available information varies from state to state. Not all states provide this search.

As with any searching, locating this information on the Internet does not necessarily constitute a thorough background investigation, but it can be a good place to start.

The Work Number

http://www.theworknumber.com

Purpose: For employment and salary verification.

Content: This site provides out-sourced employment verification services for hundreds of employers, including banks, city, state and federal agencies, and corporations of varying sizes. Its database covers more than sixty million employee records from over one thousand organizations nationwide. The database is updated directly from the employer's payroll records every pay period to provide the most recent employment information. Employers have signed up with the Work Number to relieve their human resources departments of the task of taking and handling all of the employment verification requests they receive. Pay-as-you-go employment verifications are $10 and income verifications are $13 per verification, billed to your credit card.

Our View: Even though you have to know the name of the company a prospective employee had worked for to verify employment, the service can still be a worthwhile time-saver. (That company must have contracted with the Work Number to handle its verifications for you to be able to get the information from the Work Number database.)

Tip: Click on the **Verification Demo** link on the **Verifiers** page for more information on how to order employment or income verifications. You can also order verifications by phone at 800-367-5690. There is no charge for attempting a verification for an employee not in the Work Number database.

For new or growing businesses that do not yet have a procedure manual or standard set of forms, the Internet can be a valuable resource in building such a collection. Usually, the form letters found on the Internet are nothing fancy and are a bit on the general side, but they can be a good starting point for creating your own targeted letters. See FormsGuru.com (**http://www.formsguru.com**) and Office Depot's Business Center (**http://www.officedepot.com/renderStaticPage.do?context=/ content&file=/BusinessTools/forms/default.jsp**—or visit **http://www.officedepot.com**, click on **Business Center** and then click on **Free Downloadable Forms**) for sample forms pertaining to:

- Business finance
- Compensation and benefits
- Employee management (recruiting, hiring, and termination)
- Excessive absenteeism
- No open employment positions
- Office space sublet agreement

While the Office Depot forms are all free, only some of the forms offered at FormsGuru are. Others, clearly marked by a dollar-sign icon ($), range in price from $8.99 to $25.00 each.

LawCommerce's forms library (**http://www.lawcommerce.com/ forms**) also offers a variety of forms for $25 each. While the price is reasonable for many of the forms (such as the Independent Contractor Agreement or the Consulting Agreement), the site also applies this price to government forms such as IRS tax forms and patent and trademark forms that are available free from their respective government agencies. (See Chapter 6, "Government Resources Online," for more information on locating individual agencies.) Before purchasing a form from any site, you might want to search the Internet for other free sources of similar forms.

Law-Related Job Search Sites for Employers and Employees

As it has done in so many other areas, the Internet has added a new dimension to the job market. Whether you're a lawyer looking for a new job in your current hometown, or relocating to another part of the country, or your firm needs to hire a new tax associate, there are a number of Web sites that list law related jobs. While the general employment sites such as Monster and HotJobs include many legal jobs, and should not be discounted, a legal professional seeking a new position (or a firm attempting to fill open positions) could benefit more from sites that specialize in legal employment but still feature the advanced search functions of the general employment sites. Although the specialty sites are not as well known as the general ones, no legal professional should leave them out of a search.

Legalstaff

http://www.legalstaff.com

Purpose: To conduct a job search.

Content: Legalstaff offers thousands of searchable job listings around the country. You can post a résumé, choosing to show your name or post anonymously. You can also search for employers or recruiters by location.

Our View: Legalstaff has one of the most targeted free legal job searches available on the internet. You can search by:

- Job type (such as lawyer or staff)
- Position (associate, partner, in-house)
- State
- Nearest metropolitan area (for example, there are nineteen cities listed for Texas, eighteen for California, and twelve for New York)

The **Nearest Metro** criteria allows you to search for jobs only in cities in which you're interested—either where you live, or where you'd like to relocate.

Legal Staff also offers a free **Career Agent** (registration required) that e-mails you when jobs are posted that fit certain criteria you select. For example, you could request an e-mail notice if a position for a full-time associate position, with three to nine years' experience, was posted by a law firm in Chicago.

Tip: Use the free **Career Agent** to keep up to date with new job listings of interest without having to keep checking for new postings.

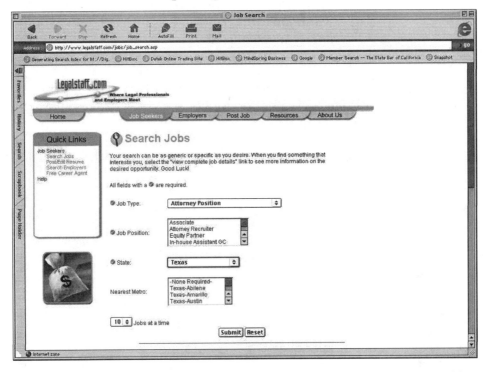

Figure 16-5. LegalStaff.com provides free online access to thousands of law related jobs around the country.

FindLaw Career Center

http://www.careers.findlaw.com

Purpose: To conduct a job search.

Content: FindLaw's career center includes listings for thousands of available jobs around the world. FindLaw also offers an employer and recruiter directory, searchable by name or location. Two of the resources that set FindLaw apart are

- Salary charts (listing first-year through eighth-year salaries for law firms by city or region).
- Greedy Associates message boards (offering anonymous postings from lawyers discussing internal firm politics, salaries, and so on, by city or region). These boards are free to read and require free registration (anonymous) to post.

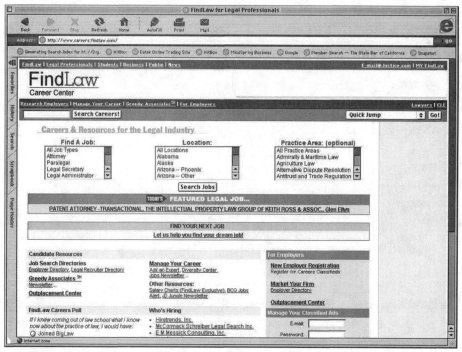

Figure 16-6. FindLaw's Career Center includes salary charts and insider information about firms, in addition to listings for thousands of available law related jobs.

Our View: FindLaw also offers flexible and targeted searching of its nearly three thousand job listings. You can search by:

- Job (such as lawyer or paralegal)
- Practice area
- Location (many states are broken down into metropolitan regions)

Tip:　　　Definitely use the salary charts and Greedy Associates message boards to collect background information on firms you may be interested in working for.

LawJobs

http://www.lawjobs.com　

Purpose:　　To conduct a job search.

Content:　　LawJobs lists nearly two thousand available positions around the country. The listings are a combination of classified advertisements placed in American Lawyer Media publications (owner of LawJobs' parent, Law.com) and positions posted directly to the site.

　　　　　　The listings are searchable by region. You can then narrow your search further, by selecting additional criteria such as practice area (select one of seventeen areas) or designate listings from employers, recruiters, or both. The results include more-detailed information regarding the position and links to more information about the employer or recruiter.

Our View:　　The site offers a good mix of tools for the job searcher. In addition to the searchable job postings, the site also has a page of law firm recruiting links to more than sixty top law firms, a geographic law firm finder, and a browsable list of recruiters and headhunters by location.

Tip:　　　While these tools are all helpful, they are not necessarily comprehensive in their depth. Use the LawJobs site in conjunction with other sites discussed in this section.

Emplawyernet

http://www.emplawyernet.com

Purpose: To conduct a job search.

Content: Emplawyernet features thousands of legal jobs across the country. To access them you have to pay a membership fee of $14.95 per month or $125.00 per year. The free membership (registration required) allows you to post a profile in the Emplawyernet database. The profile, built from a series of fill-in-the-blank fields and menu selections, becomes a *de facto* online résumé that employers can search when they have positions to fill.

Our View: While posting a free profile in the Emplawyernet database can be useful to a job search, we'd search through the free listings at other sites before signing up for paid access to their database.

Tip: You can register your profile (for free) anonymously. This way potential employers can review your qualifications and Emplawyernet will contact you if any express interest. This will keep you from "bumping into yourself" if you have already applied for a position you found elsewhere, or you wish to test the waters for a job change. If you do choose to sign up for a paid membership, see if a discount is available to members of your bar association. Emplawyernet offers discounts to ABA members and Los Angeles County Bar Association members, among others.

General Job-Search Sites

Monster

http://www.monster.com

Purpose: To conduct a job search.

Content: Monster boasts over 800,000 job listings. While they're not all law related, its job search engine allows you to specify a geographical region (Texas is divided into twelve regions) and a job category (legal). You can further customize the search by including a keyword, such as a practice area. A sample search for legal jobs in Dallas yielded 139 listings for positions ranging from associates to Judge Advocate (JAG), as well as legal secretaries, paralegals, and court clerks. Refining the search further by adding the keywords "tax" and "lawyer" returned just two results—both of which were for tax lawyers.

Our View: You can search and view the listings without registration, but if you do register (free), you can post your résumé, apply for jobs online, and have jobs e-mailed to you based on criteria you select.

Tip: You can refine the search even further by using the site's ZIP code function.

HotJobs

http://hotjobs.yahoo.com

Purpose: To conduct a job search.

Content: HotJobs lists thousands of jobs in over thirty-five categories. Here you can search for jobs by job category, company, staffing firm (recruiter or headhunter), location, or any combination. Select a state and type in the city you are interested in searching. Our sample search for legal jobs in Dallas yielded forty-seven listings for positions ranging from associates to bankruptcy specialists, as well as legal secretaries, paralegals, and firm administrators. Refining the search further by adding the keywords "tax" and "lawyer" returned just three results. (While each of the postings included the keywords "tax" and "lawyer," none was for an actual tax lawyer.)

Our View: Registering for your own personalized myHotJobs account can help you organize your job search. It also allows you to post your résumé online, allows access to statistics about the number of times an employer or recruiter reviewed your résumé, and keeps a complete history of cover letters and résumés you have sent. The site also offers a personal job search agent (requires free registration) that e-mails jobs to you that match criteria you select.

Tip: Based on the results of our sample search (compared to similar searches at other sites) it's probably a wise idea to use HotJobs in conjunction with some of the other sites discussed here, and not rely on it solely.

A natural inclination for any legal job seeker might be to check out the job listings at a well-known legal directory like Martindale-Hubbell (**http://www.martindale.com**). You should note that even though LawJobs supplies the job listings for Martindale-Hubbell's Web site, the Martindale listings do not include all of the LawJobs listings. A recent search of Martindale's job search site listed 445 lawyer job listings, while LawJobs listed 1,692. A search for lawyer jobs in Southern California produced six Martindale and ninety-three LawJobs results.

While the Internet has added a new dimension to job hunting and recruiting, online job seekers should not forget old-fashioned methods such as going directly to the source. LawJobs aids this type of search by offering direct links to the recruiting sections of more than fifty top firms (**http://www.lawjobs.com/firms.html**). You can also find a firm's Web site by conducting a search for the firm name using the Martindale-Hubbell Web site, or the Google search engine. (See Chapter 4, "Search Tools," and Chapter 3, "Search Strategies," for further details on effective Google searching.)

A visit to a targeted employer's Web site can be the beginning of a profitable information-gathering campaign. Many firms make job openings, compensation information, and benefit information available in a recruiting section on their sites.

Another old-fashioned method with an online twist is finding and registering with a traditional recruiter or headhunter. While a number of national recruiters post their openings at some of the employment sites noted above, you might also find smaller local or regional recruiters that do not post on these sites. Working with a recruiter might not be for everyone, so getting referrals from colleagues is also a good idea. Online, you can search the recruiters' listings noted in the sites above, or you might also check some of these sites listed below.

Hieros Gamos

http://www.hg.org/rec_sel.html

Purpose: To locate listings of hundreds of legal recruiters around the world.

Content: Companies range from large national recruiters such as the Affiliates (**http://www.affiliates.com**) to regional and local recruiters such as Southern California's Attorney Network (**http://www.attorney-network.com**). You can search for a specific firm if you have their name, or you can search by location.

Figure 16-7. Hieros Gamos offers a list of hundreds of legal recruiters around the world.

Our View: While the large national recruiters have the highest number of job listings, the local recruiters may have access to more jobs in their respective cities, or closer relationships with the firms listing the jobs. You can create a list of recruiters to contact (either on the Web, via e-mail, or by phone) using Hieros Gamos' recruiter search. To pull up the largest list of local recruiters, select your state from the pull-down menu and click **GO** to return the list of recruiters listed from that state.

Tip: Adding a city can narrow your search too much, since the search will not return recruiters from nearby cities (for example, results for Los Angeles will not include recruiters in nearby Santa Monica). Since links are not provided to the recruiters' Web sites, you'll have to infer the Web address from the e-mail address given for particular companies (for example, the Web site for mrosch@netforlawyers.com would be **http://www .netforlawyers.com**).

The Affiliates

http://www.affiliates.com

Purpose: To conduct a job search.

Content: The Affiliates lists thousands of jobs across North America. The company breaks down its listings of legal (and other) jobs into logical categories (attorney, licensed, 10+ years experience; attorney, licensed, 0-3 years experience; file clerk; and so on). Their database is searchable by location, category, and keyword.

Our View: A search for jobs for "attorney, licensed, 0-3 years experience" returned more than sixty results, including Seattle, Washington; McLean, Virginia; and Canada. These included full-time and part-time positions, as well as temporary and contract lawyer positions. A more targeted search for "attorney, licensed, 0-3 years experience" in New York City with the added keyword "litigation" produced no results. Oddly, however, removing the keyword "litigation" did return a listing for a contract lawyer position for a commercial litigation attorney, licensed, 0-3 years experience.

Tip: Leave keywords out of your search for more results.

Legal job seekers can also use the Internet to research salaries, firm culture, and the outlook for employment in different geographic and practice areas. Salary information from a wide variety of firms in California is provided at the FindLaw Career Center site (**http://careers.findlaw .com**), for example. Data is obtained from the recruiting pages of the law firms' own sites as well as from lawyers who are, or were, associated with the firms they write about. Monster.com also offers a **Get the salary you deserve!** link that leads you through a series of questions regarding the job you're seeking (type, location, level, and so on), your background, and your education, in order to deliver a report on the range of salaries to expect (or to ask for).

Continuing Legal Education Sources

Online continuing legal education (CLE) comes in a variety of styles. As audio and video on the Internet have become easier for users to access, state and local bar associations have moved into the business of providing online (recorded) versions of their live seminars for CLE credit. Other providers offer an online version of the article and quiz format that is familiar from its use in any number of legal print publications. Whatever the format, online CLE offers you the opportunity to acquire new, useful information (and satisfy your state's CLE requirement) at a time and place that is convenient to you. Despite this convenience, the ABA's 2001 Legal Technology Survey found that while the majority of lawyers have embraced electronic communication methods such as e-mail (87.25% of respondents reported sending e-mails with attachments), only a small portion (21.8%) have enrolled in any CLE courses offered online.

Just like live seminars, online CLE programs cover a wide spectrum of topics—from general law office management and research skills to reviews of the latest substantive legal or legislative developments. Below are some of the best-known multistate providers of online CLE courses.

You might also want to check with your own state and local bar associations to see if they offer CLE courses online.

CLE Now!

http://www.abanet.org/cle/clenow

Content: The ABA's CLE Now! offers topics covering a wide range of law practice management and litigation-related subjects. The programs are presented as RealAudio streams (requiring the RealOne player, a free download). The free programs vary in length from forty-one to eighty-four minutes long. The ABA also offers CLE online in a variety of other media formats. Most of those programs are not free (though some of them are discounted to ABA members or members of certain ABA sections).

Cost: Free for ABA members.

ABA Connection

http://www.abanet.org/cle/connection.html#previous

Content: Recorded versions of the ABA's monthly mandatory CLE (MCLE) teleconferences are available via the Internet.

Cost: Free for ABA members.

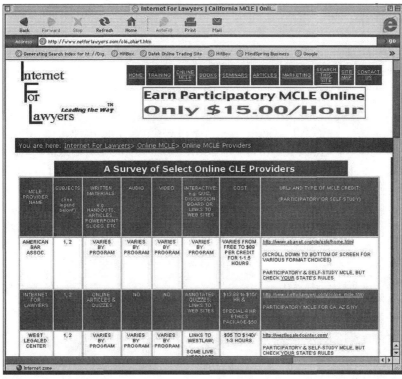

Figure 16-8. Internet For Lawyers provides an online chart comparing approx-imately one dozen local and national providers of online CLE (**http://www.net forlawyers.com/cle_chart.htm**).

Internet For Lawyers

http://www.netforlawyers.com/online_mcle.htm

Content: The site offers text-based quizzes covering a total of nine hours of general, legal ethics, substance abuse educa-tion, and law practice management credits. The quizzes combine a comprehensive article with locating material from outside Web sources.

    These quizzes lead you through the functions of other Web sites where you can find important free resources useful to your practice while also satisfying your CLE requirements.

Cost: Credit can cost as little as $13.88 per hour when submit-ting all nine hours ($15.00 per hour when submitted sep-arately). Payment can be made by credit card or check.

Law.com

http://store.law.com/seminars

Content: Law.com offers a combination of streaming audio, streaming video, and e-mail panel and discussion courses. Each Law.com panel and discussion course includes panelist bios, library documents, seminar discussions, and links to relevant statutes, case law, and Internet resources. Courses run for two weeks, and you can join in at any time. A course agenda for the two weeks is posted and a moderator leads the discussion daily (via e-mail). Cyber attendees join in the discussion via e-mail.

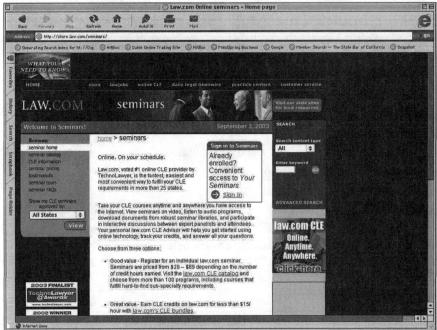

Figure 16-9. Law.com offers online CLE in a variety of formats, including streaming audio, streaming video, and e-mail panel discussions.

Cost: Prices range between $29 to $69 for courses lasting one to three hours. Preset bundles (offered on a state-by-state basis) can bring the price down to $15 per hour. Group pricing is also available for blocks of one hundred or more hours.

FindLaw

http://www.findlaw.com/07cle/cle

Content: FindLaw's online text-based CLE courses are comprised of an annotated quiz with a Web surfing component. The quizzes provide a brief overview of a site and then send lawyers to those sites to answer questions. Find-Law's courses focus on teaching you about legal research sites available on the Internet—from health care law, California law, and federal law, to cyberspace law and environmental law.

Cost: To earn one hour of credit, you can mail in, fax, or e-mail the answers to the ten-question quiz, along with a $35 check or credit card information.

Taecan

http://www.taecan.com

Content: Taecan has teamed up with more than two dozen state and local bar associations and private MCLE providers to deliver streaming audio and video versions of programs that the providers have previously presented live.

Cost: Fees per seminar range from $25 to $50 per hour (depending on the provider). Discounts are available to individuals who purchase multiple hours or to firms purchasing large blocks of seminars.

Figure 16-10. Legalspan offers CLE programming from numerous state and local bar associations.

Legalspan

http://www.legalspan.com

Content: Legalspan has also teamed up with more than two dozen state and local bar associations and private MCLE providers to deliver streaming audio and video versions of programs that the providers have previously presented live. The company's virtual seminar room offers a 3-D image of a seminar room on the user's computer, the ability to see and hear the speaker, and read their accompanying PowerPoint presentation slides and handouts, all at one time and within one computer screen. If you're watching a live seminar, you can send questions to the speaker's teleprompter. If you're watching a recorded seminar, you can e-mail the speaker with any questions and will receive a response at a later date.

Cost: Prices vary depending on the provider. Most courses cost approximately $25 to $30 per hour. Once paid for, the courses can be accessed for three months.

ABA Online CLE

http://www.abanet.org/cle/ecle/home.html **$**

Content: The ABA cosponsors online audio and video seminars (some with slides) with a variety of partners, ranging from ABA sections to outside groups. Questions and exercises are mixed throughout the audio and video programs. Written materials are also available for download. The programs are searchable by topic or browsable by title.

Cost: Prices range from $59 to $89 for one to one-and-a-half hours. Pricing is in three tiers: the highest price for non-ABA members, a discount of $10 for ABA members, and a discount of $20 for ABA section members if their section sponsored the seminar.

Practising Law Institute (PLI)

http://www.pli.edu

Content: PLI offers streaming audio and video online versions of their live programs, as well as live webcasts of seminars as they are being presented. They also include links to related written materials from PLI, other non-PLI Web-based resources, and an online discussion group.

Cost: The streaming previously-presented programs are mostly priced at $750, but can go up to $1,295 for a two-day seminar. Prices for webcasts of live events are higher, up to $1,695 for a two-day seminar.

West LegalEdcenter

http://www.westlegaledcenter.com

Content: West LegalEdcenter has over one thousand accredited audio and video online CLE programs (and some live webcasts) from over sixty-five local, state, and national providers, ranging from the ABA to the Women's Bar Association of the State of New York

Cost: Prices vary widely, sometimes depending on the format or whether you are a member of a specific bar. For example, the fifteen West LegalEdcenter courses listed on the State Bar of California page offer a one-hour course priced as low as $35. A three-and-a-quarter-hour audio course is offered for $125, while the same course on video is priced at $140. Another example of the price variation is a one-and-a-half-hour audio course for $115, but priced at $75 for members of the ABA Section on Public Contract Law.

*CHAPTER*SEVENTEEN

Statistical Research

Various organizations compile statistics on an unimaginable number of topics. Depending on the types of matters you handle, you can use statistics to prove (or disprove) an argument or better illustrate a point. As the oft-quoted American humorist Evan Esar defined it, the science of statistics is "the only science that enables different experts using the same figures to draw different conclusions."

Statistics Metasites

From the Census Bureau to the FBI, this country's most prolific gatherer of statistical information is probably the U.S. government. The first stop for federal statistical information has to be FedStats at **http://www.fedstats.gov**. You can search by topic, keyword (click on **Search across agency websites**), or by agency name. Searches can be limited to regions. The choice of topics appears limitless, from **Adoption** to **Women-Owned Businesses**. See below for more information on selected statistics data available on the Internet.

For nonfederal statistics, your first stop should be the University of Michigan Documents Center site, Statistical Resources on the Web (**http://www.lib.umich.edu/govdocs/stats.html**).

The University of Michigan Documents Center site categorizes its links into a broad array of nearly three hundred topics ranging from **Abortion** to **World-Village**. Additionally, the site offers an Experimen-

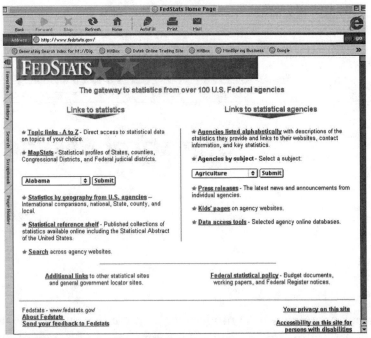

Figure 17-1. FedStats links to the statistical databases from more than seventy federal agencies.

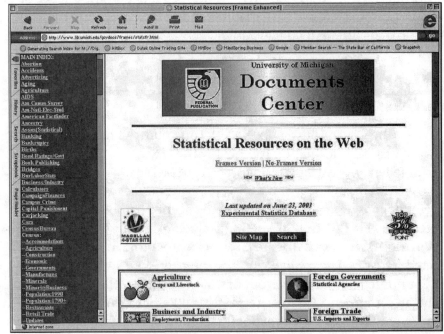

Figure 17-2. The University of Michigan Documents Center, Statistical Resources on the Web, links to state, local, and foreign governmental statistical databases, as well as to many nongovernmental databases, such as private nonprofits.

tal Statistics Database (the link is in the center of the home page) that may still need a bit of work. For example, a search for documents containing "work" and "injury" in the title or description returned no results, while a search for just "injury" returned two results for two documents from two different government agency Web sites; however, neither of the links to those documents was still accurate. Try some sample searches of the experimental database for yourself, but you may have your best results browsing the extensive list of topics.

Judicial Statistics Sites

Federal Court Management Statistics

http://www.uscourts.gov/fcmstat/index.html

Purpose: To locate information regarding the U.S. District Courts and Courts of Appeals.

Content: This site offers statistical information regarding the operation and caseloads of all the U.S. District Courts and Courts of Appeals. After clicking on **District Courts** or **Courts of Appeals** for a particular year, you can pick the court about which you want more information (such as Ninth Circuit or Texas Northern). Results are returned in a spreadsheet format in your browser window.

Information returned includes overall caseload statistics, actions per active judge, and median time from notice to disposition, among other useful data. The report also includes comparative data in each category back to 1997.

Our View: For the courts of appeals, you can view information for a single circuit or all twelve. For the district courts, you can request information for one district, or aggregated data for all of the districts. There is no way to pick and choose the districts to compile an original report for multiple districts of your choosing. Only aggregated information for the courts is available. No judge-specific information is offered.

Tip: To view results in your browser, do *not* check the **Open in spreadsheet format** option beneath the court name.

U.S. Sentencing Commission (USSC) Annual Reports

http://www.ussc.gov/annrpts.htm

Purpose: To locate statistics on the application of the federal sentencing guidelines.

Content: Each year the U.S. Sentencing Commission compiles its annual "Sourcebook of Federal Sentencing Statistics" containing data on the application of federal sentencing guidelines on a national level, as well as statistics broken down by district and circuit. The report's other statistics (arranged nationally—by offense, by district, or by circuit) include:

- Demographic information on offenders
- Guilty pleas
- Average length of sentence
- Sentencing appeals

Our View: The Sentencing Commission has broken down the information far enough that you can get a pretty good picture of what your client might expect to face in the courts. For example, selecting the Illinois Northern district court link in Appendix B of the 2001 report, you can learn that of the 274 offenders brought before the court on drug offenses during the reporting period, 269 received prison time—with 127 of those receiving more than 60 months. None of the 274 received probation only, and only one received a sentence that combined probation and confinement.

Tip: Note that the 2001 "Sourcebook of Federal Sentencing
              Statistics" contains a *major* typographical error. Repeat-
              edly, throughout the document, it states that it covers the
              period from October 1, 2001, through September 30, *2001*
              instead of October 1, 2001, through September 30, *2002*.

Federal Justice Statistics Resource Center (FJSRC)

http://fjsrc.urban.org/noframe/wqs/q_intro.htm

Purpose: To locate information regarding offenders in the federal
              justice system.

Content: The site contains "comprehensive information describ-
              ing suspects and defendants processed in the Federal
              criminal justice system" compiled by the Bureau of Jus-
              tice Statistics (BJS). Specific data sets for the most recent
              available year include:

              • Executive Office for U.S. Attorneys (EOUSA)—sus-
                pects in matters received and concluded by the U.S.
                Attorneys office
              • Administrative Office of the U.S. Courts (AOUSC)—
                ongoing and completed cases in the U. S. District
                Courts
              • U.S. Sentencing Commission (USSC)—defendants
                sentenced
              • Federal Bureau of Prisons (BOP)—inmates entering
                and exiting the federal prison system, and total
                inmate population at fiscal year end

              To query the database you must:

              • Select a year
              • Select a data set
              • Select a variable
              • Check one or more value boxes
              • Click the **Go** button
              • Click **Frequency**

To view a list of the searchable variables in each of the data sets, and a description of each, click the **Data Dictionary** link on the left-hand side of the screen. Then select a **Year** and **Data Dictionary** and click the **Submit** button. Then select a specific data for which to retrieve the list of variables and their explanations, and click the **Submit** button.

Our View: There is a lot of useful information contained in the FJSRC data sets, but it's not that easy to get at. Each source, each dataset, and each subcategory must be queried separately. It is much easier to retrieve information from the USSC (see the listing above).

Tip: Check the site's list of **Easy Query** questions at **http://fjsrc.urban.org/noframe/wqs/easy_q.cfm** for the answers to some of the more frequently asked questions. These questions and their answers also serve as a *de facto* tutorial for searching the individual datasets. Along with the answers to the questions, this page also delivers instructions on how you could have constructed the search yourself.

Federal District Court Civil Trials

http://teddy.law.cornell.edu:8090/questtr7900.htm

Purpose: To determine detailed (nonidentifying) information about completed civil trials in the federal district court system for 1978-2000.

Content: Two professors at the Cornell University School of Law, Theodore Eisenberg and Kevin M. Clermont, have developed a search interface for federal district court civil case information. The data is gathered by the Administrative Office of the United States Courts, based on forms completed by the clerks of each court for each completed case.

Our View: You can narrow your search to particular types of cases by selecting numerous criteria (you can make more than one selection per criteria by holding down the *Ctrl* key while clicking the selection):

- Category (such as real property or torts)
- Year (1978-2000)
- District
- Jurisdictional basis (such as federal question, U.S. defendant)
- Route to court (such as original proceeding, removal from state court)
- Trial type (judge only, jury)
  From those criteria, you then choose the type of infor-mation you want to know about those cases:
- Frequency
- Duration
- Judgment
- Amount demanded
- Amount awarded
- Basis for aggregation (such as case category, district, trial mode [judge versus jury])

For example, for all civil Racketeer Influenced and Corrupt Organizations Act (RICO) trials in 2000 in the Central District of California (CACD) resting on a particular jurisdictional basis, you can determine the total number of such cases, the length of time they were on the docket, and information about the amount of monetary awards to successful plaintiffs. This data can give you a feel for the amount of time a case may take to make it through the courts.

Tip: You might compare result of jury trials against results from judge trials to help decide which might better serve your client.

California (**http://www.courtinfo.ca.gov/reference/3_stats.htm**), Illinois (**http://www.state.il.us/court/AppellateCourt/CaseloadStat_ default.htm**), and New Jersey (**http://www.judiciary.state.nj.us/ mcs/mcstats.htm**) are some of the states that also provide access to this type of statistical information regarding their courts. A Google search for the terms "court" and "statistics" and the name of your state should return a link to the site containing the data if it is available. Also see the entry regarding Syracuse University's TRACfed Web site (**http://tracfed.syr.edu**), and the federal judicial statistics available there, in Chapter 6, "Government Resources Online."

Crime Statistics Sites

FBI Uniform Crime Report (UCR)

http://www.fbi.gov/ucr/ucr.htm

Purpose: To locate information regarding serious crime in the U.S.

Content: This site provides access to the FBI Uniform Crime Reports back to 1995. The UCR program was initiated in 1929 to collect information on serious crimes in the following categories:

- Homicide
- Forcible rape
- Robbery
- Aggravated assault
- Burglary
- Theft
- Auto theft
- Arson

Additionally, the program collects information on hate crimes and on persons arrested for twenty-two other less-serious crime categories. Hate crime offenses cover incidents motivated by race, religion, sexual orientation, and ethnicity or national origin.

Our View: While it appears that this page links directly to the UCR data, it actually links to the FBI press releases summarizing the findings contained in the UCR for each respective year. Those press releases point to national trends in the crimes tracked by the program. You can access the actual UCR data from a link in the press release.

The raw data (number of occurrences in each category per city) are included in an alphabetical list of cities and towns (of over 100,000 population) in a separate PDF document.

Tip: Each year's UCR data offers a comparison to the data
                 from the previous year, and you can download UCR data
                 from earlier years (back to 1995) and chart your own,
                 longer-term trends for the cities and offenses covered in
                 the reports.

Demographic Statistics Sites

U.S. Census Bureau

http://www.census.gov

Purpose: To locate information regarding people and business in
                 the U.S.

Content: Every ten years the Census Bureau collects data about
                 the people and economy of the United States. Addition-
                 ally, the Census Bureau, along with the Bureau of Labor
                 Statistics, conducts a monthly Current Population Sur-
                 vey that collects data from fifty thousand households.

Our View: The Census Bureau has sliced and diced its data on the
                 U.S. population in myriad useful ways.

                 Information on people is available in nearly forty cate-
                 gories ranging from **Age** to **Working at Home**, in
                 addition to general population profiles and projections.
                 (Click **People** on the site's home page to access these.)

                 For more information on business and economic data
                 from the Census Bureau, see the entry on its Economic
                 Census below.

Tip: For detailed state-by-state demographic data (or county-
                 by-county), see **http://quickfacts.census.gov/qfd**. For
                 example, selecting **California** from the pull-down
                 menu in the upper left-hand corner returns a page of
                 data for the state. You can further target the data by
                 selecting a county from the pull-down menu on the left.
                 All the data is also downloadable as Microsoft Excel files,
                 or as raw data.

U.S. Census Bureau's Statistical Abstract of the United States

http://www.census.gov/statab/www

Purpose: To locate information regarding people and business in the U.S.

Content: This site is an online version of the *National Data Book,* which contains a collection of statistics on social and economic conditions in the United States. Selected international data is also included.

Our View: Even though there is no search engine available for the *Data Book,* it is still fairly easy to use. The book is divided into thirty-one sections detailing various segments of the U.S. population, culture, and economy. Topics covered range from the **Current Population** and **Vital Statistics** (birth, death, mortality) to **Banking** or **Entertainment**. The topics are presented in numerical order (as organized in the print edition of the book) with links to PDF versions of the corresponding data in the two most recent editions.

Tip: Also see the Guide to State Statistical Abstracts (**http://www.census.gov/statab/www/stateabs.html**), the County and City Data Book (**http://www.census.gov/statab/www/ccdb.html**), and USA Statistics in Brief (**http://www.census.gov/statab/www/brief.html**).

Business, Economy, and Labor Statistics Sites

U.S. Census Bureau's Economic Census

http://www.census.gov/epcd/www/econ97.html

Purpose: To locate information and trends related to business in the U.S.

Content: Every five years the Census Bureau profiles the economy of the United States at the national and local levels. Survey forms are sent to five million businesses, and the data is available at this site.

Our View: You can view economic status reports by NAICS code (the North American Industry Classification System that has replaced the older Standard Industrial Classification [SIC] system), at nearly any level. You can retrieve data for the entire nation, down to a single ZIP code (depending on the size of the locale you're interested in).

The most recent survey was conducted in 2002.

Tip: Download the PDF files and print them yourself, rather than paying the Bureau's print-on-demand fee (which ranges from $25 to $150, depending on the report requested).

U.S. Department of Labor Bureau of Labor Statistics (BLS)

http://www.bls.gov

Purpose: To locate information and trends related to business and labor in the U.S.

Content: The BLS offers myriad statistics related to commerce, the economy, and the workforce.

Our View: Like the Census Bureau, the BLS has analyzed its data in dozens of useful ways. Reports range from state-by-state reviews of wages, earnings, and benefits to labor and productivity costs for employers across the country.

The topics are arrayed on the home page in broad categories, as noted above. Each broad category carries clickable subheadings of specific data available pertaining to that topic.

Figure 17-3. The Bureau of Labor Statistics Web site offers business and economical statistics in dozens of categories.

Tip: For workers' compensation or other workplace injury cases, search for specific reports, such as "Amputations: A Continuing Workplace Hazard" (**http://www.bls.gov/ opub/cwc/sh20030114ar01p1.htm**), that may help support your case (or refute the opposition's). Click **Search** in the upper right-hand corner of the home page to conduct keyword searches of the entire site to locate such materials.

Foreign and International Statistics Sites

U.S. Census Bureau International Database Summaries

http://www.census.gov/ipc/www/idbsum.html

Purpose:	To determine population information regarding foreign countries.
Content:	The site offers a database of population information summaries, viewable by country.
Our View:	Selecting a country from the scrollable list brings up a summary of population data for that country that includes births and deaths, life expectancy, and a breakdown by age and gender.
Tip:	In addition to current population data, the reports also include information back to 1950 and projections to 2040.

U.S. Census Bureau Foreign Trade Statistics

http://www.census.gov/foreign-trade/www

Purpose:	To determine import and export activity and volume.
Content:	The site offers a database of merchandise shipments to and from the U.S. Data is collected from import and export declarations filed with U.S. Customs and other government agencies.
Our View:	You can retrieve data regarding the value of commodities shipped to and from the U.S. for the most recent five years. Select **Country Trade Data Updated** and then **Imports** or **Exports** to view an alphabetical list of

countries doing business with the U.S. Selecting a specific country displays a chart containing the dollar values of materials, ranging from **Wheat** to **Military Apparel**, sent to or from the U.S. (depending on whether you've selected exports or imports respectively).

Tip: Select **State Export Data Updated** on the site's home page to view tables of exports from each state either by the country exported to or the commodity exported. (Data is shown for the top twenty-five export countries or top twenty-five export commodities only.) More in-depth data regarding which states exported which commodities to which countries is not available here.

For additional foreign and international statistics, see Chapter 15, "Foreign and International Research."

Transportation Statistics

For auto, aircraft, and train accident statistics, see Chapter 18, "Transportation Research."

CHAPTER**EIGHTEEN**

Transportation Research

Lawyers of many different disciplines can find a wealth of transportation-related information to help them in specific cases.

For example, a worker's compensation, personal injury, or insurance defense lawyer might use auto, plane, and train accident statistics and trends to bolster certain cases.

A products liability, class action, or personal injury lawyer could help make his case (or weaken the opposition's) with information on the number of other, similar complaints filed regarding a particular model of car.

A family law lawyer might wish to determine if the client's spouse owns any major personal property that the client is not aware of, such as a plane, boat, or luxury or sports car. (While airplane registration is available online for free, pleasure boat registration is handled at the state level in a manner similar to motor vehicle registration. Like car registration and licensing records, boat registration records are covered under the Driver's Privacy Protection Act [DPPA]. For more information on accessing motor vehicle records at the state level and the DPPA, see Chapter 8, "Accessing Public Records.")

Starting-Point Web Sites for Transportation Research

TranStats (U.S. Department Of Transportation's [DOT] Intermodal Transportation Database)

http://www.transtats.bts.gov

Purpose: To locate transportation data and statistics for air, road, and rail transportation.

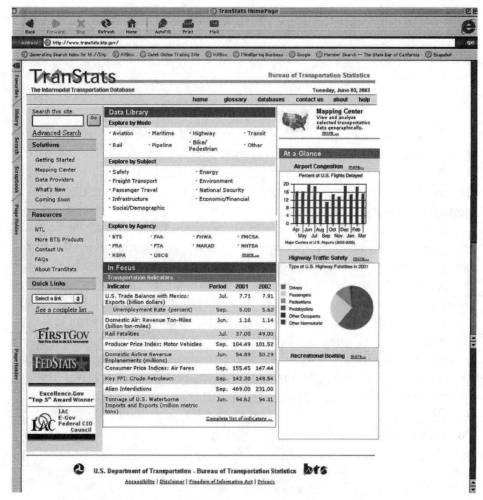

Figure 18-1. The U.S. Department of Transportation's TranStats database contains information regarding planes, trains, automobiles, and even oil and gas pipelines.

Content: TranStats is a metasite of government agencies and Web sites containing information on all conceivable modes of transportation, including:

- Aviation
- Maritime
- Highway
- Rail
- Bike and pedestrian
- Pipeline
- Transit

The site also has a number of preset **Explore by Subject** listings:

- Safety
- Freight transport
- Passenger travel
- Infrastructure
- Economic and financial
- Social and demographic
- Energy
- Environment
- National security

Our View: TranStats is an excellent one-stop shop for transportation data. For example, clicking on **Highway** brings up a number of data sets related to over-the-road transportation (for cars, trucks, and buses). The available data cover a wide range of topics from the **Commodity Flow Survey** (data on commodity shipments by industry, including hazardous materials) to the **Hazardous Materials Incidents Reporting System** (which includes information on hazardous materials spills occurring during transit). For a description of the data held in each of the listed sources, click on its name. For a more in-depth description of the government program responsible for collecting the data, click the **Profile** link. To actually view any information from the databases, you must click the **Download** link for that database. Then you can select the fields you want to include (using check boxes), and select locations, date ranges, and other limiters (from pull-down menus at the top of the database download page). Data is downloaded in the CSV (Comma Separated Values) format which can be opened using Microsoft Excel or other spreadsheet or statistics software.

Tip: Click **Glossary** at the top of the page for a dictionary of transportation-related terms.

Center for Transportation Analysis (CTA)

http://www-cta.ornl.gov/Index.html

Purpose: To locate information on intermodal (air, road, and rail) transportation.

Content: The CTA conducts research and develops new methods for "the efficient, safe and free movement of people and goods in our Nation's transportation systems." The site links to various publications and research information produced by the CTA, dealing with the interstate highway system, traffic safety, air safety and air traffic management, military transportation and distribution, and highway security, among other areas.

Our View: Click on **On-Line Tools** to access surveys and reports such as:

- The National Household Travel Survey
- Nationwide Personal Transportation Survey
- Projecting Fatalities in Crashes Involving Older Drivers

Tip: Of particular interest is the **Intelligent Transportation System (ITS) Deployment Tracking** Web site, which tracks the implementation of the ITS initiative in seventy-eight major metropolitan areas. The ITS uses "the latest in computers, electronics, communications and safety systems . . . to better manage and improve how transportation providers such as governments, transit agencies and truckers offer services to the public." These include electronic traffic monitoring on highways and major streets, electronic toll collection, and so on. Progress is tracked through periodic surveys. The survey results, along with charts and other data, are available here, as well as blank and completed survey forms.

Transportation Acronyms

Bureau of Transportation Statistics Transportation Acronym Guide

http://www.bts.gov/btsprod/tag

Purpose: To decode transportation-related acronyms.

Content: The site offers a searchable and browsable list of hundreds of transportation related acronyms.

Our View: After clicking on **Search TAG**, you can either enter the acronym you're trying to decode in the **Acronym** box, or the full word or phrase into the **Definition** box. The acronym and its definition are returned, along with the guide's source for the information. The sources can be decoded by clicking on **Source Index**.

Tip: This guide might come in handy as you access some of the other sites discussed in this section. The agency also maintains a glossary of transportation expressions at **http://www.bts.gov/btsprod/expr**.

Airplanes

Bureau of Transportation Statistics Airline Information

http://www.bts.gov/oai

Purpose: To locate traffic, market, and financial statistics about specific airlines and the airline industry as a whole.

Content: This site provides access to numerous reports regarding the air transportation industry, ranging from financial statistics and fuel costs and consumption to on-time performance and number of employees per carrier.

Our View: If you're looking for general information on the state of the airline industry, or financial information on specific airlines, this is the place for you.

Tip: To view flight durations between major airports (based on major airlines' published schedules), and how those flight durations have changed over the years, click on **Airport-Pair Elapsed Time for the Months of February in Years Indicated.**

Transportation Security Administration (TSA)

http://www.tsa.dot.gov/public

Purpose: To locate information regarding airport security requirements and special considerations for air travelers.

Content: This site offers a clearinghouse for information related to the rapidly evolving policies of this nascent federal agency. It also provides administration news, tips on travel preparedness (such as packing and security screenings), links to U.S. Code sections related to the administration's operation, and claim forms for items lost or damaged as a result of TSA screening, among other information.

Our View: Here you'll get the definitive answer to the question, "Do I have to take my shoes off before going through the metal detector?" among others. (For the record: it's currently not required, though recommended in certain instances, depending on the particular shoes you're wearing . . .)

Tip: The clickable subject links near the top of the Web site's home page are too broad to really help locate the information you may need (**Travelers & Consumers, Law & Policy,** and **Security & Law Enforcement**, among others). Clicking on **Site Map** makes it easier to find the information you're looking for.

U.S. Aircraft Ownership and Pilot Registration

FAA Aircraft Registry Inquiry

http://162.58.35.241/acdatabase

Purpose: To locate aircraft assets and owners via registration information.

Content: The FAA database site offers ten different ways to search for aircraft information, including:

- Ownership (by name)
- N-Number (registration number)
- Serial number

Our View: The FAA site contains information not included in the Landings.com database (below). Recent searches at the FAA site turned up information on re-registered N-Numbers and additional owner names that were not included in search results conducted at Landings.com (see below). For example, a search for an old airplane registration number turned up information that the plane had been exported to Australia. The search also provided the name and address of the last U.S. owner before the plane was exported.

Tip:
- A name search to determine if an individual is a licensed pilot is not included at the site. Up-to-date pilot licensing data is available for download as a *large* data file from the FAA at **http://registry.faa.gov/ amdata.asp**. The data is updated monthly.
- Use this site in conjunction with the Landings site.

Landings

http://www.landings.com

Purpose: To locate aircraft assets and owners via registration information.

Content: The site maintains databases of aircraft (airplanes and helicopters) and pilot registrations in the United States (and nine other countries around the world). It also provides links to the registration databases of another twenty countries.

The four most useful searches are

- Licensing (by name)
- Ownership (by name)
- N-Number
- Serial number

To search this site's databases, click on **Databases** at the top of the home page.

Our View: This site is particularly useful for uncovering assets, if you suspect someone might own an aircraft, or when you are trying to locate someone who you know does own one, or is at least a registered pilot. While the information contained in the site's databases comes from the FAA, there is additional information included in some search results at the FAA site that is not found when conducting similar searches at the Landings site.

Tip:
- Landings allows you to construct fairly sophisticated searches using numerous search operators (wild cards, anchors, and so on). Click on the **Unix style regular expression link** on the Search page to read more about them.
- Use in conjunction with the FAA site above.
- Clicking on the **Calculators** link brings up a list of links to many useful applications that supply the distance between two airports and distance between two

locations. The latter requires you enter the exact longitude and latitude coordinates, which you can determine utilizing a Global Positioning System (GPS) device.

Tracking Planes In Flight

Cheaptickets.com Flight Tracker

http://www.cheaptickets.com (\$)
(click on **FlightTracker** under **Travel Resources** on the upper right-hand side of the home page)

Purpose: To track commercial flights while they're in the air.

Content: Travel planning site Cheaptickets.com offers a unique flight tracker that gives the real-time location of any airborne North American commercial airliner.

Our View: You can locate the flight you're interested in by entering the airline and flight number, if you know it, or by entering the departure and arrival cities and the departure time.

Available information includes:

- Location
- Altitude
- Speed
- Equipment (type of plane)

Information can be viewed as text or as a graphical representation of the plane over a map of the U.S. (to indicate position). Control panel dials indicate speed, altitude and direction.

Tip: Entering the airline name and flight number delivers the best results. A search with the airline and flight number correctly located a Los Angeles-to-Minneapolis America

West flight on a layover on the ground in Phoenix. Searching for the same flight with just the Los Angeles departure time and Minneapolis destination did not return information on the target flight. (This presumably is due to this particular flight being redesignated as a Phoenix-to-Minneapolis flight after the layover.)

Locating U.S. Airports

AirNav.com

http://www.airnav.com/airports

Purpose: To find information on general, commercial, and private airports.

Content: AirNav offers a searchable and browsable list of general aviation, commercial, and private airports and heliports in the U.S.

Our View: It's not necessary to know the airport's official designation (LAX, JFK, and so on) to retrieve information. You can enter a city name in the site's search box, or click on **Browse by U.S. State** to view an alphabetical lists of all of the facilities in each state.

Tip: Click on **Advanced Search** to locate airports within a radius you select of any city, town, or latitude and longitude coordinates you specify.

U.S. Aircraft Safety and Accidents

National Transportation Safety Board (Aviation)

http://www.ntsb.gov/aviation/aviation.htm

Purpose: For detailed information regarding aircraft accidents.

Content: This site provides access to aviation accident statistics, information on major accident investigations, and a searchable database of the synopses of over 140,000 U.S. aircraft accidents dating back to 1962.

Our View: Accident statistics are available for the period 1983-2002, broken down by numerous criteria (such as airlines, nonscheduled service, fatalities only). Statistics are also available for the current month and year to date.

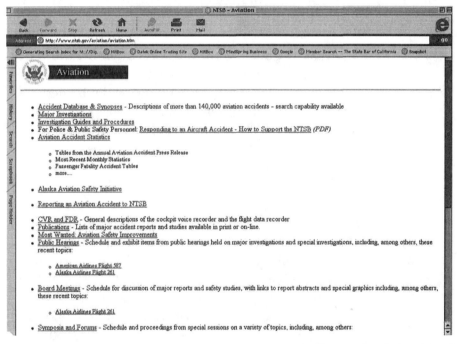

Figure 18-2. The Aviation section of the National Transportation Safety Board's Web site includes detailed information regarding plane accidents since 1962, and information regarding the agency's investigative procedures, among other useful information.

From the link marked **Accident Database & Synopses,** you can search for information on specific accidents using a variety of data fields, including a date range, city, state, aircraft category, severity of accident, and so on. You can also browse lists of accidents, listed month-by-month, back to 1962. Links are also provided to the preliminary or final reports on the accident as they are available. Additionally, by clicking on the **Completed Investigations** link, you learn which cases are expected to have additional information released in the near future.

The individual records for each aircraft accident can hold quite a bit of narrative information. Even the preliminary reports contained on this site contain more information than the preliminary reports contained on the FAA Office of Accident Investigation (OAI) Web site (see below).

Tip:

- Review all details in these reports carefully, and verify them from multiple sources when possible. Each preliminary record carries the following disclaimer: "This is preliminary information, subject to change, and may contain errors. Any errors in this report will be corrected when the final report has been completed." And apparently for good reason. One recent preliminary accident report indicated in two places that there were no injuries, while in the narrative of the same report, it stated that both occupants of the aircraft had been "fatally injured." Another recent NTSB preliminary report indicated that a particular accident had occurred at "1200 Alaska Daylight Time" (noon), "80 miles northwest of Skwentna, Alaska," while the FAA OAI (see below) preliminary report indicated that the same accident occurred at "2000 hours . . . 10 miles east of Farewell, Alaska." (Although it is not noted anywhere on the site, or in the reports, the FAA OAI site apparently utilizes Greenwich Mean Time to make note of times.)
- While the month-by-month chronological list of accident information (**http://www.ntsb.gov/ntsb/month.asp**) is listed as being updated daily, more complete information on recent aircraft accidents can be found at the FAA Office of Accident Investigation (OAI) site below.

FAA Office of Accident Investigation (OAI)

http://www1.faa.gov/avr/aai/aaihome.htm

Purpose: For preliminary information regarding recent aircraft accidents.

Content: Information is available for the most recent ten days only. Click on the **Preliminary Accident Data and Incident Data** link in the upper left-hand corner to access the reports.

Our View: The grid of dates for the past ten days indicates the number of incidents on each day. One confusing and annoying feature about the grid is that the date indicated is the **Date Reports Entered**, which in most cases is not the date that the accident took place. (The date the report was entered is usually the day after the accident took place, but can sometimes be later.) The grid further breaks the information down by fatal and nonfatal accidents. You can also view the accidents occurring in fixed-wing aircraft (planes) or rotorcraft (helicopters) by manufacturer. (Reports marked with an asterisk [*] signify updates to the reports since they were first filed.)

Another confusing and annoying feature of these reports is that the FAA apparently uses Greenwich Mean Time to denote the time of day these accidents occur (although they don't bother to tell you that on the site).

Tip: ● For a copy of the FAA publication *Aircraft Accident and Incident Notification, Investigation and Reporting,* click the link on the left-hand side of the site's home page.
● For additional information regarding specific accidents (or any accident more than ten days old), the FAA suggests contacting the NTSB. (For more information on aircraft accident information available online from the NTSB, see above.)

- For a TIP regarding inconsistencies in the data held in these preliminary reports, see the entry for the NTSB Aviation Web site above.

FAA Airworthiness Directives

http://www.faa.gov
(click on **Airworthiness Directives** under Regulatory/Advisory)

Purpose: To locate FAA-issued safety notices for specific aircrafts or parts.

Content: Like automobile recalls, the FAA issues Airworthiness Directives ordering the repair, replacement, or alteration of specific aircraft parts or mechanisms. This database contains the FAA's current Airworthiness Directives in a searchable and browsable format. You can:

- Conduct full text searches
- View emergency directives (issued in the last ten days)
- View new directives (issued in the last sixty days)
- Browse by manufacturer name or directive number

Our View: Determining the airworthiness of an aircraft could hold the solution if the aircraft has caused damage or injury. If a directive had been issued and the aircraft's current (or previous) owner had not made the mandated repairs, negligence might also be involved. The FAA regularly issues these directives, and they remain in force until they are superceded by a subsequent directive. Some directives have been in force since the 1940s, according to the FAA site.

Tip: Use the keyword search function. Click on **Search Help** for information on Boolean, phrase, and wild card searching.

Plane Crash Info

http://planecrashinfo.com

Purpose: For background information regarding past plane crashes.

Content: This site contains a database of more than three thousand plane crashes from the first airplane fatality on September 17, 1908 (in which Orville Wright suffered several broken bones) to the present. Accident information can be browsed by:

- Date
- Airline and operator
- Aircraft type

The latest accidents are featured on the front page, with photos and details (as available).

Our View: The site's statistics can be helpful in getting an overview of air fatalities, and more.

Tip: The transcripts and audio of air traffic control dialogue and cockpit voice recorder from selected crashes (in the aptly named **Last Words** section) is both disturbing and morbidly fascinating.

Trains

Federal Railroad Administration

http://www.fra.dot.gov/site

Purpose: To locate information regarding railroad safety, accidents, and rail lines

Content: The site contains passenger and freight railroad accident and safety data, along with a railroad library covering the history of railroad development.

Our View: Clicking on the **Data Central** button shows links to some of the site's most useful data. Then follow the **Safety Data** link to access searchable databases of train accidents and accident trends. Summary and detailed reports of train accidents and casualties can also be found by clicking the **Safety Data** link.

Tip: View and download accident trend graphs and charts (1993 to the last fiscal year) for use at settlement, mediation, or trial.

Amtrak

http://www.amtrak.com

Purpose: To locate information related to the Amtrak rail line.

Content: Set up much like an airline Web site, the site offers train schedules, routes, and the ability to make and pay for reservations.

Our View: This site is set up to serve the Amtrak clientele, and attract new riders.

Tip: Under **Travel Tools**, use the **MapQuest Station Finder** link to input an address and find the closest Amtrak train station. You can also use the **Check Train Status** link to determine if a specific train has left or will arrive at its destination on time.

Automobiles

National Highway Transportation Safety Agency (NHTSA)
Office of Defects Investigation

To search:
To request information not included in the free searches: **$**
http://www.odi.nhtsa.dot.gov

Purpose:	To locate information regarding automobile recalls, service bulletins, or ongoing investigations of potential vehicle defects.
Content:	The site offers searchable databases of:

- Consumer complaints (since 1995)
- Defect investigations (since 1972)
- Vehicle and equipment recalls (since 1966)
- Technical service bulletins (since 1995)

Each of the databases is searched in the same way. Rather than entering search terms, you drill down by selecting the type of information (such as vehicle, tires, or equipment), year, make, model, and component (such as airbag or parking brake). If you do not select a component, all of the records related to the vehicle you selected will be displayed. For example, a search for consumer complaints regarding the 2000 Ford Taurus returned 612 complaints. Selecting the component **Vehicle Speed Control: Accelerator Pedal** returned ten results dealing specifically with that component of the car.

Our View: Copies of most service bulletins and complaints can be accessed for free by clicking the **Document Search** button under the record you're interested in. If it is available, a new browser window will open with a link to a PDF version of the document. (Most identifying information on complaints has been redacted, although a dealer name, location, or vehicle identification number [VIN] may remain.)

If documents are not available free online, you can request them from the National Highway Transportation Safety Agency's (NHTSA) Office of Defects Investigation (by clicking the **Request Research** button). Charges are $38.50 for searching and copying time and $0.10 per page for copying.

Tip: Even if no recall or investigation has been launched, a search of the complaints database could turn up problems similar to those of a client experiencing problems with a vehicle.

NHTSA National Center for Statistics and Analysis State Data System

http://www-nrd.nhtsa.dot.gov/departments/nrd-30/ncsa/SDS.html

Purpose: To locate motor vehicle crash statistics from selected states.

Content: The National Center for Statistics and Analysis (NCSA) State Data System (SDS) provides motor vehicle crash data from seventeen states between 1990 and 1999. The states are California, Florida, Georgia, Illinois, Indiana, Kansas, Maryland, Michigan, Missouri, New Mexico, North Carolina, Ohio, Pennsylvania, Texas, Utah, Virginia, and Washington. (South Carolina joined the SDS in January 2003, and NHTSA is lobbying other states to supply data as well.)

Our View: The statistics are presented in a twenty-three-section document. General information can be found in sections 6 to 8, **Crashes, Vehicles,** and **People**, respectively. Other sections focus on accident causes (such as alcohol or speeding), vehicle actions and types (such as rollovers, motorcycles, or large trucks) and a breakdown by driver's age. Each section is available as a separate PDF file. For people who might use the information often, or want a personal copy, downloadable versions of the report's sections are also available from this page.

Tip: Because the sample is only for seventeen states, the SDS warns that the data is not representative of the entire country, but only of the states for which data is included.

NTSA NCSA Fatality Analysis Reporting System

http://www-fars.nhtsa.dot.gov

Purpose: To locate motor vehicle fatality statistics from all fifty states.

Content: The Fatality Analysis Reporting System (FARS) collects data on fatal motor vehicle traffic crashes from all fifty states, the District of Columbia, and Puerto Rico. This information is gathered from police accident reports, death certificates, and coroner and medical examiner reports, among other sources. Available information includes times of day, contributing factors (such as weather or alcohol), vehicle types, and so on.

Our View: The statistics are presented in five reports:

- Trends
- Crashes
- Vehicles
- People
- States

Each report has various subsections that further divide the information. For example, in the **Vehicles** report, you can view data for passenger vehicles only, for small trucks only, or for all vehicles. Similarly, in the People report, you can view statistics for fatalities to driver only, passengers, or pedestrians (among other categories), or view all categories in one report.

Tip: While the default view for each report is for the most current edition of data for the entire country, pull-down menus on the right side of the screen allow you to view any combination of states and years (back to 1994).

Insurance Institute for Highway Safety (IIHS)

http://www.hwysafety.org

Purpose: To locate crash test results for various cars by model and category.

Content: Data for the following IIHS tests are available back to 1992 for most cars:

- 40-mph offset frontal crash
- 5-mph crash
- Head restraint

Click on **Vehicle Ratings** at the top of the home page to access the data.

Our View: The IIHS are the folks who made crash test dummies famous for performing crashworthiness evaluations of automobiles, and who issue safety ratings based on those test results. You can view the results for a particular model of automobile by selecting it from the alphabetical pull-down menus. You can also view the results of vehicle categories (such as large luxury car, midsize moderately priced cars, and so on)

Clicking **IIHS Research by Topic** at the top of the home page gives you access to background information on a series of automobile-related topics, such as daytime running lights and red-light running, among others.

Tip: Was your client's car yielding to oncoming traffic or making a left turn when the other driver hit them? You may be able to prove (or disprove) that a collision your client was involved with occurred in a certain manner by comparing your accident scene photos with "control" photos of known collision damage from the Institute's tests. (Check with the IIHS regarding copyrights and usage permission before utilizing any of their photos for presentations.)

Kelley Blue Book

http://www.kbb.com

Purpose:	To determine the value of a used car (and other new car information).
Content:	Going far beyond the scope of the old-faithful print version of the *Blue Book*, the site offers:

- Used car and motorcycle prices (buying and selling)
- New car prices
- New car reviews
- Side-by-side comparisons (new and used)

Our View:	The site is easy to navigate and clearly labels the links and functions. To find out the value of a car if sold to a private party, click **Private Party Value.** To get the trade-in value likely to be offered by a dealer, click **Trade-In Value.** Once you select the pricing you want to retrieve, menu-driven pages ask for specific information on the car (such as year, make, and model) before offering up the value.

The site also allows you to compare features and options between two or more cars (new or used) Click **Side-by-Side Comparison** under the **Tools-Tips-Advice** heading.

Tip:	If you have the VIN for a particular car, you can also order a CarFax vehicle report (see below) for additional information.

Other sites offering new and used car pricing and side-by-side comparisons include Edmunds (**http://www.edmunds.com**) and Vehix (**http://www.vehix.com**).

CarFax

Instant record check: More detailed record check:

http://www.carfax.com

Purpose: To determine used car vehicle history.

Content: CarFax's database contains more than two billion
              unique vehicle records compiled from nearly eight hun-
              dred data sources (such as state vehicle registrations,
              state inspections, and fire departments).

Our View: CarFax's vehicle history reports can confirm a clean title
              history or identify serious problems with a used car,
              including salvage history, odometer fraud, flood dam-
              age, or theft. Reports are available via the CarFax Web
              site for $14.99 for a single report, or $19.99 for two
              months of unlimited reports. Just enter the VIN into the
              designated box on the home page.

Tip: The site also offers a free instant record check (which
              returns year, make, model, engine type, and body type),
              lemon check, and recall check. The results page of each
              of those searches is also an effort to sell you a full report
              on the vehicle.

NHTSA Uniform Tire Quality Grading

http://www.nhtsa.dot.gov/cars/testing/utqg

Purpose: To decode the letters and numbers on tire sidewalls.

Content: Uniform Tire Quality Grading (UTQG) is a tire informa-
              tion system designed to help buyers make relative com-
              parisons among tires. Under UTQG, tires are graded by

the manufacturers in three areas: tread wear, traction, and temperature resistance. The grades are molded into the sidewalls of the tire. This site identifies the meanings of the various codes and shows their relative locations on the tire.

Our View: The diagram at the top of the page gives a good illustration and explanation of what each of the codes on the tire represents. For a more detailed description of the tread wear, traction, and temperature resistance grades, scroll down the page.

Tip: Toward the bottom of the page, don't miss the links to charts for dozens of tire manufacturers listing the grades of each of their tires by model name and size.

Boats

As we mentioned in the beginning of this chapter, in many states, registration of recreational (and smaller commercial) boats is handled by the department of motor vehicles. (In others, it's handled by the department of fish and wildlife.) Regardless, as with driver licensing information, many states have limited the accessibility of this information to the public (such as Texas SB 95-72). Therefore, none of the states makes this information available on the Internet.

U.S. Coast Guard National Vessel Documentation Center

http://www.uscg.mil/hq/g-m/vdoc/nvdc.htm

Purpose: To locate ownership information regarding domestic commercial vessels.

Content: Vessels of five net tons or more used for fishing or "coastwise trade" (the transportation of merchandise or passengers between points in the U.S., or tow boats and tugboats operating in the U.S.) must be registered with the Coast Guard. Title abstracts can be ordered from this site.

Our View: To order an abstract, click the **Order Abstracts of Title Online** link on the left-hand side of the screen. This brings up the Coast Guard's DiY (Do it Yourself) order page. Then click the **Abstract of Title** tab at the top of the page. On the order page, enter your contact and credit card information, along with the registration number for the vessel for which you want registration information. Title abstracts cost $25 each. Copies of a ship's certificate of ownership (not available online) are $125.

Tip: These documents cannot be requested anonymously. Requesters must provide a Social Security number or tax-payer identification number when requesting these documents.

*CHAPTER*__NINETEEN__

Entertainment Industry Research and Intellectual Property

That's Entertainment: Locating Entertainment Industry Sites

What is entertainment? Depending on who is asked, the question elicits a variety of answers. For some it means attending the theater, a concert, a sporting event, the opera, or the ballet; to others it could mean watching a film or television show, listening to music (over the radio or the Internet), or playing video games. Ask a group of entertainment law lawyers to define entertainment law and their answers will be just as varied. Type "entertainment" into the Google search engine and 32,800,000 results are listed, led by E! Online. Type "entertainment law" into Google and 63,500 results are listed, with a scholarly entertainment law review listed first. From the low-brow to the high-brow, this sums up the range of information entertainment lawyers use to keep up with entertainment law and the entertainment industry in general.

When asked which resource she uses most in her entertainment law practice, Susan Kaiser (**http://www.kaisermedialaw.com**), a lawyer who has represented network-owned radio and television stations, and negotiates and drafts agreements and contracts, replied, "Probably the resource I use most is Google.com to search opposing counsel, talent names, potential clients, and law firms." Searching Google makes sense when a lawyer is trolling for any and all information, since Google, which indexes more of the Internet than any other engine, casts such a wide net. It is not surprising then that her first line of research is a general search engine instead of an entertainment related site. However, if a lawyer is seeking background information about entertainment in general, especially people, the best place to start may be in consumer entertainment sites and entertainment trade publication sites.

Entertainment Research

Consumer Sites: Television and Film

E! Online

http://www.eonline com

Purpose:	For general entertainment news and background information on celebrities.
Content:	The site content ranges from news, features, gossip, multimedia (for example, you can use keywords to find a clip), movie reviews, celebrity information, and information about shows on the E! network.
Our View:	While it can sometimes be difficult to distinguish E! Online's news from its gossip, the site's full-text searching of its extensive Hollywood coverage and its hyperlink feature (see below) make the site worthwhile.
Tip:	• A handy hyperlink feature allows users who are reading an article about a named celebrity, actor, musician, writer, or director to hyperlink to that person's biography, a chronology of the person's career, a credit list, links to other E! Online stories about that individual, online multimedia clips, and fan clubs. • Free membership entitles you to an e-newsletter and access to celebrity chats.

Entertainment Weekly (EW)

http://www.ew.com

Purpose:	For online-only entertainment news on a daily basis, and information from EW's print magazine.
Content:	EW offers the following content from its print magazine: reviews (movies, books, videos, film), some of its reporting, and an archive of all of the magazine's articles since its inception in 1990. EW's site also includes photo galleries, interviews, and video and audio clips.
Our View:	It's useful that the archives include both EW's articles and the online content. However, we'd prefer a more advanced search menu than the simple search box on the site's home page. Its **Monitor** service should appeal to those who are tracking (not stalking!) a particular celebrity, movie, or band (up to ten subjects). EW searches through three thousand sources to update your **Monitor** page.
Tip:	As of March 30, 2003, access was limited to print subscribers to EW and to AOL subscribers. Those who buy copies of the magazine at a newstand can also access the site with an access code found on the table of contents page.

Commercial Trade Databases

Law librarians at entertainment law firms are frequently asked to conduct background research on potential clients or opposing parties; at other times, they are asked to find contact information, perhaps to serve a complaint. To meet these queries, law librarians at entertainment law firms tend to favor two subscription sites: BaselineFT and the Internet Movie Database (IMDB) Pro.

Internet Movie Database Pro

http://www.imdb.com

Purpose: Internet Movie Database (IMDB) Pro offers access to twenty-four thousand contact and agent listings, and box-office statistics for eighteen countries (both weekly and daily for the U.S.).

Content: Nonsubscribers can access some information for free, such as IMDB's searchable archives back to 1997; celebrity news; box office information; reviews of movies, TV and videos; a picture gallery; and a film glossary. Subscriptions for individuals range from $12.95 (monthly) to $99.95 (annually). However, enterprise-wide subscribers need to contact the site for pricing.

Our View: While nonsubscribers can view more detailed information if they register (free), they still can't access as much as the Pro pay subscribers (for example, they can't access the database of contact and agent listings). It's worth paying for a Pro subscription just to avoid wading through continual pop-up ads at the free site.

Tip: Use **Power Searching (http://us.imdb.com/list)** when you have limited clues about what you're looking for (such as a movie with the word "Africa" for which the genre is adventure) or when you want to create a list (such as every horror film, in black and white, from Japan). For other sophisticated searches, go to **http://us.imdb.com/ search** and click on one of the **Popular Searches** or **Advanced Searches** (choose **people working together** to find movies in which certain people costarred).

BaselineFT

http://www.baseline.hollywood.com

Purpose: Locate information regarding the entertainment industry.

Content: BaselineFT's databases contain 1.5 million records with 7,000 biographies; credits for 900,000 actors, producers, directors, and crew members; and contact information for companies, executives, and talent.

Baseline also includes archives of Paul Kagan Associate's Motion Picture Investor database, the *Hollywood Reporter* (THR) and *Variety*. A daily e-mail provides updates about films and television programs in development and in production, and current entertainment news. Other information and statistics, such as the Star Salary Report, are available. The cost of BaselineFT is $99.00 per year for companies and $69.00 for individuals and nonprofits, plus a per-document fee that can range from $1.25 for current weekly *Variety* stories to $79.00 for the Star Salary Report.

Our View: This is a useful site for the following reasons:

- Its extensive database of biographies, credits, contacts, and hard-to-find information (such as the Star Salary Report)
- The ability to search THR back to May 1988 (which is three years further back than the archives at THR's own site)
- The ability to conduct simultaneous searches of the archives and current issues of the various databases, along with the Motion Picture Investor database

Tip: For those who do not have individual subscriptions to *Variety* or THR, one subscription to BaselineFT might be all you need (unless you need to go back further than 1991 for *Variety*).

Trade Publication Sites

Television And Film

The Hollywood Reporter (THR)

http://www.hollywoodreporter.com

Purpose: For archives of past stories (back to early 1991) and continual updating throughout the day.

Content: Online viewers may find that the stories are longer than those found in the print version. The subscription portion of the site also includes the *Blu-Book Production Directory*, a news scroll, box office charts, production listings, and script sales.

Our View: With full access at $14.95 monthly (which includes the first ten full-text displays of news stories, archived items, and production listings for free), the site is a must for entertainment research. (Any displays beyond the first ten are charged at $0.10 to $0.25 each.)

Figure 19-1. Search the Hollywood Reporter's archive of news, reviews, and features dating back to 1991 or search a separate database of reviews and columnists.

Tip: The archives can be found by clicking on the **Advanced Search** link on the right side of the home page or by scrolling down and clicking on **Archives** on the left side of the page (under Resources). Search the archives by keywords, byline, or date. (Nonsubscribers have free access to parts of the site. For instance, they can read the headlines and abstracts of current articles (and the archives back to 1991), and the weekly box office charts (but not the daily charts). They have full access to PR Newswire.)

Variety

http://www.variety.com

Purpose: Locate entertainment industry news and information back to 1914.

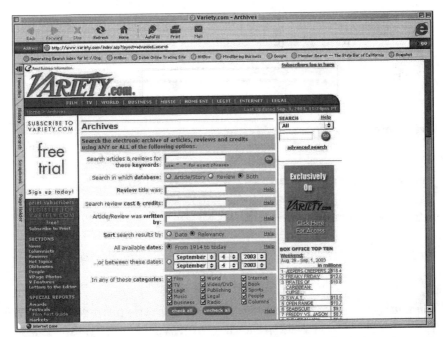

Figure 19-2. Search Variety.com for articles or reviews by keywords, cast and credit, title of review, or name of reviewer or article author. You can also limit by date.

Content: Visitors to Variety.com will find credits, classified ads, obituaries, and photos. On the legal pages, entertainment-law related jobs are posted free. Nonsubscribers can read the headlines and abstracts of current and archived articles for free. Also, Variety.com subscribers can sign up for various free e-newsletters with topics ranging from film news to box office numbers.

Our View: While Variety.com has similar resources as THR, its archive goes back much further—to 1914—and has more search options.

With access to Variety's Web site free to print subscribers, and its deep archives back to 1914, this is also a must site for entertainment lawyers. The cost of an on-line-only subscription is $259.00 per year. Although more costly than THR, there is no per-display charge. For those with an occasional need, the $3.95 per day charge is a boon. A free sixty-day trial subscription is also available. For those who like to receive free newsletters e-mailed daily, Variety is your choice over THR.

Tip: To search by a variety of search options, click on **advanced search** on the right side of the home page, under Search. You can sort results by relevancy or date.

Television and Interactive Media

Television Week (formerly Electronic Media)

http://www.tvweek.com

Purpose: For coverage of broadcast and cable television, and the interactive media industry.

Content: Every Monday, top stories from the print edition of *Television Week* are added to TVWeek.com. The site is also updated every day with breaking news. Subscribers to the print version can search the Internet archives back to 1999. Subscriptions run $119 per year.

Our View: This is one of the few subscription sites where nonsubscribers will discover that "more" actually means more. When nonsubscribers read the abstract of a story, and then click on **more**, it links them to the full story for free (back five days). At most other sites, clicking on **more** results in a page asking the visitor to log-in, or subscribe and provide a credit card number.

Television and Radio

Broadcasting & Cable

http://www.broadcastingcable.com

Purpose: For news and feature stories about broadcast and cable television, and the radio industry.

Content: Full online access is free to subscribers of the print edition ($179 per year) or runs $14.95 per month for on-line-only subscribers. A free trial is available.

Our View: Between this site and TVWeek.com, nonsubscribers are better off visiting TVWeek.com for free access to full-text stories of the past five days since Broadcasting & Cable's site offers nonsubscribers only abstracts. But, for those involved in the radio industry and those who find a free daily newsletter useful, BroadcastingCable.com is the better choice.

Tip: The site also offers a free daily e-mail newsletter of the industries' top headlines.

Guild Information

Transactional entertainment lawyers spend a lot of time drafting agreements and searching for forms for both general business matters and entertainment-specific industry matters. Finding a good source of sample business forms and knowing where to find guild agreements, guild forms, and other guild information can speed up the process. For general business forms, The 'Lectric Law Library (**http://lectlaw.com/form.html**), a site with free and fee-based forms, is favored by an associate of the authors who is a cable television network vice-president for legal and business affairs. For entertainment-specific forms and agreements, the major Hollywood creative guilds' sites should be consulted (see below).

The Directors Guild (DGA)

Nonmembers and members:
Members only: (requires DGA membership)

http://www.dga.org

Purpose:	Locate information related to Directors and the Directors Guild.
Content:	The site has a Members Only section and a section for both members and nonmembers. It offers the full text of the guild's agreements (basic, commercial, documentary, and so on) and a variety of forms (such as deal memos, signatory compliance forms, and residual reporting forms).
	Also available are the "minimums" (rate cards of directors' fees) to be paid by signatory companies to DGA members. Additionally, the site offers a searchable database of guild members, and a browsable list of signatory agencies.
Our View:	This is a useful site that has recently added multimedia, links to member's Web sites, and the DGA magazine. It

will soon be adding members' demo reels and its Women and Ethnic Minority contact list (which is now on the members' part of the site but will soon be added to the public part of the site).

Tip: To link to different sections of the site, use the tabs on the bottom of the page. There is a DGA Members Only section of the Web site with information not available to the public (for example, an interactive calendar of events, committee meeting information, and so on) and a more detailed version of the searchable database of members found on the public side of the site.

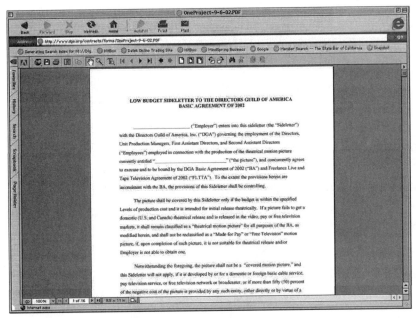

Figure 19-3. The DGA site links to a variety of contracts, from signatory documents, to rate cards, to residuals department forms. This is one of the signatory documents, the Low Budget Sideletter.

Writers Guild of America (WGA)

http://www.wga.org

(some material only available to WGA members)

Purpose: For resources for writers (and about writers), for members, and for producers.

Content: The site has its resources logically categorized by clickable tabs such as **For Writers** (agreements, forms, minimums, and a list of signatory agencies); **About Writers** (such as a list of agents by location); **For Members** (a daily list of industry news and information directly affecting WGA members) and **For Producers**. The WGA also offers a searchable database to determine whether a certain production was under a WGA contract (although the results do not include the name of the guild signatory that produced the work).

Our View: The site would be more useful if search results included the name of the guild signatory that produced the work.

Screen Actors Guild (SAG)

http://new.sag.org/sagWebApp/index.jsp

(some material only available to WGA members)   **$**

Purpose: Locate information regarding actors, talent agents, and the Screen Actors Guild.

Content: The top tabs point you to news and events, SAG membership benefits, FAQs, information about SAG (such as its constitution), and contacts. On the left-hand side of the home page, near the bottom, you will find **SAG Basics**, which includes **Contract Information, Signatory Information, Rate Information,** and **Talent agent Information**. There are searchable databases in the **Talent Agent** and the **Signatory Information** sections. For example, you can search the signatory database by the title, keyword, or production

ID of the film or television show to determine whether a certain production was produced under a contract from SAG.

Our View: The site is geared to SAG members and anyone who needs access to SAG's forms and contracts. Part of the site is password-protected and is for members only.

The site has many useful forms, contracts, and information about signatories and agents, but like the WGA site, the signatory results do not include the name of the guild signatory that produced the work. It would be more useful if the results included the name of the guild signatory that produced the work.

Tip: The site also has an internal search engine.

Well-Known Legal Site Reveals Its Hollywood Secret

A vice-president of legal and business affairs at a major cable television network lists a nonentertainment site as his first line of entertainment law research: FindLaw.com, and especially FindLaw's search engine, LawCrawler (**http://lawcrawler.findlaw.com**). And by digging deeper, he discovered FindLaw's "Hollywood secret": even though it's primarily a legal research site, it has a rather large entertainment and sports law and news component at its Entertainment and Sports Law page (see **http://www.findlaw.com/01topics/12entertainsport/index.html**). Lawyers can also subscribe to a free weekly entertainment law newsletter (**http://newsletters.findlaw.com/sample/elegal.html**) or a free sports law newsletter (**http://newsletters.findlaw.com/sample/sports.html**), each delivered via e-mail.

Music Industry Sites

Entertainment lawyers in the music industry can bookmark the following free sites to link to countless music publishing, U.S. copyright and licensing, songwriting rights, and music rights resources:

- The National Music Publisher's Association's music links page at **http://www.nmpa.org/links.html**
- Kohn On Music Licensing at **http://kohnmusic.com**
- Worldwide Internet Music Resources at the Indiana University School of Music at **http://www.music.indiana.edu/ music_resources**

Performing rights organizations' sites, such as ASCAP (the American Society Of Composers, Authors And Publishers) and BMI (Broadcast Music, Inc.), have free lookup databases of licensed song titles with the publishers' contact data displayed. ASCAP's database can be searched by title, performers, writers, publishers, or administrators, and T-codes (**http://www.ascap.com/ace/search.cfm?mode=search**). BMI's free lookup database (**http://www.bmi.com/licensing**) may not be obvious to searchers. It can be found on the top left side of BMI's home page and is labeled **Repertoire**. To begin, use the drop-down menu to search by artist, publisher, title, or writer.

Phoning Celebrities Overseas

Entertainment lawyers who regularly phone people (especially celebrities) outside the U.S. should bookmark the World Clock at Time-anddate.com (**http://www.timeanddate.com/worldclock**). A vice-president at a cable network that has offices worldwide touts this site because it saves him the embarrassment of waking someone up in the middle of the night. Besides mere embarrassment, we know someone who was promoted to his boss's job (after being at the company for just a few weeks) when his boss was fired for accidentally waking up a celebrity overseas in the middle of the night.

Entertainment Law Employment and Opportunity Sites

For those entertainment lawyers who are job seeking, a visit to Ifcome.com, an entertainment gossip site reporting on employment openings and "opportunities" (inferred from the gossip about who has left what job), is in order. Ifcome.com reports on business and legal affairs job openings and opportunities in television, entertainment, motion pictures, Internet, new media and dot-coms (**http://www.ifcome.com**).

The Truly Entertaining (in Other Words, Pure Gossip)

For truly entertaining information, check out these sites: FindLaw's FBI celebrity files (**http://news.findlaw.com/legalnews/ entertainment/fbi**); Mugshots.org's postings of celebrity mug shots (**http://mugshots.org**), especially Larry King's mug shot (**http://mugshots.org/hollywood/larry-king.html**); and the Smoking Gun (**http://www.thesmokinggun.com/backstagetour/index.html**) that "brings you exclusive documents—cool, confidential, quirky—that can't be found elsewhere on the Web." At the Smoking Gun site, read what stars demand in their contract riders: prune juice (Kansas), or an arrangement of tulips, roses, gardenias, and lilies (Janet Jackson).

Intellectual Property

A large component of entertainment law also deals with intellectual property (IP) law (especially copyright and trademark). But lawyers outside these two fields might also find a tour through the copyright, trademark, and patent databases fruitful. For example, a family law lawyer might use one of the databases to see if the other spouse has any intellectual property that may have some worth and be added to the marital estate.

Trademarks

For a basic trademark search, Susan Kaiser (**www.kaisermedialaw .com**), a lawyer who has represented network-owned radio and television stations and negotiates and drafts agreements and contracts, searches the U.S. Patent and Trademark Office site (see the listing below). Although she wouldn't file a trademark application based only upon this search, she gets a sense of whether it's a good idea to then conduct a full-fledged search at a pay site, such as Thompson & Thompson (**http://www.ttlaw .com/trademarks.htm**). Other pay sites for patents and trademarks are Thomson Derwent (**http://www.derwent.com**), which has subsumed the

former free Delphion.com site, and LexisNexis
(**http://www.lexisnexis.com/patentservices/default.asp**).

U.S. Patent and Trademark Office (USPTO)

http://www.uspto.gov/main/trademarks.htm

Purpose: To learn about trademarks, to search trademarks, to file
trademark applications, and to track the status of an
application.

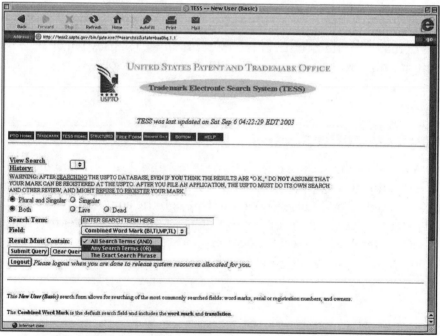

Figure 19-4. This is an example of a TESS basic search form. Enter your search
terms; choose a field; and either choose the Boolean connector AND or OR,
or search by an exact phrase.

Content: Users can view the *Trademark Manual of Examining Procedure* online to learn about trademarks. It contains specific rules and regulations for filing a trademark application. The Trademark Electronic Search System (TESS),
which has over three million pending, registered, and
dead federal trademarks, is used to search trademarks.

There are several ways to search the TESS database: by using a basic form (enter search words and then select an option to search on all words, any word, or the exact phrase), a Boolean form (link search words with Boolean and proximity connectors, such as AND, OR, ADJ), or an advanced form (to link together search words with Boolean connectors and to restrict the search words to specific fields—such as the attorney of record field or owner field).

Our View: Trademark searching can be very tricky and TESS has done a good job at providing detailed help screens and sample searches to assist with the variety of search strategies, such as searching by truncating words, searching word patterns, or limiting words to their plural or singular format only, and so on. Some things to be aware of with TESS: it will not recognize phrases unless the words are surrounded by quotation marks, and TESS infers the OR connector unless the searcher uses another connector between each word (or uses quotation marks to show the words are to be searched as a phrase).

Tip: Take advantage of the **View Search History** link to view a record of all your searches done during your current session and then print them out for your files.

State Trademarks

States have their own trademark registration procedures. See the **State Trademarks** site (**http://statetm.tripod.com**) for links to the various state trademark offices.

Patents

U.S. Patent and Trademark Office

http://www.uspto.gov/main/patents.htm

Purpose: To search for patents and published patent applications, to view the ***Official Gazette,*** to locate guides about the patenting process, to locate rules and laws about patents, to file patents and track their status, and so on.

Content: Patents from 1790 through 1975 are searchable by patent number and current U.S. classification only, while patents from 1976 to the present are full-text searchable.

Our View: There are plenty of help screens to make the searching easier. To search for patents or published patent applications, begin searching by choosing the range of dates, then enter your terms and select your fields (such as all fields, inventor name, and so on). Both the patents and published patent applications offer quick searching (using up to two terms and up to two fields) and advanced searching (using multiple terms and fields). Search patents by patent number and search patent applications by published application number or document number.

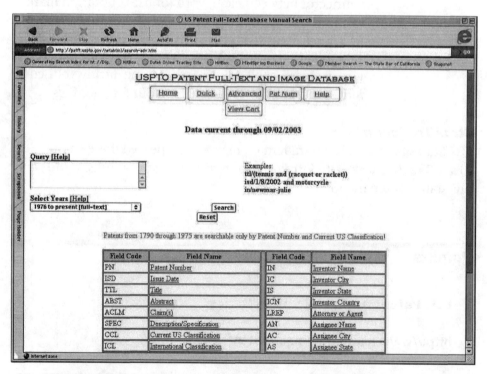

Figure 19-5. This shows the USPTO's advanced search query box and also provides an example of how to build your search. Click on **Pat Num** or **Quick** to choose another search mode.

Tip: You'll need special plug-ins to view images of the patents.

Copyrights

Those delving into copyright issues such as registrations and owner-ship documents will now find a Web-based alternative to the dreaded dial-up LOCIS Search System of the U.S. Copyright Office. The new Web-based system is called (aptly enough) Copyright Search.

Library of Congress Copyright Search

http://www.loc.gov/copyright/search

Purpose: Copyright Search has three databases: (1) a catch-all database for books, films, maps, music, and so on; (2) a serials database; and (3) a documents database (with legal records about transfers of copyrights, termination notices, statements about whether an author is alive or dead or about an erroneous name in a copyright notice, and documents identifying anonymous or pseudony-mous authors).

Content: The databases go back to 1978, but it can take recent reg-istrations several months to appear. The book database is searchable by author, title, claimant, or registration number, or by a combined search. The serials database is searchable by author, title, claimant, or International Standard Serial Number (ISSN), while the documents database is searchable by title, assignor, assignee, or doc-ument number.

Our View: Because the database only goes back to 1978 and because it takes a few months for new registrations to be entered, lawyers who want to contact a live person for further inquiries can now e-mail or chat for free with the Library of Congress's virtual librarian at **http://www.loc.gov/rr/askalib**.

Tip: A vice president of legal affairs at a cable network explained that he also finds the **Library of Congress Online Catalog (http://catalog.loc.gov)** to be useful to see if there are any other details about a publication other than what the copyright search displays.

The Copyright and Fair Use site (**http://fairuse.stanford.edu**) was recently revamped by Tim Stanley, FindLaw's cofounder. It is a joint project of Stanford University Libraries, NOLO, and Justia. It includes an overview of copyright law and links to laws, cases, treaties, current legislation, articles, mailing lists, and more. It also offers (for free) Stanford's Fair Use Monthly Newsletter.

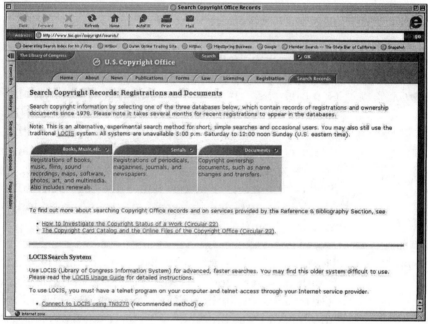

Figure 19-6. There are three separate databases to search at the U.S. Copyright Office Website—depending on whether you want to search books and music, serials, or documents.

IP Web Sites

Aside from the "official" government sites for searching (and learning about) copyrights, patents, and trademarks, there are various non-governmental sites where you can learn about these areas of law. Many of the IP sites now are geared to the digital world, offering information about issues such as software, webcasting, and so on. Some useful free IP sites are listed below.

IP Metasites

KuesterLaw, the Technology Law Resource (**http://www.kuesterlaw .com**), links to reams of technology law information, especially patent, copyright, and trademark law. There are links to leading IP cases and statutes, government sites, and various other IP resources such as law reviews and articles. According to site owner Jeffrey R. Kuester, the site is "reportedly the most linked-to intellectual property website on the Internet."

FindLaw also has many IP links (**http://www.findlaw.com/01top ics/23intellectprop**) and so does Hieros Gamos (**http://www.hg.org/ intell.html**). Hieros Gamos also links to many IP treaties.

IP Books

Digital Law Online (**http://digital-law-online.info**) is a full-text on-line version of the treatise *Legal Protection of Digital Information*, written by University of Utah School of Computing Professor Lee A. Hollaar. (Professor Hollaar was a technical consultant to the plaintiff states in the Microsoft antitrust litigation.)

IP Articles

Although searching the Thomson Derwent site is not free, reading articles about patent law is (**http://www.derwent.com/ipmatters**).

IP Blogs

Patent Project, lawyer Joseph M. Gusmano's blog, is meant to help you keep up to date with patent decisions and information from the U.S. Patent and Trademark Office (**http://patents.gusmanolaw.com**). Gusmano's Trademark Project purports to do the same with trademarks (**http://trademarks.gusmanolaw.com**).

Index

Selected Books From . . .
THE ABA LAW PRACTICE MANAGEMENT SECTION

The ABA Guide to Lawyer Trust Accounts.
Details ways that lawyers should manage trust accounts to comply with ethical & statutory requirements.

Changing Jobs, 3rd Edition. A handbook designed to help lawyers make changes in their professional careers. Includes career planning advice from dozens of experts.

Collecting Your Fee: Getting Paid From Intake to Invoice. Author Ed Poll outlines the basics and the systems you need to set in place to ultimately increase your bottom line and keep your clients happy while doing it. Learn how to increase your collections, decrease your accounts receivable, and keep your clients happy. CD-ROM with sample forms, letters, and agreements is included.

Compensation Plans for Law Firms, 3rd Ed.
This third edition discusses the basics for a fair and simple compensation system for partners, of counsel, associates, paralegals, and staff.

Complete Guide to Marketing Your Law Practice. Filled with dozens of fresh and innovative ideas, this book features the strategies form the country's top legal marketers.

Complete Internet Handbook for Lawyers. A thorough orientation to the Internet, including e-mail, search engines, conducting research and marketing on the Internet, publicizing a Web site, Net ethics, security, viruses, and more. Features a updated, companion Web site with forms you can download and customize.

Do-It-Yourself Public Relations. A hands-on guide (and diskette!) for lawyers with public relations ideas, sample letters, and forms.

Easy Self-Audits for the Busy Law Office.
Dozens of evaluation tools help you determine what's working (and what's not) in your law office or legal department. You'll discover several opportunities for improving productivity and efficiency along the way!

Effective Yellow Pages Advertising for Lawyers: The Complete Guide to Creating Winning Ads.
This new book by Kerry Randall, "the world's foremost expert on Yellow Pages advertising," shows you how to create more powerful Yellow Pages advertising—the best *lawyers* do not get the most calls; the best *ads* get the most calls.

Essential Formbook: Comprehensive Management Tools for Lawyers, Vols. I & II.
Useful to legal practitioners of all specialties and sizes, the first two volumes of The Essential Formbook include more than 100 forms, checklists, and sample documents. And, with all the forms on disk, it's easy to modify them to match your needs.

Flying Solo: A Survival Guide for the Solo Lawyer, Third Edition. This book gives solos, as well as small firms, all the information needed to build a successful practice. Contains 55 chapters covering office location, billing and cash flow, computers and equipment, and much more.

Handling Personnel Issues in the Law Office.
Packed with tips on "safely" and legally recruiting, hiring, training, managing, and terminating employees.

HotDocs in One Hour for Lawyers, Second Edition. Offers simple instructions, ranging from generating a document from a template to inserting conditional text and creating dialogs.

How to Build and Manage an Employment Law Practice. Provides clear guidance and valuable tips for solo or small employment law practices, including preparation, marketing, accepting cases, and managing workload and finances. Includes several time-saving "fill in the blank" forms.

How to Build and Manage a Personal Injury Practice. Features all of the tactics, technology, and tools needed for a profitable practice, including hot to: write a sound business plan, develop a financial forecast, choose office space, market your practice, and more.

How to Start and Build a Law Practice, Fourth Edition. Jay Foonberg's classic guide has been completely updated and expanded! Features 128 chapters, including 30 new ones, that reveal secrets to successful planning, marketing, billing, client relations, and much more. Chock-full of forms, sample letters, and checklists, including a sample business plan, "The Foonberg Law Office Management Checklist," and more.

Law Office Policy and Procedures Manual, 4th Ed. A model for law office policies and procedures (includes diskette). Covers law office organization, management, personnel policies, financial management, technology, and communications systems.

Law Office Procedures Manual for Solos and Small Firms, Second Edition. Use this manual as is or customize it using the book's diskette. Includes general office policies on confidentiality, employee compensation, sick leave, sexual harassment, billing, and more.

The Lawyer's Guide to Extranets: Breaking Down Walls, Building Client Connections. Well-run extranets can result in significant expansion in clientele and profitability for a law firm. This book takes you step-by-step through the issues of implementing an extranet.

The Lawyer's Guide to Marketing on the Internet, Second Edition. This book provides you with countless Internet marketing possibilities and shows you how to effectively and efficiently market your law practice on the Internet.

Legal Career Guide: From Law Student to Lawyer, Fourth Edition is a step-by-step guide for planning a law career, preparing and executing a job search, and moving into the market. This book is perfect for students currently choosing a career path, or simply deciding if law school is right for them.

Making Partner: A Guide for Law Firm Associates, Second Edition. If you are serious about making partner, this book will help you formulate your step-by-step plan and be your guide for years to come for your decisions and actions within your firm.

Managing Partner 101: A Guide to Successful Law Firm Leadership, Second Edition is designed to help managing partners, lawyers, and other legal professionals understand the role and responsibilities of a law firm's managing partner.

Persuasive Computer Presentations: The Essential Guide for Lawyers explains the advantages of computer presentation resources, how to use them, what they can do, and the legal issues involved in their use. It covers how to use computer presentations in the courtroom and during meetings, pretrial, and seminars.

Running a Law Practice on a Shoestring. Offers a crash course in successful entrepreneurship. Features money-saving tips on office space, computer equipment, travel, furniture, staffing, and more.

Successful Client Newsletters. Written for lawyers, editors, writers, and marketers, this book can help you to start a newsletter from scratch, redesign an existing one, or improve your current practices in design, production, and marketing.

Telecommuting for Lawyers. Discover methods for implementing a successful telecommuting program that can lead to increased productivity, improved work product, higher revenues, lower overhead costs, and better communications. Addressing both law firms and telecommuters, this guide covers start-up, budgeting, setting policies, selecting participants, training, and technology.

Through the Client's Eyes, Second Edition. Includes an overview of client relations and sample letters, surveys, and self-assessment questions to gauge your client relations acumen.

Wills, Trusts, and Technology. Reveals why you should automate your estates practice; identifies what should be automated; explains how to select the right software; and helps you get up and running with the software you select.

Winning Alternatives to the Billable Hour: Strategies that Work, Second Edition. This book explains how it is possible to change from hourly based billing to a system that recognizes your legal expertise, as well as your efficiency, and delivery winning billing solutions—for you and your client.

Women Rainmakers' Best Marketing Tips, Second Edition. This book contains well over a hundred tips you can put to use right away that will have a positive effect on your marketing strategy. Anyone involved in marketing a firm can benefit from the down-to-earth advice in this book.

Order Form

Qty	Title	LPM Price	Reg Price	Total
_____	ABA Guide to Lawyer Trust Accounts (5110374)	69.95	79.95	$_____
_____	ABA Guide to Prof. Managers in the Law Office (5110373)	69.95	79.95	$_____
_____	Anatomy of a Law Firm Merger, Second Edition (5110434)	74.95	89.95	$_____
_____	Changing Jobs, 3rd Ed.(511-0425)	39.95	49.95	_____
_____	Compensation Plans for Lawyers, 3rd Ed. (5110452)	84.95	99.95	$_____
_____	Complete Guide to Marketing Your Law Practice (5110428)	74.95	89.95	$_____
_____	Complete Internet Handbook for Lawyers (5110413)	39.95	49.95	$_____
_____	Computerized Case Management Systems (5110409)	39.95	49.95	$_____
_____	Connecting with Your Client (5110378)	54.95	64.95	$_____
_____	Do-It-Yourself Public Relations (5110352)	69.95	79.95	$_____
_____	Easy Self Audits for the Busy Law Firm (511-0420P)	99.95	84.95	$_____
_____	Essential Formbook, Vols. I and II	*Please call for information*		
_____	Flying Solo, Third Edition (511-0463)	79.95	89.95	$_____
_____	Handling Personnel Issues in the Law Office (5110381)	59.95	69.95	$_____
_____	HotDocs in One Hour for Lawyers, Second Edition (5110464)	29.95	34.95	$_____
_____	How to Build & Manage an Employment Law Practice (5110389)	44.95	54.95	$_____
_____	How to Build & Manage a Personal Injury Practice (5110386)	44.95	54.95	$_____
_____	How to Start & Build a Law Practice, Fourth Edition (5110415)	57.95	69.95	$_____
_____	Law Firm Partnership Guide: Getting Started (5110363)	64.95	74.95	$_____
_____	Law Firm Partnership Guide: Strengthening Your Firm (5110391)	64.95	74.95	$_____
_____	Law Office Policy & Procedures Manual, 4th Ed. (5110441)	109.95	129.95	$_____
_____	Law Office Staff Manual for Solos & Small Firms (5110445)	59.95	69.95	$_____
_____	Lawyer's Guide to Marketing on the Internet, 2nd Ed. (5110484)	69.95	79.95	$_____
_____	Living with the Law (5110379)	59.95	69.95	$_____
_____	Making Partner, Second Edition (511-0482)	39.95	49.95	$_____
_____	Managing Partner 101, Second Edition (5110451)	44.95	49.95	$_____
_____	Persuasive Computer Presentations (511-0462)	69.95	79.95	$_____
_____	Practicing Law Without Clients (5110376)	49.95	59.95	$_____
_____	Running a Law Practice on a Shoestring (5110387)	39.95	49.95	$_____
_____	Successful Client Newsletters (5110396)	39.95	44.95	$_____
_____	Telecommuting for Lawyers (5110401)	39.95	49.95	$_____
_____	Through the Client's Eyes, Second Ed. (5110480)	69.95	79.95	$_____
_____	Wills, Trusts, and Technology (5430377)	74.95	84.95	$_____
_____	Winning Alternatives to the Billable Hour, Second Ed (5110483)	129.95	149.95	$_____

*Handling

$10.00-$24.99 .... $3.95
$25.00-$49.99 .... $4.95
$50.00+ $5.95   MD residents add 5%

**Tax

DC residents add 5.75%
IL residents add 8.75%

Subtotal

*Handling $_____
**Tax $_____
TOTAL $_____

PAYMENT

☐ Check enclosed (to the ABA) ~ ☐ Bill Me
☐ Visa   ☐ MasterCard   ☐ American Express

_____

Account Number   Exp. Date Signature

Name _____ Firm _____
Address _____
City _____ State _____ Zip _____
Phone Number _____ E-mail address _____

Mail: ABA Publication Orders, P.O. Box 10892, Chicago, Illinois 60610-0892
◆ **Phone: (800) 285-2221** ◆ **FAX: (312) 988-5568**
E-Mail: service@abanet.org ◆ **Internet: http://www.abanet.org/lpm/catalog**

Source Code: 22AEND499

CUSTOMER COMMENT FORM

Title of Book: _____

We've tried to make this publication as useful, accurate, and readable as possible. Please take 5 minutes to tell us if we succeeded. Your comments and suggestions will help us improve our publications. Thank you!

1. How did you acquire this publication:

☐ by mail order   ☐ at a meeting/convention   ☐ as a gift

☐ by phone order   ☐ at a bookstore   ☐ don't know

☐ other: (describe) _____

Please rate this publication as follows:

	Excellent	Good	Fair	Poor	Not Applicable
Readability: Was the book easy to read and understand?	☐	☐	☐	☐	☐
Examples/Cases: Were they helpful, practical? Were there enough?	☐	☐	☐	☐	☐
Content: Did the book meet your expectations? Did it cover the subject adequately?	☐	☐	☐	☐	☐
Organization and clarity: Was the sequence of text logical? Was it easy to find what you wanted to know?	☐	☐	☐	☐	☐
Illustrations/forms/checklists: Were they clear and useful? Were there enough?	☐	☐	☐	☐	☐
Physical attractiveness: What did you think of the appearance of the publication (typesetting, printing, etc.)?	☐	☐	☐	☐	☐

Would you recommend this book to another attorney/administrator? ☐ Yes ☐ No

How could this publication be improved? What else would you like to see in it?

_____
_____
_____

Do you have other comments or suggestions? _____
_____
_____

Name _____
Firm/Company _____
Address _____
City/State/Zip _____
Phone _____
Firm Size: _____ Area of specialization: _____

We appreciate your time and help.

Fold

NO POSTAGE
NECESSARY
IF MAILED
IN THE
UNITED STATES

BUSINESS REPLY MAIL

FIRST CLASS   PERMIT NO. 16471   CHICAGO, ILLINOIS

. POSTAGE WILL BE PAID BY ADDRESSEE

AMERICAN BAR ASSOCIATION
PPM, 8th FLOOR
750 N. LAKE SHORE DRIVE
CHICAGO, ILLINOIS 60611-9851

Fold

LawPracticeManagementSection

MARKETING • MANAGEMENT • TECHNOLOGY • FINANCE

JOIN the ABA Law Practice Management Section (LPM) and receive significant discounts on future LPM book purchases! You'll also get direct access to marketing, management, technology, and finance tools that help lawyers and other professionals meet the demands of today's challenging legal environment.

Exclusive Membership Benefits Include:

- **Law Practice Magazine**
  Eight annual issues of our award-winning *Law Practice* magazine, full of insightful articles and practical tips on Marketing/Client Development, Practice Management, Legal Technology, and Finance.
- **ABA TECHSHOW®**
  Receive a $100 discount on ABA TECHSHOW, the world's largest legal technology conference!
- **LPM Book Discount**
  LPM has over eighty titles in print! Books topics cover the four core areas of law practice management – marketing, management, technology, and finance – as well as legal career issues.
- **Law Practice Today**
  LPM's unique web-based magazine in which the features change weekly! Law Practice Today covers all the hot topics in law practice management *today* – current issues, current challenges, current solutions.
- **Discounted CLE & Other Educational Opportunities**
  The Law Practice Management Section sponsors more than 100 educational sessions annually. LPM also offers other live programs, teleconferences and web cast seminars.
- **LawPractice.news**
  This monthly eUpdate brings information on Section news and activities, educational opportunities, and details on book releases and special offers.

Complete the membership application below.

Applicable Dues:
o$40 for ABA members   o$5 for ABA Law Student Division members

(ABA Membership is a prerequisite to membership in the Section. To join the ABA, call the Service Center at 1-800-285-2221.)

Method of Payment:
oBill me   Charge to my: oVisa   oMasterCard   oAmerican Express

Card number _____   Exp. Date _____

Signature _____   Date _____

Applicant's Information (please print):
Name _____   ABA I.D. number _____

Firm/Organization _____

Address _____   City/State/Zip _____

Telephone _____FAX_____   Email _____

Fax your application to 312-988-5528 or join by phone: 1-800-285-2221, TDD 312-988-5168
Join online at www.lawpractice.org.

About the CD

The accompanying CD contains a hyperlinked index of Web sites listed in the book (**Fact Finding on the Internet Index.pdf**), as well as the following checklists from the book: Internet Methodology Checklist (**Internet Methodology Checklist.doc**); Internet Source Credibility Checklist (**Internet Source Credibility Checklist.doc**); Search Strategy Checklist (**Search Strategy Checklist.doc**); and the Checklist for Finding Company Information (**Checklist for Finding Company Information.doc**).

For additional information about the files on the CD, please open and read the "readme.doc" file on the CD.

NOTE: The set of files on the CD may only be used on a single computer or moved to and used on another computer. Under no circumstances may the set of files be used on more than one computer at one time. If you are interested in obtaining a license to use the set of files on a local network, please contact: Director, Copyrights and Contracts, American Bar Association, 750 N. Lake Shore Drive, Chicago, IL 60611, (312) 988-6101. **Please read the license and warranty statements on the following page before using this CD.**

**Defending Liberty
Pursuing Justice**

CD-ROM to accompany
**The Lawyer's Guide to Fact Finding on the Internet,
Second Edition**

WARNING: Opening this package indicates your understanding and acceptance of the following Terms and Conditions.

READ THE FOLLOWING TERMS AND CONDITIONS BEFORE OPENING THIS SEALED PACKAGE. IF YOU DO NOT AGREE WITH THEM, PROMPTLY RETURN THE UNOPENED PACKAGE TO EITHER THE PARTY FROM WHOM IT WAS ACQUIRED OR TO THE AMERICAN BAR ASSOCIATION AND YOUR MONEY WILL BE RETURNED.

The document files in this package are a proprietary product of the American Bar Association and are protected by Copyright Law. The American Bar Association retains title to and ownership of these files.

License
You may use this set of files on a single computer or move it to and use it on another computer, but under no circumstances may you use the set of files on more than one computer at the same time. You may copy the files either in support of your use of the files on a single computer or for backup purposes. If you are interested in obtaining a license to use the set of files on a local network, please contact: Manager, Publication Policies & Contracting, American Bar Association, 750 N. Lake Shore Drive, Chicago, IL 60611, (312) 988-6101.

You may permanently transfer the set of files to another party if the other party agrees to accept the terms and conditions of this License Agreement. If you transfer the set of files, you must at the same time transfer all copies of the files to the same party or destroy those not transferred. Such transfer terminates your license. You may not rent, lease, assign or otherwise transfer the files except as stated in this paragraph.

You may modify these files for your own use within the provisions of this License Agreement. You may not redistribute any modified files.

Warranty
If a CD-ROM in this package is defective, the American Bar Association will replace it at no charge if the defective diskette is returned to the American Bar Association within 60 days from the date of acquisition.

American Bar Association warrants that these files will perform in substantial compliance with the documentation supplied in this package. However, the American Bar Association does not warrant these forms as to the correctness of the legal material contained therein. If you report a significant defect in performance in writing to the American Bar Association, and the American Bar Association is not able to correct it within 60 days, you may return the CD, including all copies and documentation, to the American Bar Association and the American Bar Association will refund your money.

Any files that you modify will no longer be covered under this warranty even if they were modified in accordance with the License Agreement and product documentation.

IN NO EVENT WILL THE AMERICAN BAR ASSOCIATION, ITS OFFICERS, MEMBERS, OR EMPLOYEES BE LIABLE TO YOU FOR ANY DAMAGES, INCLUDING LOST PROFITS, LOST SAVINGS OR OTHER INCIDENTAL OR CONSEQUENTIAL DAMAGES ARISING OUT OF YOUR USE OR INABILITY TO USE THESE FILES EVEN IF THE AMERICAN BAR ASSOCIATION OR AN AUTHORIZED AMERICAN BAR ASSOCIATION REPRESENTATIVE HAS BEEN ADVISED OF THE POSSIBILITY OF SUCH DAMAGES, OR FOR ANY CLAIM BY ANY OTHER PARTY. SOME STATES DO NOT ALLOW THE LIMITATION OR EXCLUSION OF LIABILITY FOR INCIDENTAL OR CONSEQUENTIAL DAMAGES, IN WHICH CASE THIS LIMITATION MAY NOT APPLY TO YOU.